The RoutledgeFalmer Reader in Education Policy and Politics

The RoutledgeFalmer Reader in Education Policy and Politics brings together selected papers from leading scholars to address the most significant recent development in educational policy and politics: the impact of globalisation. The papers discuss, document and analyse evidence of globalisation's effects on the new direction of education policies and practices and in the production of globalised agendas for the redesign of state provision and the governance of education.

However, while acknowledging the importance of globalisation for educational policy and politics, this collection also interrogates its complexity. The articles in this Reader therefore do not allow globalisation to function performatively, as a script that simply produces neo-liberal politics and economics in education. Instead, the collection offers resources for the deconstruction of that neo-liberal script, by charting the possibilities of globalisation 'from below', and providing material on the rebalancing of national and global functions that offer possibilities for diverse and divergent education policies.

The Reader is organised in two parts. The first part, 'The Global Framing of Education Policy and Politics', provides a selection of articles that interrogate globalisation and its effects from a variety of analytical perspectives and explore what kind of politics are possible in the framing context of globalisation. The second part, 'Vernacular Politics, Policies and Processes', documents and discusses different types of engagement with politics and policy in a variety of settings and sectors, including numerous European and Pacific Rim policy contexts.

This important collection underlines the need to approach globalisation, education policy and politics from numerous perspectives and offers analytical, empirical and theoretical resources for the reframing of contemporary education politics. Students of education policy and politics will find this Reader an invaluable resource for understanding, theorising and researching in these academic fields.

Bob Lingard is Andrew Bell Professor of Education in the Moray House School of Education, University of Edinburgh.

Jenny Ozga is Professor of Education Research and Director of the Centre for Educational Sociology (CES), the Moray House School of Education, University of Edinburgh.

Readers in Education

The RoutledgeFalmer Reader in Gender & Education
Edited by Madeleine Arnot and Mairtin Mac an Ghaill

The RoutledgeFalmer Reader in Higher Education
Edited by Malcolm Tight

The RoutledgeFalmer Reader in History of Education
Edited by Gary McCulloch

The RoutledgeFalmer Reader in Inclusive Education
Edited by Keith Topping and Sheelagh Maloney

The RoutledgeFalmer Reader in Language and Literacy
Edited by Teresa Grainger

The RoutledgeFalmer Reader in Multicultural Education
Edited by Gloria Ladson-Billings and David Gillborn

The RoutledgeFalmer Reader in Philosophy of Education
Edited by Wilfred Carr

The RoutledgeFalmer Reader in Psychology of Education
Edited by Harry Daniels and Anne Edwards

The RoutledgeFalmer Reader in Science Education
Edited by John Gilbert

The RoutledgeFalmer Reader in Sociology of Education
Edited by Stephen J. Ball

The RoutledgeFalmer Reader in Teaching and Learning
Edited by E. C. Wragg

The RoutledgeFalmer Reader in Education Policy and Politics
Edited by Bob Lingard and Jenny Ozga

The RoutledgeFalmer Reader in Education Policy and Politics

Edited by
Bob Lingard and Jenny Ozga

LONDON AND NEW YORK

First published 2007
by Routledge
2 Park Square, Milton Park, Abingdon, Oxon OX14 4RN

Simultaneously published in the USA and Canada
by Routledge
270 Madison Ave, New York, NY 10016

*Routledge is an imprint of the Taylor & Francis Group,
an informa business*

© 2007 Edited by Bob Lingard and Jenny Ozga

Typeset in Sabon by
Newgen Imaging Systems (P) Ltd, Chennai, India
Printed and bound in Great Britain by
The Cromwell Press, Trowbridge, Wiltshire

British Library Cataloguing in Publication Data
A catalogue record for this book is available
from the British Library

Library of Congress Cataloging in Publication Data
   The RoutledgeFalmer reader in education policy and politics /
edited by Bob Lingard and Jenny Ozga
      p. cm. – (Readers in education)
   Includes bibliographical references and index.
   1. Education and state. I. Lingard, Bob. II. Ozga, Jennifer.

LC71.R68 2006
379–dc22   2006046224

ISBN10: 0–415–34573–1 (hbk)
ISBN10: 0–415–34574–X (pbk)

ISBN13: 978–0–415–34573–6 (hbk)
ISBN13: 978–0–415–34574–3 (pbk)

September 24, 2007

CONTENTS

ILLUSTRATIONS

Figures

Tables

ACKNOWLEDGEMENTS

Chapter 6, *After the marketplace: evidence, social science and educational research* by Alan Luke is reproduced from *The Australian Educational Researcher* (2003) with the kind permission of The Australian Educational Researcher.

Chapter 7, *Globalization and educational policy making: a case study* by Sandra Taylor and Miriam Henry is reproduced from *Educational Theory* (2000) with the kind permission of the Philosophy of Education Society.

Chapter 9, *National and Global Competition in Higher Education* by Simon Marginson is reproduced from *The Australian Educational Researcher* (2004) with the kind permission of The Australian Educational Researcher.

All other chapters are reproduced with kind permission of Taylor & Francis Ltd.

disability. There are Readers in this series that are devoted to these significant issues. Nor do we consider curriculum and pedagogy, which have been constituted as intellectual fields outside the purview of education policy and politics. Although in some ways it could be argued that curricula, usually rearticulated as syllabuses, are the major policy documents which enter schools, curriculum studies has developed as a separate intellectual field from that of the study of education policy, and we do not engage with it here.

Education policy as a field, in respect of schooling at least, deals with all texts, apart from curricula, which seek to frame, constitute and change educational practices. Education policy includes all sectors of education, but now, in the context of the so-called knowledge or learning society, it also includes policy produced in parts of the state other than education ministries. This 'totally pedagogised society' (Bernstein 2001) or 'pedagogisation of everyday life', as it has been referred to (Thomson 2006, 324), is 'effected on the one hand via media and the changing role of cultural institutions and digitised knowledge "archives", and on the other through the continued intrusion of schooling into family lives and training into work/underemployment/ unemployment' (Thomson 2006, 324). The totally pedagogised society demands the deparochialising of policy research in another way, namely, through the extension and refocusing of its institutional gaze.

We take an ecumenical view, however, of what can and should be regarded as policy texts, regarding them as any 'vehicle or medium for carrying and transmitting a policy message' (Ozga 2000, 33). Thus texts may include a speech by a Minister for Education, a press release by a senior education bureaucrat, as well as formal, 'official' policy texts. We also include the processes involved in the production of a policy text and those involved in its practice in our definition of education policy and recognise that contestation is usually involved at all stages of production and implementation, as well as in relation to the discourses which frame the actual written text. As observed elsewhere:

> In summary, then, we want to stress that policy is more than simply the policy text; it also involves processes prior to the articulation of the text and the processes which continue after the text has been produced, both in modifications to it as a statement of values and desired action, and in actual practice. Furthermore, contestation is involved right from the moment of appearance of an issue on the policy agenda, through the initiation of action to the inevitable trade-offs involved in formulation and implementation. Contestation is played out in regard to whose voices are heard and whose values are recognised or 'authoritatively allocated' in the policy and which groups ultimately benefit as a result of the policy.
>
> (Taylor *et al.* 1997, 28–9)

This process/text definition of education policy indicates the politics involved in the production and implementation of a policy and in the actual purposes and language of the policy text. The resulting compromises inevitably mean that policy texts are usually heteroglossic in character, discursively suturing together differing interests to achieve apparent consensus and legitimacy.

Public policy, that is, policy produced by governments, concerns the myriad of elements that constitute educational systems, but we also need to recognise the politics of non-decision making. As Dye (1992, 2) noted some time ago, public policy can be regarded as 'whatever governments choose to do, or not to do'. If we work with a broad definition of politics as practices and discourses to do with power (in its structural possessed, concentrated and congealed, as well as poststructural dispersed,

INTRODUCTION
Reading education policy and politics
Bob Lingard and Jenny Ozga

Education policy and politics together constitute a vast field of research and intellectual endeavour, so that any attempt to produce a 'representative' selection is bound to be limited by the space available, and by the always imperfect knowledge of the editors. Furthermore, the education policy/politics relationship works in different ways within different intellectual and national traditions. In the US, for instance, a particular version of education politics has been closely aligned with the field of educational administration, which has morphed into the field of educational management and leadership. In the UK context, education politics is more closely aligned with sociology of education broadly conceived. Yet even here there is complexity. The education polices of the Thatcher regime saw sociologists of education in England focus more on education policy in response to political attacks on the intellectual project of the sociology of education and the enhanced significance of policy as the steering mechanism within restructured educational systems. This trend has not developed in quite the same way in other parts of the UK, where educational politics may be more significant in the context of political devolution.

Of course we do not intend to tie developments in the study of education policy and politics closely to geographical areas, though there is, perhaps, a tendency in Anglophone literatures to assume the centrality of preoccupations which may be rather exclusively and narrowly 'local'. Indeed, following Appadurai (2001), we argue that even in the contemporary context of globalisation the fields of education policy and politics need to be 'deparochialised'. We should, perhaps, note that Appadurai sees evidence of parochialism in apparently 'international' locations and perspectives: he is not making a criticism of small or 'peripheral' locations, and nor are we. Commenting on the international circulation of ideas, Bourdieu (1996, 220) noted how 'Intellectual life, like all other social spaces, is a home to nationalism and imperialism' and that 'a truly scientific internationalism' requires a concerted political and intellectual project. We believe that the papers selected for this volume are 'scientifically international' and that they encapsulate or help to sustain a coherent political and intellectual project: that particular quality of scientific internationalism has guided our selection.

In this introduction we seek to explain that argument a little further, by setting out the selection principles and devices used for pulling together this particular collection. Such principles of selection mean that the collection is not comprehensive; it does not provide what might be regarded as a set of canonical or standard texts in the field of education policy and politics; and it is not explicitly intended as a methodological guide to researching education policy and politics. Nor does it attempt to cover specific interests or specific polices around matters such as gender, race, ethnicity or relational and practice forms) and questions of who benefits from particular social arrangements, then education policies are evidently political. And what governments do *not* do in education is important as part of the politics of non-decision making, which also have political effects. In a somewhat narrower public policy sense, education policy can be seen as politics and specifically politics of education mediated by the logics of practice of the bureaucratic field within the education state. We have then the politics of education policy and education policy as politics. We work with both the narrower and the broader considerations of education politics in this collection, but our selection tends towards the broader conceptualisation of education politics, and thus contributes to the coherent 'project' that Bourdieu called for.

In more conventional terms, education policy has been characterised as the authoritative allocation of values within education systems. Immediately this raises political questions to do with 'whose values?', 'who has the authority – the legitimate right to exercise power – to allocate their values?' and 'who benefits from the outcomes of such allocation?' These are complex questions which cannot be addressed here, but suffice to say that a consideration of them today takes us well beyond local and national education systems and out to the global and to analyses of international organisations such as the Organisation for Economic and Cultural Development (OECD), UNESCO and World Bank, to regional agreements such as the North American Free Trade Agreement (NAFTA) and the Asia Pacific Economic Cooperation (APEC) and to emergent supranational political organisations such as the European Union.

We have already mentioned the bureaucratic field within the education state. The state generally and the education state specifically have been restructured over the past decades under new public management with the movement of hybridised private sector management forms into the public sector. Any contemporary account of education policy and politics *has* to consider the effects of these new state forms and practices. Usually this new public management within the state has been framed by a contemporary version of neo-liberal politics and economics, which privilege the market over the state and indeed want to marketise aspects of the state and its polices, including within the education state, and which regard competition and individual responsibility as central to the production of a buoyant economy and society. This neo-liberal state steers at a distance via policy frameworks through an emphasis on product accountability, resulting in the rise of a culture of performativity and audit. This politics has seen a concerted attack upon the Keynesian welfare state, on its principles of state before market and social justice conception of collective responsibility for all citizens. Education policy has been intimately involved with and affected by the political struggles over the workings and effects of the post-Keynesian, neo-liberal state.

The paradigmatic changes alluded to earlier, namely, the impact of education policy effects from beyond the nation, new state structures and practices and neo-liberal politics often involving marketisation and new forms of accountability, are effects in complex, mediated and non-straightforward ways of what has been called 'globalisation'. These changes contingent upon globalisation demand some necessary analytic moves within the field of education politics and policy. Indeed, as suggested earlier, education policy in devolved education systems as a result of such changes has become more significant in the steering of educational practices and is part of what has been described as a move from government to governance, dependant on new self-governing subjectivities rather than more direct bureaucratic restraints.

One useful approach to education policy suggests the need to analyse context, texts and consequences (Taylor *et al.* 1997); today the context includes the global. Another useful approach talks of a policy cycle moving through three cycles of influence, production and practice (Ball 1994). Today, researching the context of influence demands that we take account of the global, as does consideration of policy text production, while local factors may have more immediate effects on policy practice. Consideration of the 'global' requires a social science-based understanding of the phenomenon of *globalisation* in all its complexity (Thomson 2006).

As indicated above, it is this phenomenon of globalisation and responses to it, which we have used broadly as a selection device for the papers included in this collection. While it would be naively historicist to suggest a date for the emergence of this phenomenon of globalisation, the papers selected for this collection basically deal with related changes in education policy across the last couple of decades or so, set against globalisation and its accompanying dominant ideology of neo-liberalism in the context of the end of the Cold War, attacks upon the Keynesian welfare state, new forms of governance and the more recent emergence of the so-called *war on terror*.

Now, as Bourdieu (2003) has presciently argued, globalisation as a concept often works performatively in a political fashion to elide other more analytical meanings and to privilege globalisation read as only neo-liberal economics and politics. There are, however, political forms of resistance to neo-liberal economic globalisation, which Held and McGrew (2002) pursue in their book, *Globalization/Anti-Globalization*, and which are often described under the epithet, 'globalisation from below' as opposed to 'globalisation from above'. Pat Thomson (2006) has also suggested that the concept of *globalisation* is an open signifier through which political work can be done. This reader offers resources for the deconstruction of that performative, neo-liberal sense of globalisation (see also Olssen *et al.* 2004.) The chapters document and critique the neo-liberal restructuring of education and its playing out in the new focus and enhanced significance and steering capacity of education policy. The papers utilise analytical, sociological and political science meanings of the concept of globalisation and recognise the complex interplay of its economic, political, cultural, technological, phenomenological and social elements. They chart their effects on education policy production and demonstrate its rearticulation as micro-economic human capital development, quite narrowly conceived.

We hope that the Reader is organised in a way that sustains an informed engagement with globalisation and its effects on education politics and policy. Explanation of contemporary policy changes in education as *globalisation* can be intellectually lazy. Such talk often reifies globalisation, reads off education policy developments in a functionalist way from arguments about the logics of global capitalism and fails to consider the mechanisms through which globalisation factors affect policy and policy production within the nation and at other sub-national levels (Rizvi 2004; Thomson 2006). None of this, of course, is to deny the effects of highly mobile global capital and transnational corporations, or of international and supranational agencies, or of globalisation read simply as neo-liberal economics and politics, but rather to emphasise the need to understand how these effects work.

Furthermore, as we have suggested, there is a tendency to see globalisation as writing the education policy script for nation states, rather than as a force that may destabilise nation states and displace them as the 'natural' site and scale of politics. The displacement of the nation state may open up alternative spaces and produce a rebalancing of national and global functions that offers possibilities for diverse and divergent politics. The Reader attempts to capture some of the productive tension that exists in this process of rebalancing and rescaling. It does this by dividing the material into two sections.

Part 1 The Global Framing of Education Policy and Politics brings together a number of contributions which interrogate globalisation and its effects in theoretically and empirically sophisticated ways. The first chapter comes from Anna Yeatman's groundbreaking book *Postmodern Revisionings of the Political*, in which she discusses the kind of politics that are possible in the provisional and fragmented conditions of postmodernity. This chapter is intended to provide a framing for our entire selection in the Reader, in that it offers a clear analysis of the ways in which the condition of post-modernity transforms politics into a set of provisional and pragmatic adaptations to conditions of contestation. This transformation displaces professional expertise and state-centred politics, and relocates democratic politics in shifting and changing public spaces, in networks and interlocking fields of force that include the local, the context-bound and the conjunctural. These possibilities, and the difficulties that they encounter and throw up, provide the productive tension between policy and politics that runs through the Reader.

Fazal Rizvi provides a postcolonial reading of globalization in his piece on 'Debating Globalization and Education after September 11' which draws attention to the strengthening of the nation state in its new administrative, cultural and coercive functions in the 'war on terror'. Next we turn to Stephen Ball's influential essay on 'Big policies/Small world', which sets out the common elements in contemporary education policy, but also pays attention to possibilities of translation and recontextualisation. Roger Dale's argument for attention to the ways in which globalisation processes actually impact on national agendas comes next, his 'Specifying Globalisation effects on national policy: a focus on the mechanisms' succeeds in clarifying the concept of globalisation and its effects by subjecting the mechanisms which deliver its effects at national level to close scrutiny.

The final contribution in this part 'Globalisation, Education Policy and Politics' was written by us for this volume and seeks to review the context of education politics and policy with attention to the new constitution of education politics in globalised conditions, to international and transnational agencies and to the use of data in governing along with a discussion of local mediation and recontextualisation of global trends.

Taken together these chapters provide a comprehensive overview of the effects of globalisation on education policy making. They also, importantly, address the consequences for educational politics. They do this in different ways: either by outlining the ways in which agenda setting and the rules of the game are changing, or by identifying possibilities for new social movements to engage in a politics of representation, or by illuminating both the transnational and international pressures for homogeneity and the local and dispersed forces that are energised by such pressures.

In the second part of the book: *Vernacular Politics, Policies and Processes* we attempt a closer focus on the local and specific – not just in particular national, regional or local contexts, but in relation to key policy areas in education, and through exploration of various degrees of engagement with politics and policy. The section begins with a piece by Allan Luke, in which the challenges facing educators in Australia and elsewhere are outlined, and an evidence-based approach to policy is advocated – but one that is not restricted to performance-related 'evidence', and that embraces social, community and governmental action. Taylor and Henry next provide a case study of education policy making in the context of globalisation through exploration of the impact of OECD in shaping Australian education policy. This case study, while by no means underestimating the effect of the OECD as a powerful transnational agency, also illuminates the possibilities of counterhegemonic discourses. Lisbeth Lundahl develops this theme in her chapter 'Swedish, European, Global', which illustrates the rapid entry of neo-liberal agendas into the Swedish policy context, but also explores the ways in which Swedish policy in education has a strongly internal, or self-referential character. Globalisation in action forms the focus of Simon Marginson's chapter on national and global competition in higher education, where we see the flow of students and resources across the globe and their impacts on university positioning in national and global markets. The theme of international flows and trends is continued in the next chapter by Selwyn and Brown, on 'Education, nation states and the globalisation of information networks' which compares education networking in seven countries, identifying differences in the ways in which education is being constructed within these 'networked' societies.

The need to manage politics in the new conditions is illuminated in the article by Sharon Gewirtz, Marny Dickson and Sally Power, which considers the constitutive role of 'spin' in the education policy process, and finds that *spin* is an inherent and signifi-cant element of policy making, in the context of the New Labour government in England. Remaining in England, the piece by Stewart Ranson that follows is preoccu-pied with the shifts in accountability that have characterised neo-liberal governance of education: Ranson underlines the possibilities of change that may be offered by the contradictions of the new governance regime. His arguments, like Yeatman's, identify the fragile and compromised nature of the public sphere, but highlight the possibilities of community governance. This understanding of politics 'from below' is found, too, in the next chapter, by Trevor Gale, on 'Realising Policy: the who and how of policy production', in which the struggle and conflict involved in making policy, and the strategies of different actors are documented and analysed. The penultimate paper, by Terri Seddon, Stephen Billet and Alie Clemans on 'A Politics of Social Partnerships' focuses on the productive possibilities created in social partnerships and conceptualises the workings of social partnerships using contrasting analytical approaches, with the intention of identifying possibilities for practical politics. This paper sustains a complex analysis of social partnerships that allows for the re-framing of politics, rather than a reading of such partnerships as forms of neo-liberal governance. The final chapter in the Reader, by Agnès van Zanten, takes the work of Bourdieu as a complex but useful resource for education politics that can sustain political and pedagogical action.

This collection, then, follows a principle of selection that draws its inspiration from Yeatman's essay on revisioning the political. While we emphasise the contribution that we hope this collection makes to education politics, it is also intended to raise ques-tions about some of the more traditional approaches to education policy, especially those that saw 'politics' as outside or above that policy-making process, and thus produced an edited or cleaned up account of policy making. For example, in some of the traditional policy literature, a distinction is drawn between *analysis of* and *analysis for* policy (Gordon *et al.* 1977), with the former constructed as the more academic task, with the latter referring to research/policy work involved in the production of actual policies within the educational state. We would want to reject such a clear dis-tinction here and suggest that *analysis of* policy should be as important to policy mak-ers, broadly and inclusively defined, particularly in raising awareness and encouraging a critical research habitus, as more focused *analysis for* policy. We believe the papers in this collection dealing with global policy frames (Part I) and those dealing with vernacular policy outcomes (Part II) contribute to these broader under-standings, which like all good theory and good research are practical in their own kinds of ways.

Such considerations carry particular salience today when governments often speak of the need for evidence-based policy, a governmental rearticulation of *analysis for* policy. Such research usually takes the research problems constructed by those commissioning as a non-contestable given, rather than deconstructing the problem as constructed by the policy process as the first step in rigorous educational policy analysis. We note, though, that there are other ways of constructing evidence–based policy and we prefer the more recent articulation of 'evidence–informed' policy, which concedes implicitly the necessity of values in policy making. Policy making in education is a political and normative activity.

These matters of research policy in education in the context of neo-liberal readings of globalisation and the framing by governments of research agendas are addressed in some detail in the collection edited by Jenny Ozga, Terri Seddon and Tom Popkewitz (2006), *Education Research and Policy Steering the Knowledge-Based Economy*, the *World Yearbook of Education 2006*. The paper by Allan Luke and David Hogan in that collection, where educational policy making is defined as 'the prescriptive regulation of flows of human resources, discourse and capital across educational systems towards normative social, economic and cultural ends' (2006, 170), argues a strong case for the use of an eclectic melange of 'multidisciplinary, critical and interpretive' research to inform policy production in education. As they rightly point out, 'current debates over what counts as evidence in state policy formation are indeed debates over what counts as educational research' (Luke and Hogan 2006: 170). Their thesis is not only an academic one; rather they outline an innovative approach to evidence-informed policy making in contemporary Singaporean education, providing more evidence of the need to deparochialise the gaze of educational policy and politics research, as we have attempted to do in this collection.

References

Appadurai, A. (1996) *Modernity at Large* (Minneapolis, MN: University of Minnesota Press).

Appadurai, A. (2001) 'Grassroots globalization and the research imagination', in A. Appadurai (ed.) *Globalization* (Durham, NC: Duke University Press).

Ball, S. (1994) *Education Reform: A Critical and Post-structural Approach* (Buckingham: Open University Press).

Bernstein, B. (2001) 'From pedagogies to knowledge', in A. Morais, I. Neves, B. Davies and H. Daniels (eds), *Towards a Sociology of Pedagogy: The Contribution of Basil Bernstein to Research* (New York: Peter Lang).

Bourdieu, P. (1996) 'The social conditions of the international circulation of ideas', in R.Shusterman (ed.), *Bourdieu: A Critical Reader* (Oxford: Blackwell).

Bourdieu, P. (2003) *Firing Back: Against the Tyranny of the Market 2* (London: Verso).

Brown, P., Halsey, A.H., Lauder, H. and Stuart Wells, A. (1997) 'The transformation of education and society: an introduction', in A. H. Halsey, H. Lauder, P. Brown and A. Stuart Wells (eds), *Education: Culture, Economy and Society* (Oxford: Oxford University Press).

Dale, R. (1997) 'The state and the governance of education: an analysis of the restructuring of the state-education relation', in A. H. Halsey, H. Lauder, P. Brown and A. Stuart Wells (eds), *Education: Culture, Economy and Society* (Oxford: Oxford University Press).

Dye, T. (1992) (7th edn) *Understanding Public Policy* (Englewood Cliffs, NJ: Prentice-Hall).

Gordon, I., Lewis, J. and Young, R. (1977) 'Perspectives on policy analysis', *Public Administration Bulletin*, 25: 26–35.

Held, D. and McGrew, A. (2002) *Globalization/Anti-Globalization* (Oxford: Polity Press).

Lawn, M. and Lingard, B. (2001) 'Constructing a European policy space in educational governance: the role of transnational policy actors', *European Educational Research Journal*, 1(2): 290–307.

Lingard, B., Rawolle, S. and Taylor, S. (2005) 'Globalizing policy sociology in education: working with Bourdieu', *Journal of Education Policy*, 20 (6): 759–77.

Luke, A. and Hogan, D. (2006) 'Redesigning what counts as evidence in educational policy: the Singapore model', in J. Ozga, T. Seddon and T. Popkewitz (eds), *Education Research and Policy Steering the Knowledge-Based Economy* (London: Routledge).

Olssen, M., Codd, J. and O'Neill (2004) *Education Policy Globalization, Citizenship and Democracy* (London: Sage).

Ozga, J. (2000) *Policy Research in Educational Settings contested terrain* (Buckingham: Open University Press).

Ozga, J., Seddon, T. and Popkewitz, T. (eds) (2006) *Education Research and Policy Steering the Knowledge-Based Economy* (London: Routledge).

Rizvi, F. (2004) 'Theorizing the global convergence of restructuring policies in education', in S. Lindblad and T. Popkewitz (eds), *Educational Restructuring: International Perspectives on Travelling Policies* (Greenwich, CT: Information Age Publishing).

Seddon, T. (1994) *Context and Beyond: Reframing the Theory and Practice of Education* (London: Falmer Press).

Steiner-Khamsi, G., Silova, I. and Johnson, E. M. (2006) 'Neoliberalism liberally applied: educational policy borrowing in Central Asia', in J. Ozga, T. Seddon and T. Popkewitz (eds), *Education Research and Policy Steering the Knowledge-Based Economy* (London: Routledge).

Taylor, S. (1997) 'Critical policy analysis: exploring contexts, texts and consequences', *Discourse*, 23(13): 23–5.

Taylor, S., Rizvi, F., Lingard, B. and Henry, M. (1997) *Educational Policy and the Politics of Change* (London: Routledge).

Thomson, P. (2006) 'Policy scholarship against de-politicisation', in J. Ozga, T. Seddon and T. Popkewitz (eds) *Education Research and Policy Steering the Knowledge-Based Economy* (London: Routledge).

Yeatman, A. (1994) *Postmodern Revisionings of the Political* (New York: Routledge).

PART I

THE GLOBAL FRAMING OF
EDUCATION POLICY AND POLITICS

CHAPTER 1

POSTMODERNITY AND REVISIONING THE POLITICAL

Anna Yeatman

Yeatman, A. (1994) *Postmodern Revisionings of the Political*
(New York: Routledge), pp. 106–22

I

> There is no reason, only reasons.
>
> (Jean-Francois Lyotard in Van Riejen
> and Veerman, *An Interview with
> Jean-Francois Lyotard* 1988)

Postmodernity is the condition we are in now, a condition under which there is no operative consensus concerning the ultimate or transcendental grounds of truth and justice. This is why Lyotard (1984) identifies the postmodern condition with a crisis of narratives, or more specifically, of meta-narratives, stories which ground truth and justice in some kind of metaphysical presence such as Reason, Nature or God.

Where there can be no consensus derived from a shared culture of orientation to such transcendental grounds, the consequence for truth and justice is simple. Some other approach than that of basing them in shared transcendental grounds has to be found. If this approach is consensualist in the sense of requiring agreement on how to approach decisions concerning truth and justice, there is no guarantee that this agreement is anything more than a highly provisional and pragmatic adaptation to the conditions of contestation over these values, and how they are to be interpreted.

Here I want to discuss the kind of politics that such provisional and pragmatic adaptation involves. Because it is politics rather than knowledge that is of concern, truth enters the picture only as it is one of the criteria in relation to which the legitimacy of claims on political process are assessed and judged. For example, in the politics of needs formation in an area such as home and community care for people who are disabled seriously enough to need help in the tasks of everyday living, there are patterned disagreements between how these individuals judge their needs, and how their needs are judged by the professionals involved (gerontologists, specialists in palliative care, physiotherapists and so on).

The professionals deal in the business of what they like to think are real or objective needs, that is, needs as assessed in accordance with the knowledge base of the profession concerned. The disabled individuals think of these needs as their own, as taking on shape and existence through the way that they give voice to them: they are their expressed needs. Moreover, they accord themselves a special kind of expertise with regard to these needs: who can know them better than the person experiencing the needs? Then there are the informal carers, that is, spouses, close kin and sometimes friends who provide personally-oriented, regular assistance to the disabled individuals with whom they are connected. They have a carer's construction of the disabled individual's needs: a construction which is that of a close, personally involved observer, whose own needs are implicated in how the burden of meeting this individual's needs is distributed. The perspectives of the professional service deliverer, the carer and the needy person on the latter's needs and how they might best be met are irreducibly multiple, and often conflict.

One can make a policy decision, as the Commonwealth Government of Australia has done, to make the principle of determining how an individual's need is to be provided for one of responding to the expressed needs of the individual. This principle operates as a guideline in respect of determining how to weight these various judgments as to what the need is, and, correlatively, how it might be best met. Such a principle does not, however, resolve the ongoing tensions between the different perspectives on need. All it does and can do is to provide a principle of regulation of what I call the politics of needs formation. This example is a good one for other reasons as well. The Commonwealth Government's policy of guiding services to work with the expressed needs of individuals in the home and community care area is in line with the general emphasis of the relevant bureaucratic department (the Department of Health, Housing and Community Services) on user rights. This, in turn, is in line with contemporaneous expectations of democratic service delivery: there have been a number of social movements contesting professional domination in needs formation, not least of these being the disabled people's movements of the 1970s and 1980s. These expectations have destabilized the welfare state culture of needs definition in which expert professional opinion guided the way that policy-makers framed needs and the services responding to those needs. This was a centric culture of scientifically informed needs formation which preempted an open politics of needs formation in favor of professional expertise. It is a political culture which favors the rhetoric of rational consensus. Once there is an open and legitimate difference of perspectives on needs formation the rhetoric of rational consensus is no longer operable. It is supplanted by a rhetoric of negotiated needs settlement where the principle of user rights provides guidance toward achievement of an effective and practical compromise between these perspectives. Each perspective is necessary because it provides a basic piece of information about the context which informs the needs concerned...

The value of this example is also to underline how 'the' polity has lost a clearly bounded centricity. It has become a more or less (dis)continuous series of politics. These polities are not given but struggled for: they arise out of what Alberto Melucci (1988, 258–60) calls the opening of 'public spaces'. This particular example of a polity involves the interpenetration of the state and everyday life in respect of areas of individual need usually reserved for what we would term personal privacy (e.g. the activities of an individual being washed, fed, toiletted, and so on). It is an example which is outside the scope of the classical liberal and republican democratic polity of modernity. In this polity, needs of the kind to which I am referring were left to the private and natural business of the internal life of households. They were ministered to by those whose life was contained within the private world of the household (wives, mothers, daughters and servants). These non-citizens permitted the citizens, the heads of' households, to represent the business of the polity as both quite separate from these private needs, and as much more important than them. Theirs was a unieity [sic] of rationalist hubris and public prestige, stable as long as their own status as masters of their own culture and independent property owners remained unthreatened.

A number of left, masculinist commentators (Larch, Leach, and Donzelot) have pointed out that it was the professionals who laid the foundations of the welfare state and who undermined the integrity of this classical picture of a neat division between things public and things private. Male doctors who were licensed by the state toward the end of the nineteenth century, and who began to legitimize the intervention of the state into private lives in the areas of public and maternal/infant health, embarked on a treacherous alliance with, especially, middle-class mothers to undermine the patriarchal privilege of heads of households. The development of a universal, compulsory public school system worked in the same direction. However, the compromise between property rights and social rights which the welfare state represented maintained a principle of patriarchal determination of needs. This time it was expressed on behalf of a corporate representation of households-the state-and, in due measure, involved a transfer of rights from individual heads of households to the state in respect of the members of households. Corporate patriarchalism functioned thus to emancipate those who had been subject to the individual patriarchal householder's will. This is why interventionist doctors found ready allies amongst many, though largely amongst middle-class, women. It is also why such *fin-de-siecle* social scientists as Emile Durkheim, committed to the path of rational social reform, argued for a positive theory of right against the doctrine of natural right...Durkheim-in his lectures published as *Professional Ethics and Civic Morals* argued that these clear instances of the state bestowing rights on individuals showed that right is always a matter of positive law. Natural right, which seems to indicate that law merely reflects rather than creates the rights of individuals, is a doctrine that does not accord with the facts. Durkheim offers a benign view of the modern interventionist state, one uncomplicated by late-twentieth-century awareness that the positive constitution of rights by the state comes at the expense of the bureaucratization of the spheres in which they operate.

At the same time, this construction of the polity in the form of the welfare state is considerably more relevant than the older liberal/republican democratic construction of the polity. Where the latter offers a very simple picture of the business of governance as essentially no more than the making and enforcement of law, the former shows how the interventionist state makes the executive and administrative aspects of governance just as central to the life of the polity as the legislative aspects. This begins to complicate the principle of representative government: the legislature may be representative, but to what extent is this true of the executive, let alone of the large and complex organizations that the administration of the state has come to involve'? Moreover, an interventionist state politicizes by naming hitherto nonpolitical areas of social life and drawing them within the ambit of policy (see Yeatman 1990, chapter 8). The increasing reach of policy both deprivatizes and denatures aspects of social life hitherto regulated within the local patriarchal and customary communities of families, firms and service provision. In so doing, policy constitutes all who come within its reach as potential political actors who can open this area to a politics of voice and representation.

As we have seen with the example of the area of home and community care, a politics of voice and representation introduces the principle of irresolvable difference into the way that political process and decisions operate. This principle destabilizes and delegitimizes the paternalism of the state which it had borrowed from the patriarchal, paternalist authority of private households. This means that paternalism is no longer adequate to the vertical integration functions of social and political control at a time when the state is subject to an historically unparalleled politics of voice and representation. For paternalism, the state substitutes performativity as the principle which legitimizes both its control functions, and the way in which those functions operate to contain the influence of the horizontally integrated, democratic politics of social movements and their claims on the state. The state is thereby subject to the contradictory dynamics of performativity and democratization. Performativity has the singular virtue of supplying a meta-discourse for public policy. Thus it can subsume and transform substantive democratizing claims within a managerialist-functionalist rhetoric. Performativity is a systems-orientation: instead of the state appearing as the enlightened and paternal command of shared community, the state is equated with the require-ments of a system for ongoing integrity and viability. This is a cybernetic model: 'The true goal of the system, the reason it programs itself like a computer, is the optimization of the global relationship between input and output-in other words, performativity' (Lyotard 1984, 11).

II

> The decision makers…allocate our lives for the growth of power.
> (Jean-Francois Lyotard, *The Postmodern Condition* 1984)

Performativity as a principle of governance depends on the existence of jurisdic-tional boundaries of the state which permit it to be thought of as a discrete system. However, the very nature of the cybernetic metaphor makes these boundaries open to input and output flows of information, capital and population within which the regulative presence of the boundaries operates like a program in relation to these flows, and where the limits of the program are set, reviewed and revised in state policy decisions. Performativity is a principle of governance which establishes strictly functional relations between a state and its inside and outside environments. Democracy and social welfare are operationalized in terms of these functional relations. The rhetoric of the state addressed to its own internal population takes on the features of an instrumentally rational orientation to the terms of economic competition between states and/or states allied together in trading blocks: Cerny (1990, chapter 8) refers to this development as a shift from the welfare to the competition state: Cerny (1990, 230) argues that: 'As the world economy is char-acterized by increasing interpenetration and the crystallization of transnational markets and structures, the state itself is having to act more and more like a market player, that shapes its policies to promote, control, and maximize returns from market forces in an international setting.'

Clear criteria (immigration policy) of who are/are not legitimate citizens of the state are maintained primarily as a strong regulative control over who is permitted access to this community of goods and services. Policy concerning such access is defined almost completely in terms of the performativity requirements of a competition state. For those who are legitimate members of the state, their shared identity is not that of the social citizens of the welfare state, but that of actual or potential contributors to the performativity of the competition state. The trend is thus to turn all nationals into contributors (an active labor market policy), and to define out of existence non-contributors. As Lyotard (1984, xxiv) correctly discerns, the application of the criterion of optimizing the system's performance 'to all of our games necessarily entails a certain level of terror, whether soft or hard: be operational (that is commensurable) or disappear.'

A state which is oriented in terms of the culture of performativity is a secretive state, oriented to making discreet deals with corporate players who can significantly affect the performativity of this state-centric system. Information is openly shared by the state with its internal environment only to the extent that it furthers strategies of political and social management of the actors within this environment. The consequence of this is that a great deal of the business of the state is private rather than public. Or, to put it more accurately, this business becomes public only as social movements and their minority party representatives within the legislature contest state decisions, and, by so doing, drag them into the visibility of openly contested political representations.

In this context democratic politics is centered in the evanescent openings of public spaces which the new social movements achieve in their contestation of the state's definition of the situation. By turning the techno(econo)cratic representations of state policy into openly contested political issues, they convert performative decisions into rhetorical praxis. Democratic struggle is centered on attempting and effecting this conversion. A politics of representation depends on making issues visible by opening up public spaces. This is why the state has encouraged a high degree of concentration and centralization of print and electronic media capital. However, even within the controlling ambience of a partnership between the state and media corporate players, representational control is never complete. As Michael Ryan (1989, chapter 6) argues, vertical use of rhetoric to control meaning by condensing it within a governing metaphor for example, the USA as the liberator of a Kuwait from a Hitler-like Saddam Hussein-can never foreclose horizontal use of rhetoric where metonymy can develop meanings which work against the vertical integration and condensation of meaning. For example, if the USA state, led by ex-CIA Director Bush, emphasized the liberator ideal of US Manifest Destiny, then it is all too easy for it to become hoist on its own petard in relation to those audiences to whom its rhetoric is addressed. This is what happened with US intervention in Vietnam, when the corruption and antidemocratic features of the Diem regime in South Vietnam belied all the rhetoric on behalf of defending the forces of democracy against those of totalitarianism. Equally, while the Bush-led USA state was intent on ensuring that it was the controlling leader of any liberating intervention in the Gulf (Middle East), it was unable to control the metonymic properties of liberation rhetoric, and thus to explain why it was that it abandoned the Kurds, who rose up against Hussein only to draw down upon themselves his counterforce and military terror.

It will be clear from what I have argued that the performative state has an historical symbiosis with the centricity of both the classical bourgeois liberal/ republican state and of the welfare state. The system that is the reference point for the performative criteria of efficiency, economy and effectiveness borrows its cultural and structural integrity from these earlier phases of the modern state's existence. The performative, competition state represents itself as the natural development of the *burgerliche* culture of public man and of the social citizenship of the welfare state. This representation is an exercise in performativity. It is not substantively anchored in the current commitments and *modus operandi of* the state. State-sponsored police terror, as well as addictive behaviors (alcohol and other drugs, gambling); are used to control and marginalize those who are destined to be non-contributors. The prisons fill up, legal due process becomes a matter of privilege rather than of right, and the Redferns or Harlems of this world are subject to police terror raids that are never called properly to public account.

The performative state empties the formally instituted public sphere of substantive politicized content. Executive decision-making is undertaken in relation to a series of disciplinary instruments, with regard to internal party discussion and parliamentary process: these ensure that public debate and information sharing are never developed beyond a strictly limited theatrical intimation of debate and information sharing. The performative state is the response of vertically integrated control agendas to the conditions of postmodernity. If there cannot be a substantive community of ends shared by a legitimate elite of master subject citizens (the private proprietors of households), and the dissonance of irresolvably multiple perspectives of difference is introduced, the most sensible move is to abandon the substantive game of modern citizenship in favor of performativity.

At the same time, the terms of struggle for democratic politics have changed in ways that are congruent with dissonance, dissension, multiplicity, and difference. They are not oriented to the development and stability of a single political arena or public sphere, if only for the reason that their motivating agendas combine to indicate a complexity and multiplicity that is not containable within the one public space. For all these reasons, democratic discourse that is oriented in terms of a centric public sphere is truly anachronistic.

III

> Thus the society of the future falls less within the province of a Newtonian anthropology...than a pragmatics of language particles. There are many different language games-and heterogeneity of elements. They only give rise to institutions in patches – local determinism.
>
> (Jean-Francois Lyotard, *The Postmodern Condition* 1984)

Lyotard (1984, 17) argues that, under postmodern conditions, the social becomes 'flexible networks of language games'. Politics thus becomes the more or less extensive politicization of these networks, and the situation of the language tames involved within public space. A democratic politics is oriented in principle to the development of this politicization within both specific language games, for instance, the language game of service-delivery or the language game of academic pedagogy, and across such flexible networks of language games. It is important to enquire how this democratic politics is situated in respect of a performative culture of governance. Performativity is one type of rhetorical practice: open dialogue, discussion, dissension and sharing of information is mother. Where the former reifies certain values, such as efficiency, the latter develops rhetorical praxis by asking basic questions like: efficient in relation to what ends, whose ends, and what time scale (short, medium, long term)?

As we have seen, performativity involves the use of terror, but there are important limits on how far the business of governance can be brought within the ambit of the principle of performativity and its distinctive form of terror. As both Lyotard (1984, 15) and Melucci (1988, 249; 1989, 207) argue, the steering capacity of the system is improved by allowing performativity to be substituted for by the politicization of particular issue areas. With the kind of complexity that the contemporary state has to deal with, and where policy decisions serve to effectively reduce this complexity by making provisional commitments, this reduction needs to be well informed if it is to work. Social movements are both reliable and creative in making visible the issues that have to be faced. For example, it is no good thinking that aged care service delivery can work in one mode if it turns out to be culturally unacceptable to those who need the service.

Melucci's characterization of the 'new' social movements, which are engaged as contestants of the performative state, emphasizes their primary feature as movements engaged in symbolic challenge. These movements open and develop a politics of representation, and thereby contribute to converting performative decisions into rhetorical praxis. Melucci (1988, 247) states:

> The modern contemporary phenomena to which I refer (in particular the women's movement, the environmental 'movements', the forms of youth collective action and the mobilizations in favor of peace) are not concerned primarily with citizenship. This is not to say that this theme has disappeared. In the collective action of women, for example, the problem of rights, inequality and exclusion constitute a large part of the mobilization process. But what women, along with other contemporary political actors, have achieved is above all to practice alternative definitions of sense: in other words, they have created meanings and definitions of identity which contrast with the increasing determination of individual and collective life by impersonal technocratic power.

These movements are themselves flexible networks of language games rather than a precisely bounded, hierarchically integrated organizational presence. They are subject to an internal politics of multiple and conflicting representations of why they exist, what it is that they should do, and how they should operate. Perhaps more significantly, a good deal of movement activity is submerged within the commonsense of everyday life. This permits dissenting constructions of the movement's politics to assume peaceful coexistence in the form of different and plural ways of conducting everyday life.

Mobilization is in terms of a flexible, networked membership, and it is understood that the sites of struggle are themselves multiple. Accordingly, for these movements, there is not public space neatly sequestered and bounded in relation to private space. Kitchen table conversation can become a public space, not because those using it are planning their next political action, but because their discussion and debate are politicizing their interaction and relationships. With feminism, for example, public spaces open up in respect of how housework is distributed, and how sexuality is expressed.

These are movements grounded in everyday life: recall the disability movements and their inevitable immersion in fundamental issues of embodiment and survival. They enjoy a resilience because of this. If, for the time being, a movement loses visibility on a larger canvas – for example, the performance art of street demonstrations, which gains prime time electronic media coverage – and if the state substitutes performative criteria for the movement's presence within substantive policy, it is still developing and experimenting within what Melucci terms the latency of everyday life. It is this that makes these movements such a rich source of system innovation and development. As Melucci (1989, 208) puts it:

> The submerged networks of social movements are laboratories of experience. New problems and questions are posed. New answers are invented and tested, and reality is perceived and named in different ways.
>
> All these experiences are displayed publicly only within particular conjunctures and only by means of the organizing activities described by resource organization theory. But none of this public activity would be possible without the laboratory experiences of the submerged networks.[1]

Social movements and their capacity to open up public spaces of openly contested representations are, then, necessary for the principle of performativity to operate. They enhance what Melucci (1989, 207) terms the 'already high learning capacity' or 'reflexivity' of complex systems. This is why, instead of responding to the backward looking nostalgia of conservative groups for racial homogeneity, the state maintains an equal opportunity relationship to difference, thereby maintaining open access to critical information about the changing demographics, markets and environments of the system. It is also why the public management of relatively new service areas such as home and community care maintains a consultative relationship to the field of consumers and carers.

Performativity thus depends on the perviousness of the policy-making capacities of the state to social movements which represent emergent demands and issues for the system. For this reason, a performative state cannot insulate itself against politics. If performative terror lies in the rationality of 'be operational (that is, commensurable) or disappear', the requirement to be operational simultaneously militates against the adoption of widely visible, class-nondiscriminatory and systemic terror. For these reasons the perfonnative state is more of a democratic than a police state. It maintains rhetorical continuity with the traditions of liberal/republican democracy and with social democracy as a way of both signalling and explaining its perviousness to social movements.

Melucci (1988) sees social movements as engaging in primarily symbolic contestation which challenges dominant representations, the effect of which is to make power visible and accountable within the public space opened up by this contestation. The decision-makers absorb this contestation within policies which take up as well as neutralize the challenge. These policies are the negotiated settlements to which I have referred above: 'They have to be redefined continually and rapidly because the differences change, the conflicts shift, the agreements cease to satisfy and new forms of domination are constantly emerging' (Melucci 1988, 251).

Their force is local in both a temporal and relational sense, temporally local, for the reasons Melucci has just indicated, and relationally local, because the fields of force out of which negotiated settlements come are themselves local in relation to the system. Performativity is the only principle available which permits some degree of commensurability across different context of pressure for complexity-reducing decisions. It thereby assumes a pan-local force, which does not shield it from being upset in a particular, local context of struggle.

Melucci and Lyotard emphasize the relational properties of symbolic contestation and language games. This is a semiotic politics which shows how it is possible that social movements can convert dominant codes and powerful organizations to their own purposes, purposes, it is clear, that are no more exclusively within the control of those movements than dominant agendas are within the control of those movements, rhetorical antagonists. In this sense, symbolic cooptation can work in both directions. This is why Melucci *(*1989, 208, emphasis in the original) distinguishes his view of power from that of Foucault, Deleuze and Guattari: 'They share a one-dimensional view of power-as the construction and administration of subjects-whereas reality as we experience it in complex societies is in my opinion the resultant of powerful organizations which attempt to define the meaning of reality *and* actors and networks of actors who use the resources of these same organizations to define reality in novel ways.'

Local determinism is a principle of institutionalization which elides the two alternatives Adam Smith offered in *The Wealth of Nations:* the invisible hand of the market, or the 'men of system' who attempt to arrange society as though it were pieces on a chess board in accordance with a grand plan or vision. For Smith, the former option had the singular virtue of working through the intentionality of individuals participating in a self-interested relationship to exchange transactions with others. Local determinism indicates a different principle of sociality: a language game: 'the question of the social bond, insofar as it is a question, is itself a language game, the game of inquiry. It immediately positions the person who asks, as well as the addressee and the referent asked about: it is already the social bond' (Lyotard 1984, 15).

A language game is institutionalized when it functions according to constraints which regulate what is admissible within the game and how moves in the game are to be made (Lyotard 1984, 17). As with the policies Melucci discusses, this institutionalization has a provisional and conjunctural character: 'the limits the institution imposes on potential language "moves" are never established once and for all (even if they have been formally defined)'[2] (Lyotard 1984, 17). As Lyotard argues, the limits themselves are the stakes in the game. The language game of home and community care service delivery is one in which the limits are under constant tussle. Not least do these concern, as we have seen, who is authorized to speak, and on behalf of whom. In aged care, most medical professionals would like to reinstate a game in which the needy individuals are positioned as 'patients', as those of whom questions may be asked by the professional but who are accorded no right to ask questions themselves of the professional or any other participant in the service delivery language game.

IV

> We must arrive at an idea and practice of justice that is not linked to that of consensus.
>
> (Jean-Francois Lyotard, *The Postmodern Condition* 1984)

What, indeed, is the status of justice under the conditions of postmodern politics? I have argued that postmodern politics is constituted by a field of tension and conflict between, on the one hand, an open politics of voice and representation, and, on the other, performativity as a principle of selective closure in respect of the information overload and social complexity which confronts the contemporary state. I have suggested also that the new social movements of the kind which are theorized by Melucci are movements oriented within an imaginary of resistance to domination combined with a commitment to self determination. Moreover, these movements situate themselves within a polyphony of different movement claims to self-determination and resistance to the performative terror of the state. That is, they share a practical understanding of the universality of the political ethic which informs these claims: they understand both their affinity with each other as similar though distinct claimants of this kind, and they are aware that the state is either relatively open to the ethos they share, or closed.

At the same time, these movements do not resile from their differences, which make their claims of self-determination and resistance to domination non-additive and non-totalizable. They are not subsumable within a single culture, ethos, or vision of emancipation or self-determination. There is no way they could agree on a shared conception of justice, although it is possible for them to explore the connections and even the overlaps between their respective conceptions of justice...

Difference in, and sometimes connections between, emancipatory agendas indicate a kind of universalism. This is not, however, the universalism of a modern, rationalist emancipatory politics. The legitimacy of these multiple and different emancipatory claims does not reside in reason. There is no shared community of reason because there is no collective, universal subject.

In this context, should reason be claimed by adherents to modernist emancipatory traditions as the arbiter of political claims, it must be perceived as an arbitrary closure of debate, an exclusion of difference, a nostalgic assertion of a homogeneous subject that has lost all credibility. The construction of a collective homogeneous subject becomes perforce a politics of the right, which moves to defend not the universality of the human subject but the particularity of the Western (white, European) subject against those who are represented, in Margaret Thatcher's phrase, as belonging to 'alien cultures'. The right appropriates the language of difference and resituates it within an unapologetic celebration of Western racism. Thus, while the integration of Europe is bringing the dismantling of intra-European national restrictions on the movement of Europeans within Europe, immigration restrictions on the entry of non-Europeans (blacks, Third World peoples) have intensified. If the Kurds, or any other people within what Western racism terms 'the Third World', should become persecuted and subject to genocidal terror, they are not to be accorded refuge as immigrants within the nations of the West.

Western racism thus appropriates from modern social science the imaginary of a differential common culture and defends its integrity against alien incursions. This is a consensualism of a familiar kind: by excluding the alien other, differences at home are also suppressed, and the order of the modern West is upheld.

This point underlines a critical feature of the new social movements and their espousal of a non-consensualist politics of difference. These movements do not conduct themselves in terms of an homogeneous movement identity in relation to which individual adherents discipline and subject themselves. They eschew the idea of a shared or common culture. Instead, the identity of a movement arises out of a politics of affinity (Haraway 1990) between subjects who continually reinterpret the movement and its goals in relation to the changing character of their own personal histories:

> In other words, these different forms of consciousness are grounded...In one's personal history; but that history – one's identity – is interpreted or reconstructed by each of us within the horizon of meanings and knowledges available in the culture at given historical moments, a horizon that also includes modes of political commitment and struggle. Self and identity, in other words, are always grasped and understood within particular discursive configurations. Consciousness, therefore, is never fixed, never attained once and for all, because discursive boundaries change with historical conditions.
> (de Lauretis 1986, 8; and see Martin and Mohanty 1986)

A self which is discursively oriented to 'the understanding of identity as multiple and even self-contradictory' (de Lauretis 1986, 9) is clearly incapable of practicing the disciplinary self-government of a self oriented within a culture of self-mastery (mastery by reason of the passions, instincts or drives). The former self is one which understands and resists the exclusionary terror of self-mastery whereby the integrity of a self is established through the exclusion and repression of all that is rigidly deemed non-self....

A non-consensualist politics of difference develops rhetorical procedures which problematize a subject speaking on behalf of another, and which put a premium on subjects finding their own 'voice' within whatever politics of representation is at hand. Within this politics, subjects are understood to be discursively positioned within the conjunctural historical moment of contested narratives of who they are and where they are going. Thus, with feminism operating as a discursive intervention within this contestation, females are accorded a shared positioning as women. It follows that, in any cross-gender politics, women trust be accorded a voice in that politics. From the point of view of this politics, how women distribute the representation of this voice amongst themselves is up to them. Necessarily, however, this representation is subject to an internal feminist politics of difference, and of making those who speak as women accountable to their complex and differentiated constituency. This is achieved by ensuring that as many differently positioned women speak 'on behalf of women' as there are discursively posited differences among women. They may arrive at a negotiated settlement of their differences in what is represented, not as unicity, but as a claim on cross-gender political process which they share for the time being.

It is important to understand that a negotiated settlement may, more often than not, represent a willingness to achieve pragmatic compromise in relation to coexistent and different views of justice. ... Within the spirit of this kind of politics, 'tradition' or 'identity' are invoked in order to Around claims, but, as we have seen, there is a non-essentialist understanding of tradition and identity. These are subject to the conjunctural rhetorical play of the claims themselves, and this is understood, up to a point, by the players.

V

A recognition of the heteromorphous nature of language games is a first step in that direction. This obviously implies a renunciation of terror, which assumes that they are isomorphic and tries to make them so. The second step is the principle that any consensus on the rules defusing *a* game and the 'moves' playable within it must be local, in other words, agreed on by its present players and subject to eventual cancellation. The orientation then favors a multiplicity of finite meta-arguments, by which I mean argumentation that concerns metaprescriptives and is limited in space and time.

(Jean-Francois Lyotard, *The Postmodern Condition* 1984)

I have undertaken here a series of meditations on and applications of Lyotard's *The Postmodern Condition* with the intention of outlining some of the most important aspects of a postmodern politics. This *is a* politics which comprises a number of interlocking fields of force. One such field opposes the principle of performativity to that of rhetorical praxis. This field is bound up with the politics of the state, where the state is the site of struggle. Another field opposes a consensualist politics of difference on behalf of the West to a non-consensualist politics which is oriented within a postcolonial ethos. A further field opposes modernist rhetorics of democratic, rationalist consensus to postmodern rhetorics of local, conjunctural, multiple agreements, context-bound, and varying by context.

These fields of force evoke, as they reinterpret and resituate, modern visions and traditions of politics. At the same time, they are still barely theorized. Dominant constructions of the polity and politics arc still those of Western modernity. There is good reason for this: it is a functional state of affairs for those who experience a non-consensualist politics of difference as cultural loss. However, many so situated are still committed to democratic values in ways which permit new learning. It is important that those of us situated so as to find, rather than to lose, voice in the new politics proceed to reflect on and theorize it. Only then can we offer a bridge from a modern to a postmodern democratic politics. Only then also can our reflection on emergent practice permit us to develop and refine our strategic interventions.

Notes

1 'Resource mobilization theory emphasizes the fundamental importance of factors such as the availability of resources – recruitment networks, the costs and benefits of participation, organizations, funding and the availability of professionals – in analyzing the growth of new social movements' (Interviewers, in Melucci 1989, 192).
2 'Reciprocally, it can be said that the boundaries only stabilize when they cease to be stakes in the game' (Lyotard 1984, 17).

References

Cerny, P. (1990) *The Changing Architecture of Politics: Structure, Agency and the Future of the State* (London: Sage).

de Laurentis, T. (1986) 'Feminist? Critical Studies: Issues, Terms and Contexts' in T. de Laurentis (ed.), *Feminist Studies/Critical Studies* (Bloomington: Indiana University Press).

Donzelot, J. (1979) *The Policing of Families* (London: Hutchinson).

Durkheim, E. (1957) *Professional Ethics and Civic Morals* (London: Routledge and Kegan Paul).

Haraway, D. (1990) 'A Manifesto for Cyborgs: Science, Technology and Socialist Feminism in the 1980s' in L. Nicholson (ed.), *Feminism/Postmodernism* (New York and London: Routledge), pp. 190–233.

Lash, C. (1977) *Haven in a Heartless World: the Family Besieged* (New York: Basic Books).

Leach, W. (1980) *True Love and Perfect Union: the Feminist Reform of Sex and Society* (New York: Basic Books).

Lyotard, J.-F. (1984) *The Postmodern Condition* (Manchester: Manchester University Press).

Martin, B. and Mohanty, C. (1986) 'Feminist Politics: What's Home got to do with it?' in T. De Laurentis (ed.), *Feminist Studies/Critical Studies* (Bloomington: Indian University Press).

Melucci, A. (1988) 'Social Movements and the Democratization of Everyday Life' in I. Keane (ed.), *Civil Society and the State* (London: Verso).

Melucci, A. (1989) *Nomads of the Present* (London: Hutchinson).

Ryan, M. (1989) *Politics and Culture: Working Hypotheses for a Post-Revolutionary Society* (London: Macmillan).

Van Reijen, W. and Veerman, D. (1988) 'An Interview with Jean-Francois Lyotard' *Theory, Culture and Society*, 5: 277–309.

Yeatman, A. (1990) *Bureaucrats, Technocrats, Femocrats: Essays on the Contemporary Australian State* (Sydney: Allen & Lenwin).

CHAPTER 2

DEBATING GLOBALIZATION AND EDUCATION AFTER SEPTEMBER 11

Fazal Rizvi

Comparative Education, May 2004, 40(2): 157–71

Over the past decade, there has been no other concept in social, political and educational theory as widely and passionately debated as globalization. Not only has globalization become a buzzword, it has also divided theorists and practitioners alike along highly ideological lines. Deep disputes have emerged surrounding the historical and cultural origins of globalization, as well as its political consequences. Little consensus exists with respect to not only definitions and explanations of globalization but also its implications for policy, and prescriptions for a 'new world order'. Globalization has been linked to almost every purported social change in recent years, from an emergent knowledge economy, the declining authority of the state and the demise of traditional cultural practices to the spread of neo-liberal economic regimes and the advent of a postmodern consumer culture. In normative terms, some have viewed globalization as a major new source for optimism in the world, while others have seen it in entirely negative terms. As Scholte (2000) points out, 'some people have associated "globalization" with progress, prosperity and peace. For others, however, the word has conjured up deprivation, disaster and doom' (p. 14). What is beyond doubt is that globalization is a thoroughly contested subject.

Not surprisingly, therefore, globalization has been much debated in comparative education, with respect to the ways in which it has affected different policy communities, as well as its implications for the direction and politics of educational change (see Burbules and Torres 2000). Ball (1998) has used the notion of globalization to show how it can be used to compare and analyse educational policies. Arnove and Torres (1999) have suggested that the very notion of comparison needs to be re-thought, as a dialectic between the global and the local. Stromquist (2002) has explored some of the ways in which issues of power, technology and knowledge are interconnected in the globalized world. Tikly (2001) has used a range of insights from recent postcolonial theories to develop a conceptual framework for understanding the relationship between globalization and low-income, postcolonial societies. In doing this, he has argued that the response to globalization in different regions of the world is 'a product of economic, political and cultural factors and studying the impact of globalization on each region draws attention to different aspects of the postcolonial condition' (p. 152). His postcolonial analysis seeks to 're-narrativize' the globalization story from the perspective of the historically marginalized parts of the world. It uncovers the various formations of the global western hegemony, and highlights the manner in which it has been and can be resisted.

Tikly's (2001) postcolonial analysis appears to accept, as do most recent analyses in comparative education, that while the notion of globalization needs to be approached cautiously, it nonetheless represents something new about the manner in which the world is now organized and the ways in which local and national communities relate to each other. Much of the debate in comparative education surrounds the contentious issue of the nature and extent to which nation states still maintain some authority to work in line with their own policy priorities, determined in terms of their own distinctive cultural and historical traditions, rather than simply submitting to a certain framework of policy prescriptions laid down by political structures operating beyond the nation states. It is argued that not only do international organizations like the World Bank and the OECD now have the capacity to constrain national policy options, a new global hegemonic discourse of education also limits policy innovation at the local and national levels (see Henry *et al.* 2001). Whatever the debates, it is clear that global processes can no longer be overlooked when determining or analysing educational policies.

Of course, the processes of globalization do not only affect educational policy and practice through education's links to economic and political realities, but extend also to issues of governance. But perhaps even more significantly cultural globalization has greater impact on educational practice because education operates within a broader cultural field that includes mass media and, an increasingly globalized consumer culture (see Kenway and Bullen 2001). Indeed, as authors like Hall (1996) and Waters (1995) explain, it is the cultural flows between nations that above all typify the current phase of globalization. Accordingly, there has been much discussion about the possible homogenization of culture; and of the ways in which the current cultural flows are uni-directional – from 'the West' to 'the Rest'. This debate underlines asymmetries of power that exist in the modern world system, as has been demonstrated by numerous postcolonial analyses in recent years (e.g. Hoogvelt 1997).

Asymmetries of power are also inherent in the ways in which the global media has now become hegemonic, and in the manner in which particular cultural practices and identities of the global elite have become increasingly 'deterritorialized'. Bauman (2000) has drawn a useful distinction between 'tourists' and 'vagabonds' to show the uneven impact of globalization on people's life options and chances. Appudarai (1996) has argued that the current phase of globalization is marked by the accelerated pace at which cultural exchanges take place, and by the scale and the complexity of these exchanges, leading to both greater homogeneity and heterogeneity of culture, with more people than ever before becoming involved with more than one culture.

Some of these exchanges across national boundaries are as old as human society itself. But it was not until the late 1980s that the rapid expansion of these exchanges was widely recognized. With this recognition emerged an overarching and ubiquitous discourse of globalization that sought to capture a wide variety of historical changes taking place at the global level. Until the early 1990s, the term 'globalization' was not widely used in policy and academic circles. Its emergence therefore needs to be understood historically: what explains the development of the discourse of globalization, as well as its popularity and academic institutionalization?

Part of the explanation lies in the rise of new information technologies that linked people from around the world with each other in unprecedented ways. But beyond this, in my view, a persuasive historical analysis ties the rise of the discourse of globalization to the end of the cold war. The fall of the Soviet Bloc meant that the world no longer had two super powers but only one, and that in the ideological battle between capitalism and communism, the West could finally claim a victory. It was now possible for the leaders of multinational corporations to represent the world economic system as 'globally integrated'. New right thinkers too could now declare 'the end of history' (Fukuyama 1992), trumpeting the triumph of a 'new world order' where, so it was believed, old ideological disputes had all but been settled.

The arrival of the 'new world order' was symbolized by the collapse of the Berlin Wall and the spread of neo-liberal economic principles into the former Soviet Bloc countries, and also to most parts of the developing world. Politicians were able to use the term 'globalization' freely to explain economic shifts and articulate their ideological commitment to economic restructuring in a language that was assumed to be technical rather than political. The discourse of globalization was thus institutionalized around a set of converging ideas, based loosely upon neo-liberal economic theories, popularized a decade earlier by President Reagan in the USA and Prime Minister Thatcher in the UK. Central to these theories was the view that national boundaries represented a major impediment to the development of a truly free market, in which capital could move around the globe more freely.

A number of writers on globalization (e.g. Mann 2000) believed that the future of the nation state as a self-contained entity had itself become problematic. Globalization, it was argued not only by right wing ideologues such as Fukuyama but also left-leaning theorists like Held (1991), signalled the end of major national divisions in respect of political and economic action, as well as cultural reproduction and consumption. Waters (1995) argued that globalization was not just an economic force, describing the worldwide expansion of interconnected economic relations and markets, but also a cultural phenomenon that could no longer be contained within the boundaries of the nation state. Ideas, knowledge, attitudes, media and cultural commodities now spread around the world across once unbridgeable temporal and spatial distances. According to Giddens (1994), globalization was really about transformation of time and space. More precisely, globalization involved 'action at a distance' (p. 4) – its intensification over recent years owed much 'to the emergence of means of instantaneous global communication and mass transportation'. The idea of 'action at a distance' referred to the interconnectedness of economic, political and cultural activities across the globe.

However, while it could hardly be denied that advances in technologies made flows of capital, people and ideas across the globe much more feasible than ever before, what these arguments about time-space compression did not reveal was the extent to which globalization was inextricably linked to the expansion of capitalist ideologies and practices. Critics point out that globalization is not simply about movement and flows, but needs to be interpreted also as a hegemonic project, constituted by the power of capital. Hardt and Negri (2000, 180), for example, refer to this as an imperial project, globally networked, but located within 'the regime of American constitutional history'. Other critics belonging to the antiglobalization movement highlight the need to understand globalization not simply in terms of its processes but also as a historical phenomenon that serves a particular set of powerful corporate interests (see, for example, Klein 2000). Towards the end of 1990s, the arguments of the anti-globalization movement could no longer be ignored, for its robust global organization took the debates beyond the journals and the universities and into the streets.

By the time the twin towers in New York so tragically fell on September 11, 2001, the debate about globalization had become entrenched in academic circles and public imagination alike. But just as the fall of the Berlin Wall had historically given rise to a new discourse of globalization and of 'global integration', so too it is now an open question as to the extent to which the tragic events of September 11 might serve to reshape academic and popular debates about globalization. To what extent does September 11 and its aftermath have the potential to transform our understanding of globalization?

An enormous range of views has been put forward on the implications of September 11 for re-thinking globalization. The much admired globalization theorist, John Gray, for example, was reported in an editorial in *The Economist* in 2001 as saying that September 11 marked the end of globalization. The *New York Times* columnist, Tom Friedman, insisted, on the other hand, that some of the trends of globalization he had described in his book *The Lexus and the olive tree* (2000) were in fact confirmed by the events of September 11. A similar view was advanced by the Orientalist historian, Bernard Lewis (2002). To help us work through this diversity of views, Rosenau (2001) has made an important distinction between what might in fact have changed and a new vocabulary that has emerged in relation to globalization in the post-September 11 era. Rosenau argues that 'globalization was then [before September 11], as it is now, an interplay of frag-mentation and integration', but that a new vocabulary is now emerging with which to explore the 'habitual patterns of fragmentation and integration'.

Famously, of course, in the immediate aftermath of September 11, President George W. Bush and other political leaders around the world had argued that the world had changed for ever. It was argued that the events of September 11 had serious and far-reaching effects on the international financial markets; and that a new security regime would need to be developed to cope with forms of terrorism that operated across national spaces and that were highly mobile and flexible. In the cultural field, a series of pro- and anti-Islamic sentiments appeared in the popular media around the world; and in the USA, the symbols of patriotism became commonplace, as most people wondered about the American response to the atrocities. Calls for tolerance and understanding coincided with calls to root out the evils of terrorism. What was left in no doubt was that September 11 was an event almost as historically significant as the collapse of the Soviet Union.

More than two years later, it is now possible to ask, in a more sober fashion, how have, and indeed whether, the debates about globalization changed after September 11. What impact has September 11 and its aftermath had on the processes of globalization? Has it speeded up or slowed down globalization? What will September 11 mean for global economic integration and social disintegration and exclusion? To what extent is the cosmopolitan project inspired by globaliza-tion compromised by ensuing tensions between Islam and the West? Which aspects of globalization have been confirmed and refuted by September 11 and its after-math? And what implications has it had on the anti-globalization movement? And how are issues of educational policy and practice affected by it?

In what follows, I argue, from a postcolonial perspective, that many of the claims about the world becoming totally transformed by the events on September 11 are grossly exaggerated and simplistic. By 'postcolonial perspective' I mean a point of view of knowledges developed outside the dominant hegemonic orientation of the West. It is a perspective concerned with developing a set of guiding principles of political practice morally committed to identifying and transforming the conditions of exploitation in which large sections of the world's populations live out their daily lives. As Young (2003) points out, postcolonialism is about '... generative relations between different peoples and different cultures' (p. 7) and about a refusal to accept the superiority of western constructions of global issues.

From this perspective, while in the immediate aftermath of September 11, there was understandably some instability within the financial markets, this was to be expected given that markets operate on speculation. However, September 11 has not changed the fundamental structure of economic exchange within global capitalism. Nor have the fundamental ways in which American hegemonic power operates been disturbed. If anything, the events since September 11 have consolidated American economic power, as nations around the world have been expected to fall behind the USA in its 'war on terrorism'. The new rhetoric of security has been enormously useful to the USA in re-asserting its global authority and pre-eminence in international relations.

However, while much has remained the same, I want to suggest that the discursive field within which globalization is debated has changed in at least three significant ways. First, in the USA in particular, but elsewhere as well, there has emerged a powerful new narrative of security that appears to dwarf most other concerns about public policy and social welfare. This narrative has had major implications for the way issues of mobility of people across national-boundaries in particular are now considered. Second, the nation state itself, which some globalization theorists had claimed had begun to lose much of its authority, has made a comeback; and in the post-September 11 world, it has re-asserted much of its power, allegedly to work towards making the lives of its citizens more secure, but also to shut off democratic debate on a whole range of subjects. And finally, this new discursive field has rendered the relationship between the West and Islam into one of antagonism, representing a major impediment for the promotion of cosmopolitan ideals with which some strands of globalization theories had become associated.

The notion of a discursive field I use in this essay is based loosely on Pierre Bourdieu's concept of cultural field. Bourdieu (1977, 1990) defines cultural field as a series of rules, rituals, conventions, categories, designations and titles which constitutes an objective hierarchy, and which authorizes certain discourses and activities. Bourdieu understands the notion of cultural field to refer to fluid and dynamic, rather than static, entities. A cultural field is made up not simply of institutions and rules, but of interactions between institutions, rules and practices. My definition of discursive field is derived from this understanding, and refers to the range of assumptions that are made implicitly in debating a particular topic or issue; ideas that are presumed, and notions that are simply ruled out of the bounds of possibility. Of course, a discursive field represents an exercise in power, establishing the universalized grounds upon which further questions are permissible and may be asked, defining the parameters of acceptable images, narratives, information, voices and perspectives.

I want to argue that not only in the USA, but elsewhere as well, in countries as diverse as Russia, the UK, India, Singapore and Indonesia, a new discursive field has emerged that highlights the role that governments must play in establishing a regime of citizen protection, which does not only make them feel more secure but also promises to punish those who have caused, or have the potential to cause, them harm. This narrative of security is based on the assumption that citizens are prepared to concede to the government some of their democratic rights, with the expectation that the state will necessarily look after their interests. Within this discursive field, opposition to this assumption is not ruled out but is nevertheless considered 'unpatriotic', because it is believed to provide an unacceptable level of comfort to the enemies of the state. This discursive field is secured through a largely compliant media, which either does not permit oppositional voices, or else dismisses them as ill informed or insufficiently loyal to the nation. It is based on a presumed political 'settlement' between the people and the government.

However, this settlement serves only to 'de-politicize' legitimate public discussion about the nature and causes of terrorism, and specific policy measures needed to counter the threats of terrorism. As Jayasuriya (2002, p. 131) argues, under the cloak of security, this discursive field risks ushering in a debilitating form of 'anti-politics', which sidelines otherwise constructive opinions that are assumed somehow to be 'unpatriotic', or against the presumed national interest. According to Jayasuriya, 'some of these effects are already apparent in the US, where self-censorship in the media has made discussion of the politics of terrorism all but impossible' (p. 132). Moreover, and perhaps more seriously, the language of security has 'begun to frame facets of transnational governance in terms of "risk", thereby occluding important issues of conflict and power' (p. 132).

Spurred on by a new climate of fear, not only the USA, but also a number of its allies, such as Australia and the UK, have developed a new, highly circumscribed, conception of security, one that increasingly places less emphasis on social and historical causes of insecurity and more on policing its citizens, especially those who were already marginalized in society. As Jayasuriya (2002) observes, 'new forms of risk management involve applying risk profiles to a set of relationships, institutions, and even geographic sites, rather than endeavoring to manage to transform the behavior of people' (p. 140).

One of the consequences of the 'war on terrorism' has been to render issues of welfare, social and cultural policy, including education policy, increasingly subservient to the umbrella narrative of security. Despite the rhetoric of economic globalization, even some of the economic relations and institutions have been increasingly framed in terms of security. This has been accompanied by the growth in executive state power and the curtailment of civil liberties. As far as international and transnational networks are concerned, the narrative of security has contributed to the framing of transnational agendas, which put security 'risk' considerations above all other concerns and priorities.

An example might help here. In November 2001, the meeting of the Asia Pacific Economic Cooperation (APEC) in Shanghai, China dealt exclusively with issues of security, and the 'war on terrorism'. Coming on the heels of September 11, this was perfectly understandable. But two years later, the discussion at the APEC meeting in Bangkok, Thailand was similarly located within the same discursive field, making it clear that APEC as an economic forum has now become an arena for discussing political issues of war and security. And even when the issues of trade are considered, they are couched in terms of the security conditions that are considered to be necessary for capital accumulation and economic growth. In their final communiqué at the APEC meeting in Bangkok, the Asia-Pacific leaders vowed to intensify their 'war against terrorism', placing security permanently at the core of the agenda for their annual summits. In the process, the leaders in effect re-asserted the role the member countries were now required to play in supporting America's political priorities.

Throughout the 1990s, much of the globalization literature had suggested that the exclusive link between the nation state and political power was being broken by globalization; that sovereign states could no longer claim exclusive authority within their own geographical boundaries. It was argued that changes in international law, regional political associations, the structure of global economy and global institutions had altered the fundamental form of the state system. Writers such as Held and McGrew (2000) maintained that the right of most states to rule within circumscribed territories – their sovereignty – was on the edge of a major transformation, if not extinction. In her highly influential book, *The retreat of the State*, Susan Strange (2000) argued that politicians and governments had lost much of their authority: 'the impersonal forces of world market, integrated over the postwar period more by private enterprise in finance, industry and trade than by cooperative decisions of governments, are now more powerful than states' (p. 13).

Of course, the anti-globalization movement has long recognized this fact, and has worked towards the development of global structures that have the ability to contain some of the power of supra-national and extraterritorial agencies. Global social movements around cosmopolitan ideals rest on the premise that under global conditions, 'humankind in some respects becomes a "we" facing problems and opportunities where there are no "others"' (Giddens 1991, p. 27). Thus, attempts at the creation of social movements around such issues as global human rights, environmental concerns, anti-poverty, gender equity and AIDS prevention, especially within the Third World, exemplify the principles of cosmopolitan solidarity, beyond the authority of nation states. However, it is these oppositional attempts that have been most compromised by the new discourse of security after September 11, as the nation states have re-acquired some of the authority that they might have conceded during the latter part of the twentieth century.

What the aftermath of September 11 has made abundantly clear is that the discourse of security is now linked inextricably to the imperatives of capitalism. Without global security, neither capitalism nor America's imperial ambitions can be sustained. But if capitalist and security imperatives now span the world, they have not displaced the nation state. On the contrary, as Wood (2003) has argued, 'the more universal capitalism has become, the more it has needed an equally universal system of reliable local states' (p. 152). The rhetoric of war on terrorism suggests that it is a war without boundaries, because nation states are no longer the principal players but terrorists who work across national boundaries. However, as we have seen the main target of the war has been the nation states, albeit 'weak' ones such as Iraq and Afghanistan. This is so because it is assumed that weak states cannot contain terrorists, and that they often harbour them. Both global security and capitalism thus need strong reliable states, which do not pose great risks to economic activity. What is clear then is that global capital needs local states, even if they exercise considerable coercive powers to ensure social conditions necessary for capital accumulation.

Wood (2003) maintains that 'globalization has certainly been marked by a withdrawal of the state from its social welfare and ameliorative functions; and, for many observers, this has more than anything else created an impression of the state's decline' (p. 140). But that this impression is deceptive, for it is impossible for global structures to dispense with many of the social functions performed by the state, such as 'a minimal "safety net" of social provision that has proven to be an essential condition of economic success and social stability' (p. 140). But under the new post-September 11 conditions, states are now required to extend their functions to the fighting of the global 'war on terrorism'. Thus 'both capitalism and anti-terrorism depend more than ever on a system of multiple and more or less sovereign states' (p. 140). Wood (2003) insists that:

> The very fact that 'globalization' has extended capital's purely economic powers far beyond the range of any single nation state means that global capital

requires many nation states to perform the administrative and coercive functions that sustain the system of property and provide the kind of day-to-day regularity, predictability, and legal order that capitalism needs more than any other social form.

(p. 141)

This clearly explains the urgency with which the USA views the task of nation-building in both Iraq and Afghanistan, and possibly elsewhere as well. Here the goals of the 'war on terrorism' and global capitalism converge through a more complex understanding of the nation state, as indispensable.

In the post-September 11 world, the coercive powers of the nation state are needed also in regulating the movement of people. One of the cherished beliefs of many globalization theorists in the 1990s concerned the increased movement of people across national boundaries. According to Cohen (1997, p. 157) a globalizing economy, characterized by a new international division of labour, the activities of transnational corporations and the effects of liberal trade and capital flow policies, together with better communication and cheaper transport, led inevitably to a greater number of people crossing their national borders than ever before. People began to be mobile for a whole variety of reasons, including migration, tourism, trade and increasingly education. The number of refugees reached a level greater than at any time in human history. Additionally, new forms of transnational mobility emerged through contractual relationships of work, family visits, international education, intermittent stays abroad and sojourning. During the 1990s, and in response to the intensification of interactions between different sectors of the world economy, the bilateral agreements permitting dual, and even multiple, citizenships became commonplace. This led to the development of 'global cities', 'whose significance resides more in their global, rather than in their national role' (Cohen 1997, p. 157).

It would be wrong to assume however that global mobility was available to everyone equally. According to Bauman (2000), mobility was available only to the elite, the 'tourists' who were able to contribute in one way or another to the consumer economy. In a postmodern globalized society, the mobile tourists were the increasingly cosmopolitan, the global businessmen, global culture managers and global academics. For them 'state borders are levelled down, as they are dismantled for the world's commodities, capital and finances' (Bauman 2000, p. 89). But for the 'tourists', their Others were the 'vagabonds'; those who were not permitted to move freely – for example, the refugees for whom 'the walls built of immigration controls, of residence laws and of "clean streets" and zero tolerance policies', grow taller' (p. 87). Before September 11, those who could afford to move, and had a role to play within the global economy had little difficulty in being mobile, even if they came from the Third World elite, or indeed the Muslim world.

After September 11, much of this has changed. The issues of mobility have become much more complex. There has been general tightening up of the regulations governing transnational movement not only in the USA but also elsewhere. In the USA, the Uniting and Strengthening America by Providing Appropriate Tools Required to Intercept and Obstruct Terrorism (USA PATRIOT) Act was passed in October 2001 in a rushed session of Congress without public debate. State legislatures soon enacted similar anti-terrorist legislation, through which, the 'war on terrorism' expanded, most significantly at the state and local levels. Citizens were given the responsibility to report any 'suspect' activities. In a climate fearful of any mobility, the USA abandoned a plan, discussed by Presidents Bush and Fox only a week before September 11, to make Mexican immigration easier and more streamlined and generous.

The main purpose of the USA PATRIOT Act is to tighten the rules governing immigration and movement. But in its execution, the basic principles like due process, political freedom, and the rule of law are largely circumvented. The Due Process Clause allegedly applies to all 'persons' within the USA, including aliens, whether their presence is lawful, unlawful, temporary, or permanent. Yet, the main targets of Section 412 of the USA PATRIOT Act are the immigrants, especially those from Muslim backgrounds. The Act allows for extended, and, in some cases, indefinite, detention based on the Attorney General's untested certification that he has 'reasonable grounds to believe' that a non-citizen is engaged in terrorist activities (Cole 2002, p. 12). As a result, a disproportionately large number of Muslim immigrants and visitors have been held under the Act, sometimes as a result of minor visa violations. Muslim international students have been confronted by the brunt of the Act's excessive powers. As a result, the number of international students from Muslim countries who are either denied visas, or have simply decided not to apply, has increased significantly (Open Doors 2002).

The USA PATRIOT Act has in effect sealed the national borders of the USA that had supposedly become porous under globalization. In the USA, there has always been a tension between the two impulses at the heart of its self-definition. On the one hand, the nation has been proud of one of its most enduring founding myths, as a nation of immigrants, which has always welcomed the oppressed and needy people from around the globe. On the other hand, there have always been nativist reactions and xenophobic hostilities toward the so-called 'aliens', as threats to the 'American way of life'. Ali Behdad (1997) suggests that this latter vision of moral order involves a particular kind of 'nationalism that has always embodied a nativist or anti-foreign component to manufacture an imagined sense of community' (p. 161). In 'times of crisis', all moral ambiguity is replaced by a patriotic fervour, distrustful of particular groups of people and anxious about preserving America's sense of itself as a Christian nation, with the global mission of civilizing people around the world.

In the aftermath of September 11, the US government has communicated mixed messages about its attitude towards its own Muslim community, and Muslims abroad. On the one hand, the government has claimed repeatedly that its 'war against terrorism' is not against the Muslim religion, and that it needs the support of Muslims everywhere to help it root out terrorism. At the same time, however, many within the government have hardly disguised their support of the popular discourse that casts Muslim and Arab communities in the USA as enemies in nativist terms, which suggests that they threaten not only the American way of life but also the institutions of liberty and democracy. The historical traditions of nativism now merge with a range of uncritically espoused expressions of patriotism, love for one's home country, and national pride. As Franz (2002) puts it,

> immediately after the 'Attack on America', the confused and insecure American public, influenced by a simplified media discourse, reverted to a nativist interpretation of the events, which was soon to be buttressed by a moral righteous and infallible nationalism, in the country's retaliation efforts.
> (p. 3)

This interpretation has become a key component in the popular discursive field within which expressions of anti-terrorism are now couched. It involves abandoning some of the ideals of cosmopolitanism, and embracing a new vocabulary of nationalism, which has become a prism through which both the processes of globalization and the dynamics of international relations are to be viewed. The media in particular has been instrumental in institutionalizing this ideological field, which is predicated on a set of assumptions about one's ethical duty to support one's country against the terrorists who threaten the 'American way of life'. There is no room here for ambivalence or ambiguity . . . 'you are either with us or against us'. Those opposed to this interpretation are dismissed as either naïve or worse still as 'traitors' or 'cowards'. This moral infallibility, espoused by the media and political leadership alike, has given the American state the authority to use its power to reorder global politics and the terms of global exchange.

Yet, one of the main problems with the new language of security is that it is often couched in absolutist and binary terms. Far too often, words like 'war', 'justice', 'victory' and indeed 'security' are used as if they have single, uniform and uncontestable meanings. President Bush has himself spoken about a 'crusade against the enemies of America' and of 'eliminating evil from the world'. This rhetoric serves only to hinder democratic debate about the causes, expressions and outcomes of terrorism and a whole variety of possible remedies that could be considered to meet the new global challenges. Paradoxically this rhetoric is, in its broad linguistic structure, largely similar to that used by Al-Qaida and the militant Islam. It is a language of moral certainty and political absolutes, as Tariq Ali has so clearly observed in his book, *The clash of fundamentalisms* (2002). Steven Lukes and Nadia Urbinati (2001) have called it a 'war between absolutes'. The militant Islam speaks a language that has only one meaning, which celebrates faithfulness to its 'fundamentals'; the true meaning of Islam to which it claims to have unique access. To treat this language with disdain and with absolute conviction, while declaring 'them' to be absolutely evil is to respond in exactly the manner that Al-Qaida hopes to induce. As Lukes and Urbinati argue, 'the new terrorism therefore has an insidious power, one which derives from the non-political character of its language and objectives and which encourages its victims to use the same language. And in the victims' traditions there are, of course, ample resources of religious dogmatism from which to draw'. This dogmatism invites the translation of all human and social phenomena into religious language. In its discourse, 'just' becomes 'Good', 'wrong' becomes 'Evil', 'the political adversary' becomes 'The Infidel'. For a democratic point of view, this makes vacuous any language of a conversation across traditions.

While the religious language in which the opposition between the militant Islam and those who oppose it is expressed is broadly similar, the world they represent is polarized into a binary that only increases conflict. As Nira Yuval-Davis (2001) points out, in times of war, the pressure to conform to binary oppositions – to absorb them not only into our language but also our very thought processes is considerable. Thus the temptation to divide the world into 'civilizations' is especially great: 'us' and 'them'. Indeed, the clash of civilizations thesis, put forward by Samuel Huntington (1994), which describes the world as involving two unbridgeable blocs, religiously and culturally, has come to occupy centre stage since September 11. As recent commentators, such as Syela Benhabib (2002) observe, many people in the West appear to have accepted as fact the contention that the events of September 11 offer a belated confirmation of Huntington's thesis that the fundamental source of conflict in the new world is not primarily ideological or even economic, but cultural.

Yet this 'culturalization' of conflict is as wrong as it is dangerous. It is wrong because while the origins of some disputes are certainly cultural, prolonged conflict is always much more complex, involving factors that are not only cultural but also economic, political and ideological. Nor is it possible to differentiate one civilization from another in such a holistic and abstract manner. As Edward Said (2001) and others have pointed out, Huntington has made civilizations into 'shut down and sealed off' entities, overlooking the exchange, cross-fertilization and sharing that has always been responsible for cultural change within all communities, not only as a result of current and counter currents of trade but also colonialism.

In more normative terms, the most serious problem with the 'clash of civilizations' thesis is, as Modood (2002) points out, that it risks becoming a self-fulfilling prophecy, precisely at a time when a more complex understanding of cultural traditions and interdependence is most needed. The popular suggestion that Islam and Christianity represent two different and separate ways of looking at the world is fundamentally flawed, and serves only to reinforce the forms of fundamentalism promoted by the extremists on both sides. The idea of clash of civilizations masks close historical links that have always existed between the two traditions. It also hides the ways in which this binarism is politically constructed by both the militant Islam and those who hold Islam responsible for most of the causes of their insecurity. Ultimately, it is an ideological thesis that suggests a kind of pessimism that the world cannot afford.

In this article, I have discussed the ways in which debates about globalization have been reshaped by September 11 and its aftermath. While I reject the popular view that 'the world has changed forever', I have nevertheless argued that the discursive field within which globalization is discussed has been transformed by a new ideological narrative of global security. My analysis has sought to show how nation states continue to play a vital, though somewhat revised role, in the 're-ordered world', and in the operations of the global capitalism. I have also suggested that the post-September 11 discursive field is deeply ambivalent towards the 'clash of civilizations' thesis. On the one hand, September 11 has generated a culture of antagonism across religion and civilization divides, reinforcing divisions in a range of pernicious ways. On the other hand, it has been increasingly recognized that the future for both the West and Islam are inextricably intertwined and interdependent.

Given this analysis, education has an important role to play in what Buck-Morss (2003) has called 'thinking past the terror'. Educators clearly have to work within and understand the discursive field that has emerged since September 11, but we need, at the same time, to recognize that all discursive fields are socially and historically constructed; and that we can help communities develop alternative analyses of terror, and of global security. Buck-Morss (2003) has argued that

> September 11 has transformed irrevocably the context in which we as intellectuals speak. The acts of terror on that day were no invasion from the outside by a barbaric evil 'other' but were, rather, produced fully within a coeval and common world.
>
> (p. 81)

This acute observation highlights the need for educators to investigate the contours, complexities and contradictions of this common – interconnected and interdependent – world. We need to recognize that globalization has never been an objective historical reality, but simply a term that we use to interpret rapid changes in the world, caused by the shifting patterns of social and economic relations. If this is so, then September 11 has clearly changed some of the ways in which we must approach the study of world history and society. The long-term implications of September 11 will be determined in normative terms, by the way we are able to generate and realize new discursive fields of social change, and new realities of global democracy and justice.

References

Ali, T. (2002) *The clash of fundamentalisms* (London: Verso).

Appudarai, A. (1996) *Modernity at large: cultural dimensions of globalization* (Minneapolis, MN: Minnesota University Press).

Arnove, R. and Torres, C. (eds) (1999) *Comparative education: the dialectic between the global and the local* (Lanham, MD: Rowman & Littlefield).

Ball, S. (1998) Big policies/small world: an introduction to international perspectives in education policy, *Comparative Education*, 34(2): 119–30.

Bauman, Z. (2000) *Globalization* (Cambridge, UK: Polity Press).

Behdad, A. (1997) Nationalism and immigration to the United States, *Diaspora*, 6(2): 155–78.

Benhabib, S. (2002) 'Unholy wars. Reclaiming democratic virtues after September 11', in C. Calhoun, P. Price and A. Timmer (eds), *Understanding September 11* (New York: The New Press), pp. 241–53.

Bourdieu, P. (1977) *Outline of a theory of practice* (Cambridge: Cambridge University Press).

Bourdieu, P. (1990) *The logic of practice* (Cambridge, UK: Polity Press).

Buck-Morss, S. (2003) *Thinking past terror: Islamism and critical theory on the left* (London: Verso).

Burbules, N. and Torres, C. (eds) (2000) *Globalization and education* (London and New York: Routledge).

Cohen, R. (1997) *Global diasporas: an introduction* (Seattle, WA: University of Washington Press).

Cole, D. (3 June 2002) Operation enduring liberty, *The Nation*, pp. 11–12.

Franz, B. (2002) American patriotism and nativist fears after September 11. Available online at: http://www.braumueller.at/files/pdf/american_patriotism.pdf

Friedman, T. (2000) *The Lexus and the olive tree* (New York: Farrar Straus Giroux).

Fukuyama, F. (1992) *The end of history and the last man* (New York: Free Press).

Giddens, A. (1991) *Modernity and self-identity: self and society in the Late Modern Age* (Cambridge, UK: Polity Press).

Giddens, A. (1994) *Beyond left and right* (Cambridge, UK: Polity Press).

Hall, S. (1996) ' "When was the postcolonial?" Thinking at the limit', in I. Chamber and L. Curtis (eds), *The post-colonial question: common skies, divided horizons* (London: Routledge), pp. 242–60.

Hardt, M. and Negri, A. (2000) *Empire* (Cambridge, MA: Harvard University Press).

Held, D. (1991) 'Democracy, the nation-state and the global system', in D. Held (ed.) *Political theory today* (Cambridge: Polity Press).

Held, D. and McGrew, A. (eds) (2000) *The global transformations reader* (Cambridge, UK: Polity Press).

Henry, M., Lingard, R., Rizvi, F. and Taylor, S. (2001) *The OECD, globalization and educational policy* (Oxford: Pergamon Press).

Hoogvelt, A. (1997) *Globalization and the postcolonial world: the new political economy of development* (Basingstoke: MacMillan).

Huntington, S. (1994) *The clash of civilizations and the remaking of the world order* (New York: Simon & Schuster).

Jayasuriya, K. (2002) 'September 11, security, and the new postliberal politics of fear', in E. Hershberg and K. W. Moore (eds), *Critical views of September 11* (New York: The New Press), pp. 13–150.

Kenway, J. and Bullen, E. (2001) *Consuming children* (London: Open University Press).

Klein, N. (2000) *No logo* (London: Flamingo).

Lewis, B. (2002) *What went wrong?: Western impact and Middle Eastern response* (Oxford and New York: Oxford University Press).

Lukes, S. and Urbinati, N. (2001) Words matter. Available online at: http://www.opendemocracy.net/debates/article-2-49-116.jsp

Mann, M. (2000) 'Has globalization ended the rise and rise of the nation state', in D. Held, D. McGrew and A. McGrew (eds), *The global transformations reader* (Cambridge, UK: Polity Press), pp. 136–47.

Modood, T. (2002) 'Muslims and the politics of fear of multiculturalism in Britain', in E. Hershberg and K. W. Moore (eds), *Critical views of September 11* (New York: The New Press), pp. 193–208.

Open Doors (2002) *Report 2002*. Available online at: http://opendoors.iienetwork.org/

Rosenau, J. (2001) Notes from a conference held at George Washington University. Available online at: http://www.gwu.edu/~gwcsg/sept11.htm

Said, E. (2001, October 11–17) Edward Said on Samuel Huntington, *Al Ahram Weekly On-line*, 555, pp. 11–17.

Scholte, P. (2000) *Globalization: a critical introduction* (New York: St Martin's Press).

Strange, S. (2000) 'The declining authority of states', in Held, D. and McGrew, A. (eds), *The global transformations reader* (Cambridge, UK: Polity Press), pp. 148–55.

Stromquist, N. (2002) *Education in a globalized world: the connectivity of power, technology and knowledge* (New York: Rowman & Littlefield).

Tikly, L. (2001) 'Globalization and education in the postcolonial world: towards a conceptual framework', *Comparative Education*, 37(2): 151–71.

Waters, M. (1995) *Globalization* (London: Routledge).

Wood, E. M. (2003) *Empire of capital* (London: Verso).

Young, R. (2003) *Postcolonialism: a very short introduction* (Oxford: Oxford University Press).

Yuval-Davis, N. (2001) The binary war. Available online at: http://www.opendemocracy.net/forum/docu

CHAPTER 3

BIG POLICIES/SMALL WORLD

An introduction to international perspectives in education policy

Stephen J. Ball

Comparative Education, 1998, 34(2): 119–30

Introduction

One of the tensions which runs through all varieties of policy analysis is that between the need to attend to the local particularities of policy making and policy enactment and the need to be aware of general patterns and apparent commonalities or convergence across localities (see Whitty and Edwards (1998) for further discussion). That tension is central to this paper and this special issue. In this paper my primary emphasis is upon the general and common elements in contemporary, international education policy but I will also address the processes of translation and recontextualisation involved in the realisation or enactment of policy in specific national and local settings. However, one immediate limitation upon the generality of my discussion is its focus upon Western and Northern developed economies, although a great deal of what I have to say has considerable relevance to countries such as Colombia, Chile, Portugal, Japan and some of the ex-Warsaw Pact nations of Eastern Europe. The paper has three main sections. The first sketches in a set of generic 'problems' which constitute the contemporary social, political and economic conditions for education and social policy making. The second discusses the idea of ideological and 'magical' solutions to these problems and the dissemination of these solutions. The third and last returns to the issue of recontextualisation.

Post-modernity and the global economy

As Brown and Lauder (1996) explained, 'The significance of globalisation to questions of national educational and economic development can be summarised in terms of a change in the rules of eligibility, engagement and wealth creation' (p. 2). As regards eligibility, individual governments, even the apparently most powerful, have experienced a reduction in their ability to control or supervise the activities of multinational corporations (MNCs) and maintain the integrity of their economic borders. This results in the loss of 'Keynesian capacity', that is the ability to pursue independent reflationary policies. However, it is important not to overstate the case here and succumb to what Weiss (1997) called the 'myth of the powerless state'. She argued that within the processes of globalisation 'domestic state capacities differ' (Weiss 1997, 26) and that 'the proliferation of regional agreements suggest that we can expect to see more and more of a different kind of state taking shape in the world arena, one that is reconstituting its power at the centre of alliances formed either within or outside the state' (Weiss 1997, 27) (see also Taylor *et al*. 1997, chapter 4). In other words, we need to be wary of what Harvey (1996) called 'globaloney'. The 'globalisation thesis' can be used to explain almost anything and everything and is ubiquitous in current policy documents and policy analysis.

We also need to acknowledge here the national changes in the form and scope of state activities in many Western economies. Contracting, deregulation and privatisation have reduced, in both practical and ideological terms, the capacity for direct state intervention. That is not to say that these devices do not provide new forms of state steering and regulation (see below). The rules of engagement describe the relationship between governments, employers and workers. The key change here, at least in the West, is from a Fordist, welfare corporatism to a 'market model' wherein 'the prosperity of workers will depend on an ability to trade their skills, knowledge and entrepreneurial acumen in an unfettered global market place' (Brown and Lauder 1996, 3). And the new rules of wealth creation are replacing the logic of Fordist mass production with new 'knowledge-based' systems of flexible production.

However, there are three crucial caveats to the last point. First, Fordist production systems in the West have not so much been replaced as 'exported', cheap labour and unregulated conditions of labour in some developing economies make the relocation of mass production an attractive proposition to MNCs. Furthermore, while MNCs are increasingly dominant, a great deal of capital activity remains 'nationalistic'. Second, even within the developed Western and Asian Tiger economies the new logic of flexible specialisation and 'just-in-time' production (Swynegedouw 1986) is not an inclusive one – low-skill, insecure jobs, particularly in the service sectors, are the main areas of expansion of work in all of these economies. And these 'new' jobs are also bringing about the feminisation of the labour market. Harvey (1989) made the key point that 'Under conditions of flexible accumulation, it seems as if alternative labour systems can exist side by side within the same space in such a way as to enable capitalist entrepreneurs to choose at will between them' (p. 187). Thus, thirdly, the polarisations of Fordist/post-Fordist – modernist/post-modernist economies are not so much alternative forms of capital and regulation as 'a complex of oppositions expressive of the cultural contradictions of capitalism' (Harvey 1989, 39).

The two general points then that I want to make here are (1) that things have changed but not absolutely and (2) that while these changes have produced new 'first-order' problems, in terms of the demand for new skills for example, they have also produced new 'second-order' problems, such as threats to the maintenance of political legitimacy and authority. Not everyone has an equal 'stake' in the success of the new economic order. The core–periphery structure of the global economy and global and national labour markets appears to be closely paralleled in the emerging 'star'/'sink' school polarisations within 'market-reformed' education systems.

There is no way that I can follow through properly all aspects of this account of the role of globalisation on education in the space available here (see Harvey 1989; Brown and Lauder 1996; Taylor *et al*. 1997; Jones 1998). And, indeed, I am not concerned with conveying the full complexity of these global changes but rather with isolating some of those aspects of change which might allow us to understand the struggles taking place over education policy. However, I do want to pick out two further specific and related aspects of global change which I will suggest have particular significance in making sense of the current 'turn' in education and social policy making. They are, in short uncertainty and congestion.

Harvey (1989) suggested that the rhythm and content of daily life has become both more ephemeral and volatile. Commodity production increasingly emphasises 'the values and virtues of instantaneity and disposability' (p. 286) and is increasingly focused upon 'sign systems rather than with commodities themselves' (p. 287). The latter, among many other factors, has contributed to a 'crisis of representation' (Harvey 1989, 298). All of this provides a context for the 'crack-up of consensus' (Harvey 1989, 286). It constitutes, in part, what Pfeil (1988) called the 'postmodern structure of feeling' and forbears 'the terror of contingency from which all possibility of eventful significance has been drained' (p. 386).

> The central value system, to which capitalism has always appealed to validate and gauge its actions, is dematerialized and shifting, time horizons are collapsing, and it is hard to tell exactly what space we are in when it comes to assessing causes and effects, meanings or values.
>
> (Harvey 1989, 298)

In other words 'disorganised capitalism' (Lash and Urry 1987) may be beginning to dissolve the conditions of consensus and social cohesion upon which it depends in order to continue. One particular and very material aspect of the new politics of uncertainty is the very dramatic change in the trajectory of economic growth and patterns of employment which provided the basis for the massive post-war expansion in the middle classes and the creation of the so-called 'new middle class'. Their 'imagined futures' and those of their offspring are now under threat from the 'unmanaged congestion' in the old and new professions and in management positions (Jordon *et al.* 1994). One effect of this has been a loss of support among the new middle classes for efforts to democratise education and social policy. Education is being 'transformed back into an "oligarchic" good' (Jordon *et al.* 1994, 212) and progressive experimentation in educational methods is being replaced by a set of reinvented traditional pedagogies.

Magical solutions?

If these various 'policyscapes' (Appadurai 1990) of global change adumbrate a set of 'problems' and challenges for education and social policy, what then are the 'solutions' in play from which makers of policy might 'choose' as modes of response? As I shall go on to suggest choose is an inappropriate word here. Brown and Lauder (1996) suggested two ideal types of response: neo-Fordism, which 'can be characterised in terms of creating greater market flexibility through a reduction in social overheads and the power of trade unions, the privatisation of public utilities and the welfare state, as well as the celebration of competitive individualism' (p. 5) and post-Fordism, which can 'be defined in terms of the development of the state as a "strategic trader" shaping the direction of the national economy through investment in key economic sectors and in the development of human capital' (p. 5). This latter is close to Hutton's (1995) Rhineland model of capitalism. In practice, as is ever the case, the differences between states or political parties in these terms often seem to be more a matter of emphasis than any 'clear blue water'. While superficially at least the neo-Fordist 'solution' seems to be in the ascendant in education policy making, aspects of the post-Fordist scenario are clearly in evidence even in the practices of the most neoliberal of governments. Having said that, the differences between the positions are not insignificant.

This policy dualism is well represented in contemporary education policies which tie together individual, consumer choice in education markets with rhetorics and policies aimed at furthering national economic interests. Carter and O'Neill (1995) summarised evidence on the state of education policy making in their two-volume collection on international perspectives on educational reform by identifying what they called 'the new orthodoxy' – 'a shift is taking place' they said in the relationship between politics, government and education in complex Westernised post-industrialised countries at least (p. 9). They cited five main elements to this new orthodoxy.

1   Improving national economics by tightening the connection between schooling, employment, productivity and trade.
2   Enhancing student outcomes in employment-related skills and competencies.
3   Attaining more direct control over curriculum content and assessment.
4   Reducing the costs to government of education.
5   Increasing community input to education by more direct involvement in school decision making and pressure of market choice.

I shall return to the substance of this reform package below. Avis *et al.* (1996) made a similar claim about post-compulsory education and training and what they call the 'new consensus'. Indeed, the European Union (1995) *White Paper on Education and Training: towards the learning society* announced 'The end of the debate on educational principles' (p. 22). Concepts such as the 'learning society', the 'knowledge-based economy', etc., are potent policy condensates within this consensus. They serve and symbolise the increasing colonisation of education policy by economic policy imperatives. Levin (1998) suggests that it is sometimes the politics of the sign rather than the substance of policies that moves across national borders.

It would be ridiculous to claim that there is one or even one set of key ideas or influences which underpin this package. However, it would be equally ridiculous to ignore the links and correspondences which run through it. Five elements or sets of influences are identifiable. I will adumbrate these very crudely. Some of these have an analytic status, while others are more substantive. One is neoliberalism or what might be called the ideologies of the market. These set the spontaneous and unplanned but innovative responses of the market form over and against the partisan, inefficient bureaucracy of planned change. This has been of particular importance in the UK in the formation of those policies often referred to as 'Thatcherism' (see Ball 1990) and the UK education reforms certainly provided a test-bed to which other governments at least attended when contemplating their own reforms (see Whitty and Edwards 1998).

A second is new institutional economics, 'which sought to explain the workings of social life and its various institutions, and the construction of relationships and co-ordination of individual and collective behaviour, in terms of the choices and actions of the rational actor' (Seddon 1997, 176). This involves the use of a combination of devolution, targets and incentives to bring about institutional redesign. It draws both on recent economic theory and various industrial practices, sometimes referred to as Mitsubishi-ism – the replacement of task specification by target setting (see below). In education the impact of such ideas is evident in the myriad of 'site-based management' initiatives in countries and states around the world and the social psychology of institutional reinvention proselytised in texts on 'the self-managing school' and 'school improvement'. Chubb and Moe (1990) also articulated what they described as 'a theoretical perspective linking the organisation and performance of schools to their institutional environments' (p. 185).

A third influence, which interweaves with both of the above, is what Lyotard (1984) called performativity – 'be operational (that is, commensurable) or disappear' (p. xxiv). 'Performativity is a principle of governance which establishes strictly functional relations between a state and its inside and outside environments' (Yeatman 1994, 111). In other words performativity is a steering mechanism. A form of indirect steering or steering at a distance which replaces intervention and prescription with target setting, accountability and comparison. Furthermore, as part of the transformation of education and schooling and the expansion of the power of capital, performativity provides sign systems which 'represent' education in a self-referential and reified form for consumption. And, indeed, many of the specific technologies of performativity in education (total quality management, human resources management, etc.) are borrowed from commercial settings.

Number four, is public choice theory. This is a particularly important component of US attempts at education reform (see again Chubb and Moe 1990), but choice is a key aspect of Hayekian neoliberalism as well (see Organization for Economic Co-operation and Development (1994) for a review of choice policies in six countries).

Fifth and finally, there is new managerialism, that is the insertion of the theories and techniques of business management and the 'cult of excellence' into public sector institutions. Managerialism is, in this sense, both a delivery system and a vehicle for change. This 'new' managerialism stresses constant attention to 'quality', being close to the customer and the value of innovation (Newman and Clarke 1994, 15). In the education sector the headteacher is the main 'carrier' and embodiment of new managerialism and is crucial to the transformation of the organisational regimes of schools (Grace 1995), that is the dismantling of bureau-professional organisational regimes and their replacement with market-entrepreneurial regimes (Clarke and Newman 1992).

New management also involves 'new' forms of employee involvement, in particular through the cultivation of 'corporate culture' by means of which managers 'seek to delineate, normalize and instrumentalize the conduct of persons in order to achieve the ends they postulate as desirable' (Du Gay 1996, 61). Such developments are deeply paradoxical. On the one hand, they represent a move away from Taylorist, 'low-trust' methods of employee control. Managerial responsibilities are delegated and initiative and problem solving are highly valued. On the other hand, new forms of surveillance and self-monitoring are put in place, e.g. appraisal systems, target-setting, and output comparisons (see Muller (1998) for a discussion of different forms of self-regulation – competence based and performance based). This is what Peters and Waterman (1982) referred to as 'simultaneously loose and tight' or what Du Gay (1996) called 'controlled de-control'.

The dissemination of these influences internationally can be understood in at least two ways. Firstly and most straightforwardly, there is a flow of ideas through social and political networks; the 'inter-national circulation of ideas' (Popkewitz 1996). For example, by processes of policy borrowing (Halpin and Troyna 1995) – both the UK and New Zealand have served as 'political laboratories' for reform – and the activities of groups such as the Heritage Foundation, the Mont Pelerin Society and the Institute of Economic Affairs, although the effects here should not be over estimated. The movement of graduates, in particular from US universities, is also important (see Vanegas and Ball 1996). In some contexts this movement 'carries' ideas and creates a kind of cultural and political dependency which works to devalue or deny the feasibility of 'local' solutions. As Max-Neef *et al.* (1991) put it

> If as a Latin American economist I wish to become an expert in Latin American development problems, it is necessary to study in the United States or in Europe to be respectable in the eyes of both my Southern and Northern colleagues. It goes without saying that it is not only dangerous but absurd.
>
> (p. 98)

There is also the activity of various 'policy entrepreneurs', groups and individuals who 'sell' their solutions in the academic and political market-place – the 'self-managing school' and 'school effectiveness' and 'choice' are all current examples of such entrepreneurship which takes places through academic channels – journals, books, etc. – and via the performances of charismatic, travelling academics. (See Levin (1998) for an epidemiological account of the 'spread' of policy.)

Lastly, there is the sponsorship and, in some respects, enforcement of particular policy 'solutions' by multilateral agencies (see Jones 1998). The World Bank is particularly important here, as Jones (1998) puts it: 'The bank's preconditions for education can only be understood as an ideological stance, in promoting an integrated world system along market lines' (p. 152). However, it is equally important to understand a second aspect of the dissemination or institutionalisation of these influences upon reform; their establishment as the new orthodoxy, that is as a discursive framework within which and limited by which solutions are 'thought'. There is a concomitance if not a correspondence here between the logic of globalisation – as a world free-trading system – and the new terrain of thinking about social policy. Jones (1998) again notes that 'Notions of the public good shift in order to accommodate reduced expectations about accountability, regulation and taxation, which in turn lead to not only reduced but transformed expectations about what public services and infrastructure consist of' (p. 146). This concomitance is most obvious in what Brown and Lauder (1996) called neo-Fordism: 'the route to national salvation in the context of the global knowledge wars is through the survival of the fittest, based on an extension of parental choice in a market of competing schools, colleges and universities' (pp. 6–7). That is, 'education systems have been made objects of micro-economic reform with educational activities being turned into saleable or corporatised market products as part of a national efficiency drive' (Taylor *et al.* 1997, 77; (see Welch (1998) on 'efficiency'). Such reforms rest upon two starkly opposed chronotopics – the grey, slow bureaucracy and politically correct, committee, corridor grimness of the city hall welfare state as against the fast, adventurous, carefree, gung-ho, open-plan, computerised, individualism of choice, autonomous 'enterprises' and sudden opportunity.

This last point serves to remind us that policies are both systems of values and symbolic systems; ways of representing, accounting for and legitimating political decisions. Policies are articulated both to achieve material effects and to manufacture support for those effects. In particular, I want to suggest here that advocacy of the market or commercial form for educational reform as the 'solution' to educational problems is a form of 'policy magic' or what Stronach (1993) called 'witchcraft': 'a form of reassurance as well as a rational response to economic problems' (p. 6). One of the attractions here is the simplicity of the formula on which the magic is based.

social markets/institutional devolution = raising standards (of educational performance) = increased international competitiveness

Such simplicities have a particular attraction when set within the 'conditions of uncertainty' or what Dror (1986) called 'adversity'. In Stronach's (1993) terms the repetitive circularities of 'the market solution' display 'the logics of witchcraft and the structures of ritual' (p. 26). It links individual (choice) and institutional (autonomy/responsiveness) transformation to universal salvation: a transformation from mundane citizen to archetype, from dependent subject to active consumer/citizen, and from dull bureaucracy to innovative, entrepreneurial management (of course the policies of welfarism can be subjected to a similar sort of analysis). 'Ritual typically associates a personal with a cosmic pole, around which prosperity, morality and civilization are clustered' (Stronach 1993, 23). Minor personal and physical changes are linked to large scale transformation. Again then, all of this is founded upon the play of opposites, order against chaos and the redress of crisis. Employing a similar language, Hughes and Tight (1995) argued that concepts such as 'the stakeholder' and the 'learning society' represent powerful myths for projecting futuristic visions which determine the on going principles on which education policy and practice are based. And, as Newman (1984) put it, 'The libertarian revolt against the modern state is first and foremost a campaign for the hearts and minds of the American people' (p. 159).

For politicians the 'magic' of the market works in several senses. On the one hand, it is a 'hands off' reform, a non-interventionary intervention – a basic trope of the conjurer, now you see it now you don't!. It distances the reformer from the outcomes of reform. Blame and responsibility are also devolved or contracted out (see below). And yet, by use of target setting and performative techniques, 'steering at a distance' can be achieved, what Kikert (1991) called 'a new paradigm of public governance' (p. 1). On the other hand, these policies also carry with them political risks, in so far, as noted already, as they may disable direct forms of control and can leave the politician 'in office' but not 'in power'.

As indicated above, one key facet of the policy process and the formulation of new orthodoxies is critique. New policies feed off and gain legitimacy from the deriding and demolition of previous policies (see Ball 1990) which are thus rendered 'unthinkable'. The 'new' are marked out by and gain credence from their qualities of difference and contrast. In education in particular, part of the attraction of a new policy often rests on the specific allocation of 'blame' from which its logic derives. Blame may either be located in the malfunctions or heresies embedded in the policies it replaces and/or is redistributed by the new policy within the education system itself and is often personified – currently in the UK in the 'incompetent teacher' and 'failing school' (see Thrupp (1998) on the politics of blame).

Stated in more general terms, two complexly related policy agendas are discernible in all the heat and noise of reform. The first aims to tie education more closely to national economic interests, while the second involves a decoupling of education from direct state control. The first rests on a clear articulation and assertion by the state of its requirements of education, while the second gives at least the appearance of greater autonomy to educational institutions in the delivery of those requirements. The first involves a reaffirmation of the state functions of education as a 'public good', while the second subjects education to the disciplines of the market and the methods and values of business and redefines it as a competitive private good. In many respects educational institutions are now being expected to take on the qualities and characteristics of 'fast capitalism' (Gee and Lankshear 1995) and this involves not only changes in organisational practices and methods but also the adoption of new social relationships, values and ethical principles.

We can see these two political agendas being played out in a variety of countries in terms of an ensemble of generic policies – parental choice and institutional competition, site-based autonomy, managerialism, performative steering and curricula fundamentalism – which nonetheless have local variations, twists and nuances – hybridity – and different degrees of application – intensity. The purest and most intense versions of this ensemble are evident in places such as England, New Zealand and Alberta (Canada). Mixed and low-intensity versions are evident in places such as France, Colombia and many US and Australian states. Places such as Portugal and Sweden display hybrid but low-intensity versions. (See the discussion of recontextualisation below.)

While previous regimes of unthinkability derived rhetorical energy from the critique of élitism, one of the mechanisms involved in the establishment of the new orthodoxy in education has been a critique of the press for equity and social justice as part of the diagnosis of the existing 'inadequacies' of education – what I have elsewhere called 'the discourse of derision' (Ball 1990; see also below). The World Bank sees equity as one of the residual concerns of governments in marketised education systems. However, as a part of the logic of the new orthodoxy the social and welfare purposes of education are systematically played down directly (as in the World Bank) or, in effect, education is increasingly subject to exchange value criteria. That is, education is not simply modelled on the methods and values of capital, it is itself drawn into the commodity form. Within all this equity issues do not so much disappear entirely as become 'framed and reframed'; 'competing discourses are "stitched together" in the new policies' (Taylor 1995, 9). The meanings of equity are refracted, reworked and realised in new ways 'glossing over the different perspectives of key players' (Taylor 1995, 10).

In effect, in education and social policy generally the new orthodoxy, the market solution, is a new master narrative, a deeply fissured but primary discourse encompassing 'the very nature of economics and therefore the potential range and scope of policies themselves' (Cerny 1990, 205). The discourse constructs the topic and, as with any discourse, it appears across a range of texts, forms of conduct and at a number of different sites at any one time. Discursive events 'refer to the one and the same object . . . there is a regular style and . . . constancy of concepts . . . and "strategy" and a common institutional, administrative or political drift and pattern' (Cousins and Hussain 1984, 84–5). This discourse can be seen at work as much in the 1980s Hollywood 'male-rampage' movies (Pfeil 1995), part of what Ross (1990) described as 'the desperate attempts, under Reagan, to reconstruct the institution of national heroism, more often than not in the form of white male rogue outlaws for whom the liberal solution of "soft" state-regulated law enforcement was presented as having failed' (p. 33). Equally it can be seen in the UK in the commodification of academic research, in the celebration of the parent–chooser–hero of so many market policy texts in education, in the refurbished, customer-friendly, competitive school, the 'quality-guru' educational consultants and quick-fix policy entrepreneurs, Channel One television in US schools and 'designer-label' uniforms in Japanese high schools, 'early-learning' educational games shops and niche marketing, 'hot-house', nursery schools. 'Educational democracy is redefined as consumer democracy in the educational marketplace. *Buying* an education becomes a substitute for *getting* an education' (Kenway *et al.* 1993, 116). It is not simply that publicly provided school systems are being inducted into quasi-market practices but that education in its various forms, at many points, and in a variety of ways is inducted into the market episteme – a non-unified, multiple and complex field of play which realises a dispersion of relationships, subjectivities, values, objects, operations and concepts.

Localism and recontextualisation

While it may well be possible to discern a set of principles or a theoretical model underlying policy – neoliberalism, new institutional economics, public choice theory or whatever – these rarely if ever translate into policy texts or practice in direct or pristine form. National policy making is inevitably a process of bricolage: a matter of borrowing and copying bits and pieces of ideas from elsewhere, drawing upon and amending locally tried and tested approaches, cannibalising theories, research, trends and fashions and not infrequently flailing around for anything at all that looks as though it might work. Most policies are ramshackle, compromise, hit and miss affairs, that are reworked, tinkered with, nuanced and inflected through complex processes of influence, text production, dissemination and, ultimately, re-creation in contexts of practice (Ball 1994).

Policy ideas are also received and interpreted differently within different political architectures (Cerny 1990), national infrastructures (Hall 1986) and national ideologies – a national ideology is 'a set of values and beliefs that frames the practical thinking and action of agents of the main institutions of a nation-state at a given point in time' (van Zanten 1997, 352) and business cultures (Hampden-Turner and Trompenaars 1994). The latter conducted research on 15000 business managers in seven different countries and identified distinct contrasts in the mind-sets and ideologies of their respondents. Unfortunately, comparative educational research on the formation, reception and interpretation of policy in these terms is thin on the ground (see Dale and Ozga (1993) on the new right in the UK and New Zealand and van Zanten (1997) on the education of immigrants in France).

In our attempts to understand education policies comparatively and globally the complex relationships between ideas, the dissemination of ideas and the recontextualisation (see Bernstein 1996) of ideas remain a central task. As Bernstein (1996) put it, 'Every time a discourse moves, there is space for ideology to play' (p. 24). Recontextualisation takes place within and between both 'official' and 'pedagogic' fields, the former 'created and dominated by the state' and the latter consisting of 'pedagogues in schools and colleges, and departments of education, specialised journals, private research foundations' (Bernstein 1996, 48). These fields are constituted differently in different societies. The new orthodoxies of education policy are grafted onto and realised within very different national and cultural contexts and are affected, inflected and deflected by them. See, for example, Taylor *et al.*'s (1997) case studies of Papua New Guinea, Malaysia and Australia. They concluded that 'there is no essential determinacy to the ways in which globalisation pressures work, since for various globalisation pressures there are also sites of resistance and counter movements' (Taylor *et al.* 1997, 72). (See Colclough and Lewin (1993, 256) for a similar argument.)

The fields of recontextualisation are, as Muller (1998) puts it, 'fields of contest' involving 'various social fractions with different degrees of social power sponsoring' different 'pedagogic regimes' (p. 190). The five generic policies adumbrated above are polyvalent; they are translated into particular interactive and sustainable practices in complex ways. They interact with, interrupt or conflict with other policies in play and long-standing indigenous policy traditions. They enter rather than simply change existing power relations and cultural practices. We can generalise here from Offe's (1984) comment that

> ... the real social effects ('impact') of a law or institutional service are not determined by the wording of the laws and statutes ('policy out'), but instead are generated primarily as a consequence of social disputes and conflicts, for which state policy merely establishes the location and timing of the contest, its subject matters and 'the rules of the game'.
>
> (p. 186)

Such disputes and conflicts take place at a number of levels – national, local and institutional. Policy analysis requires an understanding that is based not on the generic or local, macro- or micro-constraint or agency but on the changing relationships between them and their inter-penetration.

Conclusion

What I have tried to do in this paper is to take several things seriously, but also take them together.

1   To recognise the 'problems' of globalisation which frame and 'produce' the contemporary 'problems' of education.
2   To identify a set of generic 'solutions' to these problems and acknowledge their effects in educational reform and restructuring.
3   However, to suggest that these 'solutions' also have a magical form and ritual function.
4   That they become an inescapable form of reassurance; they discursively constrain the possibilities of response and are borrowed, enforced and adopted through various patterns of social contact, political and cultural deference and supranational agency requirements.
5   Finally, to register nonetheless the importance of local politics and culture and tradition and the processes of interpretation and struggle involved in translating these generic solutions into practical policies and institutional practices.

I want to end by returning to the side of my argument which is concerned with the generic aspects of education policy rather than its specifics and to Offe's (1984) 'real social effects'. My point is that careful investigation of local variations, exceptions and hybridity should not divert attention from the general patterns of practical and ideological, first-and second-order effects achieved by the ensemble of influences and policy mechanisms outlined above. That is to say, even in their different realisations, this ensemble changes the way that education is organised and delivered but also changes the meaning of education and what it means to be educated and what it means to learn. One key aspect of the reworking of meanings here is the increasing commodification of knowledge (which again parallels changes in the role of knowledge in the economy). Educational provision is itself increasingly made susceptible to profit and educational processes play their part in the creation of the enterprise culture and the cultivation of enterprising subjects (see Kenway *et al.* 1993). The framework of possibilities, the vocabularies of motives and the bases of legitimation (including values and ethics) within which educational decisions are made are all discursively reformed. But crucially these mechanisms and influences are also not just about new organisational forms or 'worker incentives' or rearticulated professional ethics; they are about access to and the distribution of educational opportunity in terms of race, class, gender and physical ability. The diversi-fication and re-hierarchisation of schooling in various educational market-places display an uncanny concomitance with widespread middle-class concerns about maintaining social advantage in the face of national and international labour market congestion. Thus, both in relation to patterns of convergence in education policy and the recontexualisation of policy, we need to be asking the question, 'whose interests are served?'.

Acknowledgements

I am grateful to Alan Cribb, Ben Levin and Carol Vincent for their comments on previous drafts of this paper.

References

Appadurai, A. (1990) 'Disjuncture and difference in the Global Cultural Economy', in M. Featherstone (ed.), *Global Culture: nationalism, globalization and modernity* (Special Issue of *Theory, Culture and Society*) (London: Sage).

Avis, J., Bloomer, M., Esland, G., Gleeson, D. and Hodkinson, P. (1996) *Knowledge and Nationhood: education, politics and work* (London: Cassell).

Ball, S. J. (1990) *Politics and Policymaking in Education* (London: Routledge).

Ball, S. J. (1994) *Education Reform: a critical and post-structural approach* (Buckingham: Open University Press).

Bernstein, B. (1996) *Pedagogy, Symbolic Control and Identity* (London: Taylor & Francis).

Brown, P. and Lauder, H. (1996) Education, globalisation and economic development, *Journal of Education Policy*, 11: 1–25.

Carter, D. S. G. and O'Neill, M. H. (1995) *International Perspectives on Educational Reform and Policy Implementation* (Brighton: Falmer).

Cerny, P. (1990) *The Changing Architecture of Politics: structure, agency and the future of the state* (London: Sage).

Chubb, J. and Moe, T. (1990) *Politics, Markets and America's Schools* (Washington, DC: Brookings Institution).

Clarke, J. and Newman, J. (1992) Managing to survive: dilemmas of changing organisational forms in the public sector, in *Social Policy Association Conference* (University of Nottingham, unpublished conference paper).

Colclough, C. and Lewin, K. (1993) *Educating all the Children* (New York: Oxford University Press).

Cousins, M. and Hussain, A. (1984) *Michel Foucault* (London: Macmillan).

Dale, R. and Ozga, J. (1993) 'Two hemispheres—both new right?', in R. Lingard, J. Knight and P. Porter (eds), *Schooling Reform in Hard Times* (London: Falmer), pp. 63–85.

Dror, Y. (1986) *Policy Making under Adversity* (New Brunswick: Transaction Books).

Du Gay, P. (1996) *Consumption and Identity at Work* (London: Sage).

European Union (1995) *White Paper on Education and Training, Teaching and Learning: towards the learning society* (Brussels: European Union).

Gee, J. and Lankshear, C. (1995) 'The new work order: critical language awareness and "fast capitalism" texts', *Discourse*, 16: 5–20.

Grace, G. (1995) *School Leadership: beyond education management: an essay in policy scholarship* (London: Falmer).

Hall, P. (1986) *Governing the Economy* (Cambridge, UK: Polity Press).

Halpin, D. and Troyna, B. (1995) The politics of education policy borrowing, *Comparative Education*, 31: 303–10.

Hampden-Turner, C. and Trompenaars, F. (1994) *The Seven Cultures of Capitalism; value systems for creating wealth in the United States, Britain, Japan, Germany, France, Sweden and The Netherlands* (London: Piatkus).

Harvey, D. (1989) *The Condition of Postmodernity* (Oxford: Basil Blackwell).

Harvey, D. (1996) *Justive, Nature and the Geography of Difference* (Oxford: Basil Blackwell).

Hughes, C. and Tight, M. (1995) 'The myth of the learning society', *British Journal of Educational Studies*, 45: 290–304.

Hutton, W. (1995) *The State We're In* (London: Jonathan Cape).

Jones, P. W. (1998) 'Globalisation and Internationalism: democratic prospects for world education', *Comparative Education*, 34: 143–55.

Jordon, B., Redley, M. and James, S. (1994) *Putting the Family First: identities, decisions and citizenship* (London: University College London Press).

Kenway, J., Bigum, C. and Fitzclarence, L. (1993) 'Marketing education in the post-modern age', *Journal of Education Policy*, 8: 105–22.

Kikert, W. (1991) *Steering at a Distance; a new paradigm of public governance in Dutch Higher Education* (European Consortium for Political Research, University of Essex).

Lash, S. and Urry, J. (1987) *The End of Organised Capitalism* (Cambridge: Polity).

Levin, B. (1998) 'An epidemic of education policy: (what) can we learn from each other?', *Comparative Education*, 34: 131–41.

Lyotard, J.-F. (1984) *The Postmodern Condition: a report on knowledge* (Manchester: Manchester University Press).

Max-Neef, M.A., Elizadle, A. and Hopenhayn, M. (1991) *Human Scale Development: conception, application and further reflections* (New York: The Apex Press).

Muller, J. (1998) 'The well-tempered learner: self-regulation, pedagogical models and teacher education policy', *Comparative Education*, 34: 177–93.

Newman, J. and Clarke, J. (1994) 'Going about our business? The managerialization of public services', in J. Clarke, A. Cochrane and E. Mclaughlin (eds), *Managing Social Policy* (London: Sage).

Newman, S. (1984) *Liberalism at Wits End* (Ithaca, NY: Cornell University Press).

Offe, C. (1984) *Contradictions of the Welfare State* (London: Hutchinson).

Organisation for Economic Co-operation and Development (1994) *School, a Matter of Choice* (Paris: Organization for Economic Co-operation and Development).

Peters, T. and Waterman, R. (1982) *In Search of Excellence* (London: Harper Row).

Pfeil, F. (1988) 'Postmodernism as a "structure of feeling"', in L. Grossberg and C. Nelson (eds) *Marxism and the Interpretation of Culture* (London: Macmillan).

Pfeil, F. (1995) *White Guys: studies in postmodern domination and difference* (London: Verso).

Popkewitz, T. (1996) 'Rethinking decentralisation and state/civil society distinctions: the state as a problematic of governing', *Journal of Education Policy*, 11: 27–52.

Ross, A. (1990) 'Ballots, bullets or batman: can cultural studies do the right thing', *Screen*, 31: 17–35.

Seddon, T. (1997) 'Markets and the English: rethinking educational restructuring as institutional design', *British Journal of Sociology of Education*, 18: 165–86.

Stronach, I. (1993) 'Education, vocationalism and economic recovery: the case against witchcraft', *British Journal of Education and Work*, 3: 5–31.

Swynegedouw, E. (1986) *The Socio-spatial Implications of Innovations in Industrial Organisation* (Lille: Johns Hopkins European Centre for Regional Planning and Research).

Taylor, S. (1995) 'Critical Policy Analysis: exploring contexts, texts and consequences', *Discourse*, 18: 23–36.

Taylor, S., Rizvi, F., Lingard, B. and Henry, M. (1997) *Educational Policy and the Politics of Change* (London: Routledge).

Thrupp, M. (1998) 'Exploring the politics of blame: school inspection and its contestation in New Zealand and England', *Comparative Education*, 34: 195–209.

Vanegas, P. and Ball, S. J. (1996) The teacher as a variable in education policy, in *BERA Annual Meeting* (Lancaster, unpublished conference paper).

Van Zanten, A. (1997) 'Schooling immigrants in France in the 1990s: success or failure of the republican model of integration?', *Anthropology and Education Quarterly*, 28: 351–74.

Weiss, L. (1997) 'Globalization and the myth of the powerless state', *New Left Review*, 225: 3–27.

Welch, A. R. (1998) 'The cult of efficiency in education: comparative reflections on the reality and the rhetoric', *Comparative Education*, 34: 157–75.

Whitty, G. and Edwards, T. (1998) 'School choice policies in England and the United States: an exploration of their origins and significance', *Comparative Education*, 34: 211–27.

Yeatman, A. (1994) *Postmodern Revisionings of the Political* (New York: Routledge).

CHAPTER 4

SPECIFYING GLOBALIZATION EFFECTS ON NATIONAL POLICY

A focus on the mechanisms

Roger Dale

Journal of Education Policy, 1999, 14(1): 1–17

Introduction

There has been and continues to be an enormous amount of discussion about the nature and meaning of globalization. The recent experience of the global origins and consequences of the crash of East Asian stock markets and economies has reduced the ranks of doubters about the existence of at least some economic forces that are beyond the control of even the most powerful nation state; and it is significant that one of the most 'globalist' interpretations of the current world economy comes from an author who subsequently became Secretary for Trade in the Clinton administration (Reich 1992).

However, accepting that globalization 'exists', at least to the extent of curtailing states' capacities and policy making discretion (which was never as untrammelled for any state as is often implied, and was distinctly limited for most), is only the start of the problem. 'Globalization' is not, as sometimes appears to be implied, the answer to any questions about the nature and orientation of national policies, but it does require one to consider anew how those policies are formed, shaped and directed. The key problem then becomes understanding the nature of globalization in ways that enable one to trace more precisely how, and with what consequences, it affects national policies. If 'global' factors affect national policies, what is the nature and extent of their influence?

In addressing these questions, this paper shall argue that globalization does constitute a new and distinct form of relationship between nation states and the world economy, but that it takes many different forms. While globalization has certainly not made nation states either irrelevant or obsolete it has affected both the content and form of at least some of the policy making procedures and outcomes of all states – which is one of its defining characteristics. However, states have not been rendered impotent in the face of an overwhelming challenge, much less replaced by it; rather, while they have all retained their formal territorial sovereignty more or less intact, they have all, to a greater or lesser degree, lost some of their capacity to make national policy independently. Globalization, then, does create broadly similar patterns of challenge for states that shape their possible responses in similar ways. Absolutely central to arguments about the effect of globalization on public services like education is that those effects are largely indirect; that is to say, they are mediated through the effect of globalization on the discretion and direction of nation states. As Habermas (1996, 292) puts it, 'While the world economy operates largely uncoupled from any political frame, national governments are restricted to fostering the modernization of their national economies. As a consequence, they have to adapt national welfare systems to what is called the capacity for international competition'.

However, while globalization does represent a new set of rules, there is no reason to expect all countries to interpret those rules in identical ways, or to expect them all to play to the rules in identical ways. Indeed, it could be argued that the curtailment of individual states' policy discretion is no more likely to bring about greater convergence between their policies than the formal freedom they previously enjoyed. As will be made clear below, that freedom was often exercised through mechanisms as similar as any so far induced by globalization. It is not then so much the diversity of policy responses to globalization that is discussed here, as the effects of the different mechanisms through which those effects are delivered. This paper also suggests that the variety of mechanisms through which globalization affects national policy is itself a diversifying factor; globalization cannot be reduced to the identical imposition of the same policy on all countries.

However, while it is widely acknowledged that globalization does affect national policies in a range of areas, precisely how is rarely questioned, let alone analysed. There is increasing recognition that national differences remain despite the spread of globalization, and accompanying doubts about tendencies towards convergence. Paradoxically, however, globalization itself, and certainly the ways it affects national policy, remains homogenized. One is, in fact, faced with a classic 'black box' analysis, where input is clearly related to output, but where the means by which the transformation is brought about are not apparent (or, by implication, important).

The main argument in this paper will be that the mechanisms through which globalization affects national policy are crucially important in defining the nature of that effect. Those mechanisms are not merely neutral conduits, but modify the nature of the effect they convey. Thus, at one level the argument is that the 'delivery mechanisms' themselves have an independent influence on the message, on how globalization affects national policy, and that this is a significant source of diversity within and across the effects of globalization. It must, of course, also be noted, though this paper shall not go into this in any depth, that the nature and impact of globalization effects varies enormously across different countries, according to their position in the world and regional economies.

This paper will also suggest that the mechanisms through which globalization operate are themselves qualitatively different from traditional mechanisms of external policy influence; this argument also strengthens the conception of globalization as a distinct phenomenon. In particular, it shall be suggested that the main dimensions along which globalization mechanisms differ from 'traditional' mechanisms are that their locus of viability is external, that their scope embraces policy goals as well as policy processes, that they are externally initiated, that they draw on a wider range of forms of power, and that they cannot be directly sourced to other individual nations. Specifically, this paper shall point to variations in the mechanisms through which globalization affects education policy and argue that though these effects are largely 'indirect', the mechanisms not only produce different types of responses from the states affected but they also independently shape and channel the form and strength of the effects of globalization.

The next section briefly sets out what the author understands by globalization and suggests, in broad terms, how it might effect education policy. The second part of the paper outlines and discusses some of the precise mechanisms through which global dynamics affect national education policies. The paper will conclude with an attempt to draw conclusions about the explanatory value of this approach to understanding education policy.

Globalization

There is no space here to go into an extended analysis of the nature of globalization, or even to produce a digest of the massive literature that it has spawned. (Extended discussions of the nature of globalization and its consequences for education can be found in two complementary essays; see Dale 1998b). The purpose of this section is to set out, very briefly, what seem to be the major features of globalization as they effect the issues at hand. The absolutely basic features of globalization for this paper are that it has economic, political and cultural strands, though it is the political that is being emphasized here; that 'global' to a large extent masks the fact that three major regional economic groupings have separate, as well as collective, effects; that the impact of globalization can occur at different levels of national societies, such as the regime, sectoral (e.g. the education system) and organizational (e.g. schools, or educational bureaucracies) levels; and that the effects of globalization are mediated, in both directions and in complex ways, by existing national patterns and structures, summarized here as the societal effect and the cultural effect.

Globalization is not a homogeneous process, nor are its effects homogeneous. As well as operating through different strands, it is associated with three quite distinct forms of regionalization (in Europe, Asia and America) which themselves generate and mediate different policies and mechanisms (for an analysis of the relationship between regionalization and education policy, see Dale and Robertson (1997a)).

Globalization emerged from the particular set of circumstances that attended the decline of the post-war economic and political settlement, that centred on the set of international financial agreements and institutions known collectively as the Bretton Woods agreement. This settlement was also premised on American hegemony and a world divided into two major blocs. The conditions that gave rise to those arrangements no longer hold. The Cold War is over, American hegemony, certainly economically, is eroded and the financial agreements proved incapable of responding to new global financial forces. These factors have together eroded both individual states' capacities to control their own affairs and their mutual arrangements for the collective management of their common interests.

Turning to the political aspect of globalization, as Cerny (1997, 253) puts it:

> Globalization as a political phenomenon basically means that the shaping of the playing field of politics is increasingly determined not within insulated units, i. e. relatively autonomous and hierarchically organized structures called states; rather, it derives from a complex congeries of multilevel games played on multilayered institutional playing fields, above and across, as well as within, state boundaries.

Very simply, states' reactions to these changing circumstances can be argued to have taken two broad forms; individually they have taken on what Cerny (1997, 263 ff) calls a 'competition state' form, and collectively they have become more concerned with setting up a framework of international organizations through which they seek to establish what Rosenau refers to as 'governance without government' (Rosenau 1992). Most prominent among the organizations that are involved in attempting to install governance without government are the IMF, the OECD, G-7, the World Bank and other similar, often regional organizations, through such very different institutional forms as, e.g. the European Union, North American Free Trade Area and the Asia Development Bank. However, while all these organizations have different, albeit often overlapping, missions, approaches and capacities, they are all driven by a broad set of ideological preferences that have developed as the 'orthodox' response to the problems posed to rich countries by changing global economic circumstances. (And it should be noted that the existence of this common ideology demonstrates clearly that though those countries may have individually ceded some of their national political capacity to international organizations, they have done so voluntarily, in order to maintain their own privileged positions in the world economy; indeed, Cerny argues that this has become a significant driver of the globalization process.)

That common ideology has been given some different labels, but the most succinct summary of its key features is provided by John Williamson under the title of the 'Washington Consensus' (Williamson 1993). He isolates 10 features of the consensus, which it will be useful to bear in mind in the second half of this paper. These are: fiscal discipline, public expenditure priorities, tax reform, financial liberalization, exchange rates, trade liberalization, foreign direct investment, privatization, deregulation, and property rights. Together, these constitute the preferred ideological filters that inform the directions in which national policy decisions are to be shaped.

States' individual responses to changing global realities centre on making themselves more competitive. This has a number of specific consequences, not least for education policy; indeed, as suggested above, it could be argued that the clearest effects of globalization on education policy come from the consequences of states' reorganization of their priorities to make them more competitive, for instance in attracting Trans National Corporations to locate in their territory. The key characteristic of the competition state is that it prioritizes the economic dimensions of its activities above all others. However, this does not mean that the effects of globalization are confined to the 'regime' level of nation states. It is clear that different sectors of national societies are more likely to be influenced by changing global dynamics than others and in different ways. It is also clear that some global effects are very direct and narrowly focused on particular organizational practices; the clearest examples of these are the work practices introduced by TNCs, which can entail major, but isolated, shifts in traditional practices.

It is also essential to recognize the continuing significance of national societal and cultural effects whose prominence and importance are hardly diminished by globalization. Globalization may change the parameters and direction of state policies in similar ways but it does not inevitably override or remove existing national peculiarities (or different sectoral peculiarities within national societies). This is evident from a number of studies. For instance, Maurice *et al.*'s (1984) concept of the societal effect shows clearly the existence of nationally specific collections of organically related policies (such as legal, financial, education and training policies) that comprise structures to which innovations must accommodate. For a further elaboration of the societal approach to education see Dale (1991). Another powerful nationally mediating factor is the 'cultural effect'. This is based on the work of Hofstede (1994). Hofstede compared the values of similar people in 64 different national subsidiaries of IBM and discovered that they varied considerably in ways relevant to their performance of the same set of duties across the four major dimensions of Power Distance, Uncertainty Avoidance, Masculinity and Individualism. This provides a further demonstration of how external policies are likely to be differently interpreted and differently acted on in different countries, even at the organizational level, where their impact is most direct.

The remainder of this paper will concentrate on the mechanisms through which the effects of globalization are delivered. It will tackle this by setting out a typology of mechanisms of external influences on policy.

Dimensions of variability between external effects on national education policies

This section of the paper shall (a) compare mechanisms of externally influenced policy change that have been used before and during the phase of globalization, and (b) discuss the nature and outcomes for national education policy making of a wide range of policy transfer mechanisms. It will consider five mechanisms of external effect on education policy that could be seen to be associated, though not exclusively, with globalization, as parts of a 'globalization effect'. These are labelled 'harmonization', 'dissemination', 'standardization', 'installing interdependence' and 'imposition'. These are compared with two 'traditional' or 'orthodox' mechanisms of external effect on national education policies, 'policy borrowing' and 'policy learning' (note that the author is not suggesting that these two 'traditional' mechanisms have been eliminated or somehow outlawed in a global era; they might be expected to persist, though in forms crucially shaped by globalization).

The purpose of presenting these mechanisms of policy transfer is not so much to assess the validity or success of the approaches, as to test the idea that globalization represents a distinct phenomenon that also operates and achieves its effects through distinct mechanisms. What shall be shown in this section then is that (a) it is possible to distinguish globalization effects from more traditional effects on education policy, such as 'policy borrowing' and 'policy learning', and (b) mechanisms of globalization effects are themselves diverse rather than homogeneous.

A simplified digest and comparison of the eight mechanisms is set out in Table 4.1. The nature and consequences of the differences between the approaches are elaborated below. It will be useful to start by giving some explanation and elaboration of the dimensions on which they are compared.

The first dimension of variability, the degree to which the reforms were voluntarily accepted by the recipient nation, is included because of the common assumption that externally influenced reforms are necessarily 'forced on', or at least unwillingly accepted by, the recipient nation. That seems often to be the case with more 'conspiracy' inclined accounts of the consequences of globalization. However, as the discussion above of the nature of 'governance without government' suggests, imposition of policy is not the only way that globalization can affect education policy.

The second dimension focuses on how explicit the process is; again, this is used to highlight the apparent assumption that many reforms are introduced 'behind the back' of the recipient nation. However, on the one hand, much of the external influence may be quite explicit, as in the case of 'policy borrowing', and on the other, we should note that the external effect can be implicit without being suspicious; unconscious imitation is not unknown in many spheres of life!

The third dimension, the scope of the externally influenced reform, is extremely important. While traditionally externally influenced reforms might have been expected to be piecemeal and restricted in their scope, one cannot assume either that 'borrowing' or 'learning' are necessarily limited in scope or that the other types of effect are necessarily broad in scope. The key issue here is whether the effects are restricted to policy *programmes* and *organization* or whether they can also involve policy *goals*. Traditionally, only the former were taken to be susceptible to external influence, with goals and values remaining strictly 'internally'

Table 4.1 A typology of mechanisms of external effects on national policies

Characteristics of effect mechanisms	Mechanisms of external effects							
	Borrowing	Learning		Harmonisation	Dissemination	Standardization	Installing interdependence	Imposition
		'Normal'	'Paradigmatic'					
Nature of relationship	Voluntary	Voluntary	Formally voluntary	Formally voluntary	Formally voluntary	Formally voluntary	Voluntary	Compulsory
Explicitness of process	Explicit	Varies	Varies	Explicit	Explicit	Quite implicit	Explicit	Explicit
Scope	Particular policy process	Recognised parameters/policy process	Policy process and policy goals	Multiple policies	Multiple policies	Multiple policies	Policy goals	Particular policy goals
Locus of viability	National	National	External	Regional organization	External/national	International fora	Common heritage of humankind	International organization
Process	Borrowing/imitation	'Learning'	'Teaching'	Collective agreement	Persuasion/agenda setting	Condition of membership	Persuasion	Leverage
Parties involved	Bilateral	Bilateral/international	International	Multinational	International	Multinational	Global – 'bottom up'	Multinational
Source of initiation	Recipient	National 'policy community'	International model	Collectively by members	Supranational body	'International community'	NGos ('global civil society')	Supranational national body
Dimension of power	Conscious decision	Conscious decision	Agenda setting/rules of game	Conscious decision	Agenda setting	Rules of game	Agenda setting	All three dimensions
Nature of effect on education	Direct (on sector or organization)	Varies	Varies	Implied – regime and sector	Direct – sector	Direct – regime-sector relation	Indirect – regime direct – org.	Indirect – regime
Example from education	Scotvec in New Zealand	Human capital theory in 1960s	Increasing user charges for education	Maastricht treaty	OECD/CERI activity (see Papadopoulos 1992)	UNESCO science policy un declaration on human rights	'Green' curriculum materials	World bank education loans

determined. Peter Hall's work on policy learning does provide a partial and very significant exception to this and will be discussed further below (see Hall 1989).

The fourth dimension concerns the 'locus of viability' of the mechanism. The viability of any policy is usually assumed to be judged at a national level and according to existing national norms and expectations. The argument for political globalization suggests that that may no longer necessarily be the case, while the argument about the variability of forms of globalization also suggests that more than a simple shift from a 'national' to a 'global' locus of viability may be involved.

The fifth dimension concerns the process by which the external influence is introduced. This, too, might be expected to alter somewhat the (at least implicitly) relatively cooperative and collaborative processes that accompanied the traditional forms. However, it is important to recognize the difference between policy borrowing and policy learning as *processes* or *media* of introducing or implanting external influences on education systems and the way they are being employed here, as *models of mechanisms* for the introduction of external effects. As such, their importance exceeds the processes they embody, though it should also be noted that those processes may be employed by any of the other mechanisms listed in Table 4.1.

A further clear difference between the 'traditional' models and those associated with globalization is the range of partners to the transaction. Both 'borrowing' and 'learning' assume a relatively narrow range of partners to the relationship. These would normally be expected to be restricted to other nation states or some kind of 'policy community'. While the size and specificity of this community may vary according to whether the attempted transfer is occurring at regime, sectoral or organizational level, it might be expected to be limited by existing commonalities of interest (as implied in the term 'policy community'). At the very least it assumes some kind of mutual recognition of relevant parties, but *prima facie* something more distant and anonymous is involved in a 'global' relationship.

The sixth dimension concerns the central issue of the source of initiation of the reform; here again, it is implicit in the borrowing and learning models that it is the recipient (a more neutral and less emotive term than either beneficiary or victim!), rather than the external party, who would initiate the reform. This assumption too, is challenged by the possibility of externally initiated reforms. This may be an appropriate juncture at which to raise the issue of the difference between globalization and 'imperialism' or 'colonialism', since it is quite plausible to suggest that the difference between globalization and imperialism/colonialism is that what once happened only to third world or colonized countries is now happening to the most powerful states, previously the initiators rather than the recipients of external pressures on their national policies. In a nutshell, the difference is that globalization is not the result of the imposition of a policy by one country on another, possibly backed up by the threat of bilateral military action, but a much more supranationally constructed effect. The result may be little different as far as the recipient countries are concerned – indeed, as suggested above, the point of constructing the supra national organizations was not to weaken or dissipate the power of the already powerful states, but to strengthen their ability to respond collectively to forces that none of them could control individually any longer – but the nature of the process is significantly changed.

The seventh dimension is called 'dimension of power' after Steven Lukes' theoretical development of the forms of power (Lukes 1974). Put simply, Lukes argues that power may be exercised in three distinct ways, that vary in their visibility and explicitness. The first dimension involves the relatively 'naked' use of superior power and/or is exercised through clearly defined decision making fora. The second dimension centres around the politics of non-decision making and highlights the importance of the ability to exercise power through such means as agenda setting. The final dimension of power concerns the ability to control the 'rules of the game', the processes through which power is defined and exercised. These forms of power are successively less overt and correspondingly more difficult to counter. The increasing use of less direct means of power is a further manifestation of the changing nature of the relationship between states. Power over third world states is now much less likely to be bilaterally applied and much more likely to be achieved through a supranationally organized rearrangement of the rules of the game.

The final dimension concerns how the effect on education of the externally introduced change is mediated. Such effects are typically assumed to be direct; policy transfers are assumed to affect the appropriate policy area. However, if we confine ourselves to external effects that announce themselves as being concerned with education we will miss many of the most significant effects of extra national influences on national education systems. As argued previously, the more we confine ourselves to the level of education politics – that is, to policies and practices that are clearly of direct and immediate relevance to education policy or practice – the greater the risk that we will neglect the level at which the agenda for education politics is set, that of the politics of education. This becomes even more important when the ambit of possible external influences is extended geographically. This variable acknowledges the possibility of indirect, or implied, effects, as well as those that declare themselves explicitly. It is also important to note that the nature of the effect has to be registered at the appropriate level; it cannot be assumed that for an external factor to have an effect on an education system it has to be directed towards the education sector or even to educational organizations. Of course, these are extremely important; however, it is crucial not to neglect the consequences of changes at the regime level on education policy and practice.

A comparison of policy transfer mechanisms

The central focus of this paper is on claims about the distinctiveness of globalization as an influence shaping national education policies. The alternative view is implied by Halpin and Troyna (1995) who refer to 'policy borrowing' a 'a trend that has accelerated as the move towards a "global village" becomes an increasing reality' (304), while explanations that fall under the broad heading of 'policy learning' have been increasingly invoked to explain the apparent similarity of policy shifts carried out almost simultaneously in different countries (see Bennett and Howlett 1992). The comparison is made tighter and its potential validity enhanced if it is recognized that all the features of what is referred to above as the societal effect and the cultural effect modify, filter, channel, interpret and select from all the modes of external effect that will be discussed. That is to say, in none of the cases to be discussed is the external effect assumed to be either so compatible with existing practices, or to be so overwhelmingly imposed, that the societal effects etc. are rendered nugatory.

This latter proposition is perhaps hardest to sustain in the case of the first policy transfer mechanism to be discussed, borrowing. Here it sometimes seems to be assumed that some considerable level of relevant compatibility exists between the 'borrowing' and 'lending' partners. The representation of what transpires as 'borrowing' certainly sustains the compatibility assumption; we don't usually 'borrow' something we don't know we have a use, even a need, for, or indeed, that we won't return! And of course, borrowing implies a 'lender'. The notion of borrowing is, however, misleading. Bennett (1997) lists several terms that more accurately describe the nature of the relationship – imitation, emulation, copying. The literature on education policy borrowing reflects some of the uncertainties raised by Bennett. In particular, it tends to find evidence of 'borrowing' as such rather lacking. As Whitty *et al.* (1993) put it, describing Whitty and Edwards' work on the extent of policy borrowing between Britain and the US, in the City Technology College and Magnet school initiatives, 'policy makers in both countries were working with similar frames of reference and producing parallel policy initiatives, rather than directly "borrowing" policies from one another' (166). The policy borrowing literature is also somewhat sceptical about its success as a strategy (though there is some questioning of the exact nature of the strategic aims of 'policy borrowing'). McLean (1995, 14), for instance, argues that it simplifies the policy process, puts it out of the reach of potential opponents and is used to enable politicians to justify pre-determined reform intentions. Halpin and Troyna (1995) also emphasize the use of policy borrowing as a form of political legitimation and as driven by political expediency. However, there do exist cases of direct policy borrowing. Peddie (1991) cites several examples of policies directly borrowed by New Zealand from Britain (including the direct adoption of school designs that retained their south facing aspect!). More recently, several countries have expressed considerable interest in the German apprenticeship system, while Kappert (1997) describes New Zealand's attempts to introduce elements of both the English and Scottish systems of qualification and accreditation.

The point here, however, is not to evaluate policy borrowing as a strategy, but to compare it with globalization as a mechanism of introducing external influences to national education systems. As a mechanism of policy transfer, the key features of policy borrowing in terms of the variables outlined above are that it is carried out *voluntarily* and *explicitly*, and that its *locus of viability is national*. It involves *particular policies* that one country seeks to *imitate, emulate or copy, bilaterally*, from another. It is the *product of conscious decision making*, and it *is initiated by the recipient*. The nature of its effects on education could be expected to be *direct* and they would tend to be restricted to the sectoral or organizational level, that is to the level of education politics.

The issue of policy learning is somewhat more complex and more instructive. For one thing, it takes a wide variety of forms. In a very useful review of the policy learning literature Bennett and Howlett (1992, 289) conclude that 'the all-embracing term "policy learning" ... can be seen to actually embrace three highly complex processes: learning about organizations, learning about programs and learning about policies'. Such a broad compass means that some form of policy learning is likely to be present in any mechanism of policy transfer. This broad compass enables one to specify more closely what it is that distinguishes globalization mechanisms from traditional mechanisms. The 'compatibility' of 'policy learning' with both traditional and globalized mechanisms makes examining how it might fit into the different contexts a very effective way of comparing the two sets of mechanisms. The best way to illustrate how this might be done is through the example of the pre-eminent work of comparative policy learning, Peter Hall's edited collection of writings on the diffusion of Keynesian ideas across different countries (Hall 1989). This enables one to compare the place of policy learning in traditional and global mechanisms across five key dimensions; such a comparison enables one to reach one of the main goals of this paper, that of specifying factors that distinguish and differentiate traditional and global mechanisms.

The first variable to be considered is the locus of viability. In his concluding chapter (see especially 370–1 and Figure 14.1), Hall argues that the main factors affecting the reception of Keynesian ideas were their economic viability (their perceived ability to resolve the economic problems at hand); their political viability (their fit with existing goals and interests of the dominant party and the associations the ideas acquired in the political arena); and in particular, their 'administrative viability', 'the degree to which the new ideas fit the long-standing administrative biases of the relevant decision makers and the existing capacity of the state to implement them' (Hall 1989, 371). The emphasis here is entirely on the individual nation state as the locus of viability. The central point about globalization is the diminution of the nation state as the ultimate locus of viability over a range of policies. Thus, globalization assumes that the viability test of policy is carried out at a supranational level. Rather than having to demonstrate their compatibility with existing national state structures and practices, policies have to demonstrate their compatibility with supranational expectations. In certain policy areas, then, the adjustment is in the opposite direction to that required of Keynesian polices in the 1930s and 1940s – although, of course, the process involved may still be one that could be described as learning. In terms of the variables outlined above one can see that policy learning in the traditional mode was largely voluntary; the purpose of Hall's book is to show why some countries decided to adopt Keynesianism and others did not, which clearly assumes a high level of voluntarism. As this paper shall show, globalization mechanisms tend not to make this assumption.

The second important variable here is the dimension of power through which the desired end was to be achieved. The Keynesian case clearly rests on conscious decision making; there appear to have been significant elements of 'real' choice for the countries discussed, though the presence of Keynesian policy in some countries clearly had some effect on the broader international agenda. The means by which policy learning has been involved in accommodating globalization mechanisms of policy transfer may be rather more implicit and arms length, to be achieved through agenda setting or the rules of the game.

In the case of the source of initiation of policy change, all the countries that adopted Keynesian policies, or decided not to, essentially initiated the change themselves, rather than having it formally brought to them by a 'lender' state or a supranational body (though this is not to say that the fact that other countries were, or were not, adopting the same set of ideas was irrelevant to their decision). By contrast, it is a dominant characteristic of the globalization mechanisms that they are initiated outside the recipient country (albeit that the organization initiating the transfer or influence may well have been set up by the country and encouraged to initiate such policies). It might be noted here that while the 'borrower-lender' metaphor may not be wholly apt, it is possible and useful to distinguish the different status of 'policy learning' and 'policy teaching'. Some of the mechanisms to be discussed below display a clear and sometimes explicit teaching orientation.

The most significant differences come in the scope of the policy learning and the nature of the parties involved. As Bennett and Howlett (1992) point out, all the policy learning work they consider 'extends only to programs and ... to instruments ... and not to the adoption of new policy goals' (287). The exception to this is Peter Hall's work. Hall does recognise the possibility of policy learning extending to policy goals as well as policy instruments – and the circumstances in which he sees this as likely to occur are of considerable importance to the argument being advanced here. As Bennett and Howlett summarize his position, for Hall, 'normal politics' or policy-making is associated with learning about instruments, while learning about policy goals occurs only in special circumstances associated with shifts in 'policy paradigms' or changes in the dominant set of policy ideas which shape discourse in the policy-making process' (Bennett and Howlett 1992). The author's argument about globalization is that it induces precisely this kind of paradigm shift in national policy making assumptions. Essentially, globalization removes some matters from the control of individual states and this requires paradigm shifts in the ways that they respond through policy. One consequence of this is the achievement of a new state 'settlement', which has been described as 'the competitive-contractual state settlement' (see Dale and Robertson 1997b); this shift essentially makes international competitiveness the dominant criterion of state policy making and contractualism the dominant source of administrative bias and structural capacities.

This development, though indirect, is an extremely important consequence of globalization. A more direct and more immediately relevant consequence is the development of *supranational* responses to common problems for states in a globalized context. This represents the final major dimension of difference between globalization and 'traditional' mechanisms of policy influence. As pointed out above, what distinguishes globalization from imperialism and colonialism is that it is supranational; it is not initiated by a single country, or carried out by nations on nations, but by supranational organizations, albeit dominated by the same group of nations that were previously involved separately in bilateral mechanisms.

So, the different forms they take, especially the variations on 'governance without government', are what underlie the globalization inflected mechanisms of policy transfer and influence that will be discussed next. Before doing that this paper will very briefly summarize the implications of the comparisons of the place of policy learning in traditional and globalization mechanisms. The distinctiveness of globalization mechanisms lies in their extra-national locus of viability, their use of less 'direct' forms of power, the fact that they are externally rather than internally initiated and that their scope, as a result of the paradigm shift brought about by globalization, extends to policy goals as well as to policy processes.

The first of these mechanisms of policy transfer to be discussed is what has been called 'harmonization'. This draws largely on the model of the European Union. That development itself could be seen as a form of paradigm shift. As Brigitte Unger argues, in an article that examines the convergence effect of the EU, the installation of major policy change such as the EU requires the kind of stimulus represented by globalization to induce change in states where 'the more policy content, procedure or intended outcome affect the core of (political) institutions and the cultural values that underlie them, the stronger the resistance to change will be' (Unger 1997, 107). The EU example also requires one to focus on the different regional forms of globalization, although it is important to recognize that the harmonization mechanism is largely restricted to Europe. Grieco (1997) has suggested three dimensions for the comparison of what he refers to as the 'process of institutionalization' of economic relations between countries (and of course, the EU extends beyond economic relations). These are the 'locus of internationaliza-tion', the 'legal-organizational basis of association among partners': 'the scope of activity', the number of issues covered by regional arrangements: and the 'level of institutional authority', which refers to the amount of pooled responsibility for joint activities by national governments (Grieco 1997, 165). As Grieco emphasizes, on all these dimensions, the Asia region is relatively underdeveloped compared to America and especially Europe. For the purposes of this paper this serves to emphasize the heterogeneity of the mechanisms produced by globalization.

However, the focus here is on European integration, officially referred to as 'harmonization'. The point is that the process involved requires all member nations to cede and pool some of their national policy making capacity to the regional organization. The harmonization mechanism operates through a process of collective agreement, which may be its most important defining variable. The limit case of harmonization (or of almost any form of globalization) is monetary union or the EMU (European Monetary Union). Unger (1997, 106) refers to this:

> 'Maastricht-style convergence' as deliberate(ly) impos(ing) a set of convergence criteria on countries wanting to join the currency club...(where) convergence is not the result of imitation of technology or of market forces, but the result of political norms and collective enforcement.

It is at present unclear whether monetary union will ever be achieved or whether it will set a pattern for harmonization. Unger implies that it will not. However, as Mann (1996, 303–4) argues,

> Europe remains fundamentally an economic planning agency...The EC has not moved into class or other group relations, such as the regulation of labour relations, public order, religion, or the welfare state, though where welfare and the labour market meet in national education policy, it is active.

Unger (1997, 122) suggests, on the basis of a comparison of 14 policy fields, that,

> ...financial market liberalization, multinational firms' threats of relocation, the spread of political ideologies, and EU-harmonization laws are the main factors affecting national economic policies in (Europe). Of these, state competition for the location of firms seems to be more important for convergence than has the enforcement of EU-harmonization laws. And imitation of political ideology seems more important than market forces.

This is a very interesting list, especially in the way that it ranks the more 'imposed' and the more 'cooperative' mechanisms for change.

The next mechanism of policy transfer, dissemination, differs from harmonization mainly in the process, initiation and dimension of power dimensions. The best example here is found in the work of supranational organizations like the OECD. The OECD works predominantly through an agenda setting strategy. Most of its major documents seek to indicate to member nations likely future directions in a wide variety of policy fields. It should also be noted that the OECD's work is influential at all three major levels distinguished above, regime, sector and organization. Unusually, education has been a sector of particular interest, and the sectoral and organizational scope of the OECD approach to education has been clearly set out in a history of the organizastion's involvement in education by a member of its education secretariat (see Papadopoulos 1994). Papadopoulos (1994, 13) points out that the organization's influence on national policies:

> must be sought in terms of a 'catalytic role', through a process (whose) starting point is the identification of major new policy issues which emerge on the

educational horizon, and which might call for priority attention in the countries. These are issues which are somewhat ahead of actual country developments and thinking...These issues are then put together within a structured framework, leading to a number of questions which arise for policy-making. Arriving at a convincing statement of such issues and questions, of how and why they arise, and of their implications, is already half the work done.

And he concludes the book by stating that:

> The educational agenda for the nineties is...both fresh and exciting...It remains to be seen whether the Member countries can rise to the challenge. Certainly, the experience of the last 30 years...places the OECD in a unique position to continue its task of assisting them to do so.
>
> (Papadopoulos 1994, 195)

A key example of this mechanism would be OECD's attempts to develop international indicators of and for education systems (see CERI 1992) that go well beyond its stated function of meeting the growing demand for more and better information about the quality of education. It has clear implications for the goals as well as the processes of policy, something that is also clearly implicit in the process described by Papadopoulos. There is in both these examples an element of 'anticipatory policy convergence', or self denying policy ordinance around an internationally approved agenda.

The idea of 'standardization' draws heavily on the work of the 'global institutionalists' (see e.g. Meyer *et al*. 1992, 1997). Their fundamental argument is that,

> ...many features of the contemporary nation state derive from worldwide models constructed and propagated through global cultural and associational processes...Worldwide models (which) have become especially important... as cultural and organizational development of world society has intensified at an unprecedented rate) define and legitimate agendas for local action, shaping the structures and policies of nation-states and other national and local actors in virtually all domains of rationalized social life...the institutionalization of world models helps explain many puzzling features of contemporary societies, such as structural isomorphism in the face of enormous differences...
>
> (Meyer *et al*. 1997, 144–5)

It is fortunate, for the purposes of this paper, that the work of Meyer *et al*. has concentrated especially on the spread of a particular institutional form of education, which they take as a key example of the spread of the Western cultural project (this issue is discussed at greater length in Dale 2001). The extent of educational isomorphism is exemplified through a study of school curricula, which Meyer *et al*. (e.g. 1992) argue have shown signs of becoming common across the world. This argument and its implications are not quite as startling as may appear at first blush. Their focus is 'curriculum categories', rather than 'what is taught'. Indeed, they willingly concede that what is taught may well vary across countries. The processes they describe occur chiefly through the work of international organizations, especially those that are 'open' in their membership, such as those associated with the United Nations. Essentially, these organizations operate to bring about congruent policy changes by making, or assuming, adherence to particular broad policy principles a requisite of membership of the particular sector of the international community they represent. As Meyer *et al.* (1997, 158) put it,

> Entry into the system occurs, essentially, via application forms (to the United Nations and other world bodies) on which the applicant must demonstrate appropriately formulated assertions about sovereignty and control over population and territory, along with appropriate aims and purposes.

This may not only bring benefits, especially for smaller and poorer countries, but it almost seems to be suggested by the global institutionalists that they are not regarded as real states if they do not or have not such defining characteristics of modernity.

However, the processes through which global isomorphism comes about are not clear. Two representatives of the approach put forward two means of 'promoting attention to international norms' – that are useful with less and more developed countries respectively – 'pressure', through the imposition of costs for violation, and 'the use of the norms as "resources" that reinforce the purposes actors are already aligned around' (Strang and Chang 1993, 244). This seems somewhat *ad hoc*, however, and not as useful for the purposes of this paper as Lukes' typology, to which it can clearly be subsumed. The Strang and Chang article is, though, useful, in that it indicates that international organizations (in this case the ILO) can both apply 'progressive' norms and that they can be effective in 'bringing into line' advanced as well as developing countries. Another example that sheds some light on the process (though not explicitly) is provided in Finnemore's (1993) account of how UNESCO spread the idea of national science policy. She refers explicitly to this process as the 'teaching of norms' by international organizations. Specifically, she argues that:

> UNESCO 'taught' states the value and utility of science policy organization' and that this was 'a reflection of a new norm (that held that coordination and direction of science are necessary tasks of the modern state and that a science policy bureaucracy having certain well-specified characteristics was the appropriate means to fulfill those tasks) elaborated within the international community'.
>
> (Finnemore 1993, 466)

The success of this prescriptive policy is evident from the fact that it was successful in the Congo, which at the time had only nine scientists in R&D jobs, while in Sudan, 'UNESCO officials had trouble finding enough qualified scientists to draft a proposal for the new science policy body, let alone staff it once it was created' (Finnemore 1993, 591). Standardization, then, clearly has some of the crucial features of globalization effects – it extends to policy goals, it has an external locus of viability, and is externally initiated by a supranational body; however, it employs a rather smaller and less assertive range of dimensions of power.

The next type of mechanism is called 'Installing Interdependence'. Its starting point is the notion of the 'common heritage of humankind' (Sousa Santos 1995, 264–5). The defining feature of this mechanism is that it is driven essentially by a concern for *issues* (such as environmental, human rights, and peace) that extend beyond the scope of any nation state, rather than by a concern with international or even multinational policies and processes. Thus, it differs along several dimensions from most of the other mechanisms discussed. Its scope is very much centred on policy goals, indeed on the purpose of national policy. It is initiated by what might be referred to very loosely as 'global civil society' (though the amorphousness of this concept might be reduced through the development of the idea of a 'world polity', based around the work of Non-Governmental Organizations (see Boli and Thomas 1997)). It operates from the 'bottom up' and can pursue its ends only through persuasion. One other crucial feature of this mechanism is that it has no effective locus of viability (as is empirically evident from the 'non-results' of the many world environmental summits etc). Consequently, one might expect that its effects on education will be relatively direct and focused on sectoral, or more likely, organizational, levels, where the agenda setting possibilities of the mechanism might be most effective.

The final mechanism to be considered, 'imposition', is the one that is probably the first to come to most people's minds when they think of globalization. Despite the attention paid here to the variation in mechanisms of globalization, Unger's comments quoted above about the superior effectiveness of MNCs' threats over EU-harmonization alert to the continuing central importance of imposition. Because the mechanism of imposition has been so widely canvassed it is probably not necessary to describe it in even the sketchy amount of detail that has been used with the other, less familiar, mechanisms. The broad parameters and exemplars of imposition, such as structural adjustment and TNC leverage have been very fully documented in the literature on globalization. However, since a central aim of this paper is to indicate the diversity of globalization mechanisms, it is useful to point to the two dimensions on which imposition differs most significantly from the other mechanisms: it is the only mechanism able to compel recipient countries to take on particular policies and it is the only one that does not need to rely on some form of learning, persuasion or cooperation to bring about its desired changes.

Conclusion

This paper has attempted to open up the black box of mechanisms through which globalization affects national policies. In doing so, it has sought to demonstrate the qualitative differences implied by the term globalization and to extend the understanding of its diversifying consequences. In developing and elaborating the typology, it indicated five key dimensions on which the mechanisms associated with globalization differed significantly from those typical of 'traditional' mechanisms of policy transfer. These were the scope of the mechanisms (whether they included policy goals as well as policy processes), the locus of viability, the mode of power employed through the mechanism, the initiating source of the policy change and the nature of the parties to the exchange. Overall, this demonstrated the necessity of breaking down the gross concept of globalization along a range of dimensions if its nature and consequences are to be adequately understood and acted upon. Specifically in the field of education it has been argued that the effects of globalization are largely indirect, the result of the stances adopted by nation-states in response to globalization, rather than a direct effect of globalization. Two possible exceptions were considered. The 'global institutionalist' view that worldwide models of political institutions are leading to convergence of the categories states use to organize and define their business was seen as correct in a formal sense, but lacking in any effective and demonstrable outcomes on individual states, beyond a kind of lip service compliance. The possibility that the 'common heritage of humankind' may come increasingly to have a direct effect, unmediated by states, on education at the organizational level is suggested.

References

Bennett, C. J. (1997) 'Understanding ripple effects: The cross-national adoption of policy instruments for bureaucratic accountability', *Governance*, 10(3): 213–33.

Bennett, C. J. and Howlett, M. (1992) 'The lessons of learning: Reconciling theories of policy learning and policy change', *Policy Sciences*, 25: 275–94.

Boli, J. and Thomas, G. M. (1997) 'World culture in the World polity: A century of international non-governmental organizations', *American Sociological Review*, 62: 171–90.

Centre for educational research and innovation (1992) *The OECD International Education Indicators: A Framework for Analysis* (Paris: OECD).

Cerny, P. (1997) 'Paradoxes of the competition state: The dynamics of political globalization', *Government and Opposition*, 32(2): 251–74.

Dale, R. (1991) International Comparisons or a 'Societal Approach' for New Zealand?, Paper presented to New Zealand Planning Council Seminar on Education Models from Overseas (Wellington).

Dale, R. (1998a) Globalisation and national education policy, *Educational Theory*, 50(4): 427–448.

Dale, R. (1998b) 'Comparative education through globalisation', in J. Schriewer (ed.), *Discourse Formation in Comparative Education* (Berlin: Peter Lang).

Dale, R. and Robertson, S. (1997a) 'Resiting the nation, reshaping the state', in M. Olssen and K. Morris-Matthews (eds), *Education Policy in New Zealand* (Palmerston North: Dunmore), pp. 209–27.

Dale, R. and Robertson, S. (1997b) The contours and consequences of the competitive/contractualist state settlement. (University of Auckland School of Education, unpublished paper.)

Finnemore, M. (1993) 'International organizations as teachers of norms: The United Nations Educational, Scientific, and Cultural Organization and science policy', *International Organization*, 47(4): 565–97.

Grieco, J. (1997) 'Systematic sources of variation in regional institiutionalization in Western Europe, East Asia and the Americas', in E. O. Mansfield and H. V. Milner (eds), *The Political Economy of Regionalism* (New York: Columbia University Press), pp. 164–85.

Habermas, J. (1996) 'The European nation-state – its achievements and its limits. On the past and future of sovereignty and citizenship', in G. Balakrishnan (ed.), *Mapping the Nation* (London: Verso), pp. 281–94.

Hall, P. A. (ed.) (1989) *The Political Power of Economic Ideas: Keynesianism across Nations* (Princeton, NJ: Princeton University Press).

Halpin, D. and Troyna, B. (1995) 'The politics of education policy borrowing', *Comparative Education*, 31(3): 303–10.

Hofstede, G. (1994) 'Management scientists are human', *Management Science*, 40(1): 4–13.

Kappert, P. (1997) Educational Utopia? The New Zealand Standards Approach Considered in the Light of the German Experience in Vocational Training (Victoria University of Wellington, Unpublished PhD thesis).

Lukes, S. (1974) *Power: A Radical View* (London: Macmillan).

McLean, M. (1995) *Educational Traditions Compared* (London: David Fulton).

Mann, M. (1996) 'Nation-states in Europe and other continents: Diversifying, developing, not dying', in G. Balakrishnan (ed.), *Mapping the Nation* (London: Verso), pp. 295–316.

Maurice, M., Sellier, F. and Silvestre, J.-P. (1984), *Social Foundations of Industrial Power* (Cambridge: MIT Press).

Meyer, J. W., Kamens, D. and Benavot, A. (1992) *School Knowledge for the Masses: World Models and National Primary Curricular Categories in the Twentieth Century* (London: Falmer).

Meyer, J. W., Boli, J., Thomas, G. M. and Ramirez, F. (1997) 'World society and the nation-state', *American Journal of Sociology*, 103(1): 144–81.

Papadopoulos, G. A. (1994) *Education 1960–90: The OECD Perspective* (Paris: OECD).

Peddie, R. (1991) Comparative Studies in education: Lessons for New Zealand?, Paper presented to New Zealand Planning Council Seminar, Education Models from Overseas (Wellington).

Reich, R. (1992) *The Work of Nations* (New York: Vintage).

Rosenau, J. (ed.) (1992) *Governance Without Government: Order and Change in World Politics* (Cambridge: Cambridge University Press).

Sousa Santos, B. (1995) *Towards a New Common Sense: Law, Science and Politics in the Paradigmatic Transition* (London: Routledge).

Strang, D. and Chang, P. M. Y. (1993) 'The International Labor Organization and the welfare state: Institutional effects on national welfare spending, 1960–80', *International Organization,* 47(2): 235–62.

Unger, B. (1997) 'Limits of convergence and globalization', in S. D. Gupta (ed.), *The Political Economy of Globalization* (Boston, MA: Kluwer), pp. 99–127.

Whitty, G., Edwards, T. and Gewirtz, S. (1993) *Specialisation and Choice in Urban Education* (London: Routledge).

Williamson, J. (1993) 'Democracy and the "Washington Consensus" ', *World Development,* 21(8): 1329–36.

CHAPTER 5

GLOBALISATION, EDUCATION POLICY AND POLITICS

Jenny Ozga and Bob Lingard

Introduction

In this chapter we want to focus on some of the key features of the new landscape of education policy making evident in many countries across the globe, and, in particular, to consider their effects on the politics of education. Our argument covers three main topics: (1) a consideration of the effects of globalisation on state education policies, with specific consideration of the balance of transnational/ international forces and vernacular or indigenous capacities and responses: this relationship between the global and the local in education is a core preoccupation and relates directly to the possibilities for a politics of education; (2) consideration of the role of new technologies of governance, especially data and measurement in policy, and as a form of governing education, what might be termed 'policy as numbers' (Rose 1999), and their effects on educational politics: such considerations are located within an argument about the emergence of a globalised education policy field between global pressures and local effects and (3) discussion of the relationship between research and policy making in education, with particular emphasis on the ways in which evidence-based/informed policy making acts on and selectively steers research, and thus affects the production of independent analysis and critique of policy.

Of course an understanding of globalisation and its multiple effects frames all of this discussion. This entails challenging the political use of globalisation in the performative sense, where it is read only as neo-liberal economics and politics (Bourdieu 2003), by offering a critical social science account of globalisation and of the effects of such a discursive politics. Globalisation is understood as blurring distinctions between the international and the domestic, the global and the local and in so doing affects a new spatiality to politics. Its effects are evidenced in core economic activities (where multinationals operate across continents and capital flows across nation states) and in media and electronic communications (which make the flows of capital possible), in financial markets, the internationalisation of corporate strategies/management, the ecumenical spread of management structures and modes of policy steering across private and public sectors, the spread of worldwide patterns of consumption, the internationalisation of nation states and the diminished capacity of national governments. In recognising these effects and considering their impacts on education, we are attempting to argue for more attention to the dynamics of the relationship between globalising, economising forces and technologies of education governance, and mediating, vernacular forces and resources that affect the ways in which these play out and are made real in people's lives in schools, communities, universities and education systems. It is this struggle over meaning, resources and power that we understand as education politics and that creates the framework or conditions in which public policy, including education policy, is produced. In exploring that dynamic, and the energies that feed it, we believe that we can establish a more accurate and less pessimistic account of the educational politics and policy than that available from, for example, those who utilise 'world polity theory' (Meyer *et al.* 1997). Roger Dale (2001) characterises this as the 'Common World Educational Culture approach', which proffers an account close to Americanisation and in so doing appears to almost close down politics.

We acknowledge, nonetheless, that state capacity to make policy and to manage economic, political and social life within national boundaries is considerably affected by globalisation (Held 1995), and we see that, as a consequence, policy looks increasingly homogenous in education systems around the world. Universalising policy trends in education have been summarised by Taylor *et al.* (1997, 61), who draw attention to the ways in which political structures operating beyond nations are framing national policy options, how a global education policy community is emerging across the policy elites of international agencies (for example the OECD) and national education systems and how related globalising education policy discourses now affect policy making within nations. However we want to avoid over-privileging globalisation, or regarding it as a black box. Instead, we want to attend to context, to capture the possibilities of simultaneously 'local' and global development, and reflect the influence of historically embedded assumptions and beliefs on the mediation and translation of global policy pressures (Alexiadou and Jones 2001; Lingard 2000; Ozga 2005). We also reject the 'powerless state' argument that features in some globalisation accounts; rather we think that the state remains important, but now works in different ways beyond old bureaucratic, hierarchical structures and forms of accountability (Dale 1997), embracing the so-called new public management. We believe that context really matters, and that understanding of the resources available in specific conditions and circumstances is essential in assessing the possibilities for productive politics in the face of globalising trends and forces. As Giddens puts it in his well-known definition, which captures the interplay of global and local:

> Globalisation can thus be defined as the intensification of worldwide social relations which link distant localities in such a way that local happenings are shaped by events occurring many miles away and vice-versa. This is a dialectical process because such local happenings may move in an obverse direction from the very distanciated relations that shape them. **Local transformation is as much a part of globalisation as the lateral extension of social connections across time and space.**
>
> (Giddens 1990, 64; emphasis in original)

We need to say something more at this point about our orientations towards this topic and the resources that we are drawing on to construct this approach to education politics. We understand education, including education policy, to be contradictory in its effects and possibilities: education is simultaneously a means of improving life chances and enriching life, as well as a process that maintains inequality and sustains conservative social formations. It has the potential to be both conservative and progressive, reproductive and transgressive. The possibilities for progressive development lie in particular in the ways that education produces what Connell (1995) calls 'the capacity for social practice' or what Sen (1999) has called 'capabilities'. Connell emphasises the ways in which people's capacities for negotiation, dialogue and cooperation – for practical politics – may be developed through education, and the fact that the potential for such development is always there, even in the most inhospitable environments. Education policy can help frame the likelihood of these possibilities, but it is teacher pedagogies and curricular frameworks which put them into practice. The contrasting logics of practice inherent in processes of education policy production and teacher classroom practices possibly explain what is sometimes referred to as the infidelity to policy in its implementation. Agnès Van Zanten (2005), writing about Bourdieu as an education policy analyst, suggests that in his early work on education he saw unmediated relationships between unequal social arrangements and the reproduction of inequality through schooling. In contrast, his later, more overtly political work, which strongly critiqued neo-liberal globalisation, saw education policy as a possible mediator of such social inequalities, and recognised teachers as victims of the meaner, leaner neo-liberal state, rather than as agents who misrecognised their role in social reproduction.

In this chapter, these political orientations and possibilities of education policy connect to, and are sustained by, Anna Yeatman's (1990, 1998) work on public policy approaches and processes of policy production. She points out that most academic approaches to policy making seem to accept, without comment, its profoundly undemocratic and gendered nature. She argues that policy should be conceived as a *process* that is negotiated and struggled over, and thus it follows that policy making and the work of policy makers should be understood in relation to the extent to which they recognise and reflect democratic principles. This opens policy up to the appropriate participation of all those involved all the way through points of conception, operational formulation, implementation, delivery on the ground, consumption and evaluation, rather than separating policy from politics, which has the effect of protecting and sustaining bureaucratic logics of practice from democratic possibilities.

Such conceptualisations may appear idealistic, but there are strong arguments that support this redefinition of policy if the volatile and fissiparous issues confronting society in the context of globalisation are to be appropriately and fully considered and addressed (Sen 1999). Neo-liberal globalisation has witnessed growing inequalities within and across nations and added new dimensions of inequality, for example, around issues of mobility/immobility (Bauman 1998). Within some nations, policies on social inclusion have replaced older Keynesian welfare state concerns for equality of opportunity and even outcomes such as social exclusion has become more prevalent. Even for those in work there is a new culture of insecurity. As Rose (1999, 158) notes: 'work itself has become a vulnerable zone, one in which continued employment must ceaselessly be earned, the employment of each individual constantly assessed in the light of evaluations, appraisals, achievement of targets and so forth'.

Yet current globalised education policy seems unable to respond to these challenges in ways that go beyond preoccupation with raising attainment and improving national economic performance and competitiveness globally. Phil Brown and his colleagues (1997, 7–8) have called this the human capital development policy consensus, which has accompanied neo-liberal globalisation, describing it in the following fashion:

> The new consensus is based on the idea that as the 'walled' economies in mid-century have given way to an increasingly global economy, the power of

national government to control the outcome of economic competition has been weakened....Indeed the competitive advantage of nations is frequently redefined in terms of the quality of national education and training systems judged according to international standards.

There is clearly something missing from this dominant conception of education policy as human capital development – the all pervasive globalised educational policy discourse today, around which national education polices appear to converge. The absent element seems to be a normative vision about what educated individuals and active citizens might look like in this new globalised world and about the kinds of societies we might wish to sustain. As Allan Luke (2003, 91) puts it, current education policy agendas around the globe are

> All dressed up with multiple outcomes, voluminous curriculum documents, national testing, and so on, but without a strong normative vision of what might count as just and powerful educational systems in new economic and social conditions, in increasingly complex, risky and unjust transnational contexts.

For the most part policy makers remain heavily dependent on neo-liberal principles of system redesign that at the very least fail to provide a coherent agenda for education. They rely on a restricted form of evidence, promote reliance on performance measurement and management, and make only superficial and contradictory acknowledgement of difference and diversity. The observation from Brown and his colleagues cited above refers to comparisons with international standards. This is policy as numbers through international education indicators, such as the OECD's Programme for International Student Assessment (PISA) and the Trends in International Mathematics and Science (TIMSS), which taken together with similar national level developments constitute a central aspect of the new technologies of governance and which globally contribute to the emergent global education policy field (Lingard *et al.* 2005). The alignment of statistical collection approaches by the OECD, Eurostat, the statistical agency of the EU, and UNESCO, is also indicative of this emergent global education policy field (Lawn and Lingard 2001). Such performance data is also at times used within national systems of education to provide the basis for parental (consumer) choice of schools, perhaps most evident in the paradigm case of marketisation – England.

There is also ample evidence of shared organisational forms and processes in education: including devolution and deregulation; the redesign of education (including governance, management and institutions) that leads commentators to talk about the 'new production rules' of policy formation/implementation, reflecting strengthened corporate interests and the influence of international and supranational forces and agents on national systems (Lindblad *et al.* 2002). While these forms and rules are shared, they enter distinctive national terrains with their own education politics that continue to affect the translation of those apparently shared forms and processes into indigenous practices. This is the effect which Appadurai (1996) calls 'vernacular globalisation' to capture the complex interplay of global and local forces. Of course, different nations have varying capacities to mediate and ameliorate the effects of global pressures and globalised education policy discourses produced by agencies such as the Word Bank and OECD. As Bourdieu (1999) puts it, such discourses circulate without their context and their effects are mediated to a lesser or greater extent by what he terms, in later writing, 'national capital' (Bourdieu 2003).

To summarise the discussion so far, we draw three broad conclusions about contemporary education policy.

1 That at international level a coherent set of policy themes and processes (globalised policy discourses) has emerged, through which policy makers (at national, international and transnational levels) seek to reshape education systems.
2 That there has emerged a globalised education policy field situated between global pressures and local vernacular education policy responses.
3 That these globalised policy agendas and processes interact with traditions, ideologies, institutions and politics that have developed on national terrains, resulting in vernacular education policy outcomes.

Furthermore, as Alexiadou and Jones (2001) argue, the relationship between points (1) and (3) requires scrutiny in relation to the extent of embeddedness of 'travelling policy' within national policy elites, and differing degrees of local 'policy inflection' in which various forces (local policy communities, trade unions, social movements) are able to achieve adaptation of global agendas, or in which local policy elites integrate travelling policy with national agendas (Alexiadou and Jones 2001, 2). There is, of course, a good deal of uncertainty about how the conduits of travelling policy operate from the global through to the national (Dale 1999; Rizvi 2004; Tikly 2001) and a need for further enquiry into exactly how the design and delivery of national policy agendas responds to pressure from supranational organisations and agencies as examples of vernacular globalisation in education policy (Lingard 2000).

As we suggest earlier, there also appears to have emerged at a level beyond the nation what might be called a 'global education policy field' (Lingard *et al.* 2005), as well as other education policy spaces above the nation, such as the emergent European education policy field (Lawn and Lingard 2001). This is part of the new spatial politics associated with globalisation (Massey 1994). Often these fields are constituted in and around numbers and comparative statistical indicators of various kinds. As Henry *et al.* (2001, 95–6) observe in respect of the OECD indicators project and the annual publication of *Education at a Glance*, 'the very process of drawing in an expanding number of countries into a single comparative field is significant in itself'. They also comment that this project has ensured an epistemological consensus among OECD policy people and policy elites within and beyond member nations around the 'new and powerful paradigm of policy as numbers'. We consider this development in more detail in the Governing by Numbers section below.

Alexiadou and Jones' (2001) discussion of *travelling* and *embedded* policy takes travelling policy to refer to supra- and transnational agency activity, as well as to common agendas (for example for the reshaping of educational purposes to develop human capital for the information age and national economic competitiveness). Embedded policy is to be found in *local* spaces (which may be national, regional or local), where global policy agendas come up against existing priorities and practices. In the remainder of the chapter, we will be considering the interaction between travelling and embedded policy and the effects of that interaction on education politics and we will comment briefly on the emergent global education policy field.

Globalising/economising education policy

Globalisation foregrounds education, while at the same time challenging the traditional capacity of education systems to construct national identities. The creation of mass systems of schooling in the nineteenth century in many Western countries was linked to the creation of the 'imagined community' (Anderson 1991) of the nation through the establishment of universal literacy. New technologies challenge such spaces of containment and at the same time constitute possibilities for alternative forms of cosmopolitan citizenship linked to an emergent postnational order (Appadurai 1996). However, such progressive cosmopolitan citizenship possibilities are usually elided in the contemporary education policy consensus, which is more reductive in approach. Globalisation foregrounds education in specific ways that attempt to harness education systems to the rapid and competitive growth and transmission of technologies and knowledge linked to the national competitiveness of nations within the global economy. For example the World Bank identifies the human capital requirements of adaptability, creativity, flexibility and innovation as those to be delivered by education and asserts that such qualities are best delivered in deregulated education systems in which competition is maximised, business is embedded and an entrepreneurial habitus developed (World Bank 2002). It achieves compliance with this redesign through connecting financial assistance to particular agendas and processes (Syachaba 2006). Education policy makers promote the attractiveness of their local products in the global marketplace; attempting to tie roving capital into long-term relationships based on the satisfaction of the needs of the new knowledge economy. Those needs require that public institutions, as well as business, become attuned to continuous change; as UK Prime Minister Tony Blair argues, we must have constant improvement to cope with change.

> The modern world is swept by change. New technologies emerge constantly, new markets are opening up. There are new competitors but also great new opportunities....This world challenges business to be innovative and creative, to improve performance continuously, to build new alliances and ventures.... In government, in business, in our universities and throughout society we must do more to foster a new entrepreneurial spirit: equipping ourselves for the long-term, prepared to seize opportunities, committed to constant innovation and improved performance.
>
> (Rt Hon Tony Blair in Department for Trade and Industry 1998, foreword)

This is a policy trajectory that is preoccupied with the construction of a 'knowledge economy' and 'learning society'. Within this trajectory schooling/education/ training systems are acknowledged to be significant instruments for economic and social change: for building intellectual capital and capacity for innovation; for enhancing workforce development in ways that realise economic and, to a considerably lesser extent, social and civic outcomes; and for managing communities in ways that seek to minimise alienation and exclusion and that promote self-reliance and resourcefulness. Enterprising selves are promoted (in all senses of the word), in school, work and life. Rose (1999) has well encapsulated this new self-responsibilising individual and highlighted the link to the development of lifelong learning and need for constant reskilling across the life cycle.

> Education is no longer confined to 'schooling', with its specialized institutional sites and discrete biographical locus. The disciplinary individualization and

normalization of the school sought to install, once and for all, the capacities and competencies for social citizenship. But a new set of educational obligations are emerging that are not confined in space and time in the same ways. The new citizen is required to engage in a ceaseless work of training and retraining, skilling and reskilling, enhancement of credentials and preparation for a life of incessant job seeking: life is to become a continuous economic capitalization of the self.

(Rose 1999, 160–1)

The constituent nations of the EU all declare that they are attempting to become *knowledge economies* (KE). The OECD and the World Bank stress that education and training provide the entry requirements to participation in the new KE. Education policies linked to knowledge economies constitute a central globalised education policy discourse of the current moment, a discourse which at times circulates without reference to context, particularly in its circulation and take-up in many nations of the global south. Within this discourse, Education and Training dominate policy agendas, focussed on upskilling new knowledge workers and developing research and thus the knowledge that will secure success. Productive knowledge is believed to be the basis of national competitive advantage within the international marketplace. This policy discourse promotes a wide range of activity and justifies major shifts in national, institutional and individual practices and processes, yet remains, for the most part, decontextualised, unexamined and unspecific.

From this global discourse shared policy agendas emerge, and include national programmes of curriculum standardisation, target setting and testing, school self-management, parental choice and inter-school competition, teacher accountability, quality assurance (through inspection), performance-related pay and curricula centred on lifelong learning, preparation for work and citizenship. Policy makers at national, local and institutional levels may be understood as subscribing to these key principles in educational restructuring: a focus on education to meet economic needs, an insistence on rapid change that penetrates teacher cultures, an insistence on international competitiveness in education, so that each nation state achieves 'world-class status' as measured by international league tables of test success (e.g. by PISA and TIMSS), the privileging of business as a model for modernisation and a shift from equality of opportunity or outcome to diversity and differentiation as organising principles of provision with responsibility individualised rather than a collective state concern.

This last point illustrates the challenges to education politics in the shift to what Castells (2000) has called an informational politics in a crisis of democracy. Ideological differences (such as those shaping positions on comprehensive or selective education) are dismissed by policy makers as archaic, an action that is itself an ideological manoeuvre. Common-sense assumptions about effective management and modernisation produce 'hollowed out' terms – like client, consumer, stakeholder, excellence, leadership and entrepreneurship – that apparently require no further elaboration or scrutiny. Concepts that were once central to the organisation of public life – for example equality, justice, professionalism – are removed from use on the basis that they indicate ideological positions, while modernisation's vocabulary of economy, efficiency and entrepreneurship is advocated as if these terms represented agreed values. In some sites teachers' work is reconstituted and controlled through technised formulations of pedagogies (Alexander 2004; Hartley 2003), which disaffect the soul of the teacher in their inauthenticity (Ball 2003). Policy as numbers may also gather force in the absence of meaning as part of the performative emphasis on what works (Yeatman 1994). This is part of the process of challenging education politics, in which words are stripped of meaning, and there is inauthentic exchange that is, in Offe's terms 'cleansed of political participation' (Offe 1984, 32).

Speaking back in the vernacular

Given these homogenising forces and processes, is there any evidence of active adaptation or indigenisation of 'travelling' policy? As noted above, Appadurai argues that it is possible to identify *vernacular globalisation* in which there is change and reconfiguration in global, national and local interrelationships, but mediated by local and national history and politics (Appadurai 1996). As one of us has argued elsewhere (Lingard 2000, 81):

> Vernacular globalisation in this sense carries resonances with the idea of 'glocalisation': the way local, national, and global interrelationships are being reconstituted, but mediated by the history of the local and the national and by politics, as well as by hybridisation, an important resulting cultural feature of the multidirectional flows of cultural globalisation and the tension between homogenisation and heterogenisation.

Old notions of 'centre' and 'periphery' are collapsed in communities that are overlapping, complex and disjunctive. There are now multiple centres and with flows of people from the global south to the global north, the south is in the metropolitan centres of the north and the elites of the global south perhaps have more in common with the elites of the global north, than with their own compatriots. Globalisation produces rebalancing of national and global functions. That process of rebalancing is unsettled and fluid: it offers possibilities for transnational connections and strategies among those receiving as well as those 'making' policy: it may re-energise dormant forms of thinking and action and clarify purposes and values across varied populations and groups beyond policy elites. Different nations and different policy elites have varying capacities to respond, and different sources of 'national capital' to access (Tikly 2001).

These cultural and social effects of globalisation may foreground and render explicit *local* assumptions and beliefs that were previously hidden or inexplicit. This can have profound consequences for politics, including education politics. As globalisation encourages diverse and varied discourses that may dispute the authority of nation states, so the position and space of the nation state as the 'natural' scale of politics is disrupted (Ozga *et al.* 2006). The national scale may seek to provide a particular set of authoritative cultural scripts, but they exist alongside other scripts of greater or lesser power that have their origins in other discursive contexts operating in different scales (Djelic and Quack 2003; Prakash and Hart 1999). These alternative 'interpretive frames' provide other ways of understanding the relations of power–knowledge–organisation within different spatial registers – global, regional, local (Gibson-Graham 2003). Some theorists, including, Castells (2000, 458–9) argue that indeed power now resides in the 'networked, ahistorical' flows of globalisation, while most people still live in the 'space of places', and that a 'structural schizophrenia' between these two logics of place precipitates a breakdown in communications, which carries important political consequences.

The distinctive ways in which education is embedded in national cultures needs to be considered here in thinking about how the 'vernacular' may speak back to the global. For example, within the UK, which at one level is a nation state that is very receptive to globalising influences in economic and social policy, there are fractures and fissures that are explained and sustained by internal differences. There is what we interpret as a productive tension between education's centrality as a policy site for the Westminster (UK) government, and its simultaneous status as a location of cultural and political identity and practice in Scotland. Changing education governance and the pursuit of globalised modernising agendas in the UK take place against a background both of long-established patterns of internal variation and of new institutional arrangements and actors who are not uniformly compliant with the direction of change (Alexiadou and Ozga 2002; Ozga 2005; Paterson 2000). The modernisation process may, indeed, produce self-conscious revisiting of models and myths of governance and education that appear threatened by the market-focused radicalism of the UK centre.

Comparative research on Scotland and England carried out for the Educational Governance and Social Inclusion and Exclusion (EGSIE) project (Lindblad *et al.* 2002; Lindblad and Popkewitz 2000; Ozga 1999) suggests that there were embedded differences in assumptions about education: and that in Scotland, in contrast with England, there is a continuing adherence to education as a public good that should be supported by public institutions. These differences connect to different policy outcomes, for example in the role and influence of business interests, and in policy for social inclusion. Whereas in England government appears to offer social inclusion to its citizens on the basis of exchange (i.e. evidence of good citizenship through responsible self-management and engagement in waged work), in Scotland social inclusion is offered on the basis of entitlement (inclusion as a citizenship right) (Ozga 1999).

Such approaches to policy and politics draw on ideas about cultural identities in different national systems (Lindblad and Strandberg 1999; Popkewitz *et al.* 2000) and the relationships between those identities and assumptions about what is appropriate or desirable for education to *do*. New forms of governance must map against, overlap or conflict with existing policy patterns and processes: these may be understood as the *'collective narrative'* that relates policy to cultural identities in different national systems (Popkewitz *et al.* 1999). That collective narrative, whatever its complex cultural and social origins, was most coherently articulated by national and local policy makers, who used it to moderate and mediate travelling policy.

Where does this distinctive 'collective narrative' originate, and how might it be summarised? If we stay with the example of Scotland within the UK, its distinctiveness in education is often asserted, but its nature or extent is debated. In 1969 James Scotland identified a number of key components of that distinctiveness and pointed out that none of them were entirely for the good of the people (Scotland 1969, 7, vol. 2: quoted in Humes and Bryce 2003). He reduced these components to the following six propositions that encapsulated Scottish attitudes to education:

- Education is, and always has been, of paramount importance in any community;
- Every child should have the right to all the education of which he [*sic*] is capable;
- Such education should be provided as economically and as systematically as possible;

- The training of the intellect should take priority over all other facets of the pupil's personality;
- Experiment is to be attempted only with the greatest caution;
- The most important person in the school, no matter what theorists say, is not the pupil but the (inadequately rewarded) teacher.

(Scotland 1969, 275, vol. 2)

Humes and Bryce, in their recent review of distinctiveness from which the quotation above is taken (Humes and Bryce 2003, 108), suggest that while much has changed there is still evidence of endorsement of some of these principles, in particular the first three. They argue that education is a strong element in national consciousness and belief in education's worth and purpose is linked to a sense of national identity (p. 109). The *collective narrative* identified earlier relates to what they describe (following McPherson and Raab 1988) as a 'shaping myth' in Scotland of an egalitarian and meritocratic society, where ability and achievement rather than class or status command recognition and where provision in pursuit of improvement and the common good is made through public rather than private institutions (Humes and Bryce 2003, 109).

Since devolution, these aspects of the collective narrative could be said to have found expression in such areas as the designation of the National Priorities for Education, following widespread consultation and public debate that showed strong support for the comprehensive principle, support that remains strong at a time when the UK government is seeking to legislate for much increased diversity of school provision in England, with a plethora of Academies, Trust, Foundation and Faith Schools. The National Priorities stress the need for improvement within a framework of enhanced equality and inclusiveness: they enable central steering of the system towards goals that are debated and largely endorsed by the public; interpreted and implemented by schools and local authorities. For the most part, devolution seems to have enabled the continuation of Scottish distinctiveness in education, while simultaneously beginning to open up some of its more traditional aspects, including, perhaps, the academic bias and the caution about experimentation in the list of principles quoted above. It may also have enabled change in the traditionally rather hierarchical nature of schools and of the teaching profession, and promoted a more extended, self-directed and developmental version of professionalism. Indeed policy for the teaching profession offers another area in which distinctiveness may be discerned (Ozga 2005).

There are many other examples of what we interpret as evidence of vernacular globalisation and of *local* collective narratives modulating globalised policy discourses in education and their homogenising effects. Singapore, for example, has utilised a strong and interventionist state to respond to and instantiate globalised educational policy discourses (Brown and Lauder 2000). However, such discourses are inflected by specific Singaporean national concerns and education traditions. The influential *Thinking Schools, Learning Nation* policy is a response to globalisation, but one built on attempts to change Singaporean traditions of tight teacher control around highly structured curricula and pedagogies towards the production of new creative and adaptable Singaporean citizens and workers suitable for the globalised knowledge economy. All of this is being pursued through an interventionist state strategy, rather than a neo-liberal approach, and built upon a tradition of emphasising science and maths in schools (Brown and Lauder 2000; Koh 2004).

The small Caribbean island nation of St Lucia has developed a long-term educational strategy around the globalised educational policy discourse of lifelong learning (Jn Pierre 2006). Research indicates that the development of the policy through exhaustive consultation and its long-term, all encompassing cross-sector focus were specific strategies to seek to strengthen *national capital* (Bourdieu 2003). This attempt at strengthening national capital was a postcolonial political aspiration in an attempt to mediate some of the policy and policy implementation pressures resulting from funding from significant international donor agencies such as the World Bank. This was in some senses about creating policy space to allow a more vernacular expression of lifelong learning. At the same time, the policy dealt with a decontextualised policy discourse and gave most emphasis to human rather than social and cultural capital development. In so doing, the policy also denied various forms of indigenous knowledges, including creole language forms. The political location in the global south and a particular colonial history framed the possibilities here for vernacular globalisation. Nonetheless, we can see here again the mix of history, politics, global pressures and local aspirations, resulting in vernacular globalisation. Similar accounts emerge from research on globalisation's effects on the education of girls in Zambia, where significant contradictions are created between the economically driven modernisation agendas of the World Bank, transferred by policy elites into local cultural contexts that are energised to resist such pressures, with serious consequences for gender equality (Syachaba 2006).

All policy developments in education, even in the context of globalisation, result in vernacular manifestations; homogenising pressures result in heterogenising outcomes. As Taylor *et al.* (1997, 16) argue in respect of policy development in education, 'There is always a prior history of significant events, a particular ideological and political climate, a social and economic context.' Of course, different nations and different education systems have varying capacities to speak back in the vernacular, varying capacities to strengthen national capital, while differing political parties holding state power vary in their desire to speak back to or to accomodate globalised education policy discourses. As Tikly (2001, 152) notes, a shortcoming of much of the literature on globalisation and education is that 'the specific *contexts* to which the theory is assumed to be applicable have not been specified'. Our idea of speaking back in the vernacular is an attempt to recognise such specificities and histories, including, for the postcolonial world, a colonial past.

Governing by numbers and the new global education policy field

A focus on numbers at first glance sustains understandings of policy making that emphasise the idea of 'big' policies in the small world (Ball 1998), or the policy virus that infects and spreads across systems, and redefines education politics as the politics of education. However although the policy push for the use of indicators may be read as part of a policy agenda that seeks congruence and promotes similarity in policy making, as students of policy we need to acknowledge the idiosyncratic ways in which numbers have worked in specific education systems, and appreciate that the globalised policy push through educational indicators is read in different national and local contexts differently (Lingard and Ozga 2004). Recognition of context as significant, not incidental, requires culturally and historically informed approaches to understanding comparison that challenge some recent modes of comparative education which have become adjuncts of governance (Novoa and Yariv-Mashal 2003). International educational indicators are inherently decontextualising in their policy effects.

This is not to deny the power of numbers and the interrelationship of data production and governing strategies. As data production has increased so have new forms of governance involving a range of public and private partnerships and delivering systems and services (Kooiman 1993). The rise of the production and evaluation of data, linked to policy, also sustains the growing self-governance of active subjects (teachers, pupils, managers), both producing and using data. In a de-centred society, this process or governmentality extends governance into a system of self-regulation (Ball 1998; Rose 1992, 1996, 1999). Data collection relates to and possibly constitutes a form of governing (Desrosieres 2002; Porter 1996; Rose 1999), and connects to changing education governance and shared agendas and governing practices across Europe and beyond in pursuit of the new knowledge economy and society (see e.g. Ball 1998; Henry *et al.* 2001; Lawn and Lingard 2001). Trends towards deregulation and devolution and the steering of systems through evaluation (Lindblad and Popkewitz 2000; Lindblad *et al.* 2002) produce an increased need for information expressed as indicators, targets and benchmarks (European Commission 1998; OECD 1998). Attempts to create quasi-markets in schooling within national systems also require such performance data so as to give effect to parental choice. The emergence of the knowledge society/knowledge economy as an organising principle for education systems has also accentuated the need for information on performance, has increased the influence of transnational organisations and has given prominence to the data collection and analyses produced by CERI, OECD and UNESCO (Henry *et al.* 2001) and resulted in the alignment of statistical data collection categories which work together to effect a 'magistrature of influence' above national education policy making (Lawn and Lingard 2001).

International programmes of comparison in mathematics and literacy (OECD 2001) allow national evaluations to be compared internationally, with, some commentators argue, undesirable side effects and distortions of national systems (Goldstein 2004). Following the Lisbon European Council in 2003 and the adoption of the open method of coordination, benchmarking and indicators of progress are essential monitoring tools for European education and training systems. In the UK there is a strong movement towards evidence-based or evidence-informed policy making to drive improvement in education (Lauder *et al.* 2004; Thomas and Pring 2004). Furthermore, there is evidence that such processes do, indeed, constitute policy and alter politics. For example, there has been reshaping of the national statistical systems of OECD member countries (OECD/CERI 1995, 4), alignment of OECD, UNESCO and Eurostat statistical collections and a recent Welsh Assembly Report on Assessment (Daugherty 2004) recommended that Wales must enter the international programmes of comparison in order to make its educational standards comparable. Research on emergent European education policy showed how the collection of European educational statistics substantially affected data collection categories and policies in a range of net-benefactor EU member nations such as Portugal and Greece, which when combined with the effects of European and OECD policy reports was referred to as a *magistrature of influence*, working to reframe national educational policies (Lawn and Lingard 2001).

Numbers then have become a central element of the move from government to governance within neo-liberal policy agendas. There is, however, another effect of policy as numbers when considered globally. As mentioned already, the OECD and other international agencies have collected national data and pulled it into a single global field of comparison in a decontextualised way. The national strategies of reframed education policy as the creation of particular forms of human capital necessary for the knowledge economy and for ensuring the global competitiveness of the putatively national economy also demand global comparative data on education performance. The OECD indicators are perhaps the best case in point (Henry *et al.* 2001), including PISA, which in 2006 will cover the thirty member nations of the Organisation and twenty-eight other nations; indeed the aspirational reach here is global. It is our argument that rankings on PISA and other measures such as TIMSS together constitute an emergent global education policy field existing as an imaginary above nations (Lingard *et al.* 2005). As Rose (1999, 198) notes, numbers, like any inscription device, constitute what they appear to represent. Further, rankings on these indicator league tables demonstrate the power of a single figure, which as Rose (1999, 208) also argues is 'a rhetorical technique for "black boxing" – that is to say, rendering invisible and hence incontestable – the complex array of judgements and decisions that go into a measurement, a scale, a number'. In respect of the OECD's PISA, this amounts to a decontextualisation of national cultures and the constitution of calculable or 'irreal' spaces (Rose 1999, 212–3) within a globalised education policy field, part of the new scalar and spatial politics of globalisation.

The narrative concerning the establishment of the OECD's indicators project provided by Henry *et al.* (2001) also demonstrates the powerful influence of the USA in the creation of the project against some considerable philosophical opposition from within the OECD itself. This is a demonstration of the asymmetrical relations between nations and the power of the US in the context of globalisation and in the post-Cold War era. The OECD's Indicators work also demonstrates how the OECD, in addition to its work as think tank and as a site for the ventilation of policy options and research, has become more of a policy actor in the context of globalisation and now prioritises social efficiency over social equity concerns in its policy work (Rizvi and Lingard 2006). The OECD has been important to the constitution of the global economic field framed by neo-liberalism and to the development of the related global education policy field. However, hierarchies and power relations within the latter are not homologous with those in the former. At the current policy moment, Singapore and Finland have iconic status within the global education field because of their high-ranking performances on TIMSS and PISA respectively. Policy as numbers works as part of globalised education policy discourses, as part of the new policy settlement within nations and new forms of governance, and as argued here, as central to the emergent global education policy field.

Education research, policy and politics

This brings us to the relationship between research and policy in the globalised, economised agenda for education. Research policy has been reframed by the desire of governments for clear and reliable evidence that can inform and support policy. Education research, which has been weakened by global criticism from powerful sources close to governments and is not securely positioned within the academy, is very vulnerable to reconfiguration in this mode, as a price of survival.

While education research is particularly insecure, all research is fundamentally affected by the Knowledge Economy and related discourses. Research is, after all, the production of knowledge and is understood in KE terms as central to economic growth. Knowledge here is *internal* to, that is, part of – rather than *external* to and distinct from – economic processes, and growth is dependent on maximising the outputs of knowledge workers and the productivity of knowledge resources.

National systems seek to ensure competitive advantage through the commercial exploitation and application of knowledge. Knowledge production is brought into close relationship with economic policy; what matters is what works for the economy. Universities and their research are significant players in this policy frame. This seems to hold across the globe (Ozga *et al.* 2006). Research is both implicated within, and mediates the trajectory towards a *knowledge economy* and *learning society* through enhanced research steering practices evident in different national systems, and through the effects of supranational agencies and pressures (for example the World Bank, OECD and the American-dominated citation indices), and the impacts of emergent regional blocs (for example the European Research Area).

Across the globe there is a trend towards prioritising techno-scientific research and its modes of operation and organisation – concentrated in centres of excellence, working in teams characterised by differences in conditions of work and employment rights. These modes of work are shaping all research. A substantial study of changing research cultures in Australia (Bullen *et al.* 2004) suggests that intellectual autonomy is challenged by the need to meet industry/funder needs and that science is becoming 'less a public good than a tradable commodity'. Bullen and her colleagues quote the World Bank publication 'Building Knowledge Economies' (World Bank 2002, 21) which asserts that

> Continuous, market-driven innovation is the key to competitiveness, and thus to economic growth, in the knowledge economy. This requires not only a strong science and technology base, but, just as importantly, the capacity to link fundamental and applied research, to convert the results of that research to new products, services, processes or materials and to bring these innovations quickly to market.

However, despite shared trends in the steering of education research, and common pressures to commercialise knowledge gained from research, there are differences, within Europe and within and across national boundaries, in indigenous or vernacular education research practices and processes of research that provide different kinds of resource for informing or sustaining a politics of education. Again, we see that the rapid development and spread of processes designed to construct measurable research outcomes, to provide evidence of impact, and to focus on useful knowledge production has a double effect. On the one hand it contributes to performativity, but on the other it foregrounds questions about research purposes and embedded practices that continue to have meaning and thus may sustain a revived politics. We should remember that part of the reason that there is so much attention to steering processes in research in education is that research in education produces knowledge that is potentially extremely valuable and productive for the new knowledge economies, and this creates a particularly contested terrain of research development and practice in which specific contradictory challenges are confronted.

Education research is important because it informs, enables and sustains learning. In so doing, it may produce knowledge that is useful to and supportive of government policy. But that is not all that it does, and it cannot, by its very nature, be reduced to totally instrumental activity. Pressures for research steering in education are very high because of the instability and fluidity of the knowledges that it produces, and because less 'managed' research activities may, indeed, have considerable value in the creation of active, independent and creative thinkers and learners. There is, thus a considerable contradiction at the heart of the research steering process, and this opens up spaces for research to rediscover and render explicit its national capital, in terms that are not entirely set by globalising pressures and practices. It is possible that the processes of research steering, and the growth of competitive and selective funding, of emphasis on outputs and on impact, and on the translation of research into professional and policy communities (Ozga and Jones 2006) has in fact sharpened the focus on research purposes, on the role and nature of knowledge within and beyond the academy, and on epistemological and methodological issues that are critical of 'traditional' research practices, while cautioning against some of the trends documented here.

It could be argued that it is in the resources available to and in civil society – including, importantly, in education politics – that globalising agendas may be recontextualised and remodelled according to local and national histories, traditions and social relations. As education is now the centrally important policy area for governments in the context of globalisation, it follows that the intellectual resources available from education research to support such a politics are of increased importance.

Conclusion

In this chapter we have attempted to present a discussion of the key features of the new, globalised landscape of education policy and politics. Throughout we have attempted to develop an argument about the significance of the relationship between global and local in understanding policy and politics in education. We suggest that there is a tendency to read globalisation in education as neo-liberal politics and economics, and argue that this conceals the extent to which local, vernacular globalisation is called forth and energised in response to homogenising tendencies and trends. In particular, we attempt to stress the extent to which the performative readings of education politics and policy are dependent on selective assessments of the global condition in education, that see the world from a particular and somewhat distorted Anglo-American angle. Our core concern is to underline the significance of context, in all its complexity, not just as a location for globalising activity, but as an active element in the framing of education policy and politics.

One of the fundamental characteristics of globalisation is that it can revitalise local institutions and formations. Faced with homogenising travelling policy, particular groups or societies can be encouraged to revisit and reconstruct the value bases of their organisations and generate new energy in their production, including in schools, universities and other sites of learning.

Bibliography

Alexander, R. (2004) 'Still no Pedagogy? Principle, Pragmatism and Compliance in Primary Education', *Cambridge Journal of Education*, 34: 7–33.

Alexiadou and Jones (2001) 'Travelling Policy/Local Spaces', paper to the Congrès Marx International 111 Le Capitale et L'Humanite University of Paris X 26–29 September.

Alexiadiou, N. and Ozga, J. (2003) 'Modernising Education Governance in England and Scotland: Devolution and Control', *European Education Research Journal*, 1(4): 676–91.

Anderson, B. (1991) (Revised edition) *Imagined Communities: Reflections on the Origin and Spread of Nationalism* (London: Verso).

Appadurai, A. (1996) *Modernity at Large: Cultural Dimensions of Globalisation* (Minneapolis, MN: University of Minnesota Press).

Ball, S. J. (1998) 'Big Policies/Small World: an introduction to international perspectives in education policy', *Comparative Education*, 34(2): 119–30.

Ball, S. J. (2003) 'The Teacher's Soul and the Terrors of Performativity', *Journal of Education Policy*, 18(2): 215–28.

Bauman, Z. (1992) *Intimations of Postmodernity* (London: Routledge).

Bauman, Z. (1998) *Globalization The Human Consequences* (Cambridge: Polity Press).

Bottani, N. and Tuijnman, A. (1994) 'International education indicators: framework, development and interpretation (Chapter 1)', in OECD (ed.) *Making Education Count. Developing and Using International Indicators* (Paris: OECD), pp. 21–36.

Bourdieu, P. (1999) 'The social conditions of the international circulation of ideas', in R. Shusterman (ed.) *Bourdieu: A Critical Reader* (Oxford: Blackwell).

Bourdieu, P. (2003) *Firing Back: Against the Tyranny of the Market* (London: Verso).

Brown, P. and Lauder, H. (2000) The Future of Skill Formation in Singapore, Working Papers Series, Paper 3, School of Social Sciences, Cardiff University.

Brown, P., Halsey, A. H., Lauder, H. and Stuart Wells, A. (1997) 'The Transformation of Education and Society: An Introduction', in A. Halsey, H. Lauder, P. Brown and A. Stuart Wells (eds), *Education Culture Economy Society* (Oxford: Oxford University Press).

Bullen, E., Robb, S. and Kenway, J. (2004) ' "Creative Destruction": knowledge economy policy and the future of the arts and humanities in the academy', *Journal of Education Policy*, 19(1): 3–22.

Castells, M. (2000) (2nd edn) *The Information Age: Economy, Society, and Culture. Volume I: The Rise of the Network Society* (Oxford: Blackwell).

Connell, R. W. (1995) 'Transformative Labour', in Ginsburg, M. (ed.), *The Politics of Educators' Work and Lives* (New York: Garland Press).

Croxford, L. (December 2004) 'Performance Statistics for Local Authorities and Schools', paper for the AERS School Management and Government Project Seminar (University of Edinburgh).

Dale, R. (1997) 'The State and the Governance of Education: An analysis of the restructuring of the state-education relationship', in A. H. Halsey, H. Lauder, P. Brown and A. Stuart Wells (eds), *Education Culture Economy Society* (Oxford: Oxford University Press) pp. 273–82.

Dale, R. (1999) 'Specifying globalization effects on national policy: a focus on the mechanisms', *Journal of Education Policy*, 14(1): 1–17.

Dale, R. (2001) 'Globalization and Education: Demonstrating a "Common World Educational Culture" or Locating a "Globally Structured Educational Agenda?" ', *Educational Theory*, 50(4): 427–48.

Daugherty Assessment Review Group (2004) *Final Report*, Welsh Assembly.

Department of Trade and Industry (DTI) The Competitiveness White paper (www.dti.gov.uk/comp/competitive/wh_int1.htm).

Desjardins, R., Garrouste-Norelius, C. and Mendes, S. (2004) *Benchmarking Education and Training Systems in Europe – an international comparative study*, European Commission Directorate-General for Education and Culture.

Desrosieres, A. (2002) *The Politics of Large Numbers: A History of Statistical Reasoning*, (Cambridge: Harvard University Press).

Dicken, P., Kelly, P. F., Olds, K. and Yeung, H. W. (2001) 'Chains and Networks, Territories and Scales: toward a relational framework for analysing the global economy', *Global Networks*, 1(2): 89–112.

Djelic, M.-L. and Quack, S. (2003) Globalisation and institutions: redefining the rules of the economic game. Cheltenham: Edward Elgar.

European Commission (1998) *Statistical Indicators Benchmarking the Information Society* Information Society Technology Programme (1998–2002).

Fägerlind, I. and Strömqvist, G. (eds) (2004) Reforming higher education in the Nordic countries: Studies of changes in Denmark, Finland, Iceland, Norway and Sweden. (Paris: International Institute for Educational Planning.)

Gibson-Graham, J. K. (2003) Enabling Ethical Economies, *Critical Sociology*, 29(2): 123–61.

Giddens, A. (1990) *The Consequences of Modernity* (Cambridge: Polity Press).

Goldstein, H. (February 2004) 'Education for All: the globalization of learning targets', *Comparative Education*, 40(1): 7–14.

Hartley, D. (2003) 'New Economy, New Pedagogy', *Oxford Review of Education*, 29: 81–94.

Held, D. (1995) *Democracy and the Global Order: From the Modern State to Cosmopolitan Governance* (Stanford: Stanford University Press).

Henry, M., Lingard, B., Taylor, S. and Rizvi, F. (2001) *The OECD, Globalisation and Education Policy* (Oxford: Pergamon).

Humes, W. and Bryce, T. (2003) (eds) *Scottish Education: Post Devolution* (Edinburgh: Edinburgh University press).

Jn Pierre, K. (2006) Endikasyon Lavi Diwant: Translating the Concept of Lifelong Learning into Policy and Practice in St Lucia, PhD Thesis (University of Sheffield).

Koh, A. (2004) 'Singaporean Education in 'New Times': Global/local Imperatives', *Discourse*, 25(3): 335–49.

Kohler-Koch, B. and Eising, R. (1999) *The Transformation of Governance in the European Union* (London: Routledge/Falmer).

Kooiman, T. (ed.) (1993) *Modern Governance* (London: Sage).

Lawn, M. and Lingard, B. (2001) 'Constructing a European Policy Space in Educational Governance: the Role of Transnational Policy Actors', *European Educational Research Journal*, 1(2): 290–307.

Lauder, H., Brown, P. and Halsey, A. H. (2004) 'Sociology and political arithmetic: some principles of a new policy science, *British Journal of Sociology*, 55(1): 3–22.

Lindblad, S. and Popkewitz, T. (eds) (2000) *Public Discourses on Educational Governance and Social Integration and Exclusion*, Uppsala, Uppsala Reports on Education 36.

Lindblad, S., Ozga, J. and Zambeta, E. (2002) 'Changing Governance of Education in Europe', *European Educational Research Journal*, 1(4): 615–24.

Lindblad, S., Ozga, J. and Zambeta, E. (2003) 'Patterns of Devolution and Decentralisation of Education Governance in Europe', *European Educational Research Journal*, 1(4): 615–24.

Lingard, B. (2000) 'It is and It Isn't: Vernacular Globalization, Educational Policy, and Restructuring', in N. Burbules and C.A. Torres (eds) *Globalization and Education Critical Perspectives* (New York: Routledge), pp. 79–108.

Lingard, B. (2006) 'Globalisation, the Research Imagination and Deparochialising the Study of Education', *Globalisation, Societies and Education*, 4(2): 287–302.

Lingard, B. and Ozga, J. (2004 May 27–28) Educational Policy and Performativity: cause and effects?, Paper presented to the Governing by Numbers Workshop (University of Edinburgh).

Lingard, B., Rawolle, S. and Taylor, S. (2005) 'Globalizing Policy Sociology in Education: working with Bourdieu', *Journal of Education Policy*, 20(6): 759–77.

Luke, A. (2003) 'After the Marketplace: Evidence, Social Science and Educational Research', *Australian Educational Researcher*, 30(2): 87–107.

McPherson, A. and Raab, D. (1988) *Governing Education: a sociology of policy since 1945* (Edinburgh: Edinburgh University Press).

Massey, D. (1994) *Space Place and Gender* (Cambridge: Polity Press).

Meyer, J., Boli, J., Thomas, G. and Ramirez, F. (1997) 'World Society and the Nation State', *American Journal of Sociology*, 103(1): 144–81.

Neave, G. (1998) 'The Evaluative State Reconsidered', *European Journal of Education*, 33(3): 265–84.

Novoa, A. and Yariv-Mashal, T. (2003) 'Comparative Research in Education: a mode of governance or a historical journey?', *Comparative Education*, 39(4): 423–38.

OECD (1998) *Education at a Glance. OECD indicators 1998*. Centre for Educational Research and Innovation, Paris: OECD.

OECD (2001) *Knowledge and Skills for life: first results of Programme for International Student Assessment* (Paris: OECD).

Offe, C. (1984) *Contradictions of the Welfare State* (London: Hutchinson).

Ozga, J. (1999) 'Two Nations? Education Policy and Social Inclusion and Exclusion in Scotland and England', *Education and Social Justice*, 2(1): 44–51.

Ozga, J. (2005) 'Travelling and Embedded Policy: the case of post Devolution Scotland within the UK', in Coulby, D. and Zambeta, E. (eds) *Globalisation and Nationalism in Education* (London: Routledge).

Ozga, J. and Jones, R. (2006) 'Travelling and Embedded Policy: the case of Knowledge Transfer', *Journal of Education Policy*, 21(1): 1–19.

Ozga, J. Seddon, T. and Popkewitz, T. S. (2006) (eds) *Education Research and Policy: Steering the Knowledge based Economy* (London: Routledge).

Paterson, L. (2000) 'Civil Society and Democratic Renewal', in S. Baron, J. Field and T. Schuller (eds) *Social Capital: Critical Perspectives* (Oxford: Oxford University Press).

Pollitt, C., Girre, X., Lonsdale, J., Mul, R., Summa, H. and Waerness, M. (1998) *Performance or Compliance? Performance Audit and Public management in Five Countries* (Oxford: Oxford University Press).

Popkewitz, T. S., Lindblad, S. and Strandberg, J. (1999) *Review and Research on Education Governance and Social Integration and exclusion*, Uppsala Reports on Education No. 35, Uppsala: Uppsala University Press.

Porter, T. M. (1996) *Trust in Numbers* (Princeton: Princeton University Press).

Power, M. (1999) *The Audit Society: rituals of verification* (Oxford: Oxford University Press).

Prakash, A. and Hart, J. A. (1999) *Globalisation and Governance*, Routledge: London and New York.

Raffe, D., Croxford, L. and Brannen, K. (2000) 'Participation in Full-time Education beyond 16: A "Home International" Comparison', *Research Papers in Education*, 16(1): 43–68.

Rizvi, F. (2004) 'Debating Globalization and Education after September 11', *Comparative Education*, 40(2): 157–71.

Rizvi, F. and Lingard, B. (2006) 'Globalization and the Changing Nature of the OECD's Educational Work', in H. Lauder, P. Brown, J. Dillabough and A. H. Halsey (eds) *Education, Globalization and Social Change* (Oxford: Oxford University Press).

Rose, N. (1992). 'Governing the enterprising self', in P. Heelas and P. Morris (eds) *The values of the Enterprise Culture* (London: Routledge).

Rose, N. (1996). 'Governing "advanced" liberal democracies', in A. Barry, T. Osborne and N. Rose (eds) *Foucault and Political Reason: Liberalism, neo-liberalism and rationalities of government* (London: UCL Press).

Rose, N. (1999) *Powers of Freedom Reframing Political Thought* (Cambridge: Cambridge University Press).

Scotland, J. (1969) *The History of Scottish Education*, vol. 2 (London: University of London Press).

Sen, A. (1999) *Development as Freedom* (Oxford: Oxford University Press).

Syachaba (2006) *Globalisation and Girls' Education in Zambia* (The University of Edinburgh, Unpublished PhD Thesis).

Taylor, S., Rizvi, F., Lingard, B. and Henry, M. (1997) *Educational Policy and the Politics of Change* (London: Routledge).

Thomas, G. and Pring, R. (eds) (2004) *Evidence-based Practice in Education* (Buckingham: Open University Press).

Tikly, L. (2001) 'Globalisation and Education in the Postcolonial World: towards a conceptual framework', *Comparative Education*, 37(2): 151–71.

Urry, J. (2003) *Global Complexity* (Cambridge: Polity Press).

Van Zanten, A. (2005) 'Bourdieu as Education Policy Analyst and Expert: a rich but ambiguous legacy', *Journal of Education Policy*, 20 (6): 671–86.

Wenger, E. (1998) *Communities of practice. Learning meaning and identity* (Cambridge: Cambridge University Press).

World Bank (2002) *Constructing Knowledge Societies* (Washington: World Bank).

Yeatman, A. (1990) *Bureaucrats, Technocrats, Femocrats: Essays on the Contemporary Australian State* (Sydney: Allen and Unwin).

Yeatman, A. (1994) *Postmodern Revisionings of the Political* (New York: Routledge).

Yeatman, A. (1998) (ed.) *Activism and the Policy Process* (Sydney: Allen and Unwin).

VERNACULAR POLITICS, POLICIES AND PROCESSES

CHAPTER 6

AFTER THE MARKETPLACE

Evidence, social science and educational research[1]

Allan Luke

The Australian Educational Researcher, August 2003, 30(2): 87–107

Introduction

This is a narrative analysis of Australian educational policy, with illustrations drawn from the context of Queensland state education. I begin from two key insights on educational policy since the 1980s philosophic work of Lyotard and Foucault: (1) that state policies and their critiques actually constitute a series of overlapping discourses and, moreover, (2) that policy interventions actually have strong narrative chains, 'story grammars' about specific domains of problems and their possible solutions, about material societal and institutional conditions, and about prospective social agents and scenarios of action (Luke 1997). At the same time, the format of this paper is itself a narrative, an attempt to capture one of the dilemmas facing Australian educational researchers and teachers: that of moving between and conjoining the discourses and life worlds of policy formation and educational research.

Movement between school and academy typically is framed in the shopworn metaphor of practice and theory that Britzman's (1991) *Practice Makes Practice* so eloquently critiqued. There are complementary moves in the analysis of state, power and bureaucracy: a shunting between research and policy formation, between critique and reconstruction, with all of the issues such moves beg about points of possible appropriation and innovation, collusion and collaboration, contradiction and historical movement. This threatens the comfort zones (increasingly uncomfortable, given the latest wave of marketisation of Australian universities) of academic career pathways: worlds of performance indicators where publication, tenure, grants and so forth become both means and ends. Moves into state power and policy formation make for destabilising and irritating, risky and unpredictable shifts between forms of life, between discourses, between paradigmatic and professional communities, and they involve consequential decisions about our own life and career pathways as academics and educational researchers.

Educational policy and policy analysis are bids to reconstruct institutional syntaxes: sequences of actions, interventions and reforms with normative yet concrete material consequences. This does not deny the salience of social facts and estimable outcomes, of concrete historical moments and material conditions. Quite the contrary, policy can narratively reconfigure the way that the state, educational institutions and human actors within those institutions deploy discourses, and material and human resources towards particular regulative ends. Educational outcomes, or more accurately educational consequences, have allied historical mediations within the social fields of economies, institutional cultures and, most importantly, the life pathways to, through and around these fields. My point here is that at this historical moment movements through and across the traditionally bifurcated social fields of academy and bureaucracy, research and policy can construct new narratives.

I develop three broad claims about the challenges facing Australian education. These will be presented both as empirical *and* narrative claims.[2] They focus on the early, middle and senior years of schooling:

- The principal problems facing educators and systems in the early years are the powerful effects of *poverty*, both in its most historically persistent forms and those emergent in communities experiencing the immediate impacts of structural economic, cultural and sociodemographic change in what we could term, for want of better words, the new Australia.
- As the consequential effects of poverty wash through schools and systems at all levels, the principal challenge in the middle years is that of *pedagogy*, the building of new forms of pedagogic practice and action that might begin to turn the educational performance of the significant percentage of youth who disaffiliate from formal education.
- The major issue facing the secondary school is that of *pathways*, where the state at large is struggling to articulate and enable new pathways from school to work and further education in the face of the very new economic conditions, forms of cultural identity, practice and affiliation noted above.

I will make the polemical claim that Australian schools serve the social and economic interests of slightly more than half of all Australian youth – despite over a decade of major and costly attempts at curriculum revision, market-based reform, managerialist approaches to school management, policy revision and so forth.

I should begin by acknowledging the many educators pushing reform across Australian education: teachers strongly focused on pedagogy in classrooms, but also those civil servants and bureaucrats working in what are, for many, difficult conditions (their work is invisible to outsiders to civil service culture, is largely disrespected by the teaching workforce and unions, and goes unremarked in educational research), and those politicians who are deeply committed to understanding these dilemmas, generating innovative responses to the problems and, in effect, reinventing Australian education. Yet my purpose here is not to defend or explicate 'New Basics', 'Productive Pedagogies', 'Literate Futures' or the numerous other future-oriented reforms that have been underway in Queensland and other states.

These reforms, for all their possibilities and problems, exemplify new opportunities and challenges for educational research. As much as we may complain about the new competitive tendering environment, levels of state investment in research in all its forms increased throughout the 1990s. From my time as a Dean and later as Deputy Director General of Education in Queensland, I would estimate that levels of state investment in educational research in the mid-1990s averaged around $30 000 per annum. Those levels probably would push over a million dollars per annum per state at present, though contingent on budgetary conditions. But it is also a consequence of the same neoliberal reconstruction of educational bureaucracies. At once there is a new push for *evidence-based social policy*, an issue I will discuss at length. In response, bureaucracies are struggling to strike fine balances between the development of in-house research and analytic capacity, and the outsourcing of research and development work through consultancy and tendering. At the same time, cutbacks in the university sector and the support of pure research means that educational researchers worldwide are being pushed to undertake contract research to subsidise *any* faculty research capacity. This is a volatile and contradictory cocktail, full of possible conflicts of interest, compromise and appropriation. Taken as a state reorganisation of knowledge/power formation, it has stripped away resources for pure, foundational research and refocused them on the applied, the commodifiable and the profitable?[3] At the same time, it has had the indirect effect, however intentional, of opening public policy formation to stronger social scientific influence than the historical patriarchy, exclusivity and anti-scholasticism of civil service policy formation had previously enabled. It has created a situation where governments and systems, in many cases for the first time and with no small amount of trepidation, are reaching out to the educational research community for substantive analyses, for policy formation, for ideas about how to remake the connections between curriculum, communications media old and new, and everyday classroom practice.

How should we focus our efforts? These are as much epistemological and methodological issues as they are institutional and political. While our counterparts in the US and UK are engaged in an acrimonious debate over what might count as evidence-based educational policy, and neo-conservative groups are lobbying systematically against educational research and teacher education (Laitsch *et al.* 2002), Australian states are searching out research that can form the basis for the next cycle of educational policy. In addition to a strong, renewed national focus on classroom practice, this includes:

- localised, regionalised intergovernmental service provision and educational intervention; and, relatedly,
- rearticulation of educational sectors that historically have fallen into different ministries, fiscal and policy structures (e.g. schooling, child care, technical and vocational education, welfare services, mental health and rehabilitation, community employment).

A policy focus on new economies and cultures also requires much more programmatic research agendas on: multiliteracies, new technologies and education, as systems seek to understand digital education after the hardware and infrastructure investment; and new life pathways to and through, in and out of educational institutions, work and civic life, including a long overdue reconceptualisation of 'outcomes' and 'competences' in adult and vocational education.

These areas of research *can and must* be linked to a critical project of educational reform, a project with a renewed commitment to redressive and redistributive social justice. But it will require some careful consideration of the continued power of many of our current epistemological and methodological positions, the very positions that we tend to reproduce through the curriculum of masters degrees, professional doctorates and research supervision.

At the same time, my purpose here is to ask how educational systems can respond to conditions 'after the marketplace'. I believe that we can now assess the legacy of the last decade of neoliberal and liberal reforms: that the sum total of reforms have left us, to mix metaphors, all dressed up with multiple outcomes, voluminous curriculum documents, a *de facto* national testing system, school-based management – but without a strong normative vision of what might count as a just and powerful educational system in new economic and social conditions, an increasingly complex, risky and unjust transnational context.

This will require paradigm shift. But which of our many longstanding assumptions about educational research and reform are sustainable? These include powerful presuppositions that have guided our efforts at education for social justice for two decades:

- That quantitative research necessarily travels with neoliberal reform and is antithetical to a project of social justice.
- That qualitative research is necessarily empowering, transformative and progressive, countering existing forms of technocratic hegemony and domination.
- That the current orientations to 'outcomes' and evidence are an intrinsically reactionary focus on performativity.
- That such work by definition is narrowly psychometric in disciplinary foundation and practical orientation.

In response, we need to ask epistemic questions about what will count as 'evidence', what will count as the 'truths' that we speak to and through institutional power, and about the domains of knowledge, discourse and discipline that might enable us to mobilise educational institutions, and their complex flows of capital, bodies and discourse to begin altering visibly inequitable and unjust educational outcomes, consequences and pathways. These have been the very questions raised by the now old 'new' sociology of education for over three decades. They need to be asked again, and asked as much about our own work as researchers as about the state and its policies.

What follows proceeds in three moves: a brief review of the current US debate on evidence-based policy; a narrative, quasi-ethnographic description of the use of evidence in policy formation; and a framing of the aforementioned three key claims about the state of Australian education. Along the way, I set out to model what a more complex social science as applied to policy formation might look like, to explore the use of Bourdieuian theory as one model of policy analysis, and to use it to argue for different directions in policy and research.

On evidence-based social policy

Several weeks ago I was at Teachers College in New York discussing governmental policy responses to the complex push–pull effects of economic and cultural globalisation. Such discussions are always interesting, for they are lived moments in the curious phenomenology of globalisation, where particular analytic takes and lived experiences of the transnational are contingent on local 'optics' and available discourses (Burbules and Torres 2000). Attempts at universalising and totalising models of globalisation that 'travel well' often wind up unintentionally illustrating their own embeddedness in national or regional parochialism. This applies even to ostensibly 'critical' analyses of globalisation: Ritzer's (2000) MacDonaldisation thesis is a case in point.

The lecture was in the Chapel, next to the E. L. Thorndike building. It covered aspects of the Queensland 'New Basics' and the Singaporean 'Learning Nation, Thinking Schools' policies as responses to the pressures of the transnational. Afterwards, one American colleague commented that New Basics had 'taken

Dewey's side'. This comment was both troubling and revealing. Sixty years after John Dewey and E. L. Thorndike have left the building, the binary divide in epistemology, methodology and educational policy debates remains. Their ghosts are sustained by a persistent strain of dialectics: quantitative versus qualitative, child-centered versus behaviourist, progressivist/constructivist versus direct instruction, implicit versus explicit pedagogy, project-based work versus skills orientations – and, at different historical junctures, left versus right, liberal versus neoliberal, critical/emancipatory versus reproductionist.

In *Talks to Teachers on Psychology and to Students on Some of Life's Matters*, William James (1899/2001) – a mentor to both Dewey and Thorndike – defined pedagogy as the 'art and science' of teaching. It is this binary divide that became the hallmark of educational research at its very foundation a century ago. On one side we find the emergent twentieth century science of behaviourism, its strong focus on psychometrics, quasi-medical experimental models, and the application of these to agricultural models of treatment, the development curricular commodities and factory models of school and systems administration. This was the historical push to automate these processes of teaching and learning in the interests of the production of skilled human capital, the Fordist educational project that drives education in so many states today. In opposition is the version of progressivism that emphases holism of human capability, humanist curriculum, and symbolic interactionist models of teaching and learning yoked to the production of a democratic citizen. Their ostensive differences to the side, both models are predicated on a distinctively American pragmatist philosophy where technology, capital and an ethics of progress are realised via individuation and individualism. Let us take them as two responses to the dilemma that Dewey, Thorndike and colleagues faced: the development of a mass state system of education in response to industrial modernity, new forms of production, urbanisation, new youth identities and social formations. These were intellectual puzzles, research and policy anomalies no less daunting than those that we face today.

In 2001, the Bush administration's educational policies pushed to one side of the binary divide. The *Education Act* of 2001, commonly known as 'No Child Left Behind', set the conditions whereby government funding was tied to the adoption of reading programs 'scientifically proven to generate improved standardized test scores' (US Department of Education 2001). The move was strongly supported by number of conservative think tanks led by Reid Lyon, Diane Ravitch and others. These include the Council for Excellence in Education and the Coalition for Evidence in Education (Laitsch *et al.* 2002). In a press release to praise these groups, Rod Paige, Secretary of Education, argued that '30 years of NAEP [National Assessment of Educational Progress]' had yielded 'no progress' (US Department of Education 2001). Instead, the current policies were based on the assumption that only truly 'scientific' research would guide policy, that 'randomized controlled trials' set a 'gold standard' that had led to 'reduced unemployment, poverty, disease' and a 'decrease in coronary heart disease and stroke by over 50%'. Recent work on the interpretation of hormone replacement therapy results were cited by the Department of Education as examples of the negative effects of 'non-randomized' research.

In my own field of language and literacy education, the controversy has led to heated debate over the National Reading Panel, which argued for the efficacy of phonics instruction on the bases of a meta-analysis of 'randomised' and 'experimental' research. Critique has come from many quarters, ranging from progressivist critique, to minority educators skeptical about the differential effects of these on minority communities, to documentation the meta-analysis misinterpreted levels of significance (e.g. Garan 2001; Allington 2002).

This general approach to policy advocates a narrow version of educational 'science' that, however intentionally, abets a marketisation of educational knowledge and a political economy of textbook production, consultant training and in-service. Let me illustrate the effects by citing the case of one Oregon elementary school with whose principal I recently spoke (M. Shiroishi, personal communication, 11 November 2002). That school has a lower socioeconomic student body (73% free and reduced lunch), 45 per cent Hispanic, 5 per cent Asian-American, 43 per cent white. Its targeted Reading First federal funding of $300 000 to improve these 'at risk' children's reading performance is contingent upon the adoption and 'faithful implementation' of a 'comprehensive reading program' to be chosen from SRA/Open Court, Houghton, Harcourt, Macmillan, Reading Mastery, Rigby, Scott Foresman, Wright Group or Success for All, she explained, 'scientifically based' and therefore approved by the Oregon state department. The funds must be spent by bringing in trainers/consultants from designed multinational publishers and their local university affiliates. The target is that within two years standardised test scores will improve or the school itself will be sanctioned. Furthermore, many states have begun moving towards voucher schemes for communities such as these.

This is a consolidation of the technocratic political economy of education that Michael Apple (1981) described over two decades ago. While it is built as an ostensible response to the effects of poverty, and cultural and linguistic diversity, it chains together a new positivist educational science and a web of federally-funded industrial partnerships between university-based researchers, multinational textbook publishers, and local consultants/trainers. With more and more university researchers moving into commercial activities, many of us took part in a recent internal debate among the editorial board of *Reading Research Quarterly* about the ethics of publishing research undertaken by researchers with commercial interests in the products up for 'scientific' verification. In effect, these federal policies have created an environment where educational research risks becoming a kind of in-house product development and market research activity, with spin off consultancy and textbook endorsement fees.

But before one rushes headlong into the assumption that medical models of research are generalisable to education, we need to consider their complex strategies and political economies. First, it is worth noting that agencies like the Center for Disease Control and the World Health Organisation do not rely exclusively on randomised experimental models. Modern epidemiology and medicine uses a broad range of methodologies, from case-based work, observational ethnographies and interviews to complex social statistical analyses. Further, in the case of the tobacco and pharmaceutical industries, university researchers sponsored by commercial funds, government statutory and regulatory bodies, and of course, corporate sponsors and private developers have, at the least, a mixed track record. The Australian government recently moved to regulate the pharmaceutical industry's subsidisation of travel, vacations and other 'training' seminars for doctors and researchers. At the same time, state governments and universities actively seek the same industry's partnership in the development and commercialisation of biotechnology research.

There are additional spill-over effects into other educational areas, specifically teacher education. In California, for example, the state Department of Education has insistently vetted syllabus documents from language arts, reading and literacy methodology courses to determine if they are in compliance with the state reading strategies deemed by No Child Left Behind (Laitsch *et al.* 2002).

What has come to count as evidence-based educational policy in the US has set new benchmarks for a tight articulation of publishers, state authorities and a particular definition of 'science'. This is nothing short of a legislative codification of new definitions and interventions for what counts as success and risk. Because it is targeted at poor readers, it has had less visible impact on schools in upper socioeconomic areas, other than anecdotal evidence that the current policy push towards 'standards' is leading to an overall narrowing of the curriculum across several states.

Does evidence count in policy formation?

Critique is, of course, the easy bit. And this is not to diminish the problems with the intersections of poverty and social marginalisation, multilingualism and cultural diversity that the American state system is facing. Since Coleman's time they have been part of the complex factors that mediate equality of educational opportunity and achievement. These require vigorous policy intervention, not free market ideology. But what does this say about the viability of evidence-based policy and accountability-oriented policy? Are these irrevocably ideologically contaminated? Are they necessarily extensions of what is, at best, narrow positivism and reductionist approaches to educational assessment (Shepard 2000) or, at worst, what Gould (1981) demonstrated was a racist and patriarchal history of pseudo-science. Is the problem that US and UK policy makers 'took Thorndike's side', mandating a limiting concept of what might count as educational science? Is it possible to enlist evidence-based policy formation as part of a critical educational project?

Let me shift the narrative. In an excellent review of developments in educational ethnography, Foley, Levinson and Hurtig (2001) document the coming apart of many of the fundamental assumptions in the field. The axiom in the Meadian postwar tradition was that ethnography entailed an objectivised, rationalised subjectivity on the part of the researcher, whereby outsiders would make the familiar strange, even as they entered the field as 'participant observers'. By this account, the maintenance of a scientific distance was seen as a core component of the ethnographer's work.

Foley and colleagues go on to contrast this with the neo-essentialist claims of feminist theorists, post-colonialists, indigenous peoples and 'radical multicultural-ists': that only insiders can know cultures and have the right to speak about or on behalf of those cultures. This is a strong claim about the intrinsic validity of insiders' speaking rights and a skepticism towards the very western science that purported to be outside of what ultimately became genocidal and patriarchal bias. Indeed, the history of colonisation and patriarchy is one where women, diasporic and indigenous communities have been taken as artifact, objects of a scientific gaze to be manipulated, measured and tested. However 'scientific' these activities might have purported to be, they were indeed situated sociocultural and political practices.

Using the example of the work of D. K. Kondo (1990), Foley and colleagues go on to talk of the possibilities of what they call 'halfie' ethnographies. Working from feminist and materialist theories, Kondo undertook an ethnography of Japanese working women. Written as a Sansei woman, her story as much about her own hybridity, multiple subjectivity and travel between and across contexts as it is about a scientific object of study. One lesson from this work, and the broader corpus of cultural studies, is, of course, a critique of the concept of culture as singular, homogeneous and boundaried. The spatial metaphor of boundaried and autonomous culture was necessary to make traditional subject–object, researcher–researched, insider–outsider binaries work. The point I want to return to here concerns the movement between 'cultures' of research and policy, university and state bureaucracy. What follows is a narrative of 'in-between'-ness, a 'halfie' ethnography.

Ben Levin (Deputy Minister of Education, Manitoba), Charles Ungerleiter (previously Deputy Minister of Education, British Columbia), Roger Slee (Deputy Director General of Education, Queensland) and myself are 'tweeners'. We are educational researchers who moved into substantive positions within bureaucracies and, in several of our cases, back out again. This is perhaps a different situation that that of Garth Boomer and others who moved from broad experiences within educational systems towards academic work and writing.

As I began my brief tenure as Deputy Director General of Education in Queensland in 1999, I was still attending evening seminars and undertaking readings about how the state and policy discourse worked. Our studies included Rose's *Powers of Freedom* (1999), which draws from Foucault and the genealogical studies of mathematics and statistics by Canadian philosopher Ian Hacking. Rose documents the emergence of a modernist state that is premised on the calculability of the human subject, where 'countability' prefigures neoliberal moves towards government based on institutional performance and measurement. I also was reading recent work by Habermas (1998) which argues that legal, juridical discourse is a bridge between 'facts and norms'.

Though drawn from two competing strands of contemporary western philosophy, these works offer complementary accounts of how evidence-based social policy might work. In Rose's historical analysis, an avalanche of numbers overrides and drives the discourses of ethical decision making, taking on a life of its own in the constitution of governmentality. In Habermas' view, it is only a dialogic, hermeneutic social science that stands to mediate between facticity, in all of its various claims, and social norms. This is the formation of law, achieved through the ethical conditions and very possibility for discourse and consensus. While they offer strikingly different critiques of the state, both accounts view policy, law and social regulation as shaped and achieved through constituent discourses towards ethical and moral ends.

Moving from these discussions into the corporate boardroom of senior government bureaucracy was an out-of-body experience. What follows is a narrative composite of some of my first 'high stakes' senior policy meetings. The topic on the table was school size. Relatedly, we were discussing new school initiatives and the always politically sensitive issue of school closures. I waited for Rose's avalanche of numbers. I waited for technocratic economic rationalism. I waited for the ideal speech situation (not really). None arrived. After the fact, I made a list of the speech acts, treating them as a Habermasian taxonomy of dialogic 'truth claims'. These grounds were:

- Precedent: 'We always have done it this way.'
- Political: The unions would never let us do it. 'That constituency would never wear it.' 'We'd never get that through treasury.'
- Fiscal: 'We can't afford it.' 'Where is the money coming from?'

- Evidence: 'Look at the data.' 'Look at the test scores.'
- Philosophy: 'We believe in...'

The exchanges shifted fluidly, sometimes wildly, between the different categories, and, as is typical in face-to-face informal conversation, there was little explicit, self-conscious marking of such shifts. Curiously, the latter two categories were invoked least frequently, a pattern which developed across many such meetings.

We could undertake critical discourse analyses of policy claims, breaking them down as Aristotelian forms of knowledge, seeing them as taxonomic shifts in logical grounds, or, as Habermas might, taking them as speech acts with particular locutionary, illocutionary and perlocutionary characteristics. But I experienced them as something more akin to the ebbs and flows of what Blackmore and Sachs (1998) have referred to as the 'emotional economy' of educational administration. To a newcomer, they were more like unpredictable musical riffs, presented with affective force, their effects greatly dependent on the gendered power, position and authority of speakers. I find it curious that we generally treat classroom interaction and school leadership in such terms but fail to apply such analytic constructs to policy analysis – treating policy as a relatively simple instance of dominant ideology, as static text, rather than something which is historically produced through discourse generative zones, their everyday exchanges of capital, and face-to-face dynamics.

My point that is that policy formation entails far more arbitrary play of discourse and truth, power and knowledge than I had anticipated, notwithstanding how it is justified in press releases, *Hansard*, or green papers, or how it is critiqued. The use of evidence – whether psychometric, sociometric, factor-analytic, multilevel, case-based, ethnographic, or qualitative – appeared far less systematic, far less 'calculating' than Rose's account, and far less indicative of a dominant or even coherent ideology than I had anticipated. My experience convinced me that we could only move systematically towards the redressive educational project if, indeed, we reworked and reappropriated an evidence-based approach to policy development. Without a broad array of evidence and data – developing specific redressive strategies was difficult, arbitrary and piecemeal, more likely to entail add-on programs and token distribution of funds. But the evidence-based educational policy required is something of a very different order than No Child Left Behind.

Enlisting critical social science in policy development

In *Academic Distinctions*, James Ladwig (1996) argues for a critical realist approach to educational research that engages qualitative and quantitative, hermeneutic and positivist paradigms in a constructive dialogue about the reform of educational systems and their social consequences. Working from a different history and context, I want to take his argument a step further. We need evidence-based social policies derived, *inter alia*, from a critical, hermeneutic social science that draws from a range of disciplinary discourses and fields. Such an approach would provide a more complex, theory-driven analysis, using and triangulating a range of social statistical, demographic, economic, sociological, ethnographic as well as psychometric data sources.

It would move away from a reductionist focus on outcomes towards a broader analysis of how educationally acquired capital has material consequences in individuals' and communities pathways through and via emergent economies and institutions. It would bring to bear the kinds of multilevel statistical analysis (e.g. hierarchical modelling, cluster analysis) that have come into their own in the past decade, enabling the modeling of mediating social and educational effects, in lieu of reductionist, causal models of psychological effects. We would use ethnographic, case study and discourse analytic work to test hypotheses, to build models, and to instantiate the trends and clusters that emerge from such an analysis.

Further, such work would provide the grounds for a pedagogy about policy, giving policy makers such as those I described above meta-theoretical and taxonomic categories for marking out and comparing the various truth claims upon which decisions about flows of power are made. Using the partial Queensland data that we have, let me try to illustrate what such a view might tell us.

In most Australian states, the major policy settings for 'reform' have been in place for some years now. These consist of: (1) standardised achievement testing in literacy and numeracy; (2) the updating and implementation of curriculum documents. Under these broad auspices, 'outcomes-based education' brings together Tylerian models of curriculum with the aforementioned neoliberal policy approaches to the appraisal of student performance. At the same time, the de facto national agenda has been to move towards (3) school-based management, where principals can make semi-autonomous decisions about school programming, structures and procedures, ostensibly to ensure the improvement of (1) above and the better implementation of (2) above. The effects of this approach are compounded and, perhaps, confounded by the emergence of powerful market forces, with the Catholic and independent sectors differentially funded but less explicitly regulated in terms of testing-based performativity and curriculum compliance above. Though on different timelines in various states, this general suite of reforms has evolved for a decade.

Let me return to the three propositions about the state of Australian education. Each has policy implications, each is predicated on a mixed evidence base, and each stakes out significant directions for the educational research community.

On poverty in early childhood

My first claim is that there is no generalisable basic skills crisis in early childhood. Rather the material conditions, social relations, discourse relations, textual and social practices of 'childhood' and family are in historical transition. These changes are strongly mediated by both residual and emergent forms of poverty, both those persistent forms of class and cultural inequality that have plagued us since Karmel's time among indigenous, migrant and working-class communities, and those that are arising in the new Australian economy.

By recent estimates, 20 per cent of Queensland children are from families living at or below the nominal Henderson poverty line (Education Queensland 1999). This tends to be increasingly 'spatialised poverty' (cf. Harvey 2000), concentrated in new migrant communities, indigenous communities, and in emergent edge-cities, the cheap mortgage belts surrounding capital and provincial cities. As early as the preliminary studies for *Education 2010*, it was clear to us that specific zones of spatialised poverty required urgent concentrated, cross-governmental action and, moreover, much stronger coordination of community-based capital, rebuilding of social infrastructure and enlistment of private sector resources.

At the same time, the new suburban poor have high degrees of mobility and transience, with families shifting residence in search of work. One edge-city, predominantly white-Australian school that we visited in our consultations on 'Literate Futures' had successfully put in an early intervention reading/literacy program, only to have a 60 per cent turnover between years 3 and 6. This hindered sustainable effects of any 'single-shot' grade-level intervention.

In this demographic reality, there is some good news. On the basis of the face-to-face individual diagnostics undertaken by year 2 teachers, 72 per cent of this same student cohort was experiencing some difficulty with early reading and language (Education Queensland 2002). Nonetheless, by later in year 3, 90 per cent of these same children have achieved the state 'benchmark' for functional decoding in the year 3 testing system (MCEETYA 2001). Both of these instruments have their limitations. The former has reasonable levels of contextual and content validity, but overall validity is only as good as that which can be achieved through loose systems of teacher moderation. The latter is based on an arbitrary 'cut point' for establishing the benchmark. Nonetheless, if we disaggregate the data by location, we find that that the concentration of reading failure is in those specific zones noted above. There is a powerful connection between early achievement differentials and spatialised poverty.

As part of a richer analysis, this would suggest that a simple testing/phonics agenda might push some specific test score achievements up, as it has in some states, but is at best only a partial strategy. Certainly this has been the experience in Tasmania and other states. At worst, it may be a misgauged response in a system where teachers are actually moving 90 per cent of the student population to what are nominally basic reading levels in the first three years of instruction. Basic skills levels and instructional efficacy – as much as it might appeal to 'back to the basics' advocates – may not be the problem or the solution to sustainable gains for the lower quartile of the student cohort.

We could triangulate the above data with the largest scale discourse analytic study of early home–school transitions for lower socioeconomic and ethnic minority children in Queensland. Freebody *et al.* (1996) looked at home literacy events and 200 classroom events over an extended period. They found that the problem was more complex than the typical attribution of basic skills problems to 'deficit parenting'. Their finding confirmed aspects of the now classical match– mismatch hypothesis that successful students who come from English-as-a-first language, school-like interactional environments are better primed to succeed in school-based interaction. But they also offer an unsettling finding: that early school instruction tended to be intellectually trivial and cognitively low level, more focused on classroom management, on teaching kids procedural routines for doing lesson work and school, including worksheets, than on depth knowledge and skill development. That is, their point is that the curricular and interactional norms of schools where benchmarks of 'success' were being defined and assessed were of dubious educational value.

Moving from quantitative to qualitative, blending teacher judgement data (the Year 2 Net), psychometric data (benchmark testing) and discourse analytic work, we can set the grounds for a very different analysis and potentially more powerful policy approach than blanket test-driven endorsements of standardised programs. First, it suggests the need for a community-targeted, whole-of-government strategy for intervening in spatialised poverty – one that would attempt to coordinate a range of available capital in communities (Luke 2003). Second, it suggests that effective pedagogic reform may not centrally reside in the need for packaged, standardised commodities for the teaching of basic skills. Indeed, such an approach might effectively misdirect scarce funding and resources. This is especially the case if the pedagogical problem of intellectual demand and cognitive depth is in fact exacerbated by a basic skills orientation.

On pedagogy in the middle years

There are other key findings in the 2001 round of benchmark testing in literacy. First, there is evidence that the year 5 performance is lower in absolute terms than current year 3 performance: specifically, the overall proportion of students meeting the nominal benchmark performance in year 3 is 80 per cent (MCEETYA 2001). Although we have no longitudinal cohort data (which makes 'value adding' studies more difficult and problematic), we could hypothesise that this is an instance of a trend in US reading surveys, the 'fifth grade slump' (Calfee 2003). That is, early gains in reading and literacy established through intervention tend to residualise as we move towards the middle years of schooling.

There are a range of possible explanations for 'slump' data. The Freebody *et al.* (1996) study was broadly corroborated by the Queensland School Reform Longitudinal Study (Lingard *et al.* 2002). That study was the largest observational study of classroom practice in Australian educational history, with the coding of 1 000 classrooms. Among other findings, it found that levels of 'productive pedagogies' were low, with a slump in intellectual demand in the middle years. Lingard *et al* argue that this is a major impediment to educational achievement and outcomes, particularly among the lower achieving students. Both studies, then, suggest a very different policy challenge than the remediation of basic skills via the standardisation of teacher behaviour (Luke 2004). The policy challenge by these accounts is to develop forms of pedagogy that mobilise depth forms of knowledge and intellectual field, more complex technical skills, and substantive critical discourses as a means towards sustaining more powerful student pathways and achievements.

A recent national study of literacy and numeracy in the middle years of schooling (Luke *et al.* 2003) found that systematic data on the middle years of schooling was not available. The case studies and those data that did exist, however, indicted that there are unresolved issues in pedagogical depth and quality. This appears to form a major impediment to the translation of many of the significant gains of the middle years reforms (e.g. better social and psychological ethics of care; higher retention and student motivation, more relevant curriculum) into improved achievement and engaged life pathways, especially amongst the lower performing groups and cohorts. Yet even if we succeed modestly at changing the subject of pedagogy in the middle years, serious questions have been raised about the continued relevance and consequences of senior schooling for many students.

On pathways from school to the new economy

In the last five years, all Australian states have conducted various studies on pathways from school into further education and work. Since the late 1990s, the average Queensland year 12 cohort has numbered around 30 000 students per year. The overall percentage of Queenslanders who complete 12 years of schooling is 67 per cent, with an apparent retention of about 74 per cent from years 8–12 (Education Queensland 2002). The retention rates have been in decline nationally. In Queensland, the proportion of students who have achieved a 'sound' mark or better in three senior subjects is about two thirds; about 14 per cent do not complete any science, mathematics or technology board subjects. Typically about a third of the graduating cohort enrol in basic communications classes. About 30 per cent of the overall cohort complete VET certificate at AQF Level 1 or higher (Education Queensland 2002).

By the commencement of the senior years, a quarter of the potential school completion cohort has left the school, and governments have very limited tracking data on the life pathways of these students. Many 'disappear from the screen' of social analysis, turning up variously in data sets maintained by health, police services, unemployment and social welfare agencies. However governments have very little rigorous empirical data on how youth get from institution to institution or how and when they depart from these systems altogether.

Of those students the above data suggests that between a fifth and a third are struggling to reach levels of achievement that would secure ready pathways to further education or employment. In the case of Queensland, this situation has led to two major reports by Pitman (2003) and Gardner (2002) and a series of proposed training reforms that extend the mandatory age of schooling, a move also announced in South Australia. The Pitman study calls for a fundamental rethinking of the senior school. The senior system remains strongly geared to binary tracks that lead to traditional university entry, on the one hand, and vocational education, on the others. Yet we could ask whether this system has become dysfunctional, with almost half of the overall cohort either leaving or underprovided for.

The system maintains a 'dual pathway' route from school to work that was designed for a more stable employment market, with traditional bifurcated pathways through high stakes assessment systems to university studies and to vocational training. At the same time there is evidence of a delinearisation of school–further education–work pathways – with up to half of entering cohorts of many universities comprised of non-school leavers, a considerable number of university graduates engaging in vocational training, and increasing retraining requirements of many retrenched workers. In that delinearisation, somewhere between a quarter and half of the cohort is 'lost', with systems lacking a definitive sense of how, where and to what ends. This is not exclusively an Australian phenomenon, but reflects broader trends amongst the workforces of OECD countries.

In sum: the narrative that I have developed here is partial, raising many areas for further research and development. It suggests that schooling is struggling to come to grips with the new Australia, with its culturally and linguistically diverse population, its volatile economy characterised by new and spatialised stratifications of wealth, and new pathways from school to work, community and civic life. This is a troubling and complex picture. But I believe that it belies rather than reinforces the capacity of the species of quick fixes offered by the testing, basic-skills accountability models advocated in the approaches to evidence-based policy critiqued here. Just as medical models are limited in their power to analyse and proscribe complex social, cultural and economic problems, hypodermic models of educational treatment ultimately have limited medium to long-term efficacy.

To find productive policy alternatives requires that we anticipate the limits of particular interventions (e.g. early intervention models, phonics programs) where they are not articulated with a broader suite of systemic approaches to social policy. A critical educational project will only work if it sits within a broader social policy that brings together government and community-based resources systematically to address issues of changing demographic patterns and available community capital, social, economic, ecological as well as cultural. It would move us towards professional interventions with a sustainable focus on pedagogy and curriculum, not management and accountability. It would demand reinvention of relations *between* educational institutions, from child care to schools to vocational education. And it will require a sociological imagination capable of envisioning, designing and realising new student pathways that articulate through and around these institutions and those of new economies, with the state and private sectors providing access to enabling, combinatory forms of capital.

As a research community, we need to move towards a richer, more multidisciplinary approach to educational analysis and policy development – beyond the crude league tables and single-dimension test score analysis, and beyond critique that explicates the ideological contradictions of these policies but struggles to remake schools and systems in communities' and students' interests.

A research agenda

We talk about multiple subjectivities and new identities, about globalisation, and about the critical. These come to material ground in educational systems like ours. They are no longer abstractions or artifacts of educational theory, if they ever were. Our educational systems have struggled for over a decade to define coherent policy directions other than neoliberal marketisation, proliferation of outcomes and tests, and piecemeal responses to cultural, linguistic and epistemological diversity that have created a welter of 'add on' and 'pull out' programs. In policy making venues such as those that I have described here, the *social scientific evidence* of changed contexts and conditions facing communities and schools, state systems and bureaucracies needs to be placed on the table. And it is in the context of this evidence – about poverty, about new demographics and cultures, about available capital in social fields, about life pathways, about fair and unfair patterns of access and employment, about changing economies and institutions – that educational reform needs to be made and assessed.

We talk about our commitments to inclusion, to bringing forms of alterity, voice and identity into pedagogic and institutional fields. But strategies of educational inclusion must aim towards changed material conditions. Looking back at the postwar period, A. H. Halsey (1986, 173) commented that: 'Exhortation alone is futile, whether to altruism or to tolerance or to the recognition of the equal claim of others to share in the bounty afforded by society.' The challenge is to rebuild institutions in ways that enable changed material and social relations.

There are serious questions about current policy settings. There also must be questions about the power and value of many current research directions. I have argued here that to move forward we must look through social theoretic lenses at evidence – materialist and discourse-based evidence, quantitative and case-based, psychometric and sociometric, using multilevel models that stress mediation and contextualisation, rather than 'causal factors' – all with an eye to developing new narratives, new pathways and new policies.

We are at a difficult but defining historical moment. The events post 9/11 have had the effect of destabilising and questioning the human capital model, with issues of citizenship, ethics, human rights and identity suddenly focal to many nations. They have also underlined the potential obsolescence of our current systems and approaches. Our generational tools have been those of critique. What a powerful evidence-based educational policy needs is a rich, critical, multidisciplinary social science, rather than a reductionist and ultimately ideological, psychological reductionism. Social science needs to move beyond an analysis of the capital effects of the school to engage with the durability, redeployment and combinatory powers of different forms of educationally acquired capital in communities – global and local, virtual and real. Of governments and policy makers, we need to demand an educational policy that can be read and constructed as but one component of broader social policy and cultural strategy.

For such a task neither Dewey nor Thorndike, neither unreconstructed progressivism or born again positivism will suffice. A critical educational project for remaking Australian education can afford neither a purity of research uncontaminated by normative responsibility for what is to be done nor naive policy, based on pseudo-science and anecdote. Nor can we operate solely as insiders or outsiders in the worlds of research and policy formation. We have our work cut out for us.

Acknowledgements

Thanks to Jim Ladwig, Peter Freebody, Ray Land, Roger Slee, Mei-Ling Shiroishi, David Hogan and Gabrielle Matters for ideas and arguments that appear here; Terry Moran and Kim Bannikoff for on-the-job training; Donna Alvermann and Fazal Rizvi for critical responses; Christa van Kraayenoord, Leslie Sharpe and S. Gopinathan for resources.

Notes

1 A version of this paper was presented as The 2002 Radford Lecture, delivered at the Annual Meeting of the Australian Association for Research in Education in Brisbane. Aspects of the spoken address have been retained in this version prepared for publication.
2 Following Lyotard (1982), my assumption here is that narrative and exposition, scenario and 'science' are co-articulations of power and discourse.
3 The 'good old days' of postwar academic freedom are part professional mythology and nostalgia, and part necessary defence of a powerful vision of the university that many fought for and lost their jobs for in and around 1968, a matter that has arisen again with instances of suppression of anti-administration critique in the US post-9/11. There never was a twentieth century university uncontaminated by corporate influence, as any of our senior colleagues who lived through McCarthyism, through the enlistment and funding of universities in the work of the military–industrial complex will tell us. Long before this, Stanford and Carnegie Melon were founded from the surplus labour of migrant workers translated into corporate philanthropy. At the same time, those gains in reinventing the university post-1968 as a site for social and cultural critique remain part of the aspirations of universities worldwide, even as they enter the life worlds of performance indicators, intellectual properties and biotech.

Bibliography

Allington, R. (2002) *Big Brother and the National Reading Curriculum: How Ideology Trumped Evidence* (New York: Heineman).
Apple, M. W. (1981) *Education and Power* (New York: Routledge).
Blackmore, J. and Sachs, J. (13–17 July 1998) Performativity, passion and academic work: the making of self and self management. Paper presented at Winds of Change: Women and the Culture of Universities Conference (Sydney: University of Technology).
Britzman, D. (1991) *Practice Makes Practice* (Albany, NY: State University of New York Press).
Burbules, N. and Torres, C. (eds) (2000) *Education and Globalisation* (New York: Routledge).
Calfee, R. (30 May 2003) Introduction to the state of reading in California. Paper presented at the Conference of the University of California Literacy Consortium (Berkeley, CA).
Education Queensland (1999) *Education 2010* (Brisbane: Education Queensland).
Education Queensland (2002) *Destination 2010* (Brisbane: Education Queensland).
Foley, D. A., Levinson, B. A. and Hurtig, J. (2001) 'Anthropology goes inside: the new educational ethnography of ethnicity and gender', *Review of Research in Education*, 28: 37–98.
Freebody, P., Ludwig, C. and Gunn, S. (1996) *Everyday Literacy Practices In and Out of School in Low Socioeconomic Communities* (Brisbane: Griffith University/Department of Employment, Education and Training).

Garan, E. (2001) 'Beyond the smoke and mirrors: a critique of the National Reading Panel's findings on phonics', *Phi Delta Kappan*, 82(7): 500–6.

Gardner, M. (2002) *The Review of Pathways Articulation* (Brisbane: Queensland Government).

Gould, S. (1981) *The Mismeasure of Man* (New York: Norton).

Habermas, J. (1998) *Between Facts and Norms: Contributions to a Discourse Theory of Law and Democracy* (Boston: MIT Press).

Halsey, A. H. (1986) *Change in British Society*, 3rd edn (Oxford: Oxford University Press).

Harvey, D. (2000) 'Cosmopolitanism and the banality of geographical evils', *Public Culture*, 12(2): 529–64.

James, W. (1899/2001) *Talks to Teachers on Psychology and to Students on Some of Life's Matters* (New York: Dover Press).

Kondo, D. K. (1990) *Crafting Selves* (Chicago: University of Chicago Press).

Ladwig, J. (1996) *Academic Distinctions* (New York: Routledge).

Laitsch, D., Heilman, E. E. and Shaker, P. (2002) 'Teacher education, pro-market policy and advocacy reform', *Teaching Education* 13(3): 251–71.

Lingard, R., Ladwig, J., Mills, M., Hayes, D., Bahr, M., Chant, D., Gore, J., Christie, P. and Luke, A. (2002) *Queensland School Reform Longitudinal Study* (Brisbane: Education Queensland).

Luke, A. (1997) 'The material effects of the word: apologies, "stolen children" and public speech', *Discourse*, 18(3): 151–80.

Luke, A. (2003) 'Literacy and the other: a sociological approach to literacy research and policy in multilingual societies', *Reading Research Quarterly*, 38(1): 132–41.

Luke, A. (2004) 'Teaching after the market: from commodity to cosmopolitanism', *Teachers College Record*, 106(7): 1422–43.

Luke, A., Elkins, J., Weir, K., Land, R., Carrington, V., Dole, S., Pendergast, D., Kapitzke, C., Van Kraayenoord, C., Moni, K., McIntosh, A., Mayer, D., Bahr, M., Hunter, L., Chadbourne, R., Bean, T., Alvermann, D. and Stevens, L. (2003) *Beyond the Middle: Literacy and Numeracy for At Risk Students in the Middle Years of Schooling* (Canberra: DEST).

Lyotard, J. F. (1982) *The Postmodern Condition: A Report on Knowledge*, B. Massumi, (trans.) (Minneapolis, MN: University of Minnesota Press).

MCEETYA (2001) *National Report on Schools in Australia* (Canberra: MCEETYA).

Pitman, J. (2003) *The Senior Certificate: A New Deal* (Brisbane Queensland Government).

Ritzer, G. (2000) *The MacDonalization of Society* (New York: Pine Forge Press).

Rose, N. (1999) *Powers of Freedom* (Cambridge: Cambridge University Press).

Shepard, L. A. (2000) 'The role of assessment in a learning culture', *Educational Researcher*, 29(7): 4–14.

US Department of Education (18 November 2001) Press release: Report on scientifically based research supported by US Department of Education. Office of Public Affairs.

CHAPTER 7

GLOBALIZATION AND EDUCATIONAL POLICYMAKING

A case study

Sandra Taylor and Miriam Henry

Educational Theory, Fall 2000, 50(4): 487–503

Introduction

While there has been a burgeoning literature on globalization in recent years, the impact of globalization on education policymaking remains relatively unexplored theoretical territory. This essay seeks to contribute to this area of inquiry, drawing on research conducted on the influence of the Organization for Economic Cooperation and Development (OECD) in shaping education policy in Australia over the past two decades or so, within the context of globalization.[1] This terrain is explored here through an examination of vocational education and training policy, chosen in recognition of Roger Dale's point that some policy arenas in education are more highly charged than others with respect to globalization given their explicit links with the economy.[2] Vocational education and training is used somewhat loosely as an umbrella term for a number of cognate strands that have surfaced at different times and in different countries: for example, transition education, vocational and technical education, technical and further education, post-compulsory education and training, and lifelong learning.

Vocational education and training has been a recurring policy focus in many OECD countries over the past two decades. Hence this theme provides a useful focal point for exploring the seeming convergence of policy ideas and the implications of this for national policymaking. Such an exploration, we suggest, may help to illuminate ways in which globalization pressures are influencing the policymaking machinery of the nation-state, and the role of international organizations – specifically in this instance the OECD as a 'globalizing agency' – in mediating such pressures. Australia has been selected as the starting point for this discussion not only because it is familiar terrain for us, but also because vocational education and training has been an arena in which there has been a particularly vigorous interplay between the OECD and successive Australian governments over the past three decades. In turn, then, the OECD was chosen because this has been an international organization in which Australia has been an active participant. Not all OECD countries have such an 'organic' relationship with the Organization: increasingly, for example, the European Union has more salience for the policy stances of many European countries than does the OECD; and while the United States could be categorized as the OECD's superpower, exerting influence on the organization at the highest level, many within the United States regard the OECD's educational work as of marginal relevance and influence. Nevertheless, the argument here is that international organizations are integral to the processes of educational globalization.

Thus the case study seeks to do two things. First, it attempts to illuminate the processes of globalization in a particular policy domain (vocational education and training), drawing on the relation between one nation-state (Australia) and one international organization (the OECD). Second, it attempts to contribute to more theoretical understandings of the nature of educational globalization and the implications of this for national policymaking. The study argues that educational globalization does not necessarily imply policy homogenization, but rather that there are tensions within globalization processes that serve both to concentrate and to differentiate the policy agenda. Nor is it argued that globalization implies the surrendering of national sovereignty. However, the increasingly polycentric nature of governance and hence of policymaking is recognized.

In order to ground this discussion, we first provide a brief comment about the OECD as an international organization.

The OECD and educational policymaking

The OECD was formed in 1961 out of the prior Organization for European Economic Cooperation, established after the Second World War to assist with the economic reconstruction of Europe. Its policy agendas are framed by a 'commitment to a market economy and a pluralistic democracy' (and more recently, a respect for human rights) and a concern to foster a 'post-industrial age in which...OECD economies [can be woven] into a yet more prosperous and increasingly service-oriented world economy.'[3] Education as an activity within the OECD has been broadly legitimated on the basis of its contribution to economic growth, though such a role has not necessarily been narrowly interpreted. Indeed, the range of policy interests and stances in relation to education have been broader and more contested than the OECD's economic mission might indicate.

The OECD is essentially an intergovernmental organization, comprising twenty-nine predominantly wealthy Western countries though, since the mid-1990s, the trajectory has changed to include countries such as Mexico, the Czech Republic, Hungary, Korea, and Poland. While there are significant ideological differences among OECD countries, in particular between social democratic and market liberal orientations, decisionmaking is essentially consensual. This means that policy positions tend to be sufficiently flexible to enable individual member countries to develop their own policy stances. Unlike, say, the World Bank, the OECD has no prescriptive mandate over its member countries. Rather, it describes itself as a place for reflection, discussion, research, and analysis 'that may often help governments shape policy', exerting influence through processes of 'mutual examination by governments, multilateral surveillance and peer pressure to conform or reform'.[4]

The OECD has been variously characterized as an 'international think-tank', a 'Rich Man's Club', or 'a club of like-minded countries'.[5] Perhaps in relation to education the most apt characterization is as a catalyst for reform and change. As George Papadopoulos explains in his authoritative account of the OECD's work in education:

> The starting point is the identification of major new policy issues which emerge on the educational horizon, and which might call for priority attention in the countries.... These issues are then put together within a structured

framework, leading to a number of questions which arise for policymaking. Arriving at a convincing statement of such issues and questions, of how and why they arise, and of their implications, is already half the work done. It involves a dialectical process of Secretariat and country thinking and exchange, including a strong dose of advice from experts, and provides the basis for subsequent program planning and implementation.[6]

The OECD is also part of a growing network of international organizations which Connie McNeely and Y. K. Cha suggest may collectively serve as world-level agencies in educational policy convergence and change. They argue that international organizations influence the incorporation and diffusion of educational ideologies and practices within and among nation-states, and suggest that international organizations 'have been an important catalyst in spreading world cultural themes and accounts, and research conceptualizing them as institutionalizing mechanisms can provide important insights in the area of comparative education'.[7]

Such a description begs a number of questions that we attempt to address here. For example: How do these mechanisms of institutionalization take place? How does the dialectical relation between OECD secretariat and member country referred to by Papadopoulos work? Some of the complexity involved in thinking about these issues is usefully captured in Archer's more general conceptualization of international organizations as policy instruments of governments, policy arenas for debate, and independent policy actors. As instruments, they may serve formal diplomatic purposes while at the same time becoming 'the battleground for individual members or groups vying for influence over and control of the organization'. As policy arenas, they provide a 'meeting place where members can discuss matters of common interest' and 'a platform from which members can espouse views and…confront each other'. And as independent actors, they become an identifiable 'it,' 'distinguishable from [their] member states'.[8]

With such questions and this framework in mind, we turn to our study of vocational education and training, beginning first with policy developments in Australia.

Changing discourses of vocational education and training Australian approaches to vocational education and training: 1970s–1990s

For the purposes of this discussion, three phases of policy development in Australia are discernible: an early phase of transition education drawing on distinctly Australian traditions of reform; a middle phase dominated by concerns with youth unemployment and an acknowledgement of the underlying structural changes occurring worldwide underpinning youth unemployment; and a third phase plugging into more universal agendas of training reform in the context of Australia attempting to position itself in the global, knowledge-based economy. As will be seen, these three phases are marked by somewhat different relationships with the OECD.

Phase 1: Transition Education Policy Within Australia in the 1970s. Australia joined the OECD in 1971, ten years after the establishment of the Organization and only after the retirement of John McEwan, Deputy Prime Minister and leader of the Country Party, then a minor partner in the federal Coalition government. A staunch protectionist, McEwan vigorously opposed Australia's entry because of the OECD's free-market stance. Initially, with respect to education, links with the Organization were low key. According to some interviewees in our study, if anything the influence flowed from Australia to the OECD rather than vice versa, particularly in the schools sector around the Australian Schools Commission's innovative Disadvantaged Schools Program. The latter, which funded schools focusing on whole school change rather than individual students, 'had a very big effect on the thinking of the OECD.... The Schools Commission was regarded as a place to look to by the OECD'.[9] It was argued that education policy at that time was driven by the internal dynamics of Australian politics and an Australian tradition of reform drawing on ideas 'going back into antiquity': 'schooling was seen as a redemptive exercise, that it could make a difference for kids – that was the driving force. That's not OECD stuff, that's a hundred years of educational philosophical developments.... They go back a long way in the literature'.[10]

The Whitlam government's commissioning of an OECD educational policy review on the theme 'the transition from school to work and further education' in 1974 marked the beginning of a more active engagement with the OECD. The notion of transition education was a term that in the 1970s became associated with programs focusing on links between school and work. 'Transed' was often decried in educational circles as narrowly vocational and as a band-aid for keeping reluctant school stayers out of trouble during periods of high youth unemployment. Initially however, when the OECD review of transition education was commissioned, youth unemployment was not perceived as a significant factor. Rather, the topic was selected because 'the Australian education authorities had been conscious not only of their own shortcomings in this area but of the increasing attention that their OECD partners were paying to this subject'.[11] The topic, then, was broadly framed and the background report prepared by the Australian authorities to inform the review reflected this broad framing: 'The vocational development of an individual has to be seen as part of his total human development.... the emphasis should be on orientation to the world of work or vocational preparation generally, rather than training for a particular job'.[12]

The review itself occurred within the context of a change in government in Australia – from Labor to the Liberal/National Party Coalition – and a growing concern with youth unemployment. The OECD report noted the 'increasing unease' about the social role of education compared with the 'heady optimism' of the 1960s. However, it attempted to retain a broad focus and sought to study the linkages between education and employment systems, noting,

> It is obvious that coherent policies to facilitate the transition from school to work call for an adequate degree of coordination between education and employment policies. The examiners came to the conclusion that, as in many other countries, such coordination needs to be reinforced. That the Australian authorities share this view is shown by the fact that a national 'Committee of Inquiry into Education and Training' has now been appointed.[13]

The inquiry into education and training (the Williams Inquiry) was set up by the new Coalition government to consider the relation between education and employment. The Williams report, *Education, Training and Employment*, made only a brief reference to the OECD review's recommendations for better coordination, and was silent on matters pertaining to educational structures or policy integration (for example of education and labor market policies), by and large adopting a relatively narrow approach to the question of transition.[14] In general, it was seen in educational circles as a highly conservative document. However, it did resonate with the times, providing the impetus for the establishment of a commonwealth Transition Education Program which funded initiatives in work experience and the provision of 'alternative' vocationally oriented subjects in the largely academically oriented secondary schools.

Phase 2: Youth Policy Development in Australia, Late 1970s to Mid-1980s. By 1977 youth unemployment had become a major concern in many OECD countries, prompting bodies such as the Manpower Services Commission in the United Kingdom, the Australian Education Council, and the OECD itself to become interested in the notion of training as a means of responding to the long-term, structural nature of youth unemployment. As Margaret Vickers's discussion of the OECD influence on Australian education policy shows, the new approach was evident in the various reports surrounding Australia's second OECD country review on youth policy initiated by Peter Wilenski, Secretary to the Department of Youth Affairs in the new Hawke Labor government in 1983.[15]

The previous year, Vickers notes, Wilenski had been invited to work at the OECD in Paris to develop a comprehensive paper on youth policy. Among other things, his paper recommended an integrated approach to youth policy in areas of education, training, employment, and income support – ideas that were reflected in Australia's background report for the OECD review.[16] The background report referred to problems with the transition education approach flowing from the Williams Report, and asserted the goal of increasing participation and equity as 'a key element in the new framework of youth policies'.[17] The OECD review was consistent with this broad-based approach. It recommended a 'youth entitlement' and the development of comprehensive policies for youth, with emphasis being placed on the long-term needs of young people rather than on short-term concerns of high unemployment.[18] After 1983, Wilenski began to implement new policy directions consistent with those recommended in his OECD paper. He set up an Office of Youth Affairs, established a review of income support arrangements for young people which led to the AUS-TUDY (a student support scheme), and helped to initiate the important Kirby Review of the Labour Market, which recommended mainstream education and training to replace earlier labor market programs. Vickers suggests that the OECD, helped youth policies to be framed in a new way. She argues that Wilenksi's experiences at the OECD, plus 'the combined weight of the OECD review, together with the confluence of views expressed in the Kirby report and the income support review created a climate in which the government's plans could be enacted'.[19]

At that period there was something of an ideological tussle within the Labor government between old-style 'wets' associated with the former Whitlam era and economic 'dries'. In 1987, with the ascendance of the economic dries, traditionally separate policy areas were combined in a mega-Department of Employment, Education and Training (DEET) with John Dawkins as Minister. The amalgamation aimed 'to achieve a new coherence and consistency between our various education and labour market policies and programs' and was part of what Dawkins described as a 'vigorous programme of micro-economic reform' in Australia.[20]

Such directions had been increasingly promoted in various OECD reports.[21] However, as Dawkins himself commented, the creation of a single portfolio was a first among OECD countries and the formation of DEET was seen as 'a milestone in relations with the OECD'.[22] The new DEET structures, it was observed, 'led to a greater policy focus and interest in the OECD' and to 'a tighter control over education agendas for the OECD...compared to the old Education Department'.[23] In the words of one consultant: 'After Dawkins, the OECD links were cranked up – DEET was more active in seeking information. The riding instructions from Dawkins were stronger'.[24]

Thus from about this time onward, the OECD seems to have played a more visible role in Australian policymaking in education. This was particularly evident in relation to the government's restructuring agenda, so that Vickers, for example, argues that during this period Canberra's education bureaucrats selectively focused on aspects of the OECD agenda that emphasized the economic functions of education.[25] As one consultant observed of that time, 'Their [DEET's] key players had graced the OECD and saw in the OECD a conceptual, ideological framework of organization which could legitimate its work'.[26] Dawkins himself used the forums of the OECD to propound his own policy stances, in particular the role of education and training in skills development for the global economy, the need for educational restructuring to achieve this end, and the complementarity of economic and social purposes of education.

In 1988 Dawkins chaired a major OECD conference in Paris, 'Education and the Economy in a Changing Society'. The conference took as its theme the convergence of education and economic functions in the new global context premised on what was becoming an increasingly familiar argument about workers' skills and qualifications 'as critical determinants of effective performance of enterprises and economies'.[27] While these were also Dawkins's own ideas, on his return from Paris he was able to use the conference to legitimate and promote his educational restructuring agenda more strongly in Australia.[28]

Phase 3: Vocational Education and Training Policy Development, Late 1980s and 1990s. Arising out of the 1988 conference, the OECD initiated a three-year activity, 'The Changing Role of Vocational Education and Training' (VOTEC), aimed at examining approaches and programs in school-linked vocational education, including links to workplace training and relations between general and vocational education. Australia, having made vocational education and training a policy priority under the rubric of the national training reform agenda, was an active participant in the VOTEC activity.

In both the OECD and Australia, the equity-enhancing aspects of vocational education and training were stressed and in both places there was concern to avoid a narrow interpretation of vocationalism. In Australia, a number of reports on vocational education and training were produced emphasizing the need to bring together general and vocational education so that general education was seen as relevant to work and vocational education as broader than specific work-based skills.[29] The reports also stressed the importance of creating flexible educational pathways between school, Technical and Further Education (TAFE), higher education, and work in order to broaden young people's participation in education and training. Although the reforms were criticized for a symbolic and somewhat simplistic attention to disadvantaged groups, the essential argument was that they would lead to more generally equitable outcomes than previously because of their more inclusive education and training provisions.[30]

Similar ideas underpinned the OECD's VOTEC activity. So, for example, the final publication arising out of that activity noted that 'there should not be complete separation between general education and vocational training, and that as far as possible general education should continue during vocational training'.[31] Also noted was the underlying assumption that

> in a democratic society, policy makers have an interest in participation in VOTEC...there may be economic reasons for this policy interest.... There may also be social reasons: for example, the perception that participation in VOTEC may prevent failure and exclusion, especially among disadvantaged groups.[32]

The extent to which equity objectives and broadly defined vocational education and training goals were realizable or realized is of course another matter. In Australia, for example, equity objectives, while strongly expressed, were in fact resisted and poorly implemented given a lack of vigilance in the monitoring processes and the establishment of a more deregulatory training climate which helped to reduce monitoring capacity.[33]

Following on from the VOTEC activity, the OECD launched another project, 'Improving School-to-Work Transition'.[34] As part of this project, a thematic review of 'the transition from initial education to working life' was initiated.[35] Australia was the first country to be reviewed, in some sense completing the circle begun in 1976 when it was seen as having 'pointed the way' in taking the transition from school to work as the focus of its first OECD review.[36]

But of course, a circle is not really the appropriate metaphor to describe the policy developments that have been described here. Rather, what is evident is a chain of policy developments reflecting a mix of national, international, and global elements and an interplay of political, ideological, economic, and labor market factors impinging both on national policymaking as well as on the work of the OECD itself. This *mélange* is highlighted in the three phases of Australian policy development just recounted.

Australian policies and the OECD

In the initial phase, the OECD appeared to be a less significant source of policy ideas though the Labor government clearly regarded the Organization as sufficiently useful to commission an education policy review. Rather, the Schools Commission's work on educational disadvantage was arguably the most significant and innovative policy legacy of that time. While that work acknowledged ideas drawn from OECD reports, it drew more substantively on a long 'Australian' tradition of thinking as well as the experiences in the United States and the United Kingdom. The OECD review of transition education may have assisted Australian authorities 'by articulating problems and developing something of a national perspective', and it may have had a catalytic effect in the sense of 'establishing a basis for and encouraging further investigations and discussion'.[37] But its policy prescriptions were broadly couched, enabling differing interpretations of transition education. Given changing economic and political circumstances, a narrower version than may have been initially intended was taken up. Indeed, it would seem that in this phase the Williams Report – a creature of the conservative Coalition government then in power – had greater salience for educational policy directions than did the OECD review.

During the middle phase, links between Australia and the OECD were more closely intertwined, and the structural nature of youth unemployment was beginning to be better understood. This period marked the shift to an economically drier climate, and following 1987 and the formation of DEET, policy priorities pointed more directly toward the imperatives of a globalizing economy. The final phase marked a high point of Australia's involvement with the Organization's educational work – a long distance traveled since McEwan's protectionist opposition to the OECD. Dawkins, as education minister and then treasurer, used the forums of the OECD to promote and legitimate his policy prescriptions for educational restructuring and microeconomic reform – prescriptions that fitted the OECD liberal economic template like a glove, particularly the emphasis on human capital formation. Indeed, Dawkins helped to shape the template. Under this 'drier' Labor regime, notions of equity were harnessed to economic rationalist goals of efficiency, reflecting a similar grafting of liberal democratic ideas onto market liberal principles in the OECD.

By the 1990s, however, party political commonalities rather than differences around the new policy paradigm of human resource development framed by market liberal ideology were increasingly evident. Hence both sides of politics agreed on such matters as the necessity of a diminished role for the state in education, a market-driven system of provision, and what Bienefeld refers to as a 'cargo cult' faith in vocational education and training as the solution to the volatile demands of global labor markets.[38] Beyond this, there were relatively minor differences over how vocational education and training should be funded and how questions of access and equity should be conceptualized. In conforming to this general trend, then, Australia has been but one of many countries following a similar policy path, albeit each with its own distinctive characteristics.[39]

From where does such a path derive? It is difficult to argue that it springs entirely from an Australian tradition of reform, though there are undoubtedly particular indigenous elements in the way the ingredients are mixed. For example, the national training reform agenda drew upon on a series of local documents that collectively framed a distinctively Australian policy framework for vocational education and training. At the same time, there are elements of policy adaptation, in that the training reform agenda had its genesis in a mix of Swedish and U.K. models of vocational education and training. However, there is more at stake here than cross-national comparisons and adaptations. Rather, we suggest, the convergence of policy ideas emanates from the machinations of increasingly interlinked policy networks operating in part via international organizations – emergent global policy communities – mobilizing around key agendas. Vocational education and training, because of its explicit links with the economy, is one of these agendas.

Converging policy agendas in vocational education and training: the example of lifelong learning

Human resource development as the key to a competitive economy has become policy orthodoxy across first and third world countries alike and among international organizations as divergent as the European Union, UNESCO, the World Bank, and the OECD. For example: 'learning, expertise, and human resources – the 'human factor' as it is sometimes called – are critical elements of the well-being of our economies and society'.[40] 'The level of the competence of a country's skilled workers and technicians is centrally important to the flexibility and productivity of its labor force'.[41] And 'higher education is moving towards a mass enrollment system as modern economies become increasingly knowledge-intensive and therefore depend more on graduates of higher education, who constitute a 'thinking workforce'.[42] Of course, the significance of convergent rhetoric should not be overstated given the different reference points and constituencies of these organizations. Nevertheless, as one of our interviewees noted,

> you'll find the approach is very similar, not because there's a deliberate attempt to do that but because people working in the same field with the same knowledge basis, as it were, the same linkages, the same connections, and often consultants from countries will work for more than one of those organizations. So there's an increasing commonality of those policy interests.[43]

One example of the commonality of policy interests can be found in the notion of lifelong learning or lifelong education – a mobilizing slogan for UNESCO, the European Union, and the OECD alike and a policy mantra in many countries.[44] The emphases may of course differ:

> UNESCO's talk is more about core humanistic values....it's more utopian... It's not that we don't have our dreams, it's simply that a document like that would *never* go down in the Education Committee. Our paymaster simply expects something different. We're not in the same street as UNESCO.[45]

Nevertheless, there is considerable rhetorical convergence around notions of a 'learning society', and about flexible pathways encouraging equitable access and participation in education, now understood as extending beyond formal institutions.[46] Underpinning such rhetoric is the faith in education as a means – perhaps the prime means – of not only providing the changing skills required for an information-based economy but, more broadly, of promoting social cohesion and equity as well as personal development. Thus the stakes are high:

> A new focus for education and training policies is needed now, to develop capacities to realize the potential of the 'global information economy' and to contribute to employment, culture, democracy and, above all, social cohesion. Such policies will need to support the transition to 'learning societies' in which equal opportunities are available to all, access is open, and all individuals are encouraged and motivated to learn, in formal education as well as throughout life.... There is a need to rethink and broaden the notion of lifelong education. Not only must it adapt to changes in the nature of work, but it must also constitute a continuous process of forming whole human beings – their knowledge and aptitudes, as well as the critical faculty and the ability to act.[47]

Of course, such rhetoric is not implemented or taken up uniformly in the member countries of these organizations. But the question remains as to why such convergence has come about and of the implications of policy convergence for national policymaking. These issues are explored in more theoretical terms in the next section.

Discussion: educational globalization and national policymaking

John Prunty's definition of policy as the 'authoritative allocation of values' provides a useful starting point for this discussion.[48] At issue are two questions: Where does this authority come from? and, Whose/which values are being allocated? The most obvious answer would appear to be that authority derives from the nation-state or a subnational political unit within the nation-state, given that it is at these levels that educational policy is made and funded for implementation, and that the values enshrined in policy are those reflecting the dominant discourses – and the political compromises – within nation-states at any given time. The discussion here thus focuses, first, on issues relating to the locus of policymaking and, second, on the values underpinning education policy.

Processes of economic, cultural, and political globalization have served to reconfigure significantly the nation-state – never a stable geopolitical entity – with implications for its capacity to 'allocate values authoritatively'. Globalization theorists argue that the nation-state is of necessity becoming more porous given the expanded polity now involved in the processes of governance characteristic of political globalization.[49] Bob Deacon *et al.*, for example, in their discussion of the globalization of social policy refer to a 'new paradigm of political science [in which] tiers of government in effect give way to spheres of influence of complementary and contending local, national, supranational and global political forums'.[50] They go on to argue that 'social policy is increasingly being shaped by the politics of supranational agencies and nongovernment organizations which are increasingly the locus of future ideological and political struggles'.[51] They note that these agencies work in contradictory directions – hence, they suggest, the struggle for better global and national social policies is a struggle of values and ideas, occurring within major international organizations.[52] Thus, they conclude, 'It is no longer a matter of being 'in and against' the state but of being 'in and against' international organizations'.[53] This dichotomy seems overdrawn. More accurately, we would argue, international organizations along with those other spheres of influence operating above and below the nation-state need to be seen, analytically, as part of a reconfigured relation among state, civil society, and the economy.[54] Thus, as Paul Hirst and Graham Thompson put it, 'politics is becoming more polycentric, with states as merely one level in a complex system of overlapping and often competing agencies of governance'.[55] From this perspective, national policy directions can be seen as increasingly mediated by the stances of, on the one hand, supranational, international, and multinational bodies operating 'above' the nation-state and, on the other hand, a melange of locally based community groups, nongovernment organizations, and private enterprises operating below the level of the nation-state.

Given the accelerating pace of globalization, both materially and ideologically, making policy 'in the national interest' has therefore become, analytically and politically, a complex issue. However, we would argue that in such a context the nation-state's authority to allocate values has not ceased, but rather increasingly sits alongside other value-allocating authorities. It is possible, therefore, to argue for a strategic space for policymaking 'in the national interest' in ways that both recognize the complexities involved in conceptualizing the national/global interface and guard against what Hirst and Thomson refer to as 'the pathology of diminished expectations' of the state.[56] As Simon Marginson reminds us, the nation-state still retains an impressive portfolio of policy responsibilities – is still, in other words, a significant allocator of values, albeit within new political configurations.[57]

Now, one way of viewing the relation between the national and the global is to see globalization as a context for a relatively autonomous nation-state. Fowler, for example, suggests that, while nation-states are influenced by global forces, these are filtered through the prism of national characteristics such as economic resources, policymaking processes, and national values.[58] This is very much the OECD's stated approach. In Papadopoulos's words,

> A basic precept in the whole approach [of the OECD] is recognition of the fact that education policies are par excellence national policies reflecting the particular circumstances, traditions, and cultures of individual countries. The notion of an international education policy – even if such a thing existed, which has not been the case at least so far – is altogether foreign to this concept.[59]

From this perspective, countries are seen to engage in problems which, in light of globalization pressures, may be driven by increasingly common imperatives.

Viewed this way, the OECD as an international think-tank operates, and exerts influence, essentially as a comparative forum, enabling both a sense of national autonomy as well as a sense of commonality among the likeminded. The process of comparison may also contribute to policy borrowing or adaptation across the boundaries of nation-states, leading to 'universalizing tendencies in educational reform'.[60]

There is another way, however, of thinking about the genesis of universalizing tendencies, hinted at in this comment by Hirsch in reference to the 'strengthened international dimension' to the knowledge-base needed for policymaking. He suggests that

> Whereas policymakers in the past may have drawn from international experience sporadically, in future they may have to do so more as a matter of routine. This development raises the question of how to strengthen regular channels for disseminating all forms of educational knowledge across international frontiers. The role of 'Institutional International Mediators' of knowledge like CERI [the Centre for Educational Research and Innovation within the OECD] itself becomes interesting to evaluate in this context.[61]

Conceptualizing international organizations as 'international mediators of knowledge' suggests a different relation among the national, the international, and the global, illustrated too in the OECD's influential work on comparative educational indicators, published annually in the best-selling *Education at a Glance* series.[62] While at one level the indicators project is about comparison of national education systems, at another, normative level, it brings into play what could be called a global politics of comparison that has to do with supranational forms of agenda-setting. We do not wish to elaborate on the indicators example now, but certainly in terms of the study presented here, it could be argued that convergence around the vocational education and training agenda is explained, not simply as a result of policy-borrowing in the face of common problems, but rather by the emergence of new normative spheres of policymaking themselves a by-product of globalization.[63] We would argue, for example, that in its thematic reviews such as the one on the transition from education to work and further education, the OECD is acting as an international mediator of knowledge – an independent policy actor – rather than, simply, a comparative forum.

In this context, Kogan's evaluation in 1979 of the OECD's reviews of national education systems is apposite. In his report, Kogan noted that the idea had surfaced of conducting thematic examinations over more than one country in a way that differed from the normal 'exchange of views' on themes of common interest. The proposal for thematic reviews, he observed, 'invites the OECD to select sharp and focussed issues arising from major current policy matters that countries in common need to settle rather than simply to discuss'. This idea he firmly rejected: 'First, it will reduce the national motivation. There can be a healthy narcissism in the examination approach. Secondly, it might produce facile comparison.' [64] In Kogan's view, educational reviews should 'continue to be rooted firmly in the experiences and problems of the country examined. National histories and educational policies should not be blended into generalized metahistory'.[65] By contrast, he argued, focusing on country particularities 'would put the OECD in a strong position to give leadership to the development of policy studies that are reflexive, because empathetic to perceived needs, and not derived from the rhetoric of externally imposed change, or from the narrow imperatives of economic analysis'.[66]

Nevertheless, the OECD did move to establish thematic reviews in the 1990s – in other words to 'select sharp and focused issues...that countries *in common* need to settle' (our emphasis); put another way, its role as a policy actor, rather than simply a forum for discussion, was enhanced. Of course, thematic reviews constitute only one element of the Organization's work, but similar processes operate, we would argue, in its increasingly influential work on educational indicators.[67] The key issue here is the strengthening of the OECD's normative role in policy-making and, more broadly, of the significance of the policy stances of international organizations in the framing of national policies. At this point, we come to the 'values' side of the policy equation.

The rhetoric of human capital investment, skills formation, and lifelong learning has become so pervasive that it could be seen as constituting a global discourse, shaping the parameters of policymaking in most countries and among organizations as ideologically disparate as UNESCO, the OECD, and the World Bank.[68] These ideas circulate via what could be viewed as emergent global policy communities constituted by an overlapping membership of senior public servants, policy-makers, and advisers – part of the group referred to by Lesley Sklair as 'globalizing bureaucrats' who are 'active in powerful international organizations, notably the World Bank, IMF, and the OECD, and they also work politically through what have been termed 'corporatist' agencies that combine representatives of the state, business and labour'.[69] Sklair argues that the culture of this group, and the ideology it promotes, is a mixture of neoliberalism and global nationalism – 'the view that the best interests of the country lie in its rapid integration with the global capitalist system while maintaining its national identity'.[70] Viewed in this way, OECD policy agendas, and the very processes of comparison on which much of its reputation stands, may be seen as serving to establish a universal (Western) norm against which the policy values of individual countries are, to use Roland Robertson's term, relativized.[71] This was the stance adopted by senior UNESCO personnel we interviewed, who commented critically on the tendency for OECD norms to become filtered into developing countries via the World Bank, and the OECD's destructive – to developing nations – propagation of globalization ideology.

However, the formation of global policy discourses does not imply, first, that policy necessarily becomes homogenized. Globalization theorists argue that globalization exerts simultaneous impulses for convergence and fragmentation, for universalism and localism. Certainly in the Australian case study presented here, it can be seen that while national and global discourses became increasingly intertwined, distinctly Australian policy stances around vocational education and training continued to exist alongside, while also becoming enfolded into, the global policy paradigm of human resource development. This relates to the earlier point about the continuing strategic space for national policy development.

Second, given the inherently contested nature of policymaking, even hegemonic global policy discourses may be challenged. With respect to vocational education and training policy, the mantras of market liberalism and human capital investment are certainly powerful. But a growing body of critical research and literature casts doubt on some of the assumptions underpinning that policy paradigm. David Ashton and Francis Green, for example, suggest that links between training and profitability or economic growth 'are still largely in the realm of theoretical belief or just plain hope'.[72] Similarly, on the basis of a review of some of the research evidence, Marginson suggests that the 'popular narrative of investment in education' is one of the 'great modern myths, transcending the need for empirical verification'.[73] Further, the socially destructive fallout of economic globalization is beginning to generate a new politics around discourses of social inclusion and exclusion aimed at confronting what Sophie Bessis refers to as 'the dictatorship of the economy' and 'the reign of the *pensée unique* – a single acceptable way of viewing things – in the area of economics'.[74] Bessis's policy paper summarizes the outcomes of an international symposium hosted by UNESCO, the World Health Organization, the Commission of the European Union, and several research institutes – an indication of the heterogeneity of emergent global policy communities giving effect to challenges to policy orthodoxy. The popularization of so-called Third Way politics may represent another kind of challenge, despite criticisms that in many respects the Third Way (particularly Tony Blair's version) represents little more than face-lifted neoliberalism.

The emergence of such counterhegemonic discourses points to the possibilities for a different framing for educational policy goals, one that focuses more centrally on building social as well as economic capital – the twin rationales, as noted earlier, underpinning vocational education and training policy. Whether it is possible to marry the two impulses is of course arguable. But to conclude by broadening this discussion beyond the specifics of vocational education and training policy, the point here is that new discursive struggles are emerging within and across national and global policy communities, giving some hope as to what can be achieved at national and sub-national levels. As indicated, our belief is that the nation-state remains a prime site of policymaking. Relevant then is the issue of what kind of nation-state we are arguing for. Not all nations deliver equally. There are differences, for example, between market liberal, liberal democratic, and social democratic states; certainly we would not support the strident calls for various forms of state chauvinism. But those calls come largely from the losers of globalization and they have helped to propel, within national arenas, new policy framings. Thus we would like to think that there is the possibility of a politics of policymaking that recognizes the force of global change while challenging the ideological determinism of globalization rhetoric. Ironically, such a project aimed, at one level, at the assertion of a national interest, is increasingly likely to involve a politics transcending national borders.

Notes

1 A research project funded by the Australian Research Council, 'Globalization and Education Policy: An Exploration of the Role of the OECD in Shaping Australian Education (1984-present)', was conducted by Miriam Henry, Bob Lingard, Fazal Rizvi, and Sandra Taylor over the period 1995–98. As part of the project, interviews were carried out with bureaucrats, policy analysts, and consultants, past and present, from the OECD and relevant Australian commonwealth and state departments, and with members of other international organizations. Interview material cited in this essay is taken from notes or transcripts of those interviews. The outcomes of that research are reported in Miriam Henry, Bob Lingard, Fazal Rizvi, and Sandra Taylor (2001) *The OECD, Globalization and Policy Making in Education* (Oxford: Elsevier Science).

2 Roger Dale (1999) 'Specifying Globalization Effects on National Policy: A Focus on the Mechanisms', *Journal of Education Policy*, 14(1): 1–18.

3 OECD Brochure outlining the structure and functions of the OECD (Paris: OECD, undated, circa 1997), p. 6.

4 Ibid, 10.

5 Margaret Vickers (1996) ' "Cross-national Exchange, the OECD and Australian Education: Education at the Chateau de la Muette", Review of G. S. Papadopoulos, *Education 1960–90: The OECD Perspective'*, *Oxford Review of Education* 22 (1): 91–96 and OECD Brochure Outlining the Structure and Functions of the Organization (Paris: OECD, undated circa 1997), p. 4.

6   George Papadopoulos, *Education 1960–1990: The OECD Perspective* (Paris: OECD), p. 13. Papadopoulos was deputy director for education within the OECD until his retirement in 1990.

7   Connie McNeely and Y. K. Cha (1994) 'Worldwide Educational Convergence through International Organizations: Avenues for Research', *Education Policy Analysis Archives*, 2(4).

8   Clive Archer (1994) *Organizing Europe: The Institutions of Integration* 2nd ed. (London: Edward Arnold), pp. 9–12.

9   Interview transcript #45 (bureaucrat, 1996).

10   Ibid.

11   OECD, *Australia (1977): Transition from School to Work or Further Study* (Paris: OECD), p. 85.

12   Commonwealth Department of Education Report of the Working Party on the Transition from Secondary Education to Employment (1976) (Canberra: AGPS), pp. 91, 118.

13   OECD, *Australia*, pp. 5–6.

14   Bruce Williams (1979) *Education, Training and Employment, Report of the Committee of Inquiry into Education and Training* (Canberra: AGPS).

15   Vickers, 'Cross-national Exchange.'

16   Department of Education and Youth Affairs (1983) *Youth Policies, Programs, and Issues* (Canberra: AGPS), p. xxxii.

17   Ibid., 25.

18   OECD (1986) *Youth and Work in Australia* (Paris: OECD).

19   Vickers, 'Cross-national Exchange', p. 41.

20   Chairman's address, (1989) *Education and the Economy in a Changing Society* (Paris: OECD), p. 10.

21   See for example, *Education in Modern Society* (1985) (Paris: OECD), *Structural Adjustment and Economic Performance* (1987) (Paris: OECD) and OECD, *Education and the Economy in a Changing Society*.

22   Interview notes #65 (bureaucrat, 1996).

23   Interview notes #44 (bureaucrat, 1996) and Interview notes #31 (consultant, 1996).

24   Interview notes #35 (consultant, 1996).

25   Vickers, 'Cross-national Exchange'.

26   Interview notes #43 (consultant, 1996).

27   OECD, *Education and the Economy in a Changing Society*, p. 18.

28   Vickers, 'Cross-national Exchange', p. 43.

29   For example, Australian Education Council Review Committee, (1991) *Young People's Participation in Post-Compulsory Education and Training* (Canberra: AGPS); Australian Education Council/Ministers of Vocational Education, Employment, and Training *Putting General Education to Work. The Key Competencies Report* Canberra, (1992) AGPS and Employment And Skills Formation Council, National Board Of Employment, Education, And Training (1992) *Australian Vocational Certificate Training System* (Canberra: AGPS).

30   Sandra Taylor and Miriam Henry (1994) 'Equity and the New Post-compulsory Education and Training Policies in Australia: A Progressive or Regressive Agenda?' *Journal of Education Policy*, 9(2): 105–27.

31   Claude Pair, 'Synthesis of Country Reports', in OECD, *Pathways and Participation in Vocational And Technical Education and Training* (Paris: OECD), p. 23.

32   David Raffe (1998) 'Does Learning Begin at Home? The Use of "Home International" Comparisons in UK Policymaking', *Journal of Education Policy*, 13(5), p. 376–7.

33   Miriam Henry and Sandra Taylor (1995) 'Equity and the AVC pilots in Queensland: A Study in Policy Refraction', *Australian Educational Researcher*, 22: 85–106; and Sandra Taylor and Miriam Henry (1996), 'Reframing Equity in the Training Reform Agenda: Implications for Social Change', *Australian Vocational Education Review*, 3(2): 46–55.

34   OECD (1996) *Lifelong Learning For All* (Paris: OECD).

35   One of the major functions of the OECD is its reviews of national education systems and policies. In 1995, to supplement these traditional reviews, thematic reviews were introduced 'to give a horizontal rather than a vertical view' of key policy issues across countries or units within countries (Interview notes #2, OECD secretariat, 1995). The first thematic review was on higher education, the second on vocational education and training.

36 Papadopoulos, *Education 1960–90*, p. 148.
37 Maurice Kogan (1979) *Education Policies in Perspective: An Appraisal* (Paris: OECD).
38 Manfred Bienefeld (1996) 'Is a Strong National Economy a Utopian Goal at the End of the Twentieth Century?' in Robert Boyer and Daniel Drache (eds), *States Against Markets: The Limits of Globalization* (London: Routledge, 1999), p. 429.
39 Andy Green (1999) 'Education and Globalization in Europe and East Asia: Convergent and Divergent Trends', *Journal of Education Policy*, 14(1): 55–72.
40 OECD (1992) *High-Quality Education and Training For All* (Paris: OECD), p. 14.
41 World Bank (1991) *Vocational and Technical Education and Training: A World Bank Policy Paper* (Washington: World Bank), p. 7.
42 UNESCO (1994) *Policy Paper for Change and Development in Higher Education* (Paris: UNESCO), p. 24.
43 Interview transcript # 56 (OECD secretariat, 1995).
44 In 1994, Lifelong Education for All became a major term of reference for the UNESCO Mid-term Strategy for the period 1996–2001; in 1996 the OECD Ministerial conference on education adopted 'Making Lifelong Learning a Reality for All' as the theme of its new mandate 1997–2001; and in 1995 the European Parliament declared 1996 the 'European Year for Lifelong Learning'.
45 Interview transcript # 17 (OECD secretariat, 1997).
46 See for example OECD *Lifelong Learning For All*, pp. 15–19 and UNESCO (1996) *Medium-Term Strategy 1996–2001* (Paris: UNESCO), pp. 17–19.
47 OECD, *Lifelong Learning For All*, pp. 15, 19.
48 John Prunty (1984) *A Critical Reformulation of Educational Policy Analysis* (Geelong: Deakin University Press).
49 For example, David Held, 'Democracy and the Global System', in *Political Theory Today*, ed. David (Cambridge: Polity, 1995), pp. 207–9 and Malcolm Waters, *Globalization* (London: Routledge).
50 Bob Deacon with Michele Hulse and Paul Stubbs (1997) *Global Social Policy: International Organizations and the Future of Welfare* (London: Sage Publications), p. 6.
51 Ibid., 10.
52 Ibid., 201.
53 Ibid., 6.
54 This position is argued more cogently in Henry *et al.*, 'Globalization and Education Policy', chap. 8. The case study presented in this article focuses on the national/global interface.
55 Paul Hirst and Graham Thompson (1999) *Globalization in Question* (Cambridge: Polity Press), p. 183.
56 Ibid., 2.
57 Simon Marginson (1999) 'After Globalization: Emerging Politics of Education', *Journal of Education Policy*, 14(1): 19–32.
58 Frances Fowler, 'The International Arena: The Global Village', *Journal of Education Policy*, 9(5/6): 94.
59 Papadopoulos, *Education 1960–90*, p. 13.
60 David Halpin (1994) 'Practice and Prospects in Education Policy Research', in David Halpin and Barry Troyner (eds), *Researching Education Policy: Ethical and Methodological Issues* (London: Falmer), p. 204.
61 David Hirsch (1996) 'Report of the Maastricht Conference', in OECD, *Knowledge Bases for Education Policies* (Paris: OECD), p. 31.
62 OECD (1997) *Education at a Glance: OECD Indicators* (Paris: OECD, Centre for Educational Research and Innovation).
63 Guy Neave (1991) 'On Programmes, Universities, and Jacobins: Or, 1992 Vision and Reality for European Higher Education', *Higher Education Policy*, 4(4): 37–41 develops a similar argument with respect to the European Union's remit over higher education policy.
64 Kogan, *Education Policies in Perspective*, p. 71.
65 Ibid., 75.
66 Ibid.
67 This point is elaborated in Henry *et al.*, 'Globalization and Education Policy', chap. 5.

68 David Atchoarena, (ed.) (1994), *Policy and Planning for Vocation Education and Training: Report of a Subregional Training Workshop* (Paris: IIEP/UNESCO); OECD (1994) *Vocational Education and Training for Youth: Towards Coherent Policy and Practice* (Paris: OECD); and World Bank (1994) *Higher Education: The Lessons of Experience* (Washington: International Bank for Reconstruction and Development/ World Bank).
69 Lesley Sklair (1996) 'Conceptualizing and Researching the Transnational Capitalist Class in Australia', *Australian and New Zealand Journal of Sociology*, 32(2): 5.
70 Ibid.
71 Quoted in Waters, *Globalization*, pp. 3–4.
72 David Ashton and Francis Green (1996) *Education, Training and the Global Economy* (Cheltenham: Edward Elgar), p. 3.
73 Simon Marginson (1997) *Markets in Education* (Sydney: Allen and Unwin), pp. 117–18.
74 Sophie Bessis (1995) *From Social Exclusion to Social Cohesion: A Policy Agenda*, Management of Social Transformations Policy Papers, no. 2 (Paris: UNESCO), pp. 26, 13.

CHAPTER 8

SWEDISH, EUROPEAN, GLOBAL
The transformation of the Swedish welfare state
Lisbeth Lundahl

Coulby, D. and E. Zambeta (2005) (Eds) *World Yearbook of Education 2005: Globalization and nationalism in education* (London: Routledge Falmer) pp. 147–64

Introduction

For the better part of the twentieth century, Sweden has successfully combined capitalism and a strong social democratic welfare state. Swedish trade politics have traditionally been open and anti-protectionist. Sweden has been pragmatic and efficient in importing and making use of technical innovations and new cultural trends, not least from the USA. Swedes, however, have been much more wary of international influences which could challenge the existing welfare-state model. This may explain the hesitancy towards the project of the European Union. When Sweden entered the EU in 1995, the nation was clearly divided and in a referendum in September 2003 a majority of the Swedes voted against entering the European Monetary Union.

The aim of this chapter is to analyse how Swedish education politics respond to and act towards globalization and Europeanization in the late twentieth and early twenty-first centuries. Several researchers have pointed to the need for scientifically investigating how globalization of education is realized in the specific national and local contexts (Ball 1998; Henry *et al.* 2001; Jones 1998; Lingard and Rizvi 1998). Hence Henry *et al.* (2001) conclude:

> In education, we have witnessed the emergence of global flows of educational ideas around issues of educational governance and purposes. But how these ideas become embedded within the policy agendas of nation states is neither well researched nor well described.
>
> (p. 3)

Sweden is regarded as an example of a capitalist and social democratic welfare state that has undergone a rapid and radical transformation during the last three decades. The change follows a pattern which is similar to that in many other nations, but its meaning and concretization have to be understood in relation to the specific nature of Swedish modern history and politics. A central question is thus how Sweden opens and/or closes itself to new spaces and ideas of education policy and governance – the European and global ones.

Globalization may primarily be referred to as a process through which national economies become increasingly open to supranational influence. However, globalization is also to a great extent a political and ideological phenomenon (Mishra 1999). Both increased global competition and mobility of capital, and the far-reaching impact of neo-liberal ideology and market thinking have thus framed and transformed politics at the national and local levels in the last three decades (Ben-Elia 1996; Bogason 1996; Mishra 1999). Globalization is not a completely new phenomenon emerging in the twentieth and early twenty-first centuries. Its speed, range and impact, however, have reached new levels during this period. Europeanization may be understood both as the direct impact of EU policies and, more broadly, as the impact of European integration on national education policies and debate (Ollikainen 1999). In practice, however, it is often difficult to distinguish between effects of such policies and a more general impact of structural factors that enforce or stimulate similar developments in different countries, more or less regardless of European integration policies.

In the following section, the Swedish post-war model of welfare and economic policy is briefly outlined, in order to understand the particular historical and cultural context of educational change in Sweden. The main part of the chapter is devoted to an analysis and discussion of how global and European influences have changed and been translated into the Swedish political context.

Combined aspirations for economic growth and social welfare

The Swedish model (1930s–70s)

The Swedish labour movement has been uniquely powerful from an international perspective. The Social Democratic party has been in office since 1932 except for two periods, 1976–82 and 1991–4. Consequently, Sweden has been regarded as one of the primary examples of the social democratic, welfare-state regimes, as contrasted to the liberal welfare states (e.g. the USA, the UK and Australia), and conservative regimes (e.g. France, Austria, Italy and Germany). Social Democratic welfare regimes are characterized by universalism: the party's policies are not only targeting the most needy, but include the whole population through high economic transfers and social insurance (Esping-Andersen 1996). However, it would be misleading to emphasize only the strength of the Swedish labour movement in an analysis of the Swedish case; rather the strength and organized relations between economic and political actors more generally must be recognized.

In the 1930s, after a long period of class-based unrest and conflicts, Sweden entered an era of organized relations between capital and politics. The influential Main Agreement in 1938 between the Swedish Employers' Confederation and the Swedish Confederation of Trade Unions meant a clear division of labour in the economic sphere between the parties of the labour market and the state. The trade union movement could contribute to moderate wage demands and industrial peace because of the worker-friendly welfare policies of the Social Democratic government. The employers accepted such welfare policies in exchange for industrial peace and the absence of State interventions in the economy (Fulcher 1991; Heclo and Madsen 1987; Weir and Scocpol 1985). Supported by the trade unions, Swedish industry underwent intensive structural rationalization and transformation in the following decades, moving from production based on raw materials to high-technology production. The Social Democratic welfare policies helped reduce the negative effects of this restructuring. Both 'the Swedish model' of cooperation and division of labour between the State and social partners, and the fact that Swedish infrastructure and industry were not destroyed during the Second World War contributed to the steady economic growth and rise of living standards in Sweden in the post-war period (1945–70).

A combination of growth and welfare aspirations has been a crucial feature of Swedish post-war labour policies. In Esping-Andersen's words:

> The Swedish labour movement has had the unique capability to create a synthesis of equality and gain strivings, and of welfare and efficiency, which has been favourable to all parties. Every phase of the welfare state development has been equally characterised by its attitude to the problems of efficiency and those of power.
>
> (Esping-Andersen 1994, 77; my translation)

This thinking is well illustrated by the Social Democratic education ideology, which, albeit not uncontested, dominated Swedish education policy for a considerable part of the post-war period (Lundahl 1990). Good elementary education and equal access to secondary and higher education were regarded both as a matter of social justice, and as an important precondition for economic growth and prosperity, necessary for further welfare reforms. The gradual introduction of nine-year comprehensive education in the 1950s, confirmed by a final Parliament decision in 1962, built on such motives. The subsequent reforms of upper secondary education in the 1960s and higher and adult education in the 1970s rested on similar ideas for promoting social equality as well as economic growth. The resulting educational system had several distinctive features from an international perspective. The idea of comprehensive education was thus realized at an early stage. Even in the early 1970s, upper-secondary education included more than three-quarters of all 16–19-year-olds. For many years, Swedish vocational education was regarded as a rather extreme example of school-based vocational education and training (VET) (Jallade 1989). The reforms of adult education in the early 1970s were far-reaching in international comparison. Also, the proportion of GDP invested in education has been and still is high (Ministry of Education 2004).

The Swedish model restructured or dismantled? (1970s)

For the better part of the 1970s, economic and political instability and growing conflicts dominated the political agenda. The Social Democratic initiatives in the field of labour legislation in the first half of the 1970s were seen as harmful by industry and as a break from the traditional division of responsibilities between the State and the parties of the labour market. Similar to its sister organization in Western Germany, the Swedish Employers' Confederation (Svenska Arbetsgivareföreningen, SAF) launched an offensive to recapture the initiative of problem formulation and restore public confidence in enterprise and the market. The first non-socialist government since the 1930s came to power in 1976. Back in office in 1982, the right wing of the Social Democrats influenced governmental policies to a large extent. Now the efforts of the SAF and the Conservative party to launch 'the market project' and their critique of the welfare state were increasingly successful; ideas of deregulation and cuts in the public sector were not only voiced from the right, but were also supported by powerful actors within the Social Democratic administration. Swedish export corporations, central to the Swedish economy, increasingly invested abroad, and threatened to leave the country if the high level of taxation was not lowered. As a result, several radical tax reforms were decided in the 1980s and 1990s, reducing state taxation. During the deep recession at the beginning of the 1990s, unemployment rose from under 2 per cent to almost 10 per cent in a short time, and has remained high since then. Mishra (1999) argues that the beginning of chronic high employment and changes in the structure of taxation are the most obvious results of globalization of the Swedish welfare state. At the same time, the welfare state has not been rolled back to any substantial degree. Mishra correctly concludes:

> That this has happened only to a limited extent is due to a number of factors, chiefly political in nature. The fragmentation of the political Right, continuing support for social programmes in the country and a large and well-organized union movement are some of these. Besides, a time factor is also involved.
> (Mishra 1999, 79)

In the early 2000s, Sweden is certainly a part of economic globalization. Swedish multinational companies thus account for 25 per cent of employment in Sweden, 50 per cent of its exports and 90 per cent of Swedish industrial R&D investments. In relation to its size, Sweden was the world's largest foreign investor in the 1990s. In the early 1990s, this development was hampered for a time, but gained impetus again and took new forms. For example, nearly 50 of the offices of the biggest multinational companies moved out of Sweden between 1997 and 2000. International investments and acquisitions of Swedish companies accelerated, and in 1999 such investments accounted for 25 per cent of Swedish GDP (Tson Söderström 2001). In the same period, foreign ownership of shares in Swedish corporations quoted in the Swedish market place increased considerably, and amounted to over 40 per cent in 2000. After that, there has been some decline, but still one-third of the shares had foreign holders in 2003 (Statistics Sweden 2004).

It may seem as if Sweden no longer serves as a good example of the Social Democratic welfare state, and has moved in the direction of a liberal welfare regime. More generally this would fit well with a hypothesis of welfare regime convergence (Esping-Andersen 1996; Kautto *et al.* 2001). In their study of social and gender policies of the Nordic countries, Kautto *et al.* (2001), however, conclude that a distinct 'Nordic model' in welfare or living conditions still seems to exist. In their study of welfare policies in the EU countries, Vogel *et al.* (2003) come to similar conclusions.

Linking education more closely with the economy: education politics in the 1970s and early 2000s

As was shown above, Swedish education has generally been supposed to serve economic as well as social purposes, and this is also true of the last decades. However, economy and market ideas have pervaded education to an extent unthinkable 30 years ago. In Sweden, as in numerous other countries, efficiency and reduction of State costs, quasi-markets, accountability, comparability and increased local autonomy have been keywords of education government and reform. Education is modelled on the market and the enterprise (Ball 1998; Carter and O'Neill 1995; Daun 2002; Whitty *et al.* 1998). Even in Sweden, neo-liberalism, performativity and new managerialism have been important underlying ideas of this change (Ball 1998).

First steps of decentralization and deregulation (1975–90)

The Swedish education reforms in the 1950s and 1960s were accompanied by detailed State steering, which was regarded as essential to realize the overriding aim of equality of education. Schools and teaching were regulated and controlled through national curricula and syllabi, by specially destined State subsidies and by a vast number of other regulations concerning resources, organization, staff and daily work. In the 1970s, the public sector was repeatedly criticized from different directions, and education was often chosen as an important example of what had gone wrong with the Swedish welfare system. While people of the left argued that education did not reach its equality goals, the right maintained that Swedish education was expensive, inefficient and rigid, and did not provide young people with any alternatives. Local actors' lack of influence over education was a common theme. The Conservative party (*Moderaterna*), the Swedish Employers' Confederation, and other industrial and trade organizations, now putting education high on their agenda, played an important role in introducing a new thinking and vocabulary of education: alternatives and competition, individual choice and responsibility, competence and excellence (Lundahl 1990, 1997). During the latter half of the 1970s and in the 1980s, several steps were taken towards decentralization and increased local political control, but still the principle of a relatively strong State government was maintained in order to protect equality of education. In 1989 the employment responsibilities for school personnel were transferred from the State to the municipalities. In 1990 a new allocation system of state funding was introduced, putting an end to detailed economic steering from the state. But, on the whole, central State governance remained strong. The changes in the 1970s and 1980s did not lack explicit economic motives, and the need to reform education in order to improve Sweden's international competitiveness was sometimes expressed. But international economic comparisons were hardly put forward as a main argument; rather the stress was on the failings of the old welfare system and the educational needs of modern Sweden (Lundahl 2002a).

The 1990s: neo-liberal turn?

In September 1991, the second non-socialist government came into office since the 1930s, and in 1991–4 championed a successful neo-liberal policy, explicitly described as a part of a global system shift, 'Because it is about a genuinely radical change. A system shift more extensive than many participants of the Swedish debate seem to be aware of' (speech by Conservative Prime Minister Carl Bildt, 13 October 1993). Choice and market reforms were carried out and vouchers and generous conditions for establishing independent schools were introduced by the Conservative Minister of Education. A new funding system meant that specified subsidies from the State to the municipalities were replaced by lump sums for all responsibilities: education, care of old people and refuse collection. By now the State had relinquished practically all its earlier economic steering tools in education, and a quasi-market system had been introduced. Within a few years, Sweden went from having one of the most centralized to one of the most decentralized education systems in the Western world (OECD 2001). When the Social Democrats returned in 1994, their government politics focused on the reduction of an enormous State budget deficit, rather than on proactive welfare reforms, and few efforts were made to alter the non-socialist decisions previously taken.

However, the Swedish story is not an entirely neo-liberal one. New forms of state control over education were introduced in the 1990s, such as national tests, a new grading system and quality audits. As in other countries, proactive State regulation was replaced by retroactive surveillance (Daun 2002). Also, some education reforms of the 1990s had an explicitly inclusive character. In spring 1991, the Parliament decided to reorganize upper-secondary education into 16 national three-year programmes with a common curriculum in certain core subjects. The vocational programmes were prolonged by a third year, and their academic contents were strengthened. The reform, opposed by the non-socialist parties, was motivated by both welfare and economic/labour market factors, and thus followed a traditional Social Democratic reform formula. It was supposed to increase individual flexibility and employability as well as individual security by reducing the divisions within upper-secondary education and ensuring that all national and special programmes did qualify for higher studies (Lundahl 1998). Also, a large adult education reform ('the Rise of Knowledge') was implemented to raise the education level of people with limited schooling, and to reduce unemployment. Thus, even in the 1990s, Swedish education policy included comprehensive measures following the more traditional welfare model, as well as clearly neo-liberal reforms and decisions that weakened State governance, while emphasizing responsibility and self-regulation at local and individual level (Lundahl 2002a).

The situation at the turn of the century

In the late 1990s, the effects of the policy of economic austerity in schools were clearly visible and became important in shaping the political agenda. In many respects, social inequalities and segregation had increased in Sweden in the 1990s. Young people, immigrants, poorly educated people and single parents were hit hard by unemployment and a deterioration in living standards. A growing number of adolescents left compulsory and upper-secondary school without complete grades. Also, differences in school achievements related to gender and to social, geographical and ethnic backgrounds tended to grow. When state finances improved at the end of the 1990s and allowed for social reforms once more, special funding was directed to the municipalities in order to replenish education, health care and social care. Central economic steering was thus reintroduced to some extent. At the same time, further steps were taken towards decentralization and management by objectives. A five-year period of trials, meaning the abolition of the national timetables in compulsory schooling in one-third of the municipalities, started in 2000. Quality audits and school inspections were introduced as means of governance and control (Lundahl 2002a).

Finally, curricular reforms and State-supported school development reflect the increased needs of communication and information across nations during the last decades. Being a small country, language education has always had a prominent place in Swedish compulsory and upper-secondary education. Swedish children are now taught English from primary level through upper-secondary education, in academic as well as vocational programmes. A majority of pupils study a second foreign language in compulsory education, mostly German, French or Spanish. In the 1990s, considerable political efforts were made to improve the ICT infrastructure and competence in schools. In 1999–2000 1.7 billion Swedish crowns (approximately 170 million Euros) was invested in the largest of these projects (the IT in schools project), including competence development of 60,000 teachers (Ministry of Education 2004).

The world reflected in contemporary Swedish education politics

To what extent and how international influence and demands are reflected in contemporary Swedish education politics will now be discussed, in terms of the following aspects:

- to what extent recent Swedish education politics follow a neo-liberal, 'global' model;
- to what extent educational change *is presented and discussed* in terms of globalization/Europeanization or not;
- if international influence is presented as self-evident and inevitable;
- if international policies and/or policies of other countries are regarded as important as models for national action or not;
- to what extent the international dimension of education is a source of conflict and argument.

Global and neo-liberal – or not?

As was discussed on pp. 121–2, the links between the economy and Swedish education have been strengthened during the last decades. This has been accomplished in at least three ways:

- increased importance is attached to education as infrastructural investment, supporting economic growth;
- 'the market' and 'enterprise' serve as models for education and schools;
- education is privatized or marketed.

Ball (1998) distinguishes two related policy agendas: one aiming at closer connections between education and national economy, while the other subordinates education under a market or business logic and redefines it from a public to a competitive private good. In the first case, the grip of the State over education is still strong, but, in the second case, this grip is loosening.

Education as a factor of economic growth

As was pointed out earlier, Swedish education politics has traditionally been characterized by both motives of growth and democracy and social welfare and justice. However, the balance between them has shifted from time to time, and, in particular, the non-socialist government of 1991–4 stressed human capital and competition strongly (p. 122). The reforms of pre-school, compulsory and upper-secondary education do not represent any major breaks with the earlier thinking. For example, the upper-secondary education reforms of both 1991 and 2004 have aimed at providing academic and vocational education within rather few pro-grammes, giving broad knowledge and skills, and allowing for flexibility. This is supposed to be mutually beneficial to working life and the individual. Altogether, the State holds an indisputable central position when it comes to human capital investment.

Research and higher education politics have been increasingly pervaded by ideas of economic utility; such education and research are essential if Sweden is to assert itself internationally, and they also contribute to local and regional development. Today, universities cooperate with industry, municipalities and counties to a much higher extent than was the case 10 or 20 years ago. International exchange and competition have been central features of higher education and research for a long time, but such aspects have gradually become stronger, Sweden's membership of the EU being one, but not the sole, contributing factor.

The market and business serve as models

Adopting market and business models perhaps constitutes the most striking change of education during the last decades. As was previously pointed out, Swedish compulsory schools have become the most autonomous among the OECD countries in a short period of time. Efficiency and quality are supposed to be enhanced by local actors, who will use resources, creativity and knowledge better if they are not regulated in detail by the state. Schools should act as small enterprises, competing for pupils by good results and interesting profiles. But it should be remembered that a democratic motive has been important when schools were given more autonomy. Teachers, pupils and parents obtaining more influence over school work has been and remains a crucial idea behind decentralization and deregulation of education at the local level. Local bargaining and individual wage-setting was introduced in the 1990s and led to increased competition over and between teachers. Benchmarking has become increasingly influential as average grades and test scores of schools and municipalities are made public and are compared in the media. No general system directly linking school budgets to such results and comparisons has, however, been established. In conclusion, there are many examples of how education governance and thinking about schools has changed. The idea of 'the strong society' has largely been replaced by a market and business model. But this thinking still takes place within a system where the State decides on national objectives and controls results and quality of education, and where the local political level, the municipality, has a decisive power over resources and substantial possibilities to influence education in other respects.

Education as a part of the market

The non-socialist government (1991–4) launched several successful offensives to break the State monopoly over education and put education in a market situation. Earlier, practically all schools were publicly run; now generous rules for establishing so-called independent schools were introduced, and vouchers and possibilities of inviting tenders in certain subjects were introduced. Independent schools may be run by a number of actors: parents, teachers, private companies, religious and other organizations. Even though the number of independent schools rapidly multiplied in the 1990s and continues to increase, they only account for about 5 per cent of all primary and secondary schools. Independent schools are tax funded and essentially have to follow the national curriculum guide. This is nothing unique to Sweden; almost no recognized private schools in Europe are run without some form of subsidy (Daun 2002; Fredriksson 2003). For a long time, vocational education had been school-based and part of public upper-secondary and tertiary education. As opposed to most other countries, a vast majority of Swedish pre-schools are public. In principle, all compulsory education, school meals and school books included, is free of charge. Increasingly, however, supplementary services such as school cafeterias, cleaning and certain expert support are privatized, and a limited private sponsoring has also been introduced in some schools.

In conclusion, the major part of Swedish education still comprises 'pure public' services, and the share of 'free market' services is only marginal. But the trend goes clearly in the direction of increasing numbers of independent schools run by private companies and organizations, increasing shares of private supplementary services and a higher degree of cooperation between public education, industry and other parts of society.

The international perspective has been largely absent

By and large, Swedish education policy has tended to be treated as a Swedish matter. With the exception of higher education, the international perspective has been absent to a high degree, even after the entrance into the EU in 1995. For example, when interviewed about the most important changes of education governance in the last 10 to 15 years, leading Swedish education politicians and officials did not bring up global or European factors. When explicitly asked if international factors had been influential in the change of the 1980s and 1990s, some politicians and officials, however, argued that the OECD reports had had a certain impact.

A study of policy documents and education debates in the early 2000s leads to almost the same conclusion. Swedish education is still seldom explicitly analysed and discussed in relation to international conditions or actors. Some examples of the silences are given below. One important exception, however, is the recent interest from the Ministry of Education in the reform of higher education in accordance with the Bologna process, which received little attention in Swedish education politics and debate until 2004. This year, adjustments of the structure and grading system of higher education in accordance with the Bologna process were proposed in public reports from the official committee on postgraduate studies and the Ministry of Education (SOU 2004, 27). For the first time, the creation of a European Higher Education Area (Conference of Ministers 2003) was discussed more widely in Sweden.

Every second year since 1994, the Swedish government has presented a developmental plan for the pre-school, primary and secondary school system and for adult education. Even if the number of international references in the plans has increased, such passages are still marginal and mainly concern the position of Swedish schools in the OECD evaluations. In the developmental plan from May 2002, it is characteristically argued: 'Swedish education has accomplished a lot and is a (good) international example'. It is added, 'In spite of the fact that Swedish education asserts itself, the aim must be set higher' (Government Paper 2001/2, 188). Similar conclusions have been drawn by the Minister of Education elsewhere (Ministry of Education 2003; Östros 2003), but without further discussion of education in an international perspective. In its report, *Education in Europe: A Report on Education in Sweden and Common European Goals* (2004), the Ministry of Education, however, explicitly relates the state of Swedish education to the three strategic educational goals formulated by the Ministers of Education in the EU in 2001. Once again, the conclusion is mainly positive: 'Sweden has got a good educational system and good prerequisites. Nevertheless, hard and persistent efforts are required – in all member countries and among all actors in our country – to reach the goals put forward' (Ministry of Education 2004, 6).

The teacher education reform in 2000 and the preparations for a reform of upper-secondary education during the first years of the 2000s hardly referred to an international or EU dimension at all. When discussing Swedish upper-secondary education and VET more generally, the need to foster flexible and well-educated citizens to cope with rapid economic and technological development and changing working life has been stressed repeatedly, but as a rule without bringing up the global dimension of such processes. And in spite of VET being a central interest in youth and employment policies of the EU, explicit references have seldom been made in Sweden to European policies in this respect. The fact that career development and counselling have been put high on the agenda by OECD, the World Bank and the European Commission (Watts 2004; Watts and Sultana 2003) has hitherto received little attention by the Swedish authorities.

An inevitable change

The Swedish development of the 1980s and 1990s, with decentralization, deregulation, increased efficiency and market thinking as key elements, shows striking similarities with the so-called new orthodoxy of education politics in the USA, the UK, New Zealand and Australia (Ball 1998; Carter and O'Neill 1995). However, neither the international parallels nor common underlying mechanisms of educational change are pointed out and debated very often in the Swedish policy context. Instead, a rather anonymous, general image is recurrently given – that of a rapid transition from an industrial society to knowledge or information society, resulting in new demands on schools and education. The state neither can nor should regulate education in detail any longer (Lindblad *et al.* 2002; Lundahl 2002b). The range and possibilities of political action seem to be limited in this discourse. Politics tend to become reactive rather than proactive.

No explicit references to international models

Sweden has historically been fast to pick up new ideas and innovations from abroad. This is also the case for recent education politics. A broad range of neo-liberal and new managerial ideas and concepts have been imported in the last 20 years from the USA, the UK and New Zealand: enterprise, competition, choice and vouchers, school autonomy and school management, modern apprenticeship training, benchmarking, quality audits and control, excellence and individual responsibility. The list could be prolonged almost endlessly. In this respect, Sweden may be regarded a good example of policy borrowing. However, and this is the point, such borrowing is almost never explicit, and it is not used to legitimate policy decisions (Halpin and Troyna 1995). The most recent example is the gradual introduction of a national system of quality audit and control in Sweden, which has taken place with few references to its many international predecessors (Lundahl 2004).

Similar versus conflicting images

On the whole, the fast restructuring of Swedish education politics in the 1980s and 1990s created far less conflict and debate than might be expected. The changes of governance were formulated and elaborated both by socialist and non-socialist governments, but with somewhat different sets of arguments. Also, there have been no conflicting opinions regarding the crucial role of competence and knowledge if Sweden is going to assert itself in global economic competition. But this theme was brought up more frequently, and with more emphasis by the non-socialist government in 1991–4 than by its Social Democratic predecessors and successors.

The Bildt government thus coined a motto that Swedish education should become the best in Europe. In its analysis of future education, *Agenda 2000: Knowledge and Competence for the Next Century*, the Ministry of Education established that the Swedish economy and education had been overtaken by a number of OECD countries since 1970. Now strong measures had to be taken in order to turn Sweden into a first-order knowledge-based nation (Ds 1994, 35). Some years later, the former Conservative Minister of Education, Mr Unckel, developed these ideas in a book in which international perspectives and comparisons were at the forefront. He concluded:

> Make knowledge development a central task for Sweden...Formulate the aim that our country somewhat further on in the 2000s will be one of the world's foremost knowledge and cultural nations – and see to it that this aim is attained.
>
> (Unckel 1998, 167)

While the achievements of Swedish education in international comparisons are described rather positively in Social Democratic policy documents, OECD statistics are used to underpin non-socialist critiques against socialist economic and education policy, and to legitimate radical action.

Something borrowed and something new?
Some final remarks

The modern Swedish economy has always been highly dependent on international competition and exchange, and increasing economic globalization is a central feature of Sweden's economic development of the last decades. To a growing extent, education is regarded as a crucial factor in enhancing international competitiveness and growth. Also, the rapid educational restructuring that has taken place in Sweden in the last decades has followed similar paths to that in many other countries. I have concluded that Swedish education politics and debate often have been surprisingly silent about the international aspect. Next I will discuss this seeming paradox.

Brown and Lauder (1996) discuss education in the global economy in terms of neo-Fordist and post-Fordist routes to economic development. The first, clearly neo-liberal, route is characterized by the weakening of the power of the State and trade unions, and the celebration of privatization and competitive individualism. The post-Fordist alternative, where the State still has a crucial role in investing in strategic economic sectors, and providing the labour market with multi-skilled, highly qualified workers, comes closer to the Swedish case. In this latter sense there has not been a radical break with earlier Swedish education and economic policies. Ball (1998) distinguishes two related policy agendas: 'The first involves reaffirmation of the state functions of education as "public good", while the second subjects education to the disciplines of the market and the methods and values of business and redefines it as a competitive private good' (Ball 1998, 123). Even if the balance has shifted between the two agendas under Social Democratic and non-socialist rule, Swedish education politics has consequently sought to combine them, and in ways that are perceived as legitimate in the Swedish context. It is obvious that explicit policy borrowing (Halpin and Troyna 1995) has not been a favoured strategy; a whole range of concepts and ideas have been imported and reterritorialized, but without spelling it out. The conclusion of Steiner-Khamsi (2002) seems correct even in the Swedish case: 'It is important to point out that externalization functions as the last source of authority and tends to be activated once self-referentiality falls short of argumentation. In most instances, self-referentiality prevails and internal references are sufficient' (2002, 70). One may add: internal references seem to have been not only sufficient, but necessary, in order to convince Swedes that education reforms are legitimate. References to education policies of the Reagan, Thatcher or even Blair administrations would hardly have gained major popularity in Sweden, where a majority of the population supports the traditional welfare model (Svallfors 1999). This may also be a part of the explanation of the silence about global and European aspects of education and education politics.

However, the silence regarding EU policies and agreements needs some further analysis. Ollikainen (1999) discusses some reasons behind the success of EU programmes in Finland in the education policy field:

- A correspondence and lack of ideological conflicts between basic objectives of Finnish education policy and EU objectives. Most objectives of EU programmes have corresponded to national ones; others have been reinterpreted to match them.
- The practical conditions of EU programmes have fitted the needs of Finnish education policy well. At a time of reduced state funding of education, the EU programmes provided channels of funding.
- Finnish institutions have actively participated and succeeded well in the competition set up by the EU programmes...getting a fair amount of projects accepted became almost a matter of national pride.
- The EU programmes are perceived as bringing in something new, they...were regarded as filling an existing void in the field of educational cooperation.

In Sweden, there has been a greater reluctance or hesitation towards the EU than was the case in Finland. This may have affected the initial willingness to adopt EU policies and recommendations in the field of education too readily. In the field of education, decision-makers may furthermore, wrongly or rightly, have felt that Sweden already had reached some of the basic objectives put forward by the EU. For example, Sweden at a rather early stage had a high ratio of young people who had completed upper-secondary education and well-developed school-based VET. However, such relative advantages may disappear rapidly – and to a certain extent they already have. It is quite apparent that Sweden must relate itself more consciously and systematically to the global and European context, regardless to whether one wishes to be Swedish, European or global – or all of them.

References

Ball, S. (1998) 'Big Policies/Small World: An Introduction to International Perspectives in Education Policy', *Comparative Education*, 34: 119–30.

Ben-Elia, N. (ed.) (1996) *Strategic Changes and Organizational Reorientations in Local Government: A Cross-National Perspective* (London: Macmillan Press).

Bogason, P. (ed.) (1996) *New Modes of Local Political Organizing: Local Government Fragmentation in Scandinavia* (Commack, NY: Nova Sciences Publishers).

Brown, P. and Lauder, H. (1996) 'Education, Globalization, and Economic Development', *Journal of Education Policy*, 11: 1–24.

Carter, D. S. G. and O'Neill, M. H. (1995) *International Perspectives on Educational Reform and Policy Implementation* (London: The Falmer Press).

Conference of Ministers (19 September 2003) *Realising the European Higher Education Area*, Communiqué of the Conference of Ministers responsible for Higher Education in Berlin, Available at www.bologna-berlin2003.de/pdf/Communique1.pdf.

Daun, H. (ed.) (2002) *Educational Restructuring in the Context of Globalisation and National Policy* (London: RoutledgeFalmer).

Ds (1994) *Agenda 2000: Kunskap och kompetens för nästa århundrade (Agenda 2000: Knowledge and Competence for the Next Century)* (Stockholm: Ministry of Education (in Swedish)).

Esping-Andersen, G. (1994) 'Jämlikhet, effektivitet och makt (Equality, Efficiency and Power)', in P. Thullberg and K. Östberg (eds) *Den svenska modellen* (Lund: Studentlitteratur), pp. 75–105 (in Swedish).

Esping-Andersen, G. (1996) *The Three Worlds of Welfare Capitalism* (Cambridge: Polity Press).

Fredriksson, U. (17–20 September 2003) GATS, Education and Teacher Union Policies. Paper presented at the European Conference of Educational Research (Hamburg).

Fulcher, J. (1991) *Labour Movements, Employers and the State: Conflict and Cooperation in Britain and Sweden* (Oxford: Clarendon Press).

Government Paper (2001/2) *Utbildning för kunskap och jämlikhet: regeringens utvecklingsplan för kvalitetsarbetet i förskola, skola och vuxenutbildning (Education for Knowledge and Equality: Government Development Plan concerning Quality Work in Preschool, Primary, Secondary, and Adult Education)* (Stockholm: Ministry of Education (in Swedish)).

Halpin, D. and Troyna, B. (1995) 'The Politics of Education Policy Borrowing', *Comparative Education*, 31: 303–10.

Heclo, H. and Madsen, H. (1987) *Policy and Politics in Sweden: Principled Pragmatism* (Philadelphia, PA: Temple University Press).

Henry, M., Lingard, B., Rizvi, F. and Taylor, S. (2001) *The OECD, Globalisation and Education Policy* (Oxford: Pergamon/IAU Press).

Jallade, J.-P., (1989) 'Recent Trends in Vocational Education and Training: An Overview', *European Journal of Education*, 24 (2): 103–25.

Jones, P. W. (1998) 'Globalisation and Internationalism: Democratic Prospects for World Education', *Comparative Education*, 34 (2): 143–55.

Kautto, M., Fritzell, J., Hvinden, B., Kvist, J. and Uusitalo, H. (eds) (2001) *Nordic Welfare States in the European Context* (London: Routledge).

Lindblad, S., Lundahl, L., Lindgren, J. and Zackari, G. (2002) 'Educating for the New Sweden?', *Scandinavian Journal of Educational Research*, 46: 283–303.

Lingard, B. and Rizvi, F. (1998) 'Globalisation and the Fear of Homogenisation in Education', *Change: Transformations in Education*, 1: 62–71.

Lundahl, L. (1990) 'New Variations on Old Themes: The Swedish Conservative Party and the Battle over Comprehensive Education 1900–1985', *Journal of Education Policy*, 5: 157–66.

Lundahl, L. (1997) 'A Common Denominator? Swedish Employers, Trade Unions and Vocational Education in the Postwar Years', *International Journal of Training and Development*, 1: 91–102.

Lundahl, L. (1998) 'Still the Stepchild of Swedish Educational Politics? Vocational Education and Training in Sweden in the 1990s', *TNTEE Publications*, 1: 39–53. Available at http://tntee.umu.se/publications.

Lundahl, L. (2002a) 'From Centralisation to Decentralisation: Governance of Education in Sweden', *European Educational Research Journal*, 1 (4): 625–36.

Lundahl, L. (2002b) 'Sweden: Decentralization, Deregulation, Quasi-Markets – And Then What?', *Journal of Education Policy*, 17: 687–97.

Lundahl, L. (2004) 'Styrning med kvalitet (Governing With Quality)', in K. Holmlund (ed.) *Vad har kvalitet med skolan att göra? (What Has Quality Got to Do With Education?)*, (Lund: Studentlitteratur (in Swedish)).

Ministry of Education (2003) *Alla skolor ska vara bra skolor: regeringens kvalitets-program för skolan (All Schools Should Be Good Schools: The Government's School Development Program)* (Stockholm: Regeringskansliet (in Swedish)).

Ministry of Education (2004) *Utbildningen i Europa: en rapport om utbildningen i Sverige och de gemensamma europeiska målen (Education in Europe: A Report on Education in Sweden and the Common European Goals)*. Utbildningsdepartementets skriftserie, rapport 6 (Stockholm: Regeringskansliet (in Swedish)).

Mishra, R. (1999) *Globalization and the Welfare State* (Cheltenham: Edward Elgar).

OECD (2001) *Education at a Glance: OECD Indicators 2001* (Paris: OECD/CERI).

Ollikainen, A. (1999) *The Single Market for Education and National Educational Policy: Europeanisation of Finnish Education Discourses 1987–1997* (Åbo: Åbo Universitet, Research Unit for the Sociology of Education).

Östros, T. (2003) Lika rätt till kunskap är förutsättningar för jämlikhet (Equal Right to Knowledge is a Prerequisite of Equality), in *Skolboken. En skrift om skolans roll och om socialdemokratisk skolpolitik. (Book of Education. A publication on the Role of Education and Social Democratic Education Policy)* (Stockholm: Tankesmedjan Idé och tendens (in Swedish)).

SOU (2004) *En Ny Doktorsutbildning: kraftsamling för excellens och tillväxt. Betänkande av forskarutbildningsutredningen (New Postgraduate Education: Efforts to Promote Excellence and Growth. Report from the Committee on Postgraduate Education)* (Stockholm: Regeringskansliet (in Swedish)).

Statistics Sweden (2004) *Ägandet av aktier i bolag noterade på svensk marknadsplats 1983–2003 (Holdings of Shares in Corporations Quoted on Swedish Marketplaces 1983–2003)*. Statistics Sweden. Available online at www.scb.se/templates (in Swedish).

Steiner-Khamsi, G. (2002) 'Reterritorializing Educational Import: Explorations into the Politics of Educational Borrowing', in A. Nóvoa and M. Lawn (eds) *Fabricating Europe: The Formation of an Education Space* (Dordrecht: Kluwer Academic Publishers).

Svallfors, S. (1999) 'The Middle Class and Welfare State Retrenchment: Attitudes to Swedish Welfare Policies', in S. Svallfors and P. Taylor-Gooby (eds), *The End of the Welfare State? Responses to State Retrenchment* (London: Routledge/ESA Studies in European Society), pp. 34–51.

Tson Söderström, H. (ed.) (2001) *kluster.se. Sverige i den nya ekonomiska geografin (kluster.se. Sweden in the New Economic Geography of Europe)*. Ekonomirådets rapport (Stockholm: SNS Förlag (in Swedish)).

Unckel, P. (1998) *Kunskap som egen investering (Knowledge as Personal Investment)* (Stockholm: Timbro (in Swedish)).

Vogel, J., Svallfors, S., Theorell, T., Noll, H.-H. and Christoph, B. (2003) *European Welfare Production: Institutional Configuration and Distributional Outcome* (Dordrecht: Kluwer Academic Publishers).

Watts, A. G. (26 January 2004) Bridging Policy and Practice in Career Development: An International Perspective. Keynote address delivered at the National Consultation on Career Development (Natcon) in Ottawa, Canada.

Watts, A. G. and Sultana, R. G. (6–8 October 2003) Career Guidance Policies in 36 Countries: Contrasts and Common Themes. Paper commissioned by CEDEFOP for the Career Guidance and Public Policy: Bridging the Gap Conference, OECD and the Canadian Government in collaboration with the European Commission, the World Bank and the International Association for Educational and Vocational Guidance, Toronto, Canada.

Weir, M. and Scocpol, T. (1985) 'State Structures and the Possibilities for "Keynesian" Responses to the Great Depression in Sweden, Britain, and the United States', in P. E. Evans, D. Reuschmeyer and T. Scocpol (eds) *Bringing the State Back In* (Cambridge: Cambridge University Press).

Whitty, G., Power, S. and Halperin, D. (1998) *Devolution & Choice in Education: The School, the State and the Market* (Buckingham: Open University Press).

CHAPTER 9

NATIONAL AND GLOBAL COMPETITION IN HIGHER EDUCATION[1]

Simon Marginson

The Australian Educational Researcher, August 2004, 31(2): 1–28

Introduction

In the long building of the Australian public university system after World War Two, there were two aspects of the policies designed to provide equality of educational opportunity: the conditions governing student participation, and the conditions governing educational supply. The former received most of the direct attention, but the latter was equally important. The conditions governing participation included the cost of tuition, and scholarships and living allowances. Thus the Whitlam government of 1972–5 expanded and equalised access by abolishing tertiary tuition fees and providing living allowance support to half of the student population. Even at the end of the Whitlam years in 1975, university education was still the activity of a relatively small minority, with only about 15 per cent of those who finished school going straight to university. In equality politics the emphasis was always on the quantitative expansion of places, the socioeconomic composition of participation, and measures to broaden the access provided to the most disadvantaged groups. Here the ultimate horizon of equality of opportunity policy, so difficult to achieve, was to eliminate all social bias in entry so that the social composition of the tertiary student population would mirror that of the general community.

The conditions governing education supply included the hierarchy of secondary and tertiary institutions. After Menzies introduced state aid in 1964 the successive Australian governments were as much concerned to strengthen independent private schooling as public high schools, which tended to work against equality of opportunity, but they took a more egalitarian approach to universities. Like the national higher education systems of much of Western Europe, though unlike the USA, the 19 Australian universities were seen as more or less equivalent and interchangeable. All were expected to be world-class institutions with a common mandate in research and doctoral training. There was an informal hierarchy within the university sector; with the long established 'Sandstones' on top by virtue of their accumulated research capacities and their inherited status as the first choice for school leavers, and the newest universities at the bottom. However, while the universities competed with each other for academic prestige, as universities do, there was little economic competition as such. Universities were more than 90 per cent government funded, and the principal form of support for research activity was not project grants subject to competitive submissions, but the Commonwealth operating funding provided on the same basis to all institutions, which was relatively generous by later standards. This factor more than any other allowed the emerging universities to acquire world-class credentials quickly. By the late 1970s some postwar universities had accumulated strong reputations for innovative research and more student-focused teaching, and/or for organisational design, and threatened to challenge the status of the Sandstones. In the 1980s the best work in the field of education was often at new universities such as Deakin. In this respect the university hierarchy was contestable, not because it was subject to market competition – which would inevitably have favoured those universities that started the race in the strongest position – but because of the public funding regime and the deliberate policy of building capacity in the newer universities.

Marketisation policies

The principle of equality of opportunity continued to order educational programs into the 1980s. Nevertheless, even while educational theorists and policy makers were exploring the limits and contradictions of equality of opportunity programs, the operating conditions were being transformed by two different but overlapping sets of changes. The first set of changes was Commonwealth government marketisation; the second set was constituted by globalisation.

In 1984 and 1985 a new policy discussion began, inspired by the neo-liberal 'revolution' and policies of privatisation and deregulation set in train by the Thatcher government in the UK. In the coordinating departments of Treasury, Finance and Prime Minister and Cabinet a consensus emerged that Australia should expand tertiary participation but could no longer afford free tertiary education. It was believed that an increase in the element of market competition via tuition fees, industry funding, international marketing and private universities would produce a more efficient system. In this world view, the goal of equality of opportunity was less important; and policy interventions designed to achieve greater equality of condition were often seen as an unwarranted interference in a natural competitive market. In 1986 a Higher Education Administration Charge (HEAC) of $250 per full-time student was pressed on an unwilling Tertiary Education Commission, which knew this was the thin edge of the wedge; and in 1988 the Higher Education Contribution Scheme (HECS) was announced. The HECS was a uniform charge levied on all university students and paid to the government, not a market fee; and it was implemented by reforming Minister John Dawkins in order to finance the desired quantitative expansion in access in a manner that would minimise the barriers to students from poor families. Nevertheless, the argument for implementing the HECS centred on assumptions about the individualised rather than the collective benefits of higher education; and by normalising user contributions, plural public/private funding and the consumption paradigm, the HECS opened the way to marketised higher education (Marginson 1997a, 224–37, 1997b).

In the neo-liberal imagination society, culture and personality were mere outcomes of the economy; and global educational strategy was a trading game in which the world was nothing more than a map of opportunities for self-enrichment. If this vision of higher education seemed radically incomplete to most of those working in the system, it was sufficiently exciting to the economists who exercised control over government policies to power more than two decades of proposals for market reforms. The HEAC and the HECS were the first steps in a long series of policy changes that layered more and more aspects of market competition onto the public higher education institutions, without reducing Canberra's capacity to steer the system. The official creation of inter-university competition (1987–8), successive steps in the deregulation of international and postgraduate fees (1985–5); competitive bidding for innovation funds and staff development (1988); the centralisation of research support and its redistribution as project grants on a competitive basis, and the distribution of a proportion of operating funds on the basis of institutional research performance (from 1988); national quality assurance (1993–5, and again from 1999); the Hoare inquiry on governance (1995); the Vanstone cuts to funding, HECS increases and the introduction of up-front undergraduate fees (1996); the West report (1997–8); the leaked Kemp memo proposing a wholesale market deregulation and voucher funding (1999); the PELS loans to support the postgraduate market (2001); the Nelson inquiry (2002) and reform proposals (2003): almost *every* policy move from the mid 1980s, more so after the departure of Minister Dawkins in 1993, was powered by faith in markets and the business model of higher education. This was a faith that the three 'Cs' of competition, corporatism and consumerism would lift efficiency, performance and rates of innovation; strengthen accountability to government, students and business; and provide fiscal relief.[2]

To take the fiscal savings while compelling institutions into entrepreneurial activity, the per student value of Commonwealth operating funding was whittled away until by 2001 it had fallen to 40 per cent of the 1975 level in real terms (Marginson 2002, 114–17). By 2001 Australia spent only 0.8 per cent of GDP on the public funding of higher education (OECD 2003), which was half the level of public investment in 1975, though the national rate of participation in higher education had doubled since that time. Where the previous generation of students had paid no tuition costs at all, by the late 1990s students carried one of the highest public tuition charges in the OECD; and measures were under discussion to push tuition charges even higher.

In refashioning higher education as an economic market, neo-liberal policies affected both the conditions underlying student participation, and also the conditions underlying the supply of higher education. The first effect attracted the main political attention. It was widely expected that an increase in private costs would tend to stratify participation along socioeconomic lines, and the Commonwealth's research on the effects of the post-1996 increases in the levels of HECS found that these had the most affect on poorer students, who withdrew in disproportionate numbers from courses attracting the highest level of HECS charge (Aungles *et al.* 2002). However, arguably the more important regression from the prior conditions underlying equality of opportunity policies was the breakdown of the old semi-equality between universities, which had been dependent on public funding and its distribution on an egalitarian basis.

The global element

The traditional equality of opportunity project, like the Keynesian policies of national economic management that nurtured it, was premised on a sealed national economy and social polity. Just as national financial regulation were broken open by world financial flows in the 1980s, and techniques of business and government became increasingly shaped by cross-border imitations, national higher education systems became irreversibly affected by globalisation. Between 1990 and 2002 the number of international students enrolled in Australian universities increased from 24 998 to 185 058 (DEST 2003). Cross-border flows do not necessarily render the pursuit of equality of opportunity impossible, but the education of a growing number of international students not part of the egalitarian equation of national equality of opportunity policies tends to change the conditions under which these policies are pursued, as well as posing new problems of global inequality. Here international education was also coloured by the marketised form in which it was developed, which worked against the logic of the equality project.

In 1985 it was decided to offer international student places on a full-fee basis, additional to the domestic enrolment, at prices designed to ensure profitability. In 1988 it was decided to phase out the existing international education program premised on foreign aid objectives, with a limited number of subsidised places subject to quota, and confirm the full-fee market as the dominant framework for cross-border education. Universities were allowed to set the prices they chose and expand the number of students without limit. The growing scarcity of public funding for universities encouraged the rapid growth of international education. This subordinated egalitarian considerations within the international program and fed the more general corporatisation and marketisation of the university sector (Marginson and Considine 2000). Australian universities are more entrepreneurially aggressive than American doctoral universities (Slaughter and Leslie 1997), and there is little subsidisation by either governments or universities. While the USA provides scholarships to a quarter of its international students (IIE 2003), in Australia in 2002 the ratio of full-fee-paying places to scholarship places was 61 to 1 (DEST 2003).

This paper

This paper explores economic competition in higher education in both the national and global dimensions, up to and including the likely effects of the Nelson reforms, reflecting on the implications for the equality of opportunity project. The paper does not focus on the implications of marketisation for the distribution of opportunities to access university between social groups – as noted, this element is widely understood (albeit inadequately monitored by governments) and there are no new data to report here – but explores the element less discussed elsewhere: the implications of national and global markets for the producer hierarchy of universities.

The national market in Australia

A market is an economic system of coordination on the basis of buyer-seller relations, as distinct from a system of bureaucratic planning and administration, or communities of scholars, or democratic communal forms of education (Marginson 1997b, 27–50). Markets incorporate five distinctive features: a defined field of production/consumption; competition between producers; identifiable products ('commodities'); prices and monetary exchange between producers and consumers; and the human behaviours and values – entrepreneurship and cost minimisation in production, utility maximisation in consumption, contractual relations and so on – consistent with economic self-interest. Real life education systems normally incorporate some but not all of these features. Higher education systems typically consist of a set of producer institutions ('the market') together participating in several interlocking markets based on distinct products: undergraduate education, research degrees, research and consultancy and other services.

It is helpful to distinguish between *simple commodity production* in education – where the market is the means but not the end of production, and non-market objectives such as social access, or the formation of social leaders, or the reproduction of academic disciplines, may also come into play – and *fully capitalist production*, where the producer has no intrinsic interest in educational or social effects as such, only loyalty to the economic bottom line. The expansion of the production of individualised commodities and the accumulation of capital are ends in themselves. Fully capitalist production is fundamentally subversive of the equality of opportunity project and other common goods. It fulfils non-capitalist objectives only by accident, not by design.

In 2002, the publicly funded national Australian system covered 896 621 students enrolled in 38 public universities, three private universities and three small private colleges, with 98.2 per cent of these students in public institutions (DEST 2003). A 1999 survey identified a further 31 212 students enrolled in 79 accredited private institutions outside the national system (Watson 1999). The principal economic competitions are first, for research funding, via competitive academic schemes based on merit, and targeted research projects in the government and corporate sectors; and second, for tuition revenues from international and postgraduate students. Institutions also sell services in short courses, continuing professional education and consultancy; and compete for philanthropic support. International education is provided on a fullfee basis and designed to raise revenues. On the other hand, in undergraduate education Australian universities have been less market-like than American higher universities (though the Nelson reforms will change this: see below). The USA provides student loans for tuition, enabling a high level of student mobility and creating a quasi-voucher national market. In Australia there is a choice-based competition between universities in each capital but little national mobility. In 2002, 97 per cent of domestic undergraduates paid HECS to the government[3] rather than being subject to buyer–seller relations with their university. The cost of HECS-based courses is shared by students and the government, and the number of HECS places is capped by the government. There are three standardised levels of HECS based on field of study, at AUD $3680–6136 per full-time student per annum in 2003. HECS is a substantial charge in world terms but modified by its income-contingent character. In 2003 repayments began at an annual income of $24 365 (Nelson 2003a). HECS debts are indexed to prices with no real interest rate. This contrasts with direct fees and commercial loans in the USA.

Positional goods and positional competition

Teaching services are standardised on the basis of credentials. All programs of study offered by accredited tertiary institutions are lodged in the Australian Qualifications Framework. Here the degrees offered in all institutions are formally equivalent. Nevertheless, in the real world – in the minds of students, their families and employers of graduates – the degrees offered by different institutions are ranked hierarchically on the basis of institution and field of study. Higher education is a 'positional good' (Hirsch 1976) in which some student places are seen to offer better social status and lifetime opportunities than other places. A 1999 study of factors influencing the choices of prospective undergraduates found that 'applicants focus on broadly conceived course and institutional reputations when making their selections'. Further, 'course entry scores, and by implication university scores, serve as a proxy for quality in prospective students' eyes' (James *et al.* 1999, ix). Applicants had low detailed knowledge of the teaching quality and lifelong earnings potential of particular courses, suggesting that the student-centred piety of the quality assurance movement is largely misplaced: in a positional market choice making is focused primarily on the status of universities and degrees, not the quality of teaching.

Positional goods confer advantages on some by denying them to others. 'Positional competition...is a zero-sum game. What winners win, losers lose'

(Hirsch 1976, 52). Within any one nation (though 'within any one nation' is a significant qualification, as discussed below) there is an absolute limit on the number of positional goods at a given level of value. The number of such goods cannot be expanded without reducing unit value. For example, when everyone can enrol in medicine and become a doctor, medicine ceases to be a high-income-earning, high-status profession. Given the absolute limitation on the number of high-value positional goods, there is also a limit on the number of high-value producer institutions, and on the size of individual elite institutions. Elite institutions cannot expand production to meet the full demand, like capitalist businesses – while they enjoy higher revenues, for these institutions the lodestone is not maximum market share or maximum revenue; it is consumer preferment and social status. Thus, in a positional market, there is both competition among producers and competition among consumers. Producer universities compete for the custom of the most preferred 'customers', while student customers compete for entry to the most preferred institutions. Prestige sustains high student entry scores, and this very scarcity reproduces the prestige of the elite universities. Wealth follows prestige: wealthy families invest in high-value positions in education to maintain social leadership. Positional markets in higher education are a matching game in which the hierarchy of students/families becomes synchronised with the hierarchy of universities. In a high scarcity regime, with only a small number of high-quality/high-value institutions, the stakes in educational competition are much increased; and the more powerful social groups always enjoy advantages in that competition. When the element of positional competition dominates university, social equality of opportunity becomes almost impossible to achieve. The steeper the hierarchy of producers, the more the educational market becomes segmented vertically, the smaller the number of world-class universities becomes, and further hopes of equality of opportunity must recede.

Vertical segmentation is, however, inevitable in positional competition. The production of positional goods *necessarily* combines competition with oligopoly and market closure. Whether high tuition is charged or not, the university market is never a freely competitive market. In elite institutions, the more intense consumer competition for entry is, the *less* the elite institutions are required to court the consumer in the conventional manner, by dropping prices or providing more and better services, providing that they sustain their prestige (which again undermines the contemporary policy focus on improving teaching). Once a university obtains elite status, where it has a limited number of high value competitors, and its very status maintains student custom and research resources, to reproduce that status requires no more than ordinary prudence. At the top, the positional hierarchy in higher education tends to be very stable over time. In Australia the leading institutions are all 45 years old or more. At the bottom end of the market the positional competition operates differently. Institutions must compete hard to attract students to fill their places and secure revenues; and success is always provisional and contestable. But these institutions do not receive full recognition for the quality of good programs, because in a positional market their educational quality is over-determined by low social status. Intermediate institutions, combining some high-value scarce places with low-value access places, find it difficult to move up the ladder because of the limit to the number of high-prestige producers. They cluster as 'second choice' producers, or specialists. Positional markets segment into different groupings, with the segments aligned in a vertical hierarchy and firm barriers limiting upward movement between segments. There are four distinct segments in the Australian system. Geiger (2003, 6) cites seven in the United States.

Table 9.1 Elite higher education in the USA and Australia

United States (leading 30 institutions only, in rank order)	Australia ('Group of 8')
Princeton	*Australian National*
Harvard, Yale	*Melbourne*
Caltech, Duke, Massachusetts IT, Stanford, Pennsylvania	*Sydney*
Dartmouth	*Queensland*
Columbia, Northwestern	*Western Australia*
Chicago, Washington (St. Louis)	*New South Wales*
Cornell	*Monash*
Johns Hopkins, Rice	*Adelaide*
Brown	
Emory, Notre Dame	
U California Berkeley	
Carnegie Mellon, Vanderbilt	
Virginia	
Georgetown	
U California Los Angeles, Michigan – Ann Arbor, *Wake Forest*	
Tufts, *North Carolina – Chapel Hill*	
William and Mary	

Source: US News and World Report (2003, 82–3).

Note
Italics indicates public university.

Market segmentation in Australia

The market segmentation of the Australian system has been shaped by history and funding. The elite institutions, the 'Sandstones' or Group of 8 – Queensland, Sydney, NSW, Melbourne, Monash, Adelaide, WA and ANU – are the older foundations in the capital cities (excluding Hobart and Darwin).[4] They are defined primarily by the pattern of school leaver preferment as measured by entry scores, and research prestige and performance as measured by the quantity of research grants, publications and research students. The older universities, especially Sydney, Western Australia and Melbourne, also enjoy what are in Australian terms relatively high levels of income from donors and private investments, further insulating them from market forces.

Below the Sandstones (Table 9.1), the further segments of the Australian market are

- the 'Gumtrees', mostly the second or later universities established in each state, prior to the Dawkins reforms that began in 1987;
- the 'Unitechs', large universities of technology in each state capital, which had longstanding status as vocational institutions, and became universities after 1987;
- the 'New Universities', other institutions that also achieved university status after 1987. Some are specialist regional and/or distance education providers;[5]
- private universities. Bond has no HECS places and like Notre Dame is small and marginal to the national system (the Nelson reforms will change this: see below).

The national government's Institutional Grants Scheme (IGS), which is allocated competitively on the basis of research performance,[6] provides a useful indicator of

Table 9.2 Segments of the positional market, Australian universities, 2001–3 data

Segments and universities[7]	Med	Total students 2002	Flexible delivery share 2002 (%)	Total income 2002 ($s mill)	Intrnat'l fee share income 2002 (%)	Research students 2002 number share (%)	New ARC Disc 2003	NCG per EFT staff 2001 ($s)	IGS funds 2003 ($s m)
Sandstones									
U Melbourne	Y	39 378	3.0	856.3	13.1	3908 9.9	104	29 788	29.8
U Queensland	Y	37 498	7.5	814.5	8.0	3669 9.8	81	21 452	28.3
U Sydney	Y	42 305	3.9	816.3	9.5	3473 8.2	98	22 943	27.1
U New South Wales	Y	42 333	10.1	701.5	16.5	2669 6.3	81	23 529	25.4
Monash U	Y	52 010	23.8	735.4	15.1	2935 5.6	56	15 786	19.3
Australian National U	Y	11 979	0	461.7	4.3	1491 12.5	137	—**	16.6
U Western Australia	Y	15 885	0	360.4	8.0	1830 11.5	46	31 157	16.1
U Adelaide	Y	16 188	7.5	334.2	8.3	1512 9.3	36	32 382	15.3
Gumtrees									
U Tasmania	Y	13 750	10.9	199.7	7.1	1030 7.5	22	20 499	7.0
U Wollongong	N	18 764	1.1	210.1	20.5	1024 5.5	14	14 931	7.0
La Trobe U	N	24 930	0.7	314.0	8.1	1359 5.5	24	10 332	6.3
Macquarie U	N	27 239	17.5	295.9	18.9	1031 3.8	23	12 409	6.2
Griffith U	Y	30 969	7.5	350.7	11.6	1283 4.1	22	7996	6.1
U Newcastle	Y	23 502	7.5	256.9	10.9	1236 5.3	22	13 835	5.4
James Cook U	Y	13 189	17.0	173.5	6.2	679 5.1	6	11 040	4.9
Flinders U	Y	13 644	10.9	177.2	7.8	905 6.6	10	18 192	4.5
Murdoch U	N	12 734	24.1	156.0	10.4	761 6.0	7	14 954	4.3
U New England	N	18 202	81.9	148.3	3.9	820 4.5	9	13 880	3.8
Deakin U	N	33 033	54.7	325.8	8.5	899 2.7	11	6624	2.9
Unitechs									
Curtin U Technology	N	33 240	11.5	360.9	23.3	1592 4.8	11	6432	5.2

Queensland UT	N	39 192	15.1	365.2	15.6	1105	2.8	13	5121	4.9
U South Australia	N	30 627	22.0	286.1	15.8	1741	5.7	13	5297	4.5
Royal Melbourne IT	N	38 280	3.7	478.2	21.5	1831	4.8	15	3346	4.5
U Technology Sydney	N	29 290	0	287.7	17.1	918	3.1	13	6892	3.6
New unis										
U Western Sydney	N	35 361	4.5	296.7	12.9	942	2.7	4	5159	3.2
U Canberra	N	10 419	(0.04)	105.8	11.5	265	2.5	2	7332	1.7
Swinburne UT	N	14 404	(0.01)	233.2	14.6	537	3.7	10	6294	1.7
Victoria U Technology	N	19 475	1.9	277.8	10.5	654	3.4	1	4372	1.7
Edith Cowan U	N	23 829	24.4	202.9	12.1	824	3.5	3	3289	1.4
Northern Territory U	N	5612	26.3	91.6	2.8	213	3.8	2	7885	1.2
Southern Cross U	N	11 961	52.9	89.7	7.6	449	3.8	1	5920	1.2
Charles Sturt U	N	39 776	83.4	187.4	5.4	434	1.1	5	4132	1.2
Central Queensland	N	21 763	40.9	210.6	37.7	316	1.5	0	2995	1.0
Southern Queensland	N	24 271	81.0	118.6	13.3	326	1.3	3	3832	0.9
U Ballarat	N	6615	0	106.9	4.9	187	2.8	3	3754	0.5
U Sunshine Coast	N	3947	11.3	32.5	12.0	62	1.6	0	98	0.1
Private unis										
Aust Catholic U*	N	11 894	8.9	104.4	4.3	338	2.8	1	1496	0.5
U Notre Dame Aust	N	2832	1.7	20.2	17.7	27	1.0	0	0	0.1
Bond U	N	n.a.	n.a.	n.a.	n.a.	51	n.a.	0	n.a.	0.1
Minor sites										
(various)	—	6250	—	69.4	—	377	—	12	—	0.4
Total	—	896 621	19.2	11 614.1	12.5	45 703	5.1	921	15 165	277.6

Sources: DEST (2003), Nelson (2003a), Australian Vice-Chancellors Committee, Australian Research Council.

Notes

* Private university funded as public universities. Med = medicine faculty (Y = yes, N = no). Dollar amounts in current prices. Flexible delivery share = % of students external (distance) students and multi-modal students, distinct from internal (wholly campus-based). Research student share = number of research students as % of all students. IGS = Institutional Grants Scheme, awarded competitively on the basis of research performance (see note). NCR per EFT staff = national competitive research grants per effective full-time member of staff, teaching/research staff research only.** Not all ANU staff eligible as funded separately for research. New ARC Discov = new Australian Research Council Discovery grants, awarded on academic merit across all fields except medical sciences.

segmentation (Nelson 2003a, 103–4). In 2003 the Sandstones received between $24.8 million (Melbourne) and $15.3 million (Adelaide) in IGS grants: next were Flinders, Newcastle and Tasmania – Gumtrees with medical faculties – each with $7.0 million (see Table 9.2). The allocation of Australian Research Council Discovery grants follows a similar pattern. Research activity is open to merit-based contestation, but like school-leaver status it is also open to prestige-generates-prestige effects, and it is sensitive to the funding base. Before 1987 the Gumtrees were funded by government to conduct common good basic research in all disciplines. They now find it difficult to sustain this given that public funding is down, revenues are more dependent on competitive position, and the Sandstones are better placed to attract competitive research funding and student fees. Nevertheless, the Gumtrees mostly perform much better than the post-1987 universities in national competitive research grants per effective staff member. The Sandstones can internationalise while sustaining universal research intensity. In the other segments, when institutions concentrate on specialist areas such as fee-based international education and distance education, major ventures in either domain tend to cut into potential research capacity.

All else being equal, the steeper the hierarchy of institutions in terms of resources and status, the greater will be the vertical variation in the value of the positional goods produced in higher education, and the more positional competition will structure student and university behaviours. In Australia economic competition in higher education sustains Sandstone hegemony, to an increasing degree, at the expense of the resources and prestige of all other universities. 'True quality' is seen to be centred on fewer institutions than at any time since the formation of mass higher education. In a market where institutions draw on their competitive position to pay their own way, it is no longer possible for all universities to be world-class. There is '*comparison* in place of real commonality and generality' (Marx 1973, 161). The producer hierarchy has become steeper than before, and the dominance of the elite institutions more difficult to contest.

Implications of the Nelson reforms

The next round of marketisation, the Nelson reforms from 2005 (Nelson 2003b), will enhance these trends. In December 2003 the national parliament adopted a package of further market reforms in higher education as negotiated by the Minister for Education, Science and Training, Brendan Nelson. The new system begins in 2005. There are three main changes. First, though the HECS remains a payment from students to government, covering only a part of the cost of the student place with the balance paid by government, it will move closer to the forms of a market fee. The level of HECS will be varied freely by the universities, at up to 25 per cent above current levels, becoming $0–7670 per annum in 2005. All prestigious universities have opted for the maximum possible HECS. Second, public universities can charge direct tuition fees at whatever level they like for up to 35 per cent of the places in each course. Third, fee-paying students in both the public universities and accredited private institutions will be eligible for income-contingent loans under the government-backed FEE-HELP. Repayments under both HECS-HELP and FEE-HELP[8] will be income contingent, with no real interest rate, though students taking loans under FEE-HELP will be subject to an additional annual surcharge of $2000.

These new arrangements will create a differentiated price-based undergraduate market, based on a voucher-like system of subsidised loans. With the cost gap between full-fee places and HECS places reduced, many students will opt for fee-paying places in prestigious universities and courses rather than HECS places in less desired courses. The cost gap between HECS places in public universities and fee places in private institutions will also narrow, making a large-scale private sector viable for the first time. For students overall, costs will rise sharply. There are two compensatory policies. First, scholarships of up to $24 000 per course will be offered to a small number of students from low socioeconomic status or isolated backgrounds. Second, and much more substantially, there will be a higher income threshold for repayments under HECS and FEE-HELP. This has been fixed at an indexed $35 000 per year (a higher repayment threshold also helps to make full-fee places economically viable). Later, the government can create a unified undergraduate market, with variable levels of public subsidy per place, by lifting the cap on maximum HECS, extending HECS to the private sector, and abolishing the surcharge on FEE-HELP places.

Post-Nelson the HECS will be redefined from a student contribution to the costs of a publicly funded place to a public subsidy ('scholarship') that covers part of the private cost of fees. The Nelson package abandons the purpose that guided the HECS, namely user charges without deterrent effects. Meanwhile the Nelson reforms bring Australian cost levels and structures closer to those of the United States. The cost gap between an Australian HECS place and an American in-state public university place is largely closed; and in the longer term, full-fee places supported by FEE-HELP will allow prestige Australian universities to charge fees approaching American private sector levels in sought after faculties such as law, medicine and dentistry. A University of Sydney or Melbourne law degree at $25 000 per year exceeds the production costs but students would pay the difference as it reflects the positional value of the degree, given that most law graduates from these universities enter high-income earning careers. Thus the Nelson package tends to join the markets in elite university places in the two nations; one effect of increasing the domestic price of prestige Australian degrees will be to encourage investment in American university degrees. If families have to pay $20 000–25 000 per annum for prestige positional goods in Australia then an American doctoral university looms as an increasingly attractive alternative.

After 2005, the number of fee-based places underpinned by FEE-HELP can be expected to increase rapidly (Chapman 2003). This will expand the public subsidisation of positional investments by individuals – mostly from socially advantaged groups – through unpaid loans and administrative costs,[9] and further reduce funding for the direct grants to institutions vital to the common research and teaching infrastructure. No doubt much of the additional fee revenue will be squandered on the costs of competition, such as marketing. At the same time, fees and variable HECS will widen the resource gap between the Sandstones and other universities, as the Sandstones are best placed to charge high prices. Drawing new private investments from families used to investing in secondary education, most of the Sandstones, at least, will strengthen their resource base. Part of this will be ploughed into research capacity, including remuneration for high performers, because research is the global source of prestige and competitiveness, again widening their advantage over other universities. At the lower levels of the hierarchy, there will be a 'race to the bottom' as institutions struggle to fill their places. Both of their strategic options – varying HECS charges downwards, and investing resources in marketing – will reduce the resources for teaching and learning, and thin out their research capacity.

Table 9.3 Annual full-time undergraduate tuition costs in the USA and Australia

USA private universities (2002–03)	21% of students pay over $36 000, 68% pay over $22 500
USA public universities in-state (2002–03)	22% of students pay over $7500, 75% pay over $4500
Australian HECS (2003)	varies by course between $3680 and 6136
Australian HECS + 25% variation (2005)	varies by course between $4600 and 7670
Australian full-fees (2005)	(watch this space)

Source: For American data: Geiger (2003, 14).

Note
All data in Australian dollars with USD $1.00 = AUD $1.50; 2005 Australian charges expressed in 2003 prices.

The overall effect is to stretch the vertical hierarchy and widen the gaps between segments. Price variation enables a more differentiated set of economic choices, but matched by steep variations in educational quality. Because high-value course choices in the research-intensive universities command higher prices, and research-intensive provision itself – once government dependent, but now increasingly market dependant – is more firmly restricted, it becomes more difficult than before to access world-class education. Thus the protection and extension of market relations in education helps those with prior economic, social and cultural advantages to consolidate their position. The driving force of the Nelson reforms is the economisation of social privilege in education. Elite university education becomes continuous with independent private schooling at secondary level. First the Sandstones are restructured as a high-cost segment dependant on private investment. Second, the price mechanism is installed to mediate access and redifferentiate both consumption and production. The social pyramid becomes more closely aligned to the educational pyramid. The outcome is a neater, tighter (and fiscally cheaper) positional market: one more closed, with less competition for the Sandstones from below. The Sandstones will not need to become great innovators to maintain their domestic edge: the extent to which they are under pressure to innovate will depend on their openness to global competition. Closer market relations with leading Anglo-Australian families, and less reliance on international fee revenues, might encourage greater insularity. But unlike the USA Australia is not an imperial power; and in the longer term its university quality will be globally referenced. At the bottom of the market costs will be low, as well as quality. Total participation may not fall. The more important effect is the stratification of participation. The rising cost of HECS, fees and income-contingent loans will stream low-income families away from the high-cost, high-value places. In terms of equality of opportunity, the crucial questions become not so much whether or not there is access to higher education, but 'access to *what?*', and '*who* obtains it'? (Bastedo and Gumport 2003).

Global markets in higher education

There are two forms of global market in higher education. First, there is the market that has developed out of student movement across national borders, such as full-fee undergraduate and Masters coursework programs provided to international students in Australia. With one significant exception – international education in

Table 9.4 Principal exporters and importers of tertiary education, 2001

OECD exporter nations	International students		Nations importing from OECD	International students	
	Number	Proportion of all students		Number	Proportion of all students
USA	475 169	3.5	China	124 000	n.a.
UK	225 722	10.9	Korea	70 523	2.3
Germany	199 132	9.6	India	61 179	n.a.
France	147 402	7.3	Greece	55 074	11.4
Australia	110 789	13.9	Japan	55 041	1.4
Japan	63 637	1.6	Germany	54 489	2.6
Canada	40 667	4.6	France	47 587	2.0
Spain	39 944	2.2	Turkey	44 204	2.6
Belgium	38 150	10.6	Morocco	43 063	n.a.
Austria	31 682	12.0	Italy	41 485	2.3

Source: OECD (2003).

the leading American research universities and a handful of British institutions – this kind of global market does not replace the national markets in higher education. There is not one single unified world market with all students choosing freely between different nations. For the most part students continue to be educated within national systems, with a small but growing minority moving between national systems. The size of that minority varies by nation (see Table 9.4). In 2001, 2 per cent of students from OECD nations accessed foreign education, and foreign students constituted just over 5 per cent of students in the OECD nations. However in Malaysia in 2001 6 per cent of tertiary students moved offshore (OECD 2003); and in Australia in 2003 international students, of whom three quarters were located within Australia, constituted 22.6 per cent of all higher education students (DEST 2004).

The economic character of international education also varies. It is fully commercial in the UK, Australia and New Zealand, heavily subsidised in Japan and the USA, and free of tuition charges in parts of Germany. Nevertheless, it is meaningful to refer to a global market. There is a defined field of production (higher education) with identifiable products (degrees and diplomas) that increasingly conform to a Bachelor/Masters/Doctoral structure along American lines. Most international students pay fees. Nations and institutions compete for the status and/or revenues they bring, with some competing more vigorously than others. Students make choices between competing offerings, in which they seek to maximise individual outcomes. Essentially, what export nations provide are the positional advantages gained from global mobility, in three spheres, albeit varying by field of study. First, back in the home nation a foreign education provides skills and prestige. Second, there may be prospects of working in and migrating to the nation where the foreign education is acquired. American immigration policies encourage high-skilled graduates to stay, for example in ICTs and research. Third, there are a growing number of globally mobile jobs in fields such as business, ICTs, engineering and technologies and scientific research (OECD 2002). The language of international business and global academic life is English, so all English-speaking education systems are targeted and there is particularly strong demand for

American education (Mazzarol *et al.* 2001). The global market is especially important in nations where opportunities for upward mobility are constrained, but even where the number of tertiary places of good quality is adequate to meet demand, as in Korea and Japan, there is strong positional demand for an English-language foreign education.[10]

Within the national dimension, as noted, the number of high-value positional goods is subject to absolute limitations. This constrains the potential for high-fee, high-value places, sets limits on the number of elite producers, and rules out the potential for expansionary commercial production that at the same time enjoys high status. In the global dimension no such limits apply. As long as educational border crossing creates positional goods – as long as a foreign education leverages upward social mobility within and between nations – there is no foreseeable limit to the growth of the global positional market. The export market can expand freely without devaluing the unit value of global positional goods within producer nations such as Australia and the UK. Thus the market in international education can operate on a fully capitalist basis without immediately changing the character of the higher education of domestic students. International education has become Australia's third largest services export, and provides significant fiscal relief. In 2002, universities earned $1.45 billion in student fees, 13 per cent of revenues (DEST 2003); and Australia earned about $5 billion in total from international student spending on fees, food, transport, accommodation, living costs and entertainment, on and offshore (Nelson 2003a, 35).

International education in the American research universities and a handful of British institutions plays a special role within the market in cross-border education. In the global era, in which all research universities are networked and visible, and the leading institutions have a powerful presence throughout the world as both ideal-exemplars and practical leaders of the sector, these universities have come to constitute a worldwide market of elite institutions, attracting bright students and high achieving academic staff from every nation. The Ivy League universities value their hegemonic role, though it is largely subordinate to their national role in leadership selection and training, especially in the United States. Thus while only a small number of foreign students actually access Harvard, Stanford and Oxford each year, these universities exercise great symbolic power as producers of the highest value positional goods on offer. Increasingly, their global status overshadows the leading universities within national systems outside the USA/UK. This worldwide market does not replace the national markets, but it does subordinate them.

The second global market is constituted by doctoral training. Here there are signs that a single world market is emerging, not only subordinating the status of national systems of doctoral training but also substituting for them to an increasing extent. High achieving research students, not only from developing nations but in nations such as Australia with a viable national system of research training, are increasingly drawn to the 'world graduate school' based on the American universities, Oxford and Cambridge. 'Doctoral education, particularly in the sciences, is perhaps the most perfectly competitive market in higher education' (Geiger 2003, 3–4). It is a classic positional competition. Departments compete for the highest scoring students and students seek places in the preferred departments. Student places are scarce and are subsidised by scholarship funding, rather than subject to the expansionary capitalist dynamic of the market in vocational Masters degrees. American universities compete for the best students from everywhere: more than half their doctoral graduates in engineering are foreign, and over 30 per cent in the natural

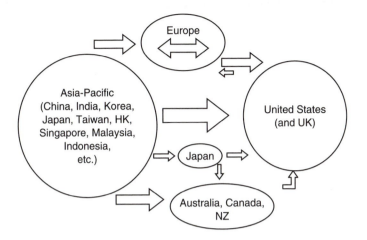

Figure 9.1 Student flows in the worldwide environment of higher education.
Source: Author.

sciences. A study by the OECD notes that, of the doctoral students in American institutions, 60 per cent or more from each of India, China, the UK, Peru, Iran, Greece, Argentina and Germany had 'firm plans' to stay in the US after finishing their studies (Tremblay 2002, 44).

Student flows in the global markets

The global markets are structured by student flows that are uneven and asymmetrical between nations (see Figure 9.1). Some nations are primarily exporters, others are primarily importers; while a third group, including Japan and parts of Europe, exhibit a pattern of more balanced two-way exchange. The diagram simplifies the picture by leaving out Latin America, Africa and central Asia, concentrating on the dynamic parts of the global market. It illustrates:

- the magnetic attraction of American higher education, which is associated with globally superior positional opportunities;
- the UK, Australia, Canada and New Zealand sitting in the American slipstream, operating on a more entrepreneurial basis than American institutions. They gain a referred power as lesser English-language educational providers and sites for migration, sometimes as a transitional stage in passage to the USA;
- the massive demand for foreign education in the Asia-Pacific. Despite the frequent movement between contiguous European countries, four of the five largest importing nations are in the Asia-Pacific – China, Korea, India and Japan – and Malaysia, Indonesia, Hong Kong and Singapore are also in the top 20 importing nations. In 2001 the English-speaking countries enrolled 71.6 per cent of international students from Asia (OECD 2003);
- the extensive student flows within Europe, largely of a non-commercial nature. European universities also educate many students from the developing world.

In the Asia-Pacific region there is immense potential for the further growth of demand for education as a global positional good (see Table 9.5). The Asia-Pacific nations constitute well over half of the world's population, including three of the four largest nations: China, India and Indonesia. Ten of the world's sixteen cities with over ten million people are in the Asia-Pacific, representing immense concentrations of present and future demand for education. In China there have been two decades of high economic growth and the nation could produce one fifth of world GDP by 2050. Expenditure on tertiary education is relatively low, and in 2000 only 8 per cent of the school leaver age group entered degree-level courses in China, a third of the level in Australia. Unmet demand in China will increase steeply because, though China will expand and upgrade domestic provision, the growth of middle-class demand for tertiary education will outstrip the roll-out of new institutions and places. Thailand and Indonesia are other countries where unmet demand can be expected to be high even without the extra incentive constituted by the positional value of foreign education. In much of the Asia-Pacific the habit of private investment is entrenched. In Korea 70 per cent of domestic expenditure on tertiary institutions is private spending, in Japan 56 per cent, in Indonesia 56 per cent, in China 43 per cent (OECD 2003).

Implications for national markets

The growth of global markets has a number of implications for national markets and the national hierarchy of universities. First, in more entrepreneurial export nations such as Australia it has encouraged the installation of business cultures within universities, with potential to transform local as well as foreign operations. In some universities, especially the more recently established ones, corporatisation is associated with the weakening of academic cultures, with negative long-term implications for research capacity (Marginson and Considine 2000). Second, the emergence of a large-scale market sector serving international students, alongside domestic students, introduces a fatal ambiguity into the old national project of equalising educational opportunities between social groups. Monitoring the social patterns of access on a national scale becomes less meaningful, especially given the increasing leakages from the national pool. The social elite has the superior option

Table 9.5 Principal sources of international students, USA and Australia, 2002

USA 2002–2003		Australia 2002	
India	74 603	Singapore	29 956
China	64 757	Hong Kong China	26 956
Korea	51 519	Malaysia	23 725
Japan	45 960	China mainland	19 596
Taiwan	28 107	Indonesia	11 981
Canada	26 513	India	8390
Mexico	12 801	USA	8325
Turkey	11 601	UK	5752
Indonesia	10 432	Thailand	5202
Thailand	9982	Taiwan	3977

Sources: IIE (2003), DEST (2003).

of investment in American education, and exercises it to a growing degree; the large number of international students muddies the waters of local merit-based competition for places; and entrepreneurial global markets popularise the notion that opportunities can be bought, encouraging the installation of local fee systems on supposed 'equity' grounds. Notwithstanding the provision of loans and scholarships, systems in which there is direct charging for tuition always favours those families with a superior capacity to pay.

Third, and on the other hand, global markets offer all institutions, elite or not, a wider set of strategic options, identities and development paths. They can specialise in international partnerships, ICT-based linkages, international marketing or a more cosmopolitan curriculum. Suddenly institutions find themselves operating in more than one sphere at the same time, using the outcomes of strategies in one sphere (resources, networks, reputation) as inputs in the other. They also face new tensions between domestic investment and global investment options. Nevertheless, and while elite status is an advantage in the global as well as national markets, universities locked out of the elite segment of their national systems can position themselves as providers of high-value positional goods for students from elsewhere. At the same time, there are limits to this. Most revenues continue to be sourced not globally, but nationally and locally, from government grants for research and teaching, and from student fees. Even in export-oriented Australia, only 13 per cent of revenues derived from international students in 2003; and institutions spend more on globally linked research activity than they generate in international research funding. Universities that have placed especially high emphasis on the global dimension, such as RMIT and Central Queensland in Australia, risk over-exposure and resource instability.

Fourth, the global market also has another and profound implication for universities in all nations other than the USA. By bringing a new and superior layer of high-value positional opportunities within view (if not necessarily within reach) of middle-class families everywhere, it relativises the local Ivy League, disturbing the traditional conservatism of national positional markets. Suddenly, venerable and unchallengeable universities become less attractive and more vulnerable; undermined by the gravitational pull of the global markets; the global character of research and judgments about the value of knowledge; and the in-your-face visibility of American institutions in a networked era. This affects both leading universities in nations such as Australia – which at least can become global players in their own right – and in developing countries, where institutions lack the capacity in research and communications technologies and the national geo-strategic power to make a ready transition into the global era, facing fewer options and more constraints (Marginson and Sawir 2006). Nevertheless, some local/national university traditions are more robust than others, some nations and institutions are more open to global influences than others, and the capacity to pursue a proactive global strategy is unevenly distributed throughout the world. Certain national governments underpin the forward strategies of their institutions in the global higher education environment (much the wisest policy), some offer their universities domestic protection from those same global market forces, and others leave it to the market to sort their universities out. Australian policies largely fall between categories two and three.

Thus, in relation to equality of opportunity, global markets have mixed effects. On the one hand, they offer the potential to free up the national hierarchy of universities, to at least some extent, while providing new positional options for middle-class families in developing nations. On the other hand, global markets undermine the old project of equalising social opportunities within national borders, and reproduce new patterns of global hierarchy and inequality in universities. Within developing nations, like global business activity, global higher education also fosters globally connected local elites, creating inequalities of opportunity between haves and have nots.

Global university hierarchy

The global markets are subject to global segmentation, in which the world market is constituted by a small number of major players, and all developed nations subordinate all developing nations: 93.5 per cent of international students are enrolled in the OECD nations. English-language nations enjoy a post-imperial advantage, and American universities are unchallengeable – at least until there are global shifts in economic and cultural power, for example, through the growth of East and Southeast Asian nations, especially China. American universities dominate institution-to-institution networking. Universities in the different global regions tend to have partial linkages with other regions but are always linked to universities in the United States, which is the global communications and business hub (Castells 2001). Recently the Shanghai Jiao Tong University Institute of Higher Education (2003) compiled a ranking of world universities based on research and academic performance.[11] The Shanghai Jiao Tong University Institute rankings found that:

- of the top 20 universities, 15 were from the USA and four from the UK. There was only one other nation in the top 20, Japan via the University of Tokyo;
- of the top 50 universities, 35 – *more than two thirds* – were from the USA;
- of the top 101 universities, almost three quarters were from the English-speaking nations: 58 from the USA, nine from the UK, four from Canada and two from Australia: the Australian National University and the University of Melbourne.[12] There were also five universities from Japan, and 23 from Western European and Israel including five from Germany, and three each from Switzerland, Sweden and the Netherlands (see Table 9.6).

Given the market power of the American universities it is ironic that Americans mostly see international education as a form of foreign aid and cultural exchange, rather than as a source of revenue. There is an intense domestic competition between the American universities for top students, leading academic staff and research reputations; but American universities do not approach global competition with the same vigour. American global hegemony is exercised without entrepreneurial marketing. It is sustained by American economic, technological, cultural and military power; by the extraordinary resources US universities command, and by their academic prestige. These universities do not have to adjust their programs or cultural ambiance to attract international support. American universities do not sell an internationalised curriculum; they freely offer themselves as the global standard. Foreign students flock to them, like the crowds of tourists streaming into Disneyland. Globalisation – in education as in other sectors – is what America does to the world, not what the world does to America.

In sum, global education is produced and consumed in terms of a worldwide university hierarchy in which not only is global equality of opportunity absent, *global educational inequality is necessary to* the commercial market in international education (though not to non-commercial educational exchange, as the heavy traffic of students in Western Europe demonstrates). Global hierarchy creates global positional goods, making it worthwhile to invest in border crossing and worthwhile for Australian universities to grow their international education enrolments. It is global socioeconomic inequality not educational quality that drives the market:

> Capital invested in foreign trade can yield a higher rate of profit... because it competes with commodities produced by other countries with less well developed production facilities, so that the more advanced country sells its goods above their value.
>
> (Marx 1981, 344–5)

Correspondingly the global educational market tends to reproduce these global inequalities of power. It maintains the unequal value of education in the developing world compared to the developed world, and sustains asymmetries in student flows, capital flows, cultural engagement and cultural respect. Students from developed nations rarely enrol in developing countries. Economic revenues flow from the developing countries to the export nations, and aid dollars rarely compensate. By spreading English language and Americanised practises, global education markets colonise non-English cultures and identities. The half a million Asian students who enter the English-speaking education systems each year come from very diverse linguistic backgrounds. Apart from English, in the Asia-Pacific there are 14 languages that are each spoken by 65 million people or more, including Putonghua (Mandarin) by 1000 million, Hindi and Urdu by 900 million, Bengali by 250 million and Indonesian/Malay by 160 million (Linguasphere Observatory 2003). All of these languages could become alternative global mediums, but the global university markets relentlessly reproduce the hegemony and homogeneity of English. The bedrock assumption of English-language universities is that native English speakers have little to learn in other languages. Along with global hegemony comes global insularity, a blindness to other languages and the cultures embedded in them, regardless of the immense richness these entail.

Yet some global educational flows are two-way; and, as emerging nations strengthen, more of their international graduates return or invest in the country of origin and feed their knowledge and skills into the national university system. In the longer term nations must develop their own national capacity in higher education to modify Americanisation and maximise their strategic options within the worldwide university network. As Singapore and Taiwan have shown, robust emerging nations can reverse the brain drain and transform their educational position. The clear losers in the global education market are those developing nations that are too weak to sustain their own national and university identities or provide sufficient opportunities to draw back their foreign-educated graduates.

For the lesser English-language providers such as Australia, the Americanised market presents more subtle difficulties for national identity and strategy. Australia has positioned itself as a high growth provider by good marketing and management, inventive off-shore engagement, a specialisation in high-volume standard-cost training in business and IT, improving non-academic services, proximity to Southeast Asia, a friendly climate and a peaceful social atmosphere, and a price advantage over the USA and UK deriving from a weak Australian dollar. IDP (2001) estimates that the average total cost of fees and living expenses in the American public universities was $19 427. It was $19 159 in the UK, where living costs are relatively high. In Australia it was $12 482, and in New Zealand $11 712. Australia's costs were therefore less than two thirds of those in the UK

Table 9.6 World's top 101 universities ranked on research and publications, according to the Shanghai Jiao Tong University Institute of Higher Education, 2003

	Institution	Nation		Institution	Nation
1	Harvard	USA	40	Utrecht	Netherlands
2	Stanford	USA	40	Southern California	USA
3	California IT	USA	43	Edinburgh	UK
4	California – Berkeley	USA	44	California – Irvine	USA
5	Cambridge	UK	45	Illinois – Urbana	USA
6	Massachusetts IT	USA		Champ.	
7	Princeton	USA	45	Zurich	Switzerland
8	Yale	USA	47	Texas – Austin	USA
9	Oxford	UK	48	Munich	Germany
10	Columbia	USA	49	Brown	USA
11	Chicago	USA	49	Australian National	Australia
12	Cornell	USA	51	Case Western	USA
13	California –	USA		Reserve	
	San Francisco		52	North Carolina –	USA
14	California –	USA		Chapel Hill	
	San Diego		53	Osaka	Japan
15	California –	USA	53	Pittsburgh	USA
	Los Angeles		55	Arizona	USA
16	Washington, Seattle	USA	55	Bristol	UK
17	Imperial College	UK	55	New York	USA
18	Pennsylvania	USA	58	Heidelberg	Germany
19	Tokyo	Japan	59	Uppsala	Sweden
20	University College	UK	60	Technical U Munich	Germany
	London		61	Rice	USA
21	Michigan –	USA	61	Carnegie Mellon	USA
	Ann Arbor		63	Oslo	Norway
22	Washington,	USA	64	Tohoku	Japan
	St. Louis		65	Paris 06	France
23	Toronto	Canada	65	Copenhagen	Denmark
24	Johns Hopkins	USA	67	Virginia	USA
25	Swiss Fed IT Zurich	Switzerland	68	Nagoya	Japan
26	California – Santa	USA	68	Sheffield	UK
	Barbara		70	Roma – La Sapienza	Italy
27	Wisconsin Madison	USA	70	Texas A &	USA
28	Rockefeller	USA		M U College Station	
29	Northwestern	USA	72	Rochester	USA
30	Kyoto	Japan	72	Paris 11	France
31	Colorado – Boulder	USA	74	Helsinki	Finland
32	Vanderbilt	USA	75	Maryland –	USA
32	Duke	USA		College Park	
34	Texas – SW Med	USA	75	Florida	USA
	Centre		75	King's College	UK
35	British Columbia	Canada		London	
36	California – Davis	USA	78	Leiden	Netherlands
37	Minnesota – Twin	USA	79	McGill	Canada
	Cities		80	Purdue – West	USA
38	Rutgers – New	USA		Lafayette	
	Brunswick		81	Ohio State –	USA
39	Karolinska I –	Sweden		Columbia	
	Stockholm		81	Utah	USA
40	Pennsylvania S – U	USA	83	Tufts	USA
	Park		84	Vienna	Austria

(*continued*)

Table 9.6 Continued

	Institution	Nation		Institution	Nation
84	Groningen	Netherlands	94	Hebrew U	Israel
86	McMaster	Canada		Jerusalem	
87	Michigan State	USA	95	Free U Berlin	Germany
88	California –	USA	96	Basel	Switzerland
	Riverside		96	Illinois – Chicago	USA
89	Manchester	UK	98	Boston	USA
90	Iowa	USA	99	North Carolina	USA
91	Gottingen	Germany		State – Raleigh	
92	Melbourne	Australia	100	Ghent	Belgium
93	Lund	Sweden	101	Emory	USA

Source: SJTUIHE (2003).

and the American public universities. It is not surprising that Australian international education is price dependent rather than quality dependent given that average student–staff ratios have risen from 12 to 21 since the mid 1980s (DEST 2004). But such a price advantage is not secure in the long term. In addition, the discipline base and countries of origin are narrowly targeted; there is no product differentiation – Australian education in business and IT is much the same as American or British education – and, because there are few educational aid dollars to finance international research degrees, the research student strand is weak. Most bright international students prefer to study in the USA and the UK. The danger for Australia is that by selling itself as 'America on the cheap' it has boxed itself into a market niche, that of the global polytechnic.

For Asia-Pacific countries, Australian international education is associated with a downgrading of global equity and other global public goods. The dichotomy of 'trade versus aid', and the policy decision to opt for the former at the expense of the latter – rather than pursue both in balanced fashion – guaranteed that. The production of global common goods in education is more effectively addressed by forms of internationalisation other than market exchange, such as scholarship programs, non-commercial student exchange, and cooperative research projects.

Notes

1 This is a revised version of the Radford Lecture delivered to the NZARE/AARE Joint Conference, Auckland, New Zealand, 29 November to 3 December 2003.
2 The only break in the pattern was the doubling of Commonwealth Australian Research Council (ARC) and National Health and Medical Research Council (NHMRC) grants in the national innovation statement of 2001; but even there market principles were applied, in that the intense competition for research funding was expected to protect the public interest.
3 Institutions are reimbursed for an amount equivalent to the HECS obligations of their students, as part of government funding.
4 The Sandstone group here includes the Australian National University, Monash University and the University of New South Wales, although these are more recent post-Second World War foundations for which (following the architectural metaphor) the title 'Redbrick' might seem more appropriate. Redbricks is the term used in Marginson and Considine (2000). However, in popular usage the term 'Sandstones' has come to include these three, sharing as they do the prestige of the older foundations, and common membership of the elite segment in the 'Group of 8'.

5 For detailed discussion of the segments in the Australian system see Marginson and Considine (2000, 175–232).
6 The IGS formula is income from research grants (60 per cent of the IGS), the number of higher degree research students (30 per cent) and publications over the previous two years (10 per cent): see Nelson (2003b, 103–4).
7 For definition and discussion of segments see Marginson (1999), Marginson and Considine (2000, 175–232).
8 The new fees/loans system from 2005 absorbs the PELS system of loans for fee-charging postgraduate courses introduced in 2002.
9 In the first full year of operation of the Commonwealth government's Postgraduate Education Loan Scheme (PELS) in 2002, 11 387 students, constituting 33 per cent of all fee-paying domestic postgraduates, took out a PELS loan at an average liability per full-time equivalent student of $10 076 for one year (Nelson 2003b, 68).
10 Like participation in higher education itself, once the acquisition of foreign education becomes a normal practice of middle-class families, it becomes not so much a method of gaining a special advantage, as a 'defensive necessity' (Hirsch 1976) for maintaining social position and retaining the effectiveness of the family business.
11 The criteria were the number of Nobel laureates associated with the university, the number of highly cited researchers (1981–1999), articles in *Nature* and *Science* (2000–2002), articles cited in the science index and the social science index, and academic performance per academic staff member using the above indicators.
12 The Shanghai Jiao Tong University Institute did not give precise rankings after 101, but bracketed the universities in groups of 50. It included a total of 12 Australian universities in the top 500, including Sydney and Queensland (between 102 and 151), Monash, NSW and Western Australia (152–200), Adelaide (201–50), Macquarie (301–50), Newcastle and Tasmania (351–400) and La Trobe (401–50). There were 160 American doctoral universities in the top 500.

References

Aungles, P., Buchanan, I., Karmel, T. and MacLachlan, M. (2002) *HECS and Opportunities in Higher Education: A Paper Investigating the Impact of the Higher Education Contributions Scheme (HECS) on the Higher Education System*, Research, Analysis and Evaluation Group, Department of Education, Science and Training (DEST), Canberra.
Bastedo, M. and P. Gumport (2003) 'Access to what? Mission differentiation and academic stratification in US public higher education', *Higher Education*, 46: 341–59.
Castells, M. (2001) *The Internet Galaxy: Reflections on the Internet, Business and Society* (Oxford: Oxford University Press).
Chapman, B. (10 December 2003) 'Hidden costs the big burden', *The Australian*, p. 36.
Department of Education, Science and Training (2003, 2004) Selected higher education statistics, viewed 2 December 2003, 21 June 2004. Available online at <http://www.dest.gov.au/highered/statinfo.htm>
Geiger, R. (October 2003) Market coordination in United States higher education. Paper presented at the seminar 'Markets in Higher Education – Mature Economies', Douro, Portugal.
Hirsch, F. (1976) *Social Limits to Growth* (Cambridge: Harvard University Press).
IDP Education Australia, with Australian Education International (2001) *Comparative Costs of Higher Education Courses for International Students in Australia, New Zealand, the United Kingdom, Canada and the United States*, IDP, Sydney.
Institute for International Education (2003) Data on international education in the USA, viewed 11 December 2003. Available online at <http://www.iie.org/>
James, R., Baldwin, G. and McInnis, C. (1999) *Which University? The Factors Influencing the Choices of Prospective Undergraduates*, Evaluations and Investigations Program, Higher Education Division, Department of Education, Science and Training (DEST), Canberra, viewed 21 June 2004. Available online at <http://www.dest.gov.au/archive/highered/eippubs/99–3/whichuni.pdf>
Linguasphere Observatory (2003) Data on world language use, viewed 15 July 2003. Available online at <http://www.linguasphere.org/>

Marginson, S. (1997a) *Educating Australia: Government, Economy and Citizen Since 1960* (Cambridge: Cambridge University Press).

Marginson, S. (1997b) *Markets in Education* (Sydney: Allen and Unwin).

Marginson, S. (1999) 'Diversity and convergence in Australian higher education', *Australian Universities Review*, 42 (1): 12–23.

Marginson, S. (2002) 'Towards a politics of the enterprise university', in S. Cooper, J. Hinkson and G. Sharp (eds), *Scholars and Entrepreneurs: The University in Crisis* (Melbourne: Arena Publications).

Marginson, S. and M. Considine, (2000) *The Enterprise University: Power, Governance and Reinvention in Australia* (Cambridge: Cambridge University Press).

Marginson, S. and E. Sawir (2006) 'University leaders' strategies in the global environment: a comparative study of Universitas Indonesia and the Australian National University', *Higher Education*, 52(2): 343–73.

Marx, K. (1973) *Grundrisse: Foundation to the Critique of Political Economy* (Harmondsworth: Penguin).

Marx, K. (1981) *Capital, Vol. 3* (Harmondsworth: Penguin).

Mazzarol, T., Soutar, G., Smart, D. and Choo, S. (2001) *Perceptions, Information and Choice: Understanding how Chinese Students Select a Country for Overseas Study*, Australian Education International, Canberra, viewed 15 July 2003. Available online at <www.dest.gov.au>

Nelson, B. (2003a) *Higher Education: Report for 2003 to 2005 Triennium*, Department of Education, Science and Training, Canberra, viewed 10 February 2004. Available online at <http://www.dest.gov.au/highered/he_report/2003_2005/pdf/triennium2003_2005.pdf>

Nelson, B. (2003b) *Our Universities: Backing Australia's Future*, Commonwealth of Australia, Canberra, viewed 21 June 2004. Available online at <http://www.backingaustraliasfuture.gov.au/policy_paper/policy_paper.pdf>

Organization for Economic Cooperation and Development (2002) *International Mobility of the Highly Skilled* (Paris: OECD).

Organization for Economic Cooperation and Development (2003) *Education at a Glance* (Paris: OECD).

Shanghai Jiao Tong University Institute of Higher Education (2003), Academic ranking of world universities – 2003, viewed 22 May 2004. Available online at <http://ed.sjtu.edu.cn/ranking.htm>

Slaughter, S. and L. Leslie, (1997) *Academic Capitalism* (Baltimore: Johns Hopkins Press).

Tremblay, K. (2002) 'Student mobility between and towards OECD countries: a comparative analysis', in OECD, *International Mobility of the Highly Skilled* (Paris: OECD).

US News and World Report (2003) America's best colleges, *US News and World Report*, special annual edition.

Watson, L. (1999) *Survey of Private Providers in Australian Higher Education 1999*, 00/4, Evaluations and Investigations Program, Higher Education Division, Department of Education, Science and Training, Canberra, viewed 11 December 2003. Available online at <http://www.dest.gov.au/archive/highered/eippubs/eip00_4/survey.pdf>

CHAPTER 10

EDUCATION, NATION STATES AND THE GLOBALIZATION OF INFORMATION NETWORKS

Neil Selwyn and Phillip Brown

Journal of Education Policy, 2000, 15(6): 661–82

Introduction

For the last 20 years the identity and sovereignty of the nation state has been brought into question by the globalization of the economy. Individual countries have been struggling to maintain their traditional decision-making power and authority against the mobilization of global financial markets and the increasing reach of the multinational corporations (Schiller 1986). The collapse of national barriers to trade, production and service delivery have been significantly advanced by the revolution in information technologies which has led to an exponential increase in global information flows (Kenway 1996). Against this background, governments around the world are developing policy initiatives aimed at improving the quality of their human resources in an attempt to win a competitive advantage in the new competition (Brown and Lauder 2000). In this way, a working familiarity with information technologies has become a key feature of both individual 'employability' and international competitiveness; thus prompting nation states to invest in information technologies as a way of delivering and extending education and training, whilst also building and developing nation-wide 'information infrastructures'.

Indeed, the recent world-wide expansion of education systems has firmly been based on a human capital approach towards economic success (Brown 1999). Thus, moves are being made in the most 'developed' countries towards implementing national standardized curricula in compulsory education, widening participation rates in tertiary and higher education as well as attempting to increase levels of 'life-long learning'. Alongside this focus on education and training, the development of advanced information networks is also taking place in most industrialized countries, usually under the objective of creating a 'national information infrastructure'. In an organizational sense, national information infrastructure (NII) policy-making encompasses all computerized networks, applications and services that citizens can use to access, create, disseminate and utilize digital information (Martinez 1997). In practice, therefore, such policies have tended to encompass the public and private diffusion of technologies as diverse as POTS (plain old telephone service), digital broadcasting, the Internet and other multimedia, in both the private and public sectors.

Given these parallel concerns of extending education *and* establishing information infrastructures, it is unsurprising that the two policy areas have rapidly converged.

The last decade has seen many developed countries initiate multi-million dollar programmes aiming to connect education systems to the Internet and other communications networks; thereby boosting the use of Information Technology (IT)[1] in both compulsory and post-compulsory education. In many cases such initiatives have been introduced with the long-term goal of establishing self-contained 'educational superhighways' (Selwyn 1999). Yet, despite an apparent commonality of purpose, the envisaged forms of these eventual educational networks and the mechanisms used to achieve them appear to vary tremendously from country to country; reflecting a variety of underlying motivations and strategies. However, given the scales of investment and the potentially far-reaching implications of such programmes, it is important to examine how information infrastructures are being created and what educational, economic, social and cultural roles governments see them playing.

This paper, therefore, offers a preliminary examination of the educational elements of NII policy-making in seven countries; Germany, Japan, Malaysia, Singapore, South Korea, United Kingdom and the United States of America and, in doing so, explores the rationales behind these different approaches to 'wiring up' their respective education systems.[2] This analysis suggests that merely viewing such policies via a narrow technologically determinist perspective, based on a linear progression of skills-upgrading and educational investment determined by the demands of technological change serves to obscure the fact that nation states continue to play a vital role in shaping NII and education networking policies. A more sophisticated approach, however, is to study these issues as an integral part of the political economy of skill formation (Brown 1999). In this way our emphasis on political economy is intended to focus attention on the role of the state in understanding the relationship between education, economy and society in different national contexts, and the extent to which globalization is leading to a convergence in national approaches to these issues. Our emphasis on skill formation is intended to examine how the apparent focus of NII policies on IT skills is related to broader issues concerning nations' attempts to develop different models of the worker/citizen in post-industrial societies and, therefore, inherently linked to issues of social inclusion and social exclusion. This analysis shows that our present empirical and theoretical understanding of these issues is extremely limited. Therefore our conclusion will outline a research agenda for the future examination of NII policies as the effects of these initiatives begin to be felt within the developed nations over the next decade.

The political economy of NII policies in seven countries

The initial task is to describe the information technology policies in each of the seven countries. This is summarized in Table 10.1, which presents the main features of educational initiatives and their relation to overarching National Information Infrastructure (NII) policies.

United States of America

The announcement in September 1993 of the 'US National Information Infrastructure' initiative by the Clinton/Gore administration (IITF 1993) has been widely acknowledged as precipitating the subsequent rush of NII policies throughout the rest of the world (e.g. Tan 1995; Langdale 1997).[3] The broad aim of the US initiative has been to create an information and communications network connecting

Table 10.1 Current NII and education policy statements in the seven countries

	NII program	Educational elements	Educations targets
USA	National Information Infrastructure	*Technology Literacy Challenge, E-Rate, Netdays*	All schools connected to the Internet by 2000. Increased IT hardware in all classrooms
UK	—	*National Grid for Learning*	All schools connected to the Internet by 2002. All teachers trained to be IT 'competent'. Development of a mosaic of on-line teaching resources
Germany	—	*Schulen ans Netz*	All schools connected to Internet by 2001
Japan	Japanese Information Infrastrcutre (JII)	—	All schools connected to Internet by 2000
Singapore	Vision of an Intelligent Island IT2000	*IT Masterplan*	All schools connected to Internet by 1998. Projected 2:1 ratio of students to computers
Malaysia	Vision 2020	*Smart Schools Initiative*	All schools established as 'Smart Schools' by 2010 with Internet access and 5:1 ratio of students to computers
South Korea	Korean Information Infrastructure (KII)	*Education Reform Plane for the Establishment of a New Education System*	Development of EDUNET and other aspects of 'cyber-education' via government directed Korean multimedia education centre

homes, businesses and public institutions to the 'Information Superhighway'. Although the US administration has expressed concern that every American citizen has equality of access to a fast and flexible network, the development and implementation of the NII has largely been left to the private sector. The Federal government sees its role as promoting the NII and creating the market conditions for private providers to flourish. In educational terms the promise of an Internet connection to every classroom in every school has been a central tenet of the official promotion of the overall policy drive. In order to facilitate this educational goal, Federal Government issued the 'Technology Literacy Challenge' (DoE 1996) which made available a projected $2 billion of funding until 2001 to provide every classroom with Internet access and 'modern multimedia computers', ensure IT training and support for all teachers and establish a network of 'effective on-line learning resources'. Subsequently, in 1998, the 'E-Rate' initiative provided up to a further $2.25 billion per annum to the Universal Services Fund; effectively offering means-tested discounts of between 20% and 90% for schools to purchase internal and external network connections. In practice the connection of US schools to the Internet has varied from state to state with many business-led 'voluntary' Net-Days taking the place of any centralized approach.

United Kingdom

In the United Kingdom an overall vision of a national information infrastructure has been a less pronounced one than in the USA. The British government have traditionally been keen to adopt a 'hands-off' approach to the construction of telecommunications and information networks. Throughout the 1980s successive Conservative governments strove to develop a telecommunications infrastructure by being a 'referee in the marketplace' (Garfield and Watson 1998); primarily overseeing the deregulation of many sectors. Nevertheless, with the election in 1997 of the New Labour administration, a more cogent sense of a NII strategy has begun to emerge. As well as encouraging cable and digital broadcasting provision the Labour government have been quick to announce the development of (primarily Internet based) ISDN networks within local and central government, Post Offices, the National Health Service and the establishment of a 'People's Network' of connected museums and libraries. However, perhaps the most developed element of this programme has been the plans for creating an educational network; the £1 billion 'National Grid for Learning' initiative. This programme aims to ensure the connection of all the country's 30,000 schools to the Internet by 2002, with 75% of teachers and 50% of pupils using individual email accounts. Nearly a quarter of this funding has been pledged to the training of teachers with consortia of private companies competing to provide 'official' on-line curriculum resources within 'Virtual Teacher Centres' and other online sites.

Germany

The general notions of 'Informationszeitalter' (age of information) and 'Gesallschaft für Informatik' (information society) have been long recognized in Germany but have proved slow in permeating official policy-making (Schidtbe 1998). However, since 1996 a German educational Internet drive has been co-ordinated under the 'Schulen ans Netz' (Schools on the Net) initiative – a joint programme between the Federal Ministry of Education, Science, Research and Technology (BMBF) and Deutsche Telekom. The Schulen ans Netz initiative was initially based around a three year plan to connect 10,000 of Germany's 45,000 schools to the 'network of networks'; involving DM36million of private funding from Deutsche Telekom and DM23million of public money from the BMBF. Yet from 1999 an additional DM100million of public and private finance has been pledged to ensure the complete connection of the German education system to the Internet by 2001. Aside from developing an overall technological infrastructure for schools the Schulen ans Netz drive also focuses on providing a 'consulting network' for schools, a programme of teacher training and the fostering of co-operation between schools, universities, libraries and companies. To this end the initiative has encompassed a range of projects designed to achieve these aims. As in the USA, education in Germany is largely a state, not federal, concern – so the initiative is largely being implemented and augmented at the State (Länder) level. However, as Breiter and Kubicek (1999) observe, the IT activities at the Länder level vary tremendously from region to region.

Singapore

Originating from 1987's National Information Technology plan, Singapore has been following the extensive centralized 'IT2000 Vision' designed to establish an 'intelligent island'. This has been based around the integration of IT into eleven major sectors, namely: government; healthcare; education; leisure and tourism; construction and real estate; financial services; manufacturing; the IT industry; publishing and media; retail and transportation. Within the IT2000 and subsequent 'Singapore One' visions education is seen as a major area in the creation of an advanced NII which aims to connect almost every home, office, factory, school and library to the Internet. In educational terms S$2billion has been committed to achieving this aim, which in 1998 led to Singapore being the first nation to provide all of its primary and secondary schools with at least one Internet connection (Research Machines 1999). The Singaporean 'Masterplan for IT in Education' outlines in further detail goals for over a quarter of the school curriculum to be technologically based with an eventual target of one computer for every two students. A further S$10million has also been committed to a pilot project (the Student Teacher Workbench) aiming to provide multi-media teaching and learning materials for students and teachers.

Malaysia

Malaysia's NII policy has been formed under the aegis of 'Vision 2020'; a 25 year-plan for a 'technologically driven nation'. An integral part of Vision 2020 is the 'Multimedia Super Corridor' (MSC). Malaysia's Multimedia Super Corridor is a 15 by 50 km zone extending south from Kuala Lumpur, thus 'creating the perfect environment for companies wanting to create, distribute and employ multimedia products and services' (Ministry of Education 1998, 1). The MSC consists of developing a physical infrastructure (highway, airport, garden cities), new 'cyberlaws' to encourage electronic commerce coupled with a high capacity national telecommunications infrastructure. With this in mind, seven 'rapid development areas' have been identified: electronic government; telemedicine; a multipurpose card; research and development clusters; world-wide marketing webs; borderless marketing centres; and smart schools. A group of 90 pilot 'Smart Schools' were established by 1999, 'serving as the nucleus for the eventual roll-out of Smart School teaching concepts and materials, skills and technologies (Ministry of Education 1998, 9). It is envisaged that by 2010 all of Malaysia's 10,000 primary and secondary schools will be Smart Schools based on a radical reappraisal of teaching-learning methods, management and organization as well as technology to 'prepare for the information age': between a 1:5 and 1:1 student:computer ratio, development of local area networks (LANs), Internet and multi-media access.

Korea

With a budget of US$50billion spanning a 20-year period (1994–2015) the Republic of Korea is aiming to eventually become one of the world's five largest telecommunications countries in the new century. Development of the Korean Information Infrastructure (KII) is focused on both a 'Government' and 'Public' Information Infrastructure, initially via a smaller 'pilot community' to pre-empt a later full scale deployment. Yet, as Kim (1999) argues, belying the rapid growth of its economy the Korean education system is still viewed as largely remaining at its '19th century stage'. This is compounded by a traditional low level of public investment in education with a reliance on high levels of private, parental expenditure. This led to the 1995 'Education Reform Proposals for the Establishment of a New Education System' with its three-way focus on 'Informatization', 'Globalization' and 'Localization' of Korea's education system.

Thus within the KII programme electronic libraries and distance education have been marked as 'core applications' as well as connection of schools to the Internet (Jung 2000). In practice the Korean Multimedia Education Centre (KMEC) was launched in 1997 as a central government financed research and development institute attached to the state broadcasting company. KMEC is charged with research and development into 'cyber-education' and the operation and expansion of EDUNET; a nation-wide education information system (KMEC 1997). Alongside this body the Korean government also established the Korean Research Information Centre; described as a 'one-stop service system for a virtual research information digital library' (KRIC 1997).

Japan

Keen to reaffirm its technological reputation and position in the world, Japan is also striving to establish a 'Japanese Information Infrastructure' (JII). As Latzer (1995) details, the technical construction of the infrastructure alone is expected to cost up to 100 trillion yen with educational and health institutions connected to the Internet by 2000 and all homes by 2010. Although most of the Network is to be financed by the private sector the health and education elements of network services are government led. Indeed, the original intention to have all primary schools connected to the Internet by 2003 has since been accelerated by a combination of extra government funding and private sector commitments to offer discount rates to schools.

In educational terms the main focus of the JII drive has been on the growing needs of an 'information-orientated society', with a practical emphasis on developing information literacy and efficient use of information (McLaughlin 1999). A new IT based curriculum is due to start in all schools by 2002 and newly qualified teachers will be required to have qualifications in information systems and information retrieval from the Internet. A key feature of Japanese NII policy-making has been the different government departments involved in educational information infrastructure policies, such as the Ministry of Education, Science and Culture, the Ministry of Posts and Telecommunications and the Ministry of International Trade and Industry. As McLaughlin (1999, 229) has observed, 'these Government initiatives are not running as smoothly as it might appear...The result is a power struggle within the Ministries in the midst of the Government's drive for internationalisation'.

The nature of education network policymaking: convergence or divergence?

As these examples demonstrate, education forms an integral part of all seven nation states' visions of the emerging 'information age'. In this respect there is unequivocal evidence of an international convergence in the significance that advanced nations (including Singapore and South Korea) are now attaching to the dual roles of information technology and education in their policy responses. However, the way IT policies for education relate to broader national visions of national information infrastructures and, it follows, how the educational systems are being institutionally 'wired' within the social, political and economic fabric of nation states, offers clear evidence of divergence rather than convergence within this apparent global 'policy-scape' (Ball 1999).

What is immediately striking about these national examples is the difference between the Western economies and their East Asian competitors. In countries such as Singapore, Malaysia, Japan and South Korea education is but one integral part of broader established NII initiatives, whereas in countries such as in United Kingdom and the United States 'education superhighway' policies have been presented more as 'stand-alone' programmes which are driven by market forces under the 'remote control' of the state. This can be explained from two different perspectives. From one standpoint it can be argued that the societal rather than piecemeal approach to the development of a NII in Japan and the Asian Tiger countries is an attempt to 'catch-up' with the mature economies as found in Europe and North America, although this loses much of its plausibility in the case of Japan which has been a major international economic force for over 30 years. An explanation based on technological determinism can be used to make the converse argument that countries such as the United Kingdom are rooted in the smokestack era of industrial capitalism and have still to catch-up with the 'hi-tech' vision of countries found in East Asia that take for granted the full force of the 'information revolution' in attempts to achieve national development. Thus education can be seen as being used in the UK, Germany and USA as a 'step-up' to eventually establishing a NII. Conversely, in countries such as Singapore and Malaysia where these shifts are well established, education is merely keeping in line with other societal NII developments that are already well in place.

Both of these explanations have an element of plausibility but we want to suggest that these differences are best understood in terms of the political economy of the countries under investigation. Here we will focus on the well-established distinction between neo-liberal and developmental approaches (Ashton and Green 1996; Castells 1996). Neo-liberalism views most forms of state intervention as an impediment to the operation of the market which is seen as being the most efficient means of economic organization. Here the private interests of individuals and companies should be left to define the demand for goods and services given that the state can never achieve a monopoly of information seen to be necessary for effective state planning. In this way Moore (1998) suggests that in the neo-liberal model of policy implementation the state acts merely as a facilitator to ensure that IT markets flourish whilst the private sector determines the scope of the NII policies. Indeed, examining the policy rhetoric across the various countries, this approach is strongly reflected in both the US and UK models of implementation:

> The Federal government funded and developed early versions of the Internet for national security and research purposes. It will continue to provide funding for research and development on future Internet and high-performance computing technologies. However, most of the capital to build the computing and telecommunications infrastructure is being provided by the private sector.
>
> (US Secretariat on Electronic Commerce 1998, 50) [USA]

> The [UK] government will not attempt to replace the private sector – competitive markets will bring the greatest benefits to the economy and consumers alike.
>
> (COOI 1998, 5) [UK]

This reliance on market forces means that the connection of homes and businesses to information and communications networks has been left firmly in the hands of the private telecommunications sector; with as yet limited success. Yet, by setting educational IT up as a 'quasi-marketplace' (Le Grand and Bartlett 1993), the UK government can still exert an element of control over the formation of the National Grid for Learning policy, ensuring its successful establishment in the hope that momentum will 'trickle down' into the other, market-driven sectors. This is reflected in the continual emphasis the UK government place on the National Grid for Learning stimulating demand 'beyond the four walls' of the school into the home and wider community; acting in many ways as a government constructed flagship for a privately constructed NII.

Yet in many ways the USA provides the closest example of an ideal-typical model of neo-liberalism in respect to the development of educational networking and over-arching national information infrastructures. Indeed, in this respect a centralized approach to policy-making has been generally considered to 'run against the very grain of American culture' (Sawhney 1996). Nevertheless, even here education has assumed a heightened importance, with the Federal government paying particular attention to the connection of US schools to the Internet. Indeed, the boast of an Internet connection into every classroom is seen as embodying the public perception of the Clinton administration's drive throughout the 1990s towards a NII. Of course, perceived government involvement and concern over the educational element of NII policy has obvious political advantages. For many Western governments, pledging to 'wire up' schools carries far more electoral significance than promising to ensure the connection of the commercial sector to the Internet; hence the high profile media images of Al Gore and Bill Clinton donning hard-hats and being seen to carry rolls of ISDN cabling into American schools. In this way education is a highly visible and highly laudable arena for Western governments to be seen to launch the idea of a national information infrastructure.

If the above provides an example of the state being treated as an impediment to the operation of market efficiency, in the case of the developmental state it is seen as the supreme catalyst, with NII policy implementation firmly 'driven by the state acting in accordance with a predetermined set of objectives' (Moore 1998, 154). This model typifies the approach taken by most East-Asian governments, who have leant towards highly centralised 'visions' with strong state leadership and direction. Castells (1996) argues that a state is developmental when its main source of legitimacy is its ability to deliver consistently high rates of economic growth and modernization of the economy both domestically and in relation to the international economy. This presupposes a societal approach to which 'in East Asia took the form of the affirmation of national identity, and national culture, building or rebuilding the nation as a force in the world, in this case by means of economic competitiveness and socio-economic improvement' (Castells 1996, 182).

Thus developmental governments can be seen as taking 'a proactive central role' rather than leaving 'their national information infrastructure to the hands of the private sector' (Teo and Lim 1998, 122). For example, although differing somewhat in the degree of private involvement that has been encouraged, the Japanese strategy implies a strong belief in the 'hands on' approach to building information-communities: 'the political/administrative system, with strong central power in the hands of the ministry at the local and national level, and a unusually close relationship between the civil service and industry support this approach' (Latzer 1995, 527). Given this societal approach to NII development the education system is treated as one element of a state coordinated strategy. But as for all ideal-typical models, this broad view runs the risk of obscuring important difference in empirical realities, such as in the educational and economic policies pursued by the Asian Tiger economies. Moreover, some countries such as Germany cannot be said to have adopted either an avowedly neo-liberal or developmental model, given the importance attached to the politics of co-determination (Streeck 1992). Indeed, had we extended our focus beyond the seven major examples discussed here the number of ideal-typical models would undoubtedly increase. Nevertheless, a more detailed analysis of the seven countries presently under consideration here permits us to examine both points of convergence and divergence in education and NII initiatives.

The political economy of national information technology and educational networking strategies can be studied in greater detail through an analysis of the stated aims of the programmes in each country. A content analysis of key policy documents produced over the last decade can therefore be presented in terms of three closely inter-related dimensions: educational, economic and societal (see Figure 10.1). These themes are now discussed in more detail in the following sections.

Educational aim

The educational discourse of establishing information networks across countries and their educational systems has tended to be expressed in three different ways, namely: using IT to improve educational opportunities; using IT to improve educational standards; and, in a more radical form, using IT to remould or transform systems of education.

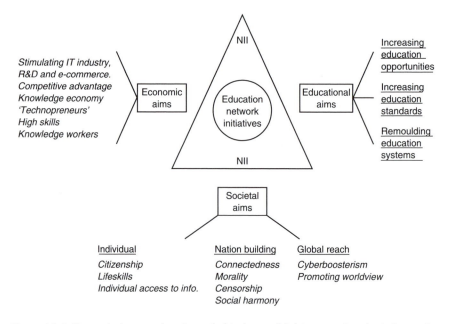

Figure 10.1 Countries' stated aims behind establishing national information infrastructures.

Firstly, in all countries education networks are being constructed under the pretext of increasing educational opportunities. Thus the UK 'Virtual Teacher Centre' and the Singaporean 'Student-Teacher Workbook' schemes are seen as vastly increasing students' and teachers' access to teaching and learning resources. Similarly, in the US connection to the Internet has been justified, among other factors, in reducing the isolation of rural isolation (Uncaplar 1999). By opening schools up to the 'world' and thereby reducing the inequalities of time and space educational super-highways are, in many cases, being presented as 'great levellers' for schools, students and teaching staff:

> The best schools, teachers, and courses would be available to all students, without regard to geography, distance, resources or disability.
>
> (ITAF 1993) [USA]

> The scope of education and learning will be extended beyond conventional teaching in classes, with students becoming able to access information from throughout the world. Remote education, joint learning with schools around the world and learning through imaginary experiences with interactive simulation will be available. As a result, more advanced and active styles of education will be realised on a practical level.
>
> (Ministry of International Trade and Industry 1994, 1.4) [Japan]

> In introducing multi-media information communication technology, the education system should be open to whoever, whatever and wherever. IT drastically changes traditional concepts of time and space in education, consequently changing the role of teachers, the concept of classrooms and educational methods and curriculum. Thus educational content, method and management must be transformed.
>
> (Kim 1999, 61) [Korea]

Coupled with this notion of achieving equality of opportunity is the argument that educational networks will lead to improving educational standards. In particular, the National Grid for Learning initiative and the associated increased use of IT in British classrooms has been consistently justified in terms of raising educational standards, most notably levels of numeracy and literacy as well as examination results:

> With Government strategy now requiring IT to be fundamental to the effectiveness of schools in the future, the task for educationalists is to ensure that the National Grid for Learning becomes a powerful vehicle for improving standards.
>
> (NCET 1997) [UK]

> The Grid has enormous potential for improving attainment, for supporting our main goal of driving up standards in schools and for delivering material which is of immediate, practical and working use to schools.
>
> (DfEE 1998) [UK]

The importance of using IT-based education as a way of improving educational standards is recognized to be important across all seven countries examined here, especially in a context of expanding opportunities for lifelong learning. In many countries, therefore, it is widely believed that this involves changing the training and work of educators themselves. Under the USA 'Technology Literacy Challenge', for example, technology training is now a prerequisite to gaining a teacher license in over half of the 50 states, whilst IT has been made an integral part of the UK training curriculum for all newly qualified teachers. In Singapore too, IT is portrayed as an 'essential' part of the teachers' role:

> Indeed, all schools will be provided with an IT-enriched infrastructure to widen and enhance the learning environment. The use of IT will strengthen the teacher's repertoire of skills, open up a much wider array of educational resources, and enable greater communication and sharing of resources both within and between schools. Within this new environment, the computer will be an essential working tool of the teacher.
>
> (NCB 1999b, 1) [Singapore]

However, the way educational standards are understood within such rhetoric varies significantly from country to country. In Britain and America the emphasis on standards directly relates to the 'basics' of numeracy and literacy, whereas in Japan, Singapore and South Korea the notion of educational standards has been extended to include creative thinking, enhance learning capability and an ability to learn independently and continuously.

> By taking maximum advantage of the advanced functions of computer software and networks, such learning activities as identifying and analysing subjects to study and expressing the results may become more advanced and active, and the capabilities of learners including their creative, intellectual and expressive powers may be dramatically enhanced.
>
> (Ministry of International Trade and Industry 1994, 2.2) [Japan]

> IT will play a critical role in fostering creative thinking, and the skills for lifelong learning. IT literacy will be a basic competency in tomorrow's workplace... students will use IT for up to 30 per cent of their curriculum time... to make sure that young people will have skills that are critical for the future – creative thinking, and the ability to learn independently and continuously.
>
> (Ministry of Education 1998, 35) [Singapore]

This emphasis on a holistic approach to educational standards and the role of IT reflects both the success these countries have achieved in international tests for numeracy and literacy, but also a belief that the emphasis on rote learning and credential competition that have characterized educational development in East Asia cannot meet the human, economic and social demands of the 'information age'.

It is therefore not surprising to find that whilst IT policies in Britain, the USA and Germany are broadly framed in terms of improving on existing educational provision, the more radical justification of using IT to fundamentally restructure national educational systems are found in East Asia. This commitment to remould the education system is epitomised by the Malaysian 'Smart Schools' programme which, as well as increasing schools' access to IT hardware and software, details comprehensive reform of teaching-learning methods, the curriculum, school management and organization strategies. The Smart School programme extends far beyond the implementation of technology in the classroom and is fundamentally based around Malaysia's 'National Philosophy of Education' which calls for schools to develop 'citizens who are knowledgeable and competent, who possess high moral standards, and who are responsible and capable of achieving high levels of personal well-being as well as being able to contribute to the harmony and betterment of the family, the society and the nation at large' (Malaysian Ministry of Education 1997, 19). This discourse of 'remoulding' education is also prevalent across East Asia:

> The substantial improvement in information processing, gathering and dispatching capacities through computers and networks will permit... developments in [Japanese] education and study, transcending the various restrictions imposed by traditional teaching in classrooms.
>
> (Ministry of International Trade and Industry 1994, 2.2) [Japan]

> The quality of [Korean] education must be raised to world level. Primary and secondary school education should be transformed from rote-learning and the cramming of fragmentary knowledge to fostering creativity and problem-solving.
>
> (Kim 1999: 62) [Korea]

The connection between education and societal goals reflected in the introduction of IT in schools, colleges and universities is, therefore, a defining feature of developmental state intervention. The importance of societal goals will receive further elaboration, but we should also not lose sight of the importance of economic goals in all the countries under investigation here.

Economic aims

Kenway (1995) argues that when examining the role of the 'information super-highway' in education it is necessary to consider the relationship between global economic markets and national information infrastructures. Issues of economic competitiveness are paramount in driving national initiatives to create electronic information networks (Schiller 1995). Thus, in the knowledge-driven economies of the future the national information infrastructure is seen as a vital source of economic competitiveness as information processing, e-commerce, and virtual networking of individuals and companies, remould the nature of business. As Castells (1996, 16) has noted: 'In the new, informational mode of development the source of productivity lies in the technology of knowledge generation, information processing, and symbolic communication'.

Investment in information technologies has therefore become a major prop in the theatre of economic conflict between nations. Failure to invest in or embrace these new technologies is not only seen as a threat to future prosperity but to lose ground in the 'head-to-head' (Thurow 1993) positional competition between national economies. This is exemplified in the United States where President Clinton explicitly framed US use of telecommunications technology in terms of 'winning' the twenty-first century:

> America's destiny is linked to our information infrastructure... The potential benefits for the nation are immense. The NII will enable US firms to compete and win in the global economy, generating good jobs for the American people and economic growth for the nation.
>
> (Information Infrastructure Task Force 1993) [USA]

This rhetoric of 'head-to-head' is also echoed in other countries:

> We want to provide an important impetus for preparing Germany's educational sector for the requirements of the 21st century – thereby providing an important basis for Germany's success in global competition between industrialised countries.
>
> (Sommer 18.4.96) [Germany]

> ...a wide ranging programme to help British businesses match the best in the world. This programme is aimed at helping the UK reverse a century of relative economic decline... call[ing] for a renewed focus on knowledge as the means of providing competitive advantage – knowledge in the broadest sense, including the skills, creativity and expertise of all those involved.
>
> (DTI 1999a, 1) [UK]

Within the discourse of comparative economic advantage, IT policies in education are typically presented as satisfying two economic criteria. Firstly, they represent a concerted attempt to change the economic 'mindset' of future workers towards a technologically based global competition. This is seen as a way of stimulating the indigenous IT industry and technological research and development, creating 'business hubs' and introducing 'e-commerce' to both public and private sectors:

> The knowledge driven economy is not simply about strengthening the science base and raising the education and skill levels of the workforce. These objectives are vitally important and central to government policy. But success in the knowledge driven economy requires a shift in the business mind set; greater receptiveness to know-how... eagerness to keep on learning at all levels in a business.
>
> (DTI 1998, 10) [UK]

In Singapore this is captured in the idea of the 'technopreneur' which involves workers in established as well as newly created businesses being able to find new ways of improving productivity or product design through the introduction of new ideas and technologies. Therefore, a major challenge in Singapore is to change the mindset of the workforce because the existing role models are seen to encourage talented young people to join the government or a large company:

> You will change the mind set by telling them that this is the next Mount Everest to climb. This is the next challenge, that we have already climbed this hill; working for a multinational, working for a government – too common... So we will want to have our engineering and science students to understand that science and technology is no longer just the creation of products, processes, services, but we should add one more thing, companies, the creation of companies.
>
> (National Science and Technology Board) [Singapore][4]

The second economic justification for investment in IT in the educational system is based on a perceived need to up-grade the skills base of emerging cohorts of pupils and students. This is captured in the notion of 'employability' and the increased importance attached to 'key' or 'core' skills, which include a working knowledge of IT:

> Those who are unable to make use of the opportunities provided by ever more powerful information and communications technology will have a very difficult time in the 21st century's labour market. And economies whose citizens are unable to handle the tools of computer and telecommunications technology will fall behind in extremely intense international competition.
>
> (Sommer 18.4.96) [Germany]

> IT skills are a key component of most jobs. By deploying these technologies as part of the learning processes in schools and beyond, we will familiarise people with them. But we need also to promote the development of IT skills more directly through basic training and by offering people the opportunity to acquire advanced skills.
>
> (COOI 1998, 11) [UK]

However, such rhetoric can be seen as part of a larger discursive construction of the new 'model' workers for the information age. In Korea, for instance, political leaders see education as a 'prime mover for continuous economic development in the information age' (Kim 1999, 56). In this respect some governments have been far more explicit in their focus on the new 'high' skills requirements of the global economy. Technologically-based education systems are thereby seen as creating the 'workforce flexibility' to counter the threat of a global labour market:

> Countries that have an insufficient supply of skilled workers will see high-skilled, high-paying jobs migrate to countries that can supply the needed talent. Those that have a surplus will find job opportunities opening for their workers in overseas organisations. Even though the United States has led the world into the digital age, we face these same realities. Without a concerted effort to develop students and workers to meet the new challenges of the digital economy, the United States could face a migration of high-skilled, high-wage jobs to other countries.
>
> (Secretariat on Electronic Commerce 1998, 49) [USA]

However, in the developmental nation states of East Asia again we find that the emphasis on future employability and the new 'model' workers incorporate the utilization of technology based education as a way of meeting their perceived need for a future workforce with creative, innovative, critical, and intellectual skills, which the system of rote learning in the past is now judged to be inadequate.

> Malaysia intends to transform its educational system, in line with and in support of the nation's drive to fulfil Vision 2020. This vision calls for sustained, productivity-driven growth, which will be achievable only with a technologically literate, critically thinking workforce prepared to participate fully in the global economy of the 21st century.
>
> (Malaysian Ministry of Education 1997, 2.1)

> The underlying philosophy of the Masterplan is that education should continually anticipate the future needs of society, and work towards fulfilling those needs. The skills required for the future will centre on thinking skills,

learning skills and communication skills. IT-based teaching and learning will be one of our key strategies for equipping our young with these skills.

(NCB 1999a, 1) [Singapore]

Societal aims

The discussion so far of educational and economic aims also point to the importance of how these relate to societal aims which will also vary according to national differences in political economy. For the purposes of this paper we have defined these differences in terms of Neo-Liberal and Developmental States models of education and the application of IT. It is worth reiterating that the clustering of countries around these models (with the exception of Germany) will inevitably obscure variations in approaches, for instance between Britain and the USA. However it is the difference in the 'piecemeal' approach apparent in our Neo-Liberal countries and the 'holistic' approaches in Japan and the Asian Tiger economies which is most striking. This conclusion is reinforced when we extend our analysis to societal aims.

What is surprising given the importance attached to globalization in each of the countries was the paucity of discussion about how IT could be used to develop a sense of global rather than national identity. There appears to be an implicit assumption that as people are exposed to new individual and social possibilities derived from other parts of the world this therefore poses a threat to national identity. The question of global citizenship is raised in the Korean literature as the following quotation describes:

> [Korean] education needs to build leadership qualities so that our students can participate as world citizens. We need to open our minds to the world, and to think and behave from the perspective of world citizens. Peace education, education for international understanding and the training of international communication skills should be promoted at every level of schooling.
>
> (Kim 1999, 62) [Korea]

But this emphasis on opening 'our minds to the world' reflects the demands of the globalization strategies of the Korean Chaebol in the 1990s. It also reflects the historical isolation of Korea, which is only recently beginning to change. Therefore, the global reach which new communication technologies permit are, at best, being used to enhance mutual understanding of different nations and cultures:

> Japan's objectives are ... to achieve the free circulation of information at home and abroad in order to strongly promote the transparency of Japanese society and to build a Japan that is open to the world.
>
> (Telecommunications Council 1994, 1) [Japan]

> Using the Internet, Korea can introduce its culture, history, artistic heritage and everything it takes pride in to global society. To make Korea better understood, we have to build ... websites.
>
> (Namgoong 1999) [Korea]

However, the societal aims of NII policy-making are also expressed in terms of citizenship, lifeskills, and individual assess to information. In some countries, therefore, there is a strong emphasis on the ameliorative effects technology can have on individual citizens; primarily in terms of righting existing 'wrongs' of industrial society. For example, the Japanese agenda for creating an 'intellectually creative society' makes much of developing an info-communications infrastructure in order to reform the socio-economic system and 'improve people's lives'. The individual and social implications of the Japanese Information Infrastructure are therefore presented in many contexts: dealing with an ageing population (both in terms of health support and encouraging increased participation in society); rectifying over-concentration in urban areas; addressing the environmental concerns from an industrial structure based on the massive consumption of resources; and, finally, realizing a 'comfortable lifestyle' (Telecommunications Council 1994).

Outside of Japan most attention has been paid to the 'forward-looking' role of educational technology in pre-empting potential problems of the emerging 'information society' for the individual citizen. Such notions have often been broadly based around the need for citizenship in the information age – in particular the 'lifeskills' needed for the twenty-first century:

> Germany's young students will be able to profit from interesting, modern instruction that impacts the real fascination of modern information technology. They will receive the opportunity to become aware, creative citizens of the information society.
>
> (Rüttgers 18.4.96) [Germany]

The issue of citizenship in an information age also returns to issues of 'opportunity' especially for lower socio-economic groups or rural communities. There is widespread concern over the creation of a 'digital underclass' of 'information-have nots'. In the German context this has been portrayed more in terms of ensuring equality of outcome, with an emphasis on teaching individuals how to use IT 'profitably' and 'appropriately':

> The aim of the initiative is to give as many young people as possible the opportunity [to use] multimedia as mental nourishment rather than junk food.
>
> (Rüttgers 18.4.96) [Germany]

However, in the UK and USA there is a focus on initially ensuring that all have access to the 'hardware' of the information age:

> Education and the information age will support and reinforce each other. The information age will transform education, at all levels and for all ages. Education in turn will equip people with the necessary skills to profit from the information age. We want to open up these opportunities to everyone.
>
> (COOI 1998, 7) [UK]

> [We aim to] extend the 'universal service' concept to ensure that information resources are available to all at affordable prices. Because information means empowerment – and employment – the government has a duty to ensure that all Americans have access to the . . . potential of the Information Age.
>
> (Information Infrastructure Task Force 1993) [USA]

In Britain and the United State this question of opportunity is not only understood as a matter of citizenship but also of nation building. The attempt to narrow educational, economic and social inequalities through new technologies is seen as a necessary feature of a cohesive society. But it is in respect to nation building that the full extent of the differences in the discursive construction of education superhighway policy-making are revealed. In the Western countries only a very loose and vague notion of nation building is alluded to, for example:

> Information technology is central to our key priority of improving education for all – making Britain better.
>
> (COOI 1998, 1) [UK]

Similarly, in America any prevailing rhetoric upon these lines lacks a collective focus, instead invoking more a sense of a nation of individuals:

> the NII promises to transform the lives of the American people. It can ameliorate the constraints of geography and economic status, and give all Americans a fair opportunity to go as far as their talents and ambitions will take them.
>
> (Information Infrastructure Task Force 1993) [USA]

However, in East Asia where the role of the developmental state is inextricably connected to issues of national identity and nation building (Brown 1999; Kam and Gopinathan 1999), the use of education to foster nation building has been extended in terms of educational superhighway construction. In the first instance this approach focuses firmly on issues of national identity.

> Japan stands at an important cross-roads. The era of constantly rising growth is past. We are seeing the twilight of the economic system that nurtured historically unparalleled, stunning economic growth during the post-war period. Having a range of burdens inherited from the past, Japan is now searching for ways to establish the foundations for its nationhood in the future.
>
> (Telecommunications Council 1994, 1) [Japan]

> Concerns and efforts to preserve our traditional culture should be strengthened in order to live with other nations harmoniously without losing our own identity.
>
> (Kim 1999, 62) [Korea]

Similarly, one of the central challenges of Malaysia's Vision 2020 is 'establishing a united Malaysia with a sense of common and shared destiny' (Lee 1999, 87). Here the development of national identity through telecommunications networks has specifically focused on overcoming regional disharmony:

> Education is an instrument for promoting and strengthening national integration by inculcating a common and shared destiny among the different ethnic groups, removing racial prejudices and encouraging racial tolerance, and establishing the use of a common national language, that is, Bahasa Malaysia.
>
> (Lee 1999, 87) [Malaysia]

Towards a research agenda

The building of national information infrastructures and educational networks is clearly a global concern. The vast sums of funding already committed will mean that NII policy-making is set to have a profound effect on educational systems the world over. We have attempted to locate such initiatives within a framework of political economy, which has focused on points of convergence and divergence to compare Neo-liberal and Developmental State models. This analysis highlights both the importance of comparative analysis and the need for detailed studies of other models which may exist, for instance, in continental Europe, Australia and the Middle East (e.g. Geray 1999). Moreover, despite the magnitude of this global drive towards the creation of education networks little is known about the relative effectiveness of these different approaches or the likely impact of networks on student/teacher attitudes, learning cultures, equity and the social construction of student 'employability'. There is also a need to further theorize the impact of 'networked education' within 'network' societies (Castells 1996). In formulating a research agenda the longitudinal nature of NII policies must be taken into account with, the effectiveness of such policies only slowly becoming apparent. The national initiatives described in this paper can be 'tracked' as they begin to be implemented and progress from policy to practice. In this way, at least five main areas of questioning readily present themselves.

The effect of NII policies on national education systems

Underlying any such analysis is the examination of the effects NII initiatives will have on different education systems as they are implemented. For instance, will the connection of classrooms to the Internet really lead to the transformation of teaching and learning that is being claimed in official policy documents? Is the introduction of 'networked education' part of a universal transformation to 'new forms' of education? Even in countries such as Singapore, which are introducing far-reaching changes aimed at transforming their educational systems through the use of new technologies, the extent to which this can overcome the inertia of 'bureaucratic' education remains to be seen (Marvin 1986). Sawheny (1996) argues that models of the 'information superhighway' may do little more than amplify the existing parameters of the quantity and speed of information transfer and overlook the new 'liberty of action' the medium potentially offers. From an educational perspective Jane Kenway and colleagues (1994) make a similar point in drawing a distinction between 'new' and merely 'pseudo' forms of education.

Therefore, to what extent can initiatives such as the National Grid for Learning, Schulen and Netz, and Smart Schools be seen as new educational forms? Do they really represent new ways of approaching curriculum and pedagogy? Are they encouraging new educational forms and values that transcend information exchange? Alternatively, do they represent the latest example of the 'technical fix' (Robins and Webster 1989) where the social and political context of 'wired education' and the way new technologies are embedded in societal institutions such as the family, school, and labour market are reduced to a technocratic model of social progress?

The establishing of educational networks – a centralization or decentralization of power?

An inherent quality of information technologies is that they can be used to centralize or decentralize decision-making and institutional power. Therefore we also need to investigate whether the installation of educational superhighways is leading to a centralization or decentralization of control over national educational systems. In changing the role of the teacher and curriculum, opening access up to resources around the world, it is commonly argued that education network programmes are effectively devolving educational power away from the centre towards the local context of the school, teacher and learner (Selwyn 2000). Government statements on these issues emphasize the 'democratization' of education and the empowerment of teachers and students. However, the counter-argument is that 'wiring up' classrooms to the Internet and provide online resources to teachers and students is a way of monopolising the power to decide what is to count as 'really useful' information and knowledge. As Kitchin (1998, 102) argues, in formulating such policies most 'governments have recognised the power of the Internet to disseminate information and political ideology'.

The scale of national investments in 'networked education' can therefore be interpreted as an attempt by nation states to counter the threat of unadulter-ated access to cyberspace and potential loss of social control (Poster 1990). By institutionalizing cyberspace in this way, governments can reassert their power over education systems. As Feenberg (1995, 88) intimates, central governments draw their power not from their direct role in the teaching process but from control of the technology of teaching; 'organisations responsible for delivering public ser-vices restructure them around technical mediations that impose centralisation and control'. Thus, programmes such as the UK National Grid for Learning could be seen as a continuation of the centralization of power and control in education that has persisted throughout the last 20 years of neo-liberal policy-making in the West.

Therefore, to what extent do NII programmes act as an illustration of how the Internet is being incorporated into systems of state power? Poster (1990, 1995) contends that IT and the Internet in particular, extends and perfects the 'capillary' extension of state power throughout the space of disciplinary society into a 'Super-Panopticon'. But it is not clear that this necessarily means that NII programmes represent 'new forms' of domination. Although the Internet may seem to challenge traditional notions of power, it is a microcosm of real-life social relations: reproducing and reinforcing existing power relations (Kitchin 1998). Equally, if education networking policy has been motivated by a desire to extend state power, it is difficult to explain why Britain and the USA have adopted a piecemeal approach with the private sector taking a major role in policy implementation. It can also be plausibly argued that government concerns about the new technologies of education reflect a genuine reduction in state control over information and knowledge. In Singapore, for instance, attempts to control access to the Internet have widely been acknowledged to have failed, which has led the Singapore government to put more emphasis on 'educating' students about how to use and interpret the information they can now receive, such as critical commentaries about the role of the ruling People's Action Party. Therefore, to what extent are new technologies of education simply new technologies of state control? Or do they represent a democratization of information and knowledge that have the potential to empower both students and teachers?

Political economy, culture and the creation of NII policy

This paper has argued that national policies of education and NII can not be understood independently of an analysis of the state, economy and society. Moreover, from this initial consideration alone, it is clear that there are important differences in the way nation states are organizing their education network initiatives. More comparative research is therefore required to understand and explain the nature of these differences. What role do cultural differences play in explaining Neo-Liberal as opposed to Developmental State models of education and technological innovation? Garfield and Watson (1998), for instance, argue that cultural difference between countries appear to be strongly reflected in NII policy mechanisms and eventual goals, from the 'village market' cultures of the USA and UK reflected in their market-driven NII policies to the Singaporean 'family' national culture reflected in the government-directed IT2000 vision. Thus, cultural variations in individualism and collectivism; norms of power distribution; political process; and short-term/long-term orientation, can affect and be affected by national information infrastructures. Equally, Japan's loftier goals of improving societal ills can be traced to its dominant national culture, along with a strong cultural faith in technology (Latzer 1995; Garfield and Watson 1998). National culture is also reflected in Singapore's overt attempts to control, and in some cases censor, individuals' access to the Internet (Birch 1998).

NII policy-making and the reskilling of national workforces

It is also important to consider the role of education networking and NII policy-making on changing the nature of the skills-base of the workforce, the reconstruction of the individual worker-citizen and, in particular the current emphasis on developing a 'high-skills' workforce. The picture of empowered knowledge workers portrayed within many countries' policy statements contrasts with the view that the 'information age' will not lead to an expansion of 'high-skilled' employment opportunities but a new cohort of information slaves rather than knowledge workers.

Therefore, how much credence is there in the argument that establishing educational networks will prepare all students for 'high skilled' employment in the 'information age'? Although computerized telecommunications undoubtedly will play a major role in the twenty-first century, it is argued that the conventional wisdom that 'all' students should be educated in preparation for a[n] information or knowledge economy ignores the limited numbers of high skilled jobs that will be required (Rumberger and Levin 1984; Apple 1997). Therefore, can it be plausibly argued that many students will require little more than a 'McDonald's level' of familiarity with technology, primarily consisting of lower order data-entry and limited problem solving skills (Neill 1995). The validity of these alternative accounts of the relationship between economic change, technology and skills remains a matter for empirical enquiry. Comparative research on skill formation in the countries included in this paper reveal important differences in skill formation strategies which in turn may have an [*sic*] sizeable impact on the relative demand for skilled workers (Lauder 1999). Therefore, an important question for future research is how the role of educational networks relates to national skill formation strategies and the emerging supply and demand of hi-tech workers.

Highways to social inclusion or exclusion?

Finally, one of the points of convergence in government education and NII policy statements is the view that new information technologies hold out the prospect of transcending social class, gender and racial differences in access to knowledge and learning opportunities. Therefore, as 'online education' becomes more widely available to those in formal and informal educational settings, we will need to study the *nature* of this access. Are the socio-economic disadvantages experienced by the poor, or those in poverty, reinforced by a lack of access to information technologies? Equally important is the issue of social class, gender and racial differences in individual responses to information technology. Do women and men, for instance, utilize new technologies in different ways and what impact does this have on access to education, training and labour market opportunities? From a comparative perspective are there national differences in the ways that social groups respond to wired education? Do such differences relate to cultural variations in attitudes to information technologies and/or reflect opportunity structures for educational or occupational advancement?

Conclusion

Concluding our analysis with a series of unanswered questions may appear perverse but we feel is necessary if progress is to be made in understanding the impact and effects of educational network policies around the world. These national visions of educational renewal will only slowly be introduced but it is imperative to begin investigating their individual, educational, economic and societal consequences. Moreover, it is clear that a comparative approach is essential to any such analysis, as developments in the UK are not occurring in isolation from what is taking place in Singapore or the USA and, indeed, policy borrowing appears to be widespread.

Our analysis suggests that although there is some evidence of policy convergence there is more evidence of divergent trends. This policy divergence does not reflect an evolutionary model of technological progression with some countries merely more advanced than others in their implementation, but rather reflects fundamental differences in political economy. It is therefore imperative that these variations in educational information infrastructures are recognized and explored. As Melody (1996, 244) argues:

> Clearly there will be as many 'information societies' as there are societies. All countries [are not trying] to charge down a single path emulating the perceived leaders in technological development at any moment in time. Rather each society will want to use the new technology and service opportunities to meet its particular priority needs and values and thus to help shape its futures. The addition of the term 'information' to 'society' should imply an expansion of the opportunities for individual societies, as well as individuals within societies, to enhance their distinctiveness in designing their own futures.

Whether this will prove to be the case is a moot point. But this initial skirmish with the comparative evidence suggests that there are differences in the way education is being constructed within 'network' societies, which could have significant long-term educational, economic and social consequences. But an obvious limitation of such policy analysis is that it is unable to tell us much about the process of converting policy into practice and the efficacy of policy in meeting its stated aims. A comparative analysis of the relationship between educational networking and wider NII programmes, of how educational networks are being introduced into schools, colleges and universities, and of how effective new educational technologies are proving (or otherwise) to be in meeting educational, economic and societal goals, is now required.

Acknowledgements

The authors are grateful to Chon Sun Ihm for his assistance in locating sources on South Korea, as well as Leon Tikly and the three anonymous referees for their helpful comments on earlier drafts of this paper.

Notes

1 Although now being referred to in some countries as ICT or CIT, this paper refers to IT to maintain a sense of continuity. Here IT is defined as encompassing multimedia in its broadest sense, acknowledging the rapid convergence of computers, telecommunications and broadcasting technologies.
2 The idea for this paper derives from an ESRC funded project 'Education & Training Markets for a High Skills Economy: a Comparative Study' (ESRC R000236664). The selection of the seven case study countries is therefore based around the project's focus on the USA, UK, Germany and East-Asian countries.
3 There are obvious exceptions to this, such as the Singapore government report A Vision of an Intelligent Island published in 1992.
4 This quote derives from an interview with the National Science and Technology Board in Singapore. This interview was conducted as part of an ESRC funded project 'Education and Training Routes to a High Skills Economy'. See *Journal of Education and Work*, Special Issue, Winter 1999.

Bibliography

Apple, M. (1997) 'The New Technology: Is it Part of the Solution or Part of the Problem in Education?' in Hawisher, G.E. and Selfe, C. (eds) *Literacy, Technology and Society: Confronting the Issues* (New Jersey: Prentice Hall).

Ashton, D. and Green, F. (1996) *Education, Training and the Global Economy* (Cheltenham: Edward Elgar).

Ball, S. J. (1999) Labour, Learning and the Economy: a policy sociology perspective. *Cambridge Journal of Education*, 29(2): 195–206.

Birch, D. (1998) Communication Policy in Asia: Limited Democracy and the Public Sphere. *Media International Australia*, 86: 87–102.

Breiter, A. and Kubicek, H. (1999) *Educational Technology and Organisational Reform in the United States: Executive Summary* (University of Bremen: Mimeo).

Brown, P. (1999) Globalisation and the Political Economy of High Skills: notes towards a comparative theory *Journal of Education and Work*, 12(3): 233–51.

Brown, P. and Lauder, H. (2000) *Capitalism and Social Progress* (Baskingstoke: Macmillan).

Castells, M. (1996) *The Rise of the Network Society* (London: Blackwells).

Central Office of Information (COOI) (1998) *Our Information Age: the Governments Vision* (London: Stationary Office).

Department for Education and Employment (1998) Blunkett Announces Details of Biggest Ever Investment in Schools Information and Communication Technology, *Press Release 184/98* (London: DfEE).

Department for Trade and Industry (1998) *Our Competitive Future: Building the Knowledge Driven Economy*, White Paper December 1998 (London: Stationary Office).

Department for Trade and Industry (1999a) *Competitiveness: Our Partnership with Business*. Available online at http://www.dti.gov.uk/comp/imp2.html

Department of Education (1996) *Getting Americas Students Ready for the 21st Century: Meeting the Technology Literacy Challenge* (Washington, DC: US Department of Education).

Feenberg, A. (1995) *Alternative Modernity: the Technical Turn in Philosophy and Social Theory* (Berkeley: University of California Press).

Garfield, M. J. and Watson, R. T. (1998) 'Differences in National Information Infrastructures: the Reflection of National Cultures', *Journal of Strategic Information Systems*, 6: 313–37.

Geray, H. (1999) 'Network Policy Formation between Idealist and Strategic Models: a Political Economy Perspective from Turkey', *Telecommunications Policy*, 23(6): 495–511.

Information Infrastructure Task Force (1993) *The National Information Infrastructure: Agenda for Action*, Washington, DC, ITAF. Available online at http://metalab.unc.edu/nii/NII-Executive-Summary.html

Jung, I. (2000) 'Korea: Can Edutopia Become a Reality?', *TechKnowLogia*, 1(2): 48–50.

Kam, H. W. and Gopinathan, S. (1999) 'Recent Developments in Education in Singapore' *School Effectiveness & School Improvement*, 10(1): 99–117.

Kenway, J. (1995) 'Reality Bytes: Education, Markets and the Information Superhighway', *Australian Educational Researcher*, 22(1): 35–65.

Kenway, J. (1996) 'The Information Superhighway and Post-Modernity: the Social Promise and the Social Price', *Comparative Education*, 32(2): 217–31.

Kenway, J., Bigum, C., Fitzclarence, L, Collier, J. and Tregenza, K. (1994) 'New Education in New Times', *Journal of Education Policy*, 9(4): 317–33.

Kim, Y. H. (1999) 'Recent Developments in Korean School Education', *School Effectiveness & School Improvement*, 10(1): 55–71

Kitchin, R. (1998) *Cyberspace: the World in the Wires* (Chichester: Wiley).

Korea Multimedia Education Centre (1997) *Korea Multimedia Education Centre* (Seocho-Gu Seoul: KMEC).

Korean Research Information Centre (1997) *Korean Research Information Centre* (Seoul: KRIC).

Langdale, J. V. (1997) 'International Competitiveness in East Asia: broadband telecommunications and interactive multimedia', *Telecommunications Policy*, 21(3): 235–49.

Latzer, M. (1995) 'Japanese Information Infrastructure Initiatives: a Politico-Economic Approach', *Telecommunications Policy*, 19(7): 515–29.

Lauder, H. (1999) 'Competitiveness and the problem of low skill equalibria: a comparative analysis', *Journal of Education and Work*, 12(3): 281–94.

Lee, M. N. N. (1999) 'Education in Malaysia: Towards Vision 2020', *School Effectiveness & School Improvement*, 10(1): 86–98.

Le Grand, J. and Bartlett, W. (1993) *Quasi Markets and Social Policy* (London: Macmillan).

McLaughlin, R. (1999) 'The Internet and Japanese Education: the Effect of Globalisation on Education Policies and Government Initiatives', *Aslib Proceedings*, 51(7): 224–32.

Malaysian Ministry of Education (1997) The Malaysian Smart School: Conceptual Blueprint (Malaysia: Dept. of Education).

Martinez, L. (1997) 'Thinking about the Information Infrastructure', *Telecommunications Policy*, 21(1): 72–3.

Marvin, C. (1986) *When Old Technologies were New: Thinking about Electronic Communication in the Late Nineteenth Century* (Oxford: Oxford University Press).

Melody, W. H. (1996) 'Toward a Framework for Designing Information Society Policies', *Telecommunications Policies*, 20(4): 243–59.

Ministry of Education (1998) *Learning to Think, Thinking to Learn: Towards Thinking Schools, Learning Nations* (Singapore: Ministry of Education). Available online at http://moe.edu.sg

Ministry of International Trade and Industry (1994) *Program for Advanced Information Infrastructure*. Available online at http://www.glocom.ac.jp

Moore, N. (1998) 'Confucius or Capitalism? Policies for an information society', in B. D. Loader (ed.), *Cyberspace Divide: Equality, Agency and Policy in the Information Society* (London: Routledge).

Namgoong, S. (1999) Minister Namgoong stresses importance of mastering English in Internet age. *Korea Herald*, 19 January 1999. Available online at http://www.koreaherald.co.kr

National Computer Board (1999a) *IT Masterplan: a summary*. Available online at http://www.moe.edu.sg/iteducation/masterplan/summary0.htm

National Computer Board (1999b) *Computer Purchase Scheme for Teachers*. Available online at http://www.moe.edu.sg/iteducation/masterplan

National Council for Educational Technology (1997) NCET – response to National Grid for Learning, *Press Release 7 October 1997* (Coventry: NCET)

Neill, M. (1995) 'Computers, Thinking and Schools in "the New World Order" ' in J. Brook and I. A. Boal. (eds), *Resisting the Virtual Life: The Culture and Politics of Information* (San Francisco: City Lights).

Poster, M. (1990) *The Mode of Information* (London: Polity).

Poster, M. (1995) *The Second Media Age* (London: Polity).

Research Machines (1999) *The RM G7 Report 1998: IT Provision in Schools* (Abingdon: Research machines).

Robins, K. and Webster, F. (1989) *The Technical Fix: Education, Computers and Industry* (Basingstoke: Macmillan).

Rumberger, R. and Levin, H. (1984) *Forecasting the Impact of New Technologies on the Future Job Market* (School of Education: Stanford University).

Rüttgers, J. (18 April 1996) *Statement by Federal Minister on the Occasion of the Launch of the 'Schools Online' Initiative*, Bonn. Available online at http://www.san-ev.de/default_en.asp

Sawhney, H. (1996) 'Information Superhighway: Metaphors as Midwives', *Media, Culture and Society*, 18: 291–314.

Schidtbe, O. (1998) 'Berlin and the Net: Prospects for Cyberdemocracy from above and below', in R. Tsagarousianou, D. Tambini and C. Bryan (eds), *Cyberdemocracy: Technology, Cities and Civic Networks* (London: Routledge).

Schiller, H. I. (1986) 'The Erosion of National Sovereignty by the World Business System', in M. Traber (ed.), *The Myth of the Information Revolution* (London: Sage).

Schiller, H. I (1995) 'The Global Information Highway: Project for an Ungovernable World', in J. Brook and I. A. Boal (eds), *Resisting the Virtual Life: The Culture and Politics of Information* (San Francisco: City Lights).

Secretariat on Electronic Commerce (1998) *The Emerging Digital Economy* (Washington, DC: US Department of Commerce).

Selwyn, N. (1998) 'A Grid for Learning or a Grid for Earning? The Significance of the Learning Grid Initiative in UK Education', *Journal of Educational Policy*, 13(3): 423–31.

Selwyn, N. (1999) 'Educational Superhighways – in the Public or Private Interest' *Internet Research: Electronic Networking Applications and Policy*, 9(3): 225–31.

Selwyn, N. (2000) 'The National Grid for Learning: Panacea or Panopticon?', *British Journal of Sociology of Education*, 21(2): 243–55.

Sommer, R. (18 April 1996) *Statement for the Start of the 'Schools Online' Initiative*, Bonn. Available online at http://www.san-ev.de/default_en.asp

Streeck, W. (1992) *Social, Institutional and Economic Performance* (London: Sage).

Tan, Z. (1995) 'Chinas Information Superhighway: what is it and who controls it?', *Telecommunications Policy*, 19(9): 721–31.

Telecommunications Council (Japan) (1994) *Reforms Towards the Intellectually Creative Society of the 21st Century: Programme for the Establishment of High-Performance Info-Communications Infrastructure* Tokyo, Telecommunications Council. Available at http://mpt.go.jp

Teo, T. and Lim, V. (1998) 'Leveraging Information Technology to Achieve the IT2000 Vision: the case study of an intelligent island', *Behaviour and Information Technology*, 17(2): 113–23.

The Presidential Commission on Education Reform (1995) *Education Reform for New Education System* (Korea: The Presidential Commission on Education Reform).

Thurow, L. (1993) *Head to Head: the coming economic battle among Japan, Europe and America* (London: Nicholas Brealey).

Uncaplar, W. (1999) 'Electronic Homesteading on the rural frontier', in M. Smith and P. Kollock (eds), *Communities in Cyberspace* (London: Routledge).

US Secretariat on Electronic Commerce (1998) *The Emerging Digital Economy* (Washington, DC: US Department of Commerce).

Utsumi, Y. (1995) GII and its Future Challenges, speech made to *Telecommunications Summit: the International Conference and Exhibition on Human Resources Development*, September 4th 1995, Bandung, Indonesia.

CHAPTER 11

UNRAVELLING A 'SPUN' POLICY

A case study of the constitutive role of 'spin' in the education policy process

Sharon Gewirtz, Marny Dickson and Sally Power

Journal of Education Policy, May 2004, 19(3): 321–42

Introduction

This paper draws on a 3-year study of the English Education Action Zones (EAZs) policy.[1] This policy was one of a number of area-based initiatives introduced in England by the New Labour[2] Government in their first term of office (1997–2001). The initial Government publicity suggested that EAZs would be 'standard bearers in a new crusade uniting business, schools, local education authorities[3] and parents to modernize education in areas of social disadvantage' (DfEE, 1998). Allocated via a process of competitive bidding, 25 'first-round' EAZs were introduced between September 1998–January 1999, followed by a further 48 'second-round' EAZs in the period September 1999–April 2000. The zones, resourced by a combination of state and private funding, were established in a mixture of urban and rural locations. The policy was short-lived, however, and has since been eclipsed by other initiatives. The purpose of this paper is not to provide an analysis or evaluation of the EAZ policy. Rather, we intend to use the case of EAZs to explore issues around the role of impression management in educational governance and the policy process. In particular, the paper is concerned with processes of governance which attempt to manage, contain or render invisible potential controversies that relate to policy development and implementation by impression management, or what has become known as 'spin'.

In the collection and analysis of the data from our study of the EAZ initiative, spin has arisen as an unexpectedly prominent theme. For example, spin was often raised explicitly by those we interviewed as an activity that they needed to be reflexive about and engage in. It was described as shaping the fortunes of the policy or, in some cases, as constituting the policy. We were often aware that we were being spun a line about the 'successes' of the policy and frequently overt attempts were made by those we were researching to try to 'persuade' us of a particular spin which we should put on our own research questions and/or reports. The following examples from the data illustrate some of the diverse articulations of the theme of spin that emerged in the course of our fieldwork. Crudely, some of these are spin, some are about spin, and one is an example of the study itself being caught up in spin:

> [Y]ou always have to have a headline for the press when you publish a bill and we decided that Education Action Zones should be the headline because a lot of the other content of the Bill was detailed stuff about the GM [grant-maintained][4]

sector becoming Foundation Schools and so on which is not very interesting at all. So...we decided to highlight them and that went really – that worked perfectly, it was a model of policy development, press announcement, got good attention, and plenty of column inches, air time, message was right...

(Civil Servant A)[5]

...[T]he whole EAZ experience has been a fun time. All Year 6 pupils in the zone went to the Dome as a learning day out. We were covering the day as journalists and interviewing people about what they thought of the trip and taking photographs...I think the EAZ is a brilliant way to boost educational standards and help all the children get a brighter future for themselves.

(Ben Borthwick, Year 7, Kingswood High School, Bransholme, Kingston Upon Hull EAZ, 'quoted' in Department for Education and Employment (DfEE)s[6] EAZs newsletter, Issue 1, Summer 2000)

It was very much the style of the early days of the government, early initiatives of the government, establishing a certain position vis-a-vis [the] public, the readership of the *Daily Mail*.[7] They were not going to be seen as going into a kind of social partnership with trades unions, teachers...they were going to be seen as sorting out, and quickly, long-standing problems, which through a mixture of action and spin, you know, would be rapidly alleviated. Even though there were long-standing problems in our education system.

(Teacher union official)

I was worried that it [joining an EAZ] could be perceived as something that a school in crisis got involved in rather than a successful school...So I was worried that that's how people within our community who we are trying to attract to the school might perceive it. It doesn't seem to have happened that way, largely because it's not been, because, as I said before, it's been presented to parents as 'we're part of an Education Action Zone – it's dynamic and we get lots of money from it!'

(Teacher, Greenbrook EAZ)

The results have gone up, you know, quite dramatically...I think the zone's contributed to it. I mean, it would be totally false for me to say it's exclusively due to the zone, because obviously the schools have, you know, greatly played a part in that and I think the schools would have a few misgivings if we presented [the improved results] as totally the impact of the zone, you know. In a sense, we were required to send the zone figures in that way to the DfEE, so it was a bit of a sort of, um, shall I say, a bit of a game...

(Seaham EAZ director)

Both schools have done lots to improve and they certainly let you know about it. I'm getting a bit suspicious with Secondary A – maybe overkill on telling us how good things are as there are still lots of problems there.

(Nairnton parent survey, 2001)

...We all know that when they work well, partnerships with businesses are empowering for young people, staff, schools, businesses, and members of the local community...One thing remains certain – the significant role that EAZs play in raising achievement and improving the life chances of young people.

(Jackie Turner, Department for Education and Skills (DfES) EAZ Education Advisor, quoted in DfES's EAZ newsletter, Issue 4, Autumn 2001)

Dear Marny

I would like to thank you on behalf of the [EAZ group] for attending the meeting on...I hope the points raised at the meeting prove useful in your continuing research into EAZs. In particular, I hope [you are] able to take on board concerns expressed by [group] members at the meeting that it appeared research findings were being compared unfavourably with claims made by ministers at the time EAZs were launched. Members believed it would be particularly unfair to draw this comparison as those working within EAZs are trying to implement the policy they were presented with, not claims made by ministers and the media...

(Extract from letter to Marny Dickson from an EAZ grouping)

There is other data in correspondence and fieldnotes which show attempts to bring influence to bear on how we represent the policy in our own research reports, but because of possible sensitivities we are not able to use it here.

These are just some examples of the various articulations of spin that have appeared across our project database, which includes press coverage of EAZs, EAZ publicity materials, interviews with DfES, LEA and union officials, EAZ directors, headteachers, teachers and EAZ partners, as well as surveys of teachers and parents. The overarching purpose of this paper is to demonstrate the crucial role played by spin in the trajectory of the EAZ policy and thereby to illustrate the complex relationship between spin and policy. In the first section, we define spin and place the concept in historical context. We then go on to explore the relationship between spin and the EAZ policy, focusing, in particular, on the double-coded nature of much of the spin, its dynamic, endemic, and constitutive characteristics, and its disciplinary nature. In doing so, we are seeking to unravel the ways in which policy 'spin' and policy 'substance' are intimately and inextricably bound up together.

Impression management and the growth of political spin

[Politicians]...like to be thought well of and want to control the message and the messengers as far as possible. There is nothing new or even disreputable about this: it comes with the job. What is new though is the systematic and professional way in which it is now undertaken. The wearisome gibes about spinners and sound bites do capture the modern enterprise of news management that is central to contemporary politics. The practitioners of these black arts are increasingly the key figures in the political world.

(Wright 1998, 20)

Contemporary usage of the term spin derives from the US. The concept of 'spin doctors' – political advisors responsible for policy presentation and information management – was first imported into Britain by a *Guardian* columnist in 1988. However, it was not until the general election campaign of 1997 that the expression became widely used within the British media to refer to the process and products of purposively managing information to cast politicians, political parties, governments, and their policies in a favourable light in the eyes of specific audiences. This is also the sense in which we use the term in this paper (although we are arguing that, in practice, policy spin and policy substance cannot be easily separated from each other, as is sometimes implied in both popular and academic discourse).[8]

Esser *et al.* (2000, 210) argue that the spin phenomenon is associated with a new political landscape which was forged in the US:

> The rules of the political game have changed: parties bring in management consultants for a more efficient party organization, advertising experts for better dealing with the mass media, and brainpower – gathered together in policy units and think tanks – for the ideological content.

Whilst 'news management is an inescapable part of politics' (Cockerill *et al.* 1984, 233) and not unique to New Labour, New Labour is frequently presented – by the media and political opponents – as being *obsessively* concerned with impression management to the detriment of both transparency and substantive policy-making. As the British political commentator, Rawnsley (2002) put it: 'Spin has come to be the shorthand which sums up New Labour's reputation for over-promising and under-achieving'. Consequently, spin has become a central plank of Conservative Party attacks on the Labour Government:

> [T]he Tories have become the greatest devotees of spin. Virtually everything they say about the Government or about themselves revolves around spin … It's not by winning policy arguments that they calculate that they will best the Government. Rather, they hope to depict New Labour as a bunch of morally bankrupt twisters who can never be expected to tell the truth about anything.
>
> (Rawnsley 2002)

Thus, it could be argued that spin itself is a spun concept. The negative connotations associated with spin – dishonesty, manipulative and/or inappropriate behaviour – mean that allegations of spin are typically used by those who are hostile to the Labour Government to challenge and undermine the authority of the 'official line' (although see note 8). Accusations of spin have proved to be a useful tool with which to discredit political opponents in the battle over public perceptions and public trust. Spin is clearly not an 'innocent' concept. Nonetheless, the growth of spin is not merely a political invention: the concept and practice of spinning reflect both qualitative and quantitative changes in the nature of media-political relations, evident particularly in the following trends:

- *The growing significance, influence and capacity of the media.* Politics has become increasingly dominated by mass media communicated messages, as television, in particular, has become the public's principal source of political information (Jones 1995). Unsurprisingly, as the role of the media has become more important, politicians have become increasingly aware of the links between media performance, policy presentation, and public perceptions. As a consequence, 'Politicians and their media advisors have become skilled at conveying their messages in ways appealing to the broadcasters' (Riddell 1998, 13). The media assumes particular importance at the time of a general election. As Barendt (1998, 108) puts it, 'Everyone knows now that elections are won by the press'. Accordingly, recent elections have become primarily media rather than party affairs and the significance of party members has declined as the role of political consultants has expanded (Esser *et al.* 2000).

- *An increased politiciztion of the news media.* Cockerill *et al.* (1984) describe a close association of particular government ministers and certain members of the press as dating back at least 100 years in Britain. However, some commentators have claimed that these relations underwent a qualitative shift in the 1970s under Prime Minister Harold Wilson at the time of the Rhodesia crisis when his press secretary, Joe Haines, is said to have established a so-called 'white commonwealth' group of favoured correspondents who could be relied on to give positive coverage to the government over this issue. This tradition is said to have continued during Margaret Thatcher's government under press secretary Bernard Ingram through to the Governments of John Major and Tony Blair (Cockerill *et al.* 1984). The creation of an 'in-group' clearly pre-supposes the existence of an 'out-group' of journalists who find their access to exclusives, interviews, and breaking stories denied if they fail to accept the government line. However, although complaints about media coverage, bullying, and intimidation have been 'part of the media scene for a long time', under the current Labour government it has been argued that what is new is 'how consistently, aggressively, and fast they complain' (Esser *et al.* 2000).

- *The professionalization of news management within political parties.* Campaign management within modern political parties is now characterized by centralized planning and controlling of communications as part of an integrated strategy that follows the pattern of commercial PR (Esser *et al.* 2000). Political parties now place professional experts in PR, marketing, advertising, and polling at the centre of their campaign teams. In Britain, this process is said to have begun in earnest under the Conservative government of Margaret Thatcher (Cockerill *et al.* 1984) and accelerated under New Labour (Esser *et al.* 2000). In addition, New Labour have been credited with creating a particularly efficient news management regime which involves the close monitoring of all media outlets and the collation of data about the inner structure of media organizations, journalists, and the electorate. The creation of detailed databases make it possible for the party to release advantageous information effectively and allow for the 'rapid rebuttal' of critics' claims. Perhaps most importantly, effective impression management requires some level of control over the messages which the media receive. In the run up to the 1997 election, Labour campaign headquarters centralized all communications to ensure that all party members stayed 'on message' in their dealings with the media – a model of news management that the party has retained in Government.

In order to understand why New Labour chose to adopt such a proactive model of impression management, it is important to understand the context in which their fear of 'bad press' developed. Pre-1997, much of the British press exhibited a longstanding antipathy towards the Labour party. Perhaps unsurprisingly, given this history of Conservative bias prior to the 1997 election, Labour spin doctors embarked on a concerted effort to win over the newspapers owned by News International, eventually winning front page endorsement by the *Sun*, Britain's highest selling – and traditionally Conservative Party-supporting – daily paper. Subsequently, political commentators have repeatedly argued that it was the superiority of the Labour media operation that secured Labour's election victory (Esser *et al.* 2000).

Rethinking spin

So, although New Labour is clearly not the first government to try and manipulate information by attempting to control journalists, suppress dissent from within the government's own ranks and control the 'information' that the government sends out, it appears to have taken impression management to new extremes. As Fairclough (2000) has argued, specifically in relation to New Labour's attempts to 'calculatively manipulate' language, it is 'the scale and intensity' which is new. There also now appears to be a greater degree of reflexivity about the process. Spin is not something the government is ashamed of. Rather, it is paraded as both a virtue and a necessity. Indeed, as Franklin (1998, 5) has pointed out, New Labour is the first government explicitly and 'genuinely committed to the belief that the presentation of policy is as important as the policy itself.'

This quote from Franklin is fairly typical of the way in which the relationship between spin and policy is constructed in the public domain and in academic analyses. That is, spin is conventionally understood as something separate from policy, as something that is 'done to' policy in order to make it attractive to particular constituencies. Those constituencies range from the whole of the 'business world' to the archetypal *Daily Mail* reader (see note 6) and middle Englander[9] and, in terms of conventional party politics, its polar opposite – the resident of Old Labour's heartlands.[10]

In this paper, we want to argue for a more complex understanding of the relationship between 'spin' and 'policy'. We want to suggest that spin needs to be understood as operating on two levels, often simultaneously. At one level, it operates as a strategy of impression management, where a range of tactics are used to attempt to control the impression that 'the public' gets of New Labour policies. However, those policies and the 'spin that represents them to 'the public' cannot be understood as distinct and separate entities because the policies cannot be neatly abstracted from the spin. Thus, at another level, we also need to focus on the *constitutive* role that spin plays. We are using the term constitutive here to highlight the way in which spin is not simply 'done to' a policy, but is also something which 'makes up' a policy. A key example here is that certain policies require the demonstration of progress and success and that this in itself becomes an intrinsic feature of the policies rather than something outside of them. This idea is developed more fully later in the paper.

Another characteristic emphasis in the current debate around spin has been the almost exclusive focus on Downing Street and the central government civil service based in Whitehall as the key sites within which spin is produced and struggled over. In this paper, we suggest that spin is more endemic to the policy process and the culture of policy making than is suggested by this focus on central government. Thus, we look more broadly at a range of sites into which the culture and practices of spin have penetrated (i.e. local authorities, zones, schools, teacher unions, private companies, as well as the DfES). In doing so, we attempt to trace the ambiguous and conflicting rationales and interests that are played out in struggles over the production of spin/policy in and across these different sites.

Not only but also

How we understand the underlying rationale for New Labour's commitment to impression management depends on which of New Labour's spins on the policy of spin we believe – as it would seem that the Government's finely tuned art of spin has also subtly been applied to the strategy of spin itself. Thus, those on 'the left' are encouraged to believe that spin is necessary to render traditional Labour policies underpinned by commitments to redistribution and social justice palatable to 'middle England' by dressing them up as being business-friendly. In contrast, the rationale for spin constructed to appeal to those on the right is that business-friendly policies need to be cloaked in a language of social justice in order to secure the support of 'the left'. New Labour's extensive use of the strategy of 'double coding' – the 'not-only-but-also' discursive repertoire (Fairclough 2000), which is particularly reflected in the discourse of the 'third way' (Blair 1998; Giddens 1998) – enables these two mutually exclusive readings of its rationale for spin to co-exist side by side.

Indeed, at its launch in 1998 the EAZ policy was presented as *emblematic* of New Labour's third way – a 'flagship' initiative which combined a commitment to social justice and inclusion with support for new modes of delivering welfare based on public – private partnerships (Gewirtz 1999). The policy, its architects claimed, would raise standards in disadvantaged areas – areas subject to nearly two decades of Conservative neglect – whilst at the same time allowing businesses to get more involved in the running of schools. DfEE officials described the initiative at its launch as 'the centrepiece of Labour's modernization agenda' (Carvel 1998) and Margaret Hodge, then Chair of the Commons Education and Employment Select Committee, argued that 'the development of the Third Way is perhaps best seen in the development of education action zones' (Hodge 1998, 15).

In his interview with us, Civil Servant A, quoted in the introduction to this paper, described the launch as a model of policy development in that it got 'good attention...plenty of column inches [and] air time' and the 'message was right'. There are a number of senses in which this civil servant thinks that the message was 'right'. As he goes on to explain, first, the policy was emblematic of New Labour's policy agenda, and, secondly, the focus on EAZs meant that attention could be deflected away from other potentially more troublesome and controversial aspects of the Bill:

> they were a symbol of New Labour because they were about innovation addressing disadvantage. They've got the sort of core Labour values of addressing disadvantage and the New Labour angle on it which is new ways of doing it, so they were a very good symbol for the reform and put the focus on achievement, whereas a lot of the Bill's actually about the technical details of governing bodies and some of which is very boring, and in any case we didn't particularly want to debate it in public at length 'cause it would all be about – if you had a big debate about that it would be about abolishing the grant maintained sector, which would not be a very constructive debate.
>
> (Civil Servant A)

The message conveyed by the announcement of the policy was also arguably 'right' in the sense that it complied with the message the Downing Street press office was insisting at that time that all departments convey (i.e. that New Labour was a 'modernizing government', 'for all the people', 'delivering on its promises', with 'mainstream policies' providing new directions for Britain (memo quoted in Franklin 1998, 12)). And the double-coded nature of the message – that EAZs were simultaneously promoting social justice *and* enterprise – enabled the policy to be received enthusiastically across the political spectrum of the mainstream media.

Thus, for example, Bright and Wintour (1998) of *The Observer*[11] could write of Britain's 'whirlwind of reform' that it was designed not only to make 'our state schools safe for Middle England', but also 'to prove that the system can deliver on its early egalitarian promise'. Whilst at the same time an article in *The Times* (O'Leary 1998) could welcome the opportunity the policy gave for allowing businesses a greater role in the provision of education, whilst acknowledging that this opportunity had not been taken up in practice.

However, whilst the policy was presented as central not only to New Labour's education agenda, but to its social policy agenda more widely, Civil Servant A claims that the initiative was not necessarily 'really' viewed as particularly central at the time. On his account, the Government had a core education agenda consisting of 'the basic approach to dealing with school standards, like putting data in a system, giving schools responsibilities, disseminating better practice, intervening where school's aren't working, the literacy strategy, the numeracy strategy', and it was this core agenda that was central. The EAZ policy, on the other hand, was simply one of a number of initiatives the Government was trying out:

> I couldn't have said in 1997 which of our policies would become the central planks and which weren't. I would always have known that the National Literacy Strategy was, and the National Numeracy Strategy were the top priority so I could have predicted that, but the others you're doing a range of things...you're trying things out and some of them will be big successes and some of them will become things you tried out but didn't work quite as you expected.
>
> (Civil Servant A)

Spin as dynamic

The spin that has been put on the policy by the DfEE/S has not been static. Whilst the double coding has been present throughout, the mix in the 'message' has shifted to some extent as the policy has developed. For example, the earlier press releases and ministerial announcements emphasized the radical nature of the policy and its potential for creating innovative approaches to tackling disadvantage, holding it up as a 'flagship', and a test-bed for the 'future of public service delivery'. In the initial bidding guidance, particular care was taken to ensure that the role of business was made to seem paramount. Indeed, according to one of the civil servants who drafted the guidance (Civil Servant B), one of the changes that the Secretary of State for Education's special advisor, Conor Ryan, made to the EAZ documentation was to change the order of the partners (schools, local education authorities (LEAs), parents, and business) so that business came first. As we shall see when we discuss the later development of the policy, in retrospect it seems that the spin doctors may have got the balance wrong and the prominence given to business backfired.

Later press releases and comments tended to be more muted, and increasingly the EAZ policy was eclipsed by another policy for improving education provision in disadvantaged areas – Excellence in Cities (EIC) – which seemed to take over as the flagship initiative.

As the EAZ policy progressed, there was also a shift in the spin away from emphasis on business leadership. For example, the press notice announcing the establishment of second round zones was headlined 'Schools leading second round of Education Action Zones' and in the text businesses were mentioned alongside (and after) parents as partners whom the *initiators* – headteachers and schools – had sought to involve. Thus, here headteachers and schools were constructed as the active agents, and parents and businesses were cast in a more passive role in the sense that they were presented as having become involved *as a consequence of* headteacher initiative.

Later press releases also focused more on the policy's 'successes'. The key discourses here were EAZs 'making a difference' and the 'celebration of success'. Thus, for instance, the press release accompanying the announcement of the second round zones provided some examples of EAZs 'making a difference both in terms of performance and securing sponsorship'. These included Wigan's 'companies in classrooms' initiative which the press notice claims had led to improvements in pupils' work. 'Parents as Educators' was identified as 'one of the key successes within the [Blackburn with Darwen] EAZ – with over 160 parents having completed the course by the end of last term – smashing the target of 60 originally set...'. The press release also claims that Newham's 'competency based staff development model...has resulted in the number of teachers leaving EAZ schools this summer down 28% on a year ago, compared with a 1% fall for the whole of Newham!' (DfEE 1999, 5). The language of 'smashing targets', 'making a difference', and the liberal use of exclamation marks has strong echoes of commercial styles of promotion.

In Autumn 2000, figures were released which purported to show that the EAZ policy was directly contributing to rising SATs[12] scores, particularly in primary schools in the zones. Issue 2 of the DfEE's newsletter for zones announced that:

> Across the country zone schools have been celebrating some encouraging GCSE[13] and KS results. These show a positive trend, with year-on-year improvements in zone schools above – and sometimes well above – the national average...On this page we pick out some of the zones where results have been particularly creditable and encouraging. If your zone has achieved similar or better results but is not featured this time – congratulations anyway!

The claims made by the DfEE about improved performance were at some variance with our own analysis of the performance data for EAZ schools which show a more mixed and uncertain picture (Power *et al.* 2003). Doubts also need to be raised about the validity of making claims about the impact of EAZs (a) over such a short timescale (the first EAZs had been up and running for less than 2 years when the initial claims about improving performance were made), and (b) when so many other changes were being implemented at the same time. Indeed, many of the headteachers we spoke to were themselves acutely aware of the impossibility of isolating out the effects of zone status when so many other government initiatives were simultaneously having an impact on schools.

One explanation for the shifts in emphasis in the spin is the negative reporting of the policy following a speech by Michael Barber (then head of the DfEE's Standards and Effectiveness Unit) to the North of England Education Conference where the bidding guidance was launched. The civil servants and teacher association officials we interviewed all saw this event as a key turning point in the policy's fortunes. In the speech, Barber had mentioned that the DfEE expected one of the first round zones to be 'led and run' by business. In response to a question from one of the delegates, Barber stated that zones could be run for profit and he provided the names of some companies which might be interested in such a possibility. The press reporting of the event that evening and the next day focused on the zones as a privatization story. According to the civil servants we interviewed, this was *seen to be* and, thus, *was* very damaging to the policy. Indeed, this 'negative' press reporting was held in large part to be responsible for the policy's demise or transformation.[14] More specifically, these civil servants were arguing that the privatization spin that the press put on Barber's speech fuelled teacher opposition to the policy which in turn hampered the activities of local EAZ partnerships, and that the speech was, therefore, a major miscalculation. As Civil Servant A commented, the DfEE had not anticipated that this was a big news story. If it had been, a Minister would have made the announcement. Furthermore, under the Government's strict press management regime, all major print and broadcast media appearances, the policy content of major speeches, press releases, new policy initiatives, and the timing of announcements must be cleared by Downing Street (the Prime Minister's office) (Mountfield 1997; cited in Franklin 1998). The launching of the bidding guidance was not considered to be a major news story, as Barber was not announcing anything that was not already in the public domain. It was thought to be 'a purely technical matter' (Civil Servant A) and so it was not felt to be necessary to clear it with Downing Street. This was, according to Civil Servant A amongst others, a mistake, which was presented to us as having 'dire consequences for the policy' because:

> ...everybody thought it was a privatization story which is how it got written. Whereas it was never a privatization story, it was never a privatization policy but that's how it got written in the press, so then the unions and the local authorities and everybody out there thinks that's what it is even though it wasn't that.
>
> (Civil Servant A)

> ...the problem with the speech was that it over-hyped the expectations for the policy...I think after that, you know, the education correspondents, having all written up this great sort of privatization story, were determined that unless there was a radical, huge privatization that the policy was going to be dumped...after that the media were totally setting the agenda on Education Action Zones. And, you know, it happens with some policies. People seem to think that we are able to greatly manipulate the agenda on these things. I would say, after January 1998 the media had total control of the agenda and I think there was almost an inevitability that they were going to damn Education Action Zones from then on in.
>
> (Civil Servant D)

The role of the private sector, on Civil Servant A's account, was 'a kind of small bit of the policy that had a huge consequence'.

One possible reading of this version of the policy's demise – as emanating from the media reporting of the North of England speech – is that it represents part of a sophisticated strategy of spin designed to deflect attention from what might be viewed as fundamental flaws in the policy by blaming 'mischievous' journalists, local government officials, and trade union activists – or a failure of spin – for the policy's demise. Such flaws include the decision to establish EAZs as separate legal entities, which resulted in enormous administrative costs; and the short time scale allowed for the establishment of the first round zones. The latter meant that many zones were established without consultation with teachers and parents, and, according to one source (Civil Servant C), in some cases applications for zone status were submitted without even headteachers knowing their schools were included in a bid. Rather than focusing on such flaws, it is arguably more convenient for those responsible for promoting New Labour policies to focus on the spin:

> So we made a mistake in the actual drafting of the policy documents. We obviously made a mistake in thinking it was a technical thing, not a press story, and we were then on the defensive and it's actually the consequence of that for the policy. You know a lot of the very shallow policy comments you get on the *Today* programme[15] and so on and you get this comment about New Labour especially that it's spin not substance, and this story's the perfect example of how you can't separate the two. They're actually – they're integrally related. If you get the story wrong it actually effects the policy, whereas if you get the story right then it gives it a really good.
>
> (Civil Servant A)

This failure of spin seems to have had knock-on effects for how the policy was subsequently spun. Thus, as we pointed out above, there was less of an emphasis on business leadership and more on the role of schools in initiating bids; there was an increased emphasis on celebrating success; and mention of EAZs became rarer as they were eclipsed by the EIC programme as the flagship policy.

At one point, the Secretary of State for Education at the time, David Blunkett, explicitly 'admitted' to the press that some of the difficulties the EAZ policy had faced stemmed from the fact that it had been 'over-hyped' at the outset. This 'admission' in itself should perhaps not simply be read as an 'innocent' expression of Blunkett's candid views on the policy. It is possible, for example – and, of course, we are speculating here – that Blunkett's 'admission' was contrived as part of a new spin strategy designed to limit the damage caused by the fact that the policy was about to be dropped by the DfEE. Certainly, the strict regime of press management emanating from Downing Street (Franklin 1998) means that we have to be sceptical about the possible existence of any innocent announcements.

Spin as endemic – the cascading culture of spin and its disciplinary nature

The DfEE/S civil servants, based in Sanctuary Buildings, used a variety of strategies to ensure that 'appropriate' messages about the EAZ policy got out. For example, all press releases and policy documents were shown to Blunkett's special advisor, Conor Ryan, so that he could check that the 'right' message was being conveyed. However, it was not just via the press that the civil servants were aiming to impress the public. The DfEE's EAZ newsletter, from which we have quoted above, was produced presumably both to raise morale in EAZs and schools at a local level and to convey the key messages about the policy that schools in turn were meant to convey to their local 'communities'.

Academic researchers were viewed as another vehicle for spin. One of the civil servants with whom we had contact (Civil Servant E) appeared to have as one of his briefs keeping an eye on academic researchers and trying to persuade them to tell the 'right' story. Thus, for example, in our meetings with this civil servant we were asked for information as to which academics were researching EAZs and who was funding them. In one meeting, one of us presented him (and the three colleagues he brought with him) with one of our interim reports. The civil servants' response to our report was that we were asking the wrong questions, and one of our research questions – which was concerned with the relationship between the state and civil society and the extent to which EAZs could be viewed as constituting testing grounds for innovations in local democratic practice and new forms of public accountability – was rather mockingly described as resembling a secondary school essay question. The stance of these civil servants reflects a view currently dominant in government circles and manifest in government policy that educational research should exclusively address questions that have an obvious and direct relevance to educational policy and practice rather than questions with a broader philosophical, political or sociological relevance (Hammersley 1997; Ozga 2000).

In a critical analysis of New Labour's approach to news management, Franklin (1998) has written of the Government's attempts to directly control journalists through a system of reward and punishment. Friendly journalists who produce pro-New Labour copy are rewarded with 'exclusives'. Those who write critical stories are ignored, harangued, or publicly humiliated (Viner 1997; cited in Franklin 1998, 7). One of the best publicized examples of New Labour's bullying news management tactics is the leaked letter sent to the BBC by New Labour's director of communications, Dave Hill. The letter was sent following an interview on the *Today* programme (see note 14) by the radio journalist John Humphrys with the then Social Security Secretary, Harriet Harman, in which Harman was pressed about the government's decision to cut benefit for lone-parent families. The letter threatened a Government withdrawal of co-operation with the programme – i.e. not allowing Ministers to appear. More sinisterly, Andrew Neil, former editor of the News International-owned *Sunday Times*, has suggested that, prior to the 1997 General Election, Tony Blair made a pact with the proprietor of News International, Rupert Murdoch, in which Blair effectively promised favourable treatment of Murdoch's media interests in return for favourable treatment of the Labour Party both in the run-up to the election and once the Party was in government (Franklin 1998).

Although the tactics used with us were not as strong armed as this, it would seem that similar tactics may be being employed with academic researchers in order to control research. This kind of approach can encourage self-censorship when researchers suspect that future research access may well be dependent on saying the 'right' things about policies (Ozga and Gewirtz 1994).

So far we have focused on Sanctuary Buildings (where the DfEE/S is located) as the key site of spin production and 'news management'. However, spin has been produced in a variety of sites. At a local level, EAZs and schools were themselves involved in developing strategies of spin. In our experience, most headteachers, whether working within an EAZ or not, are highly skilled spinners. Interviews with headteachers are frequently characterized by their attempts to present themselves and their schools in glowing terms, and this has long been the case. Indeed, it is headteachers' skills of impression management that presumably have played a key role in securing their appointment to headships in the first place. However, the EAZ policy has produced a range of additional incentives for spin. The importance of celebrating the successes of the policy was explicitly conveyed by the DfEE/S to EAZs. As Civil Servant C explains, extreme pressure was put on EAZs to demonstrate that they were 'making a difference', and this pressure was seen to have emanated from the fact that the press had initially 'savaged the policy':

> The biggest disappointment was, having launched the initiative, to see how the press just savaged it and, because the press savaged it, the politicians then wanted information to sort of defend it, so we were in a bizarre situation

where the people from above on floor 7 of Sanctuary Buildings [were] demanding facts – what has the zone achieved? And this was [at] the ... end of September [1998]. Well sorry, they've achieved, they've got a forum together. Yes, but you know, how [much] better are the results? ... I then had to go back to the project directors and they were concerned because I was asking them questions they couldn't answer, and as much as I tried to wrap it up and work with them to find creative ways to answer that question, it was unrealistic, so time scale demands were huge.

(Civil Servant C)

The EAZ directors in turn conveyed the vital importance of 'celebrating success' to headteachers who in turn impressed it upon teachers involved in aspects of local EAZ programmes.

The incentive for spin was rooted not only in direct pressure from the DfEE/S conveyed via its EAZ 'advisors', but also emanated from another form of pressure – the short term nature of EAZ funding. EAZs were initially funded for a 3-year period, potentially renewable to 5. In order to secure the extension of their funding, EAZs needed to 'demonstrate' success.

Again at this local level, academic researchers were seen to have a key role to play. Most of the initial bids for EAZ status included reference to proposed university evaluations of the zone, presumably because of the signal this gave that the zone was taking evaluation seriously and that, like the Government, the zone was committed to developing policy on the basis of 'what works'. And on several occasions we were taken to task by zone directors and/or other forum members on comments we had made in our interim reports that might have been construed in negative terms either by the DfEE/S or other readers. The letter cited in the introduction to this paper by one EAZ grouping exemplifies the kinds of attempts that have been made to influence our output. One zone director went as far as to tell us that our report on our research in that zone was inappropriate because it was not 'celebrating success'.

Other institutions which were key sites of spin production included the teacher associations and private companies. In one case – where the National Union of Teachers (NUT)[16] commissioned a report by the private consultancy firm Price Waterhouse Coopers (PWC) on the EAZ policy – there was a significant merging of such sites. Whilst the NUT has a longstanding relationship with PWC, the choice of a private company to conduct EAZ research can also be seen as part of a strategy of spin being developed by the union – a strategy perhaps designed to convince the government specifically that the research has a particular kind of credibility and more generally that the NUT is not fundamentally hostile to the private sector and, therefore, should perhaps be more trusted/listened to. The resultant document tells a story about the EAZs with its own distinctive double-coded spin, which appears to bring together the interests of the NUT and the interests of PWC – a company which has a growing financial interest in the education sector. Thus, on the one hand, the PWC/NUT report identifies professional development 'as one of the [EAZ] programme's most successful achievements':

Both the NUT survey [of teachers in EAZs] and our fieldwork indicate that [professional development] opportunities have increased significantly, that in the main these are of reasonably high quality, and that there is an increasing trend for these opportunities to be appropriately based on the needs of teachers themselves. Investment in the professional development of staff is likely to produce sustainable improvement in a way in which, for example, additional support staff does not, in that there will be a benefit after additional funding has been withdrawn.

(PWC 2001, para 29)

In terms of lessons for the profession emerging from our evaluation, the main finding is that involvement in programmes such as EAZs offers many advantages, both in terms of creating better opportunities for the pupils they teach, and in terms of their own professional development. These advantages included an increased level of collegiality, the opportunity to exercise greater creativity and the chance to see welcome additional funding directed towards the pupils.

(PWC 2001, para 43)

These comments relate closely to the NUT's agenda of persuading the government to invest more in schools and in professional development. The language of celebrating success in which they are couched can be read, at least in part, as a strategic device to persuade the government both of the legitimacy of the NUT and its specific arguments in the report. There is also an emphasis in the report on encouraging the government to 'trust teachers and others to deliver' (PWC 2001, para 41) and on success being dependent on 'an appropriate level of professional involvement and consultation...a large degree of local autonomy' (PWC 2001, para 46). The 'making a difference in the classroom' discourse, which, as noted above, was being encouraged by the DfEE, is present as well:

Our own impression is that teachers have been willing to accommodate change where they have seen a link to improving opportunities for pupils.

(PWC 2001, para 45)

At the same time, the report identifies as another of the research's 'wider messages for government' the value of business involvement:

In terms of learning points that go more widely than the EAZ programme, DfEE appears to have moved on from the model of separate statutory EAZs in terms of future area-based improvement programmes. New programmes will be either within Excellence in Cities, or in the form of Excellence Clusters, which will work within the LEA framework...However, we note that business involvement is not a requirement of the Clusters. We would ask the DfEE to consider whether there is merit in ensuring that wider partnerships with business and the community can be created and, if so, how to achieve this.

(PWC 2001, paras 38 and 39)

The conclusion elides the two codes in the double-coding, that is the two sets of concerns about the value of teacher involvement and professional development, on the one hand, and the value of business involvement, on the other, within an overall discourse of success:

The EAZ programme itself appears to have been largely successful both in involving teachers and in many of the subsequent achievement [*sic*]. It has shown there is merit in providing funds for locally managed initiatives, and that teachers, heads, businesses and pupils can benefit as a result.

(PWC 2001, para 47)

These are just some examples of the endemic nature of spin, of how it is produced in a variety of settings in addition to Whitehall.

The rationales for the spin across these settings are diverse. The rationale is often simultaneously personal and institutional – i.e. individual's jobs or opportunities for promotion, alongside the financial health or perceived success of the institution, depend, or are seen to depend, on the perceived success of the policy. This applies as much to civil servants in Sanctuary Buildings as it does to EAZ project directors, teachers, learning mentors, and support assistants. For some within the DfEE, the rationale was possibly as much about furthering the reputation of the DfEE within government, as it was about promoting the policy to 'the people'. The 'flagship' spin that was initially put on the policy helped to enable the DfEE to be viewed in turn as a flagship, can-do, archly loyal New Labour department, thus enhancing its image within government. This was an impression also promoted by the fact that the Department was the first to produce a bill – within 4 months of New Labour coming to power.

However, whilst the rationales for spin were diverse, some of the similarities in the content of the spin are striking. Thus, for example, the discourses of 'celebrating success' and 'making a difference' were just as evident in the PWC/NUT report as they were in the DfEE press releases as they were in the way in which some headteachers presented the initiative to us.

The ubiquity of spin and the similarity in its content across different sites can, we suggest, be read as a manifestation of the disciplinary nature of spin. Viewed from a Foucauldian perspective, spin can be seen to operate simultaneously as a form of both sovereign and disciplinary power.[17] We have clear evidence of *direct* pressure from DfEE officials on EAZs to promote their successes (i.e. evidence of the exertion of 'sovereign power'). However, it is also the knowledge that DfEE officials can potentially observe large swathes of EAZ activity – the knowledge of the existence of a DfEE 'gaze' – that may function to 'prompt' individuals to ensure that the 'right' message is conveyed. For example, DfEE officials are included on EAZ director appointment panels and the fora that are meant to run EAZs, and EAZs are constantly reminded of the DfEE presence through various accountability requirements including the requirement to submit performance data. Through these requirements and the frequency of the message emanating from Whitehall that success must be celebrated and that zones must demonstrate that they are 'making a difference', the DfEE has effectively constructed what Foucault called an 'inspecting gaze' –

> a gaze which each individual under its weight will end by interiorizing to the point that he is his own overseer, each individual thus exercising this surveillance over, and against, himself. A superb formula: power exercised continuously and for what turns out to be a minimal cost.
>
> (Foucault 1980, 155)

Viewed through a Foucauldian lens, then, spin can be understood as a mechanism of disciplinary power. However, those involved in implementing EAZ policy are not passive agents in all of this – unwittingly speaking and playing out the discourses that the DfEE has made available to them. There are varying degrees of reflexivity and cynicism about the process. Some of those we interviewed spoke the New Labour discourse as if it had been wholly internalized and as if it was wholeheartedly believed in. Members of this group appeared to lack any consciousness that they were even speaking a specifically New Labour discourse in the first place.

However, others were clearly aware of the strategic importance of language and were able to consciously, and sometimes cynically, move across a range of discursive repertoires for strategic purposes.

Spin as constitutive

So far we have discussed the way in which spin is used as a strategy of impression management. We have emphasized that spin is both dynamic and endemic. In the previous section we also suggested that spin acts in a disciplinary fashion. A key way in which the disciplinary ends of spin are achieved can be seen in its constitutive nature. That is the spin plays a role in creating and constituting policy realities at the same time as representing them. In order to produce the relevant spin, social and educational practices need to be transformed in particular ways.

We have numerous examples, for instance, of the way in which school practices have been re-orientated to enable EAZs to demonstrate success in the narrow performance indicators that they are expected to meet and celebrate:

> I am not convinced that some of the results being publicized by some Zone schools are true reflections of true achievement. I think there has been so much pressure to push up results that I think we've had schools making the decision that Year 2 and Year 6 are SAT years so we have deprived children of what I call [a] rich balanced curriculum, and I know that because my Year 6 teacher talks to other Year 6 teachers and knows what's going on.
>
> (Headteacher, Primary School, Nairnton)

> I do feel very cynical about it...I really thought the money was going to support [challenging] inequalities, but it wasn't, it was going to improve results. Now ultimately yes of course, children learning to read will support their life chances, but I mean current research is showing that a lot of these improvements and results are actually quite false...
>
> (Headteacher, Primary School, Wellford)

Frequently in interviews, those involved in implementing the policy at a local level complained about how the emphasis on the production, and demonstration, of short-term results had diverted attention from activities which are viewed either as intrinsically worthwhile but not relevant to SATs performance or as having a longer term benefit to those who participated.

Within the DfEE also there is evidence of the way in which spin may have played a constitutive role in the drafting of legislation. Comments made to us by Civil Servant A, quoted on p. 178 above, suggest that the highlighting of the EAZ policy in the press announcement of the Schools Standards and Framework Bill was prompted in part by concerns to deflect media and public attention away from the provisions to abolish grant-maintained schools which were included in the same Bill. The abolition of the grant-maintained sector was a sensitive issue and potentially a source of discontent with those sections of the electorate New Labour was particularly concerned to woo – i.e. 'middle England' (see note 9). However, the decision to include EAZs in the legislation in the first place may itself have been driven by concerns to deflect attention from this potentially unpopular policy. According to Civil Servant B, the civil servants working on the legislation had counselled against having primary legislation for the EAZ policy because it was viewed as simply unnecessary. Everything that ministers wanted EAZs to be able to do could, they argued, already be done under existing legislation. However, according to this civil servant's version of events, Stephen Byers, the Schools Standards minister at the time, insisted there had to be some primary legislation, and so the decision was made to set up EAZs as separate statutory bodies.

Now there are a number of possible – and not mutually exclusive – explanations for why Byers insisted on primary legislation. One interpretation given to us by one of the civil servants responsible for drafting the legislation was that this was simply an instance of macho politicking. Byers, according to this interpretation, had legislation drawn up for the reason that other men purchase large and powerful cars. A second possible explanation is that for Byers the primary purpose of EAZs was to erode the taken-for-granted assumption that LEAs should automatically be viewed as the sole provider of state schooling. On this explanation, by establishing EAZs as separate statutory bodies, the Government was paving the way for private companies to take over the running of clusters of schools from LEAs. However, as later developments showed, it was quite possible for private companies to be given a major role in the provision of schooling and to take over the running of schools from LEAs without the creation of separate statutory bodies. A third possible explanation is that, by enshrining EAZs in legislation, the Government was creating a big 'good news' story that could eclipse the bad news of the loss of resources for grant-maintained schools.

If it is the case that the EAZs were incorporated into the Bill partly for image management purposes – whether the image that was being managed was that of Byers himself or of New Labour's education reforms – then this turned out to be a costly public relations exercise. The separate statutory status of EAZs generated much red tape and was largely responsible for the high proportion of EAZ funds which were diverted to administration; and it is these excessive administration costs which appear to have contributed, at least in part, to the policy's quiet demise.

Conclusion

In this paper we have drawn attention to the dynamic, endemic, and constitutive characteristics of spin, demonstrating how spin has pervaded the EAZ policy – and the EAZ policy process – across its various sites of construction and enactment. We have suggested that, whilst key policy players might at times have exaggerated the constitutive nature of spin in some respects – by claiming that the 'transformation' of the policy was a consequence of a failure of spin – there are other ways (not acknowledged by policy makers) in which spin is constitutive which are important. In particular, the emphasis on 'celebrating success' and 'making a difference' has contributed to a refocusing of EAZ resources both on activities that can make an immediately measurable (yet perhaps superficial) difference in the classroom and on the activities involved in demonstrating success. We have also argued that the ubiquity of the celebrating success and making a difference discourses and their constitutive role might be usefully understood, in Foucauldian terms, as instances of how spin operates as a mechanism of disciplinary power.

Criticism of New Labour's pre-occupation with spin and what has been called its control freakery (see, for example, Franklin (1998) and Fairclough (2000)) has centred on its adverse implications for democracy, which has at least three key aspects. First, there is a re-surfacing of a long-standing concern about the politicization of the civil service and the fact that its traditional 'neutrality' is being even more heavily compromised than ever before, so that there is an increasing blurring of the boundaries between party political interests and the interests of 'effective' government.

Second, there is a concern that genuine public debate is being stifled because the public are being lied to or at least denied the accurate information needed to inform judgements about the value of particular policies or courses of action. This second concern has been highlighted recently by the controversy over the 'Iraq dossier' which the BBC reporter, Andrew Gilligan, accused a government adviser of 'sexing up' in order to legitimate the government's decision to send British troops to Iraq (Hutton 2004).

Thirdly, there is a concern about the impact of centralized control and government spin on the *nature* of public discourse. The concern here is that the colonization by government of large swathes of the media means that critical public debate has, to a significant extent, been stifled. Franklin (1998, 16) has argued that, in the process of colluding with the government, 'the media obfuscate rather than clarify policy choices'. This in turn has, he suggests, contributed to the production of a passive and de-politicized political culture, where 'politics, like football, has been transformed…into a largely spectator sport with viewers inclined to watch the match from the comfort of their favourite armchair rather than becoming embroiled in the game' (Franklin 1998, 17). Fairclough (2000) argues that the predominant mode of communication between the New Labour Government and the public tends to be promotional rather than dialogical.[18] For Fairclough, essential characteristics of genuine dialogue are that people are free to disagree, their differences are recognized, there is equality of opportunity for people to participate in it, and there is space for consensus but consensus cannot be guaranteed. Yet, in their communications with 'the public', for example in green papers, the government exudes certainty – 'readers are hardly ever asked, they are told. And although in the nature of things there is a great deal of uncertainty, readers are told things as if they are certain – there are no "maybes" or "perhaps". Neither questions nor "maybes" sit easily within promotion'. The government's green papers may be 'reader friendly' but they are also 'reader directive' (Fairclough 2000, 13, 136–7; see also CPPR 2002).

These are all important reasons for subjecting the role of spin in the policy process to critical scrutiny. However, our research suggests that spin has implications not only for the relationship between the government and 'the public', but also for how we understand the substantive content of policies. In evaluating policies, it is important not only to analyse their main 'planks' and see spin as something that interferes with, distorts or obscures the analysis. In addition, we need to see spin as an important object of analysis in its own right and an object which has real effects on educational and social practices.

Notes

1 See Power *et al.* (2003) for a report of the overall findings of the research. We are grateful to the UK Economic and Social Research Council for funding the study (no. R000238046), to our co-researchers, David Halpin and Geoff Whitty, for their contributions to the collection of the data we are using here, to Alan Cribb for very helpful conversations which have fed into the writing of the paper, to John Clarke, Harvey Goldstein, Peter Mitchell, George Smith, and Janet Theakston for their insightful comments on an earlier draft and to the two anonymous referees for their helpful suggestions.

2 The current British Labour party repackaged itself as 'New Labour' in the run-up to the 1997 General Election, signifying a shift away from traditional Labour connotations of working-class representation, nationalization, and overtly re-distributive policies.

This process of repackaging, of which the expression 'New Labour' is just one part, is characteristic of the current Government's pre-occupation with impression management which is the subject of this paper.

3 These are the statutory authorities traditionally responsible for the organization of educational provision at a local level in England and Wales. As a result of a series of reforms since 1988, many of their powers have been eroded through being devolved to schools or taken over by central government. In addition, the role of the private sector in the provision of educational services has increased.

4 Grant-maintained schools were state-funded schools which received their funds directly from central government and operated independently of LEAs. They had been introduced by a Conservative government in 1988 as part of a wider attempt to introduce more market 'diversity' into the education system. The Labour Government abolished the grant-maintained sector under the same legislation which established EAZs. The coming together of provisions to abolish the grant-maintained sector and to establish EAZs in the same Act of Parliament is potentially significant for understanding the spin-policy relationship, as we discuss below.

5 This paper makes use of several quotes from Civil Servant A. This reflects the fact that Civil Servant A was a key informant who was centrally involved in the development and implementation of the EAZ policy.

6 The DfEE is the government department with responsibility for education policy. It was renamed the Department for Education and Skills (DfES) in 2001.

7 Right-wing tabloid newspaper whose readership is typically viewed as emblematic of conservative-minded lower middle-class voters, whose support the Labour Party needs if the Party is to be successful in elections.

8 One of the anonymous referees asked how spin is different from propaganda. We would argue that, in essence, spin, understood as a process and product of the purposive management of information for political purposes, refers to the same phenomenon as propaganda, but it has softer, less extreme connotations. As we point out elsewhere in this paper, spin is itself a spun concept. Thus, although it has negative connotations, the connotations of 'spin' are nevertheless more positive than those of 'propaganda', and so the use of the term 'spin' rather than 'propaganda' arguably helps to make the practice of spinning a more acceptable and respectable one for politicians and their advisers to be engaged in.

9 Middle England is a term popularized by media political analysis and used to capture conservative-minded middle-class voters often associated with non-metropolitan areas and rural living.

10 Classically, urban centres of the old 'heavy' industries.

11 A centre-left Sunday broadsheet.

12 SATs (Standard Assessment Tasks) are national tests in English, Maths, and Science taken by students at the end of three 'Key Stages'. Key Stage 1 covers school years 1–2, Key Stage 2, years 3–6, and Key Stage 3, years 7–9. Schools have to set targets for the percentage of students in a given year reaching the 'expected level' in the SATs for each Key Stage and the results are published, providing a 'key indicator' used to judge the performance of schools.

13 General Certificate of Secondary Education examinations are national examinations usually taken by students at the end of Key Stage 4 (school years 10 and 11). The results are published. The percentage of students getting at least five A–C grades at GCSE is used by the government and the press as *the* key indicator for comparing the performance of secondary schools.

14 Ministers presented their decision to abandon the original EAZ concept – of EAZs covering large areas and operating as statutory bodies outside LEAs and funded in part by the private or voluntary sector – and to move to the establishment of small EAZs operating within traditional LEA structures as a transformation rather than demise of the policy.

15 BBC Radio 4's 'flagship' current affairs programme.

16 The largest teacher union in England.

17 Although there is a fuzzy boundary between the two forms of power in this instance.

18 One of the anonymous referees of this paper suggested that the dominance of promotional dialogue in the Government's communications with the public can be understood as an aspect of New Labour's transformational model of leadership which is rooted in belief and trust rather than dialogue.

References

Barendt, E. (1998) 'Judging the media: political impartiality and broadcasting', in: J. Seaton (ed.), *Politics and the media: harlots and prerogatives at the turn of the millenium* (Oxford: Blackwell), 108–16.

Blair, T. (1998) *The third way: new politics for the new century* (London: The Fabian Society).

Bright, M. and Wintour, P. (29 November 1998) Revolution in schools, *The Observer*.

Carvel, J. (7 January 1998) Labour revolt on private schools plan, *Guardian*.

Cockerill, M., Hennessy, P. and Walker, D. (1984) *Sources close to the Prime Minister: inside the hidden world of the news manipulators* (London: Macmillan).

CPPR (Centre for Public Policy Research) (2002) 'Achieving success? Discursive strategies and policy tensions in New Labour's White Paper for schools', *Education and Social Justice*, 4(1): 15–25.

DfEE (Department for Education and Employment) (23 June 1998) £75 million boosts radical education action zones to raise standards, *DfEE Press Release*.

DfEE (1999) *Schools leading second round of Education Action Zones*, Press Notice 495/99 (London, DfEE).

Esser, E., Reinemann, C. and Fan, D. (2000) 'Spin doctoring in British and German election campaigns', *Journal of Communication*, 15(2): 209–39.

Fairclough, N. (2000) *New Labour, new language* (London: Routledge).

Foucault, M. (1980) 'The eye of power', in C. Gordon (ed.) *Power/knowledge: selected interviews and other writings 1972–1977 Michel Foucault* (Brighton: Harvester).

Franklin, B. (1998) *Tough on soundbites, tough on the causes of soundbites: New Labour and news management*, Catalyst Paper 3 (London: The Catalyst Trust).

Gewirtz, S. (1999) 'Education Action Zones: emblems of the "third way"', in H. Dean and R. Woods (eds), *Social policy review 11* (Luton: Social Policy Association), pp. 145–65.

Giddens, A. (1998) *The third way: the renewal of social democracy* (Cambridge: Policy Press).

Hammersley, M. (1997) 'Educational research and teaching: a response to David Hargreaves' TTA lecture', *British Educational Research Journal*, 23(2): 141–62.

Hodge, M. (12 June 1998) A pragmatic ideology, *Times Educational Supplement*.

Hutton, B. (2004) *Report of the inquiry into the circumstances surrounding the death of Dr David Kelly C. M. G.*, HC247 (accessed 29 March 2004). Available online at <http://www.the-hutton-enquiry.org.uk/img/fullcover.gif>

Jones, N. (1995) *Soundbites and spin doctors* (London: Cassell).

Mountfield, R. (1997) *Report on the working group on the Government Information Service* (London: Cabinet Office/HMSO).

O'Leary, J. (11 September 1998) State and the obvious: private business can do it, *The Times*.

Ozga, J. (2000) *Policy research in educational settings: contested terrain* (Buckingham: Open University Press).

Ozga, J. and Gewirtz, S. (1994) 'Sex, lies and audiotape: interviewing the education policy elite', in D. Halpin and B. Troyna (eds) *Research education policy: ethical and methodological issues* (London: The Falmer Press), pp. 121–36.

Power, S., Gewirtz, S., Halpin, D. and Whitty, G. (2003) *Paving a 'third way'? A policy trajectory analysis of Education Action Zones*, ESRC end-of-award report (accessed 29 March 2004). Available online at <http://www.regard.ac.uk/research_findings/R000238046/report.pdf>

PWC (PriceWaterhouseCoopers) (2001) *Evaluation of the role of teachers in Education Action Zones*, (London: PWC).

Rawnsley, A. (14 July 2002) It's the Tories who are addicted to spin, *The Observer*.

Riddell, P. (1998) 'Members and Millbank: the media and parliament', in J. Seaton (ed.), *Politics and the media: harlots and prerogatives at the turn of the millenium* (Oxford: Blackwell), pp. 8–18.

Viner, K. (9 August 1997) The Ministry of truth, *Guardian*, p. 3.

Wright, T. (1998) 'Inside the whale: the media from Parliament', in J. Seaton (ed.) *Politics and the media: harlots and prerogatives at the turn of the millenium* (Oxford: Blackwell), pp. 19–27.

CHAPTER 12

PUBLIC ACCOUNTABILITY IN THE AGE OF NEO-LIBERAL GOVERNANCE

Stewart Ranson

Journal of Education Policy, September–October 2003, 18(5): 459–80

Introduction[1]

Autumn 2001 was the 25th anniversary of James Callaghan's speech at Ruskin College,[2] designed to promote a 'great debate' about the vocational as well as academic purposes of education, standards of achievement, appropriate teaching methods and whether there should be a core curriculum of basic knowledge. Distinctively, however, it inaugurated an era of accountability and a restructuring of the governance of education. The curriculum would no longer be the 'secret garden' of an autonomous professional community detached from public scrutiny. A public service became publicly accountable. One by one professional communities have been called to account: first the teachers and more recently social workers and doctors have attracted the anxious gaze of a society increasingly driven to impose regimes of scrutiny and regulation in the face of public concern and lost trust (O'Neill 2002b).

Since the late 1970s such regimes of public accountability have been strengthened systematically so that accountability is no longer merely an important instrument or component within the system, but constitutes the system itself. We now live in 'the audit society' (Power 1999), or 'the performative society' (Ball 2001a). Power and purpose, it will be argued, are thus brought together in the institutional arrangements of accountability in ways that cause us to focus not only upon performance of a service but also significantly upon the form and relationships of the public sphere itself.

Yet this 'revolution in accountability', though society's remedy for the loss of public trust, has, it will be argued, generated perverse unintended consequences. The preoccupation with specifying goals and tasks distorts the practice of public services as quantifiable models of quality and evaluation increasingly displaces concern for the internal goods of excellence. Moreover, the regimes of regulation designed to enhance public accountability paradoxically strengthen corporate power at the expense of the public sphere. This paper begins by developing an analytical framework, before discussing the intensifying patterns neo-liberal of accountability embodied in what has become characterized as the new public management or governance. A critique of this regime, in particular the erosion of public accountability in public–private partnerships (PPPs), will lead to discussion of an alternative model of democratic accountability appropriate to the public sphere.

Understanding accountability

Accountability is a multi-layered concept whose meanings need unravelling if sense is to be made of its emerging form (Ranson 1986[3]; Stewart 1985) and its connection to trust, the rationality of which Dunn (1988, 1996) regards as the central question of the polity.[4] To be accountable can reveal very different social relationships, of regulation as against deliberation, and relations that express different evaluative practices and criteria, of external or internal goods. These relationships and criteria embody potentially divergent modes of securing trust in the public sphere.

Relations of regulation or reason

To be accountable, conventionally, is to be '*held to account*', defining a relationship of formal control between parties, one of whom is mandatorily held to account to the other for the exercise of roles and stewardship of public resources. Such a report, moreover, is always an evaluation of performance according to established standards (Elliot 2001). A canonical elaboration of this central, judgemental dimension of 'answerability' has been Dunsire's (1978, 41):

> Being accountable may mean...no more than having to answer questions about what has happened or is happening within one's jurisdiction...But most usages require an additional implication: the answer when given, or the account when rendered, is to be evaluated by the superior or superior body measured against some standard or some expectation, and the differences noted: and then praise or blame are to be meted out and sanctions applied. It is the coupling of information with its evaluation and application of sanctions that gives 'accountability' or 'answerability' or 'responsibility' their full sense in ordinary usage.

This understanding locates accountability in the hierarchical practices of bureaucracy. Being held to account is experienced as a specific event, such as the annual appraisal, or departmental review, or the annual shareholders (or parents') meeting, in which data on performance is presented for evaluation. Public trust is secured by specifying performance and regulating compliance. It is this form of accountability, with its potentially punitive image, that has become anathema to professional communities who reject its instrumental rationale and techniques. Professionals become subjected to a process that denies their agency (cf. Elliott 2001; Fielding 2001; Gleeson and Husbands 2001).

Yet even this conception of formal accountability is rendered problematic in many parts of the public sphere given the complexity and multilateral nature of 'accountable' relationships. Teachers are accountable to governors and the local education authority (LEA) but also to parents and the students. Moreover, the patterns of expectation and answerability are reciprocal. If teachers are required to account to parents about the progress of their children, they in turn can have legitimate expectations that carers reinforce the learning process. Such complexity denies any simple linearity of answerability.

More subtle interpretations follow from the usage of '*giving an account*' which emphasizes the discursive relations of accountability. Any request 'to account' for performance is likely to lead to the giving of an account, that is, to offer a story that interprets and explains what has happened and why it has taken place.

'To be accountable for one's activities is both to explicate the reasons for them and to supply the normative grounds whereby they may be justified' (Giddens 1984). The 'partners' to education – ministers, LEAs, teachers, parents and students – may bring different interpretive schema of what is to count as the purposes and conditions of effective achievement. Once accountability is rooted in exchange of accounts of meaning and value in contexts of multiple and reciprocal answerabilities, conflicts of purpose are likely to follow. For Day and Klein (1987) their 'starting point is that accountability is all about the construction of an agreed language or currency of discourse about conduct and performance, and the criteria that should be used in assessing them.' Public trust will be established when the different participants and constituents of an institution strive to reach shared understanding and accounts about its purposes and practices. Thomas and Martin (1996) helpfully call this the 'dialogue of accountability', recalling Durkheim's (1957, 91) conception of dialogue between governors and the governed as the best means of democratic accountability.

For a number of social theorists (Habermas 1984; MacIntyre 1982, 1999; Scanlon 1998) this discursive practice of accountability is not merely confined to organizational procedure, but defines the reasonableness of communication that must inform any just civil society. The obligations we have to each other; that is, to give and take reasons/accounts for our beliefs and actions, enable mutual understanding and agreement. Accountability in this view, as discursive reason, is the very expression rather than denial of our reflective agency. Our accounts of action make intelligible their intentions and the narrative histories we have authored and are responsible for. Accountability in these interpretations is not a summons to compliance but rather provides understanding, as Shotter (1989) argues, of how we constitute the sense we have of ourselves (our identities) as well as shared ways of constructing the meanings that inform our social orders (cf. Wittgenstein 1953; Tully 1995). The positive potential of this intelligible, reflexive accountability has been neglected in much contemporary theorizing of accountability.

External or internal goods

The relations and purposes of accountability are inescapably evaluative, but the criteria and judgements vary according to the mode adopted, whether of hierarchical answerability or communicative reason. The differences are captured in MacIntyre's (1982, 1988) distinction between 'the extrinsic goods of effectiveness' (for example, wealth, status, power) and 'the internal goods of excellence'(such as realizing the virtues of justice, courage, and friendship). These goods remain endlessly in tension within institutional settings.

When the emphasis is on 'holding to account', the orientation is towards instrumentally rational goods of effectiveness (Power 1999), creating the culture and technology of 'performativity' that strives to 'optimise performance by maximising outputs (benefits) and minimising inputs (costs)' (Lyotard 1997). What begins as an approach to assessing quality gravitates to evaluation of efficiency (Elliott 2001). Measures of productivity are created to judge and control the performance of organizational 'units', rendering them continually accountable. Yet, as Foucault argues, the accounts produced typically become 'fabrications' of performance, manufactured for their effect as 'accountability' (Ball 2001a). Such regimes of accountability deny our agency, turning us into inauthentic subjects pursuing and resisting the imposition of extrinsic goods alone.[5]

Practices of communicative rationality, on the other hand, the mutual giving and taking of accounts, can presuppose a very different habitus of accountability. They entail pursuit of the goods of excellence included in MacIntyre's (1982) understanding of 'socially established co-operative activit(ies) through which goods internal to that form of activity are realized in the course of trying to achieve those standards of excellence which are appropriate to, and partially definitive of, that form of activity, with the result that human powers to achieve excellence, and human conceptions of the ends and goods involved are systematically extended'. Members of the community of practice (embracing the public as well as the profession) recognize and draw upon the authority of standards which they can trust for evaluating performance because they have been tested in deliberation. In the pursuit of excellence, internal goods replace extrinsic controls, and agency supplants alienated routines. Reflexive questioning of achievement informs the practice of mutual accountability: things can be done better, the process implies, even when they are done well. The accounting for (present) performance and the discursive negotiating and agreeing of (improved) performance are interrelated processes in the practice of excellence.

An intensifying regime of neo-liberal governance

The relations and discourses of accountability express not only the patterns of power and purpose in public services but reveal the forms of governance of the public sphere itself.[6] As Kogan (1988) argued, the task is to get clear the values that shape the developing forms of accountability and distributions of power that they embody and legitimate. The typology set out in Table 12.1 conceptualizes the practices, structures and codes of accountability[7] within two regimes of governance: the age of professionalism and the neo-liberal age.

Accountability is a *social practice* pursuing particular purposes, defined by distinctive relationships and evaluative procedures. Participating in communities of practice shapes the dispositions of its members, their taken for granted ways of perceiving, judging, imagining, and acting. These socially sanctioned practices are rendered intelligible, Foucault (1991) argues, if we recognize their twofold character as 'juridicative and veridicative'. That is on the one hand practices establish and apply norms, controls and exclusions; on the other they render true/false discourse possible. His genealogies sought to understand the descent of practices as a series of events – the controls, disciplines, regulations imposed on the members of a practice.

Structures conceptualize the organizational arrangements, the distribution of authority and power and the modes of sanction and regulation, while *cultural codes* express the regulative principles, the shared assumptions that constitute what is known and how it is to be interpreted. Yet, although particular codes are likely to dominate the informing and shaping of institutional practices and structures, other codes may be embodied in the dispositions and practices of organizational members creating potential contradictions of structuration and the possibility of challenge and change. Such contradictions form distinctive possibilities in the tensions of accountability as 'answerability' as against 'communicative action'.

The practices of accountability and the dispositions they have engendered have changed over time since the mid-1970s. It will be argued that following the demise of the age of professional accountability, a regime of neo-liberal corporate accountability has dominated the governance of education. The distinctive dimensions of this regime – of consumer choice, of contract efficiency, quality, and

Table 12.1 A typology of accountability regimes

	Age of professionlism	The age of neo-liberalism			
	Professional accountability	Consumer accountability	Contract accountability	Performative accountability	Corporate accountability
Practice					
Why: Purpose of accountability	Client need	Strengthen consumer responsiveness	Strengthen service(s) efficiency	Strengthen product quality	Control fabric/ infrastructure
Who: Relations of answerability	Schools to LEA	LEA/schools to parents	Schools to contractors	Schools to national guidelines	Schools to private/vol. corporations
What is accounted for	Pupil progress	Extent of choice	Costs/VFM efficiency	Standards	Captial
How: Rules of accountability	Professional judgement	Market competition	Competitive tendering	Public inspection	Business plan
• Criteria	Specialist knowledge	Consumer choice	Technical efficiency	National standards/ targets	Profitability
• Data	Internal reports	Public data (exam results)	Costs/VFM	Test scores/ league tables	Capital gain
Structure					
Organization	Administrative hierarchy	Administered market LMS/NC	Client-contractor	Ofsted	Public/ private partnership
Power	LEA	State/consumer	Contractor	State	Private sector
Ground of control trust/	Electoral change	Regulations/ exit	Contract	Surveillance/ regulations	Capital
Cultural code (dominant discourse; knowledge claims	Authority of specialist knowledge	Authority of calculative/instrumental rationality			
		Possessive individualism Relative competitive advantage	Input/process technical knowledge	Output; value-added; technical rationality	Surplus value/ profit

capital ownership – have been introduced at different times since 1979. While it is possible to periodize their inception, it is necessary to see them as, over time, extending and intensifying into a coherent regime of regulation. Thus understanding of the present modes can only be understood by clarifying the historical and political conditions which have shaped them. Nevertheless, possibilities of change may lie in the contradictions of accountability within the regime of governance.

Professional accountability (late 1970s)

The post-war world constituted a political order of social democracy based upon the principles of justice and equality of opportunity and designed to ameliorate class disadvantage and class division (cf. Perkin 1988). Public goods were conceived as requiring collective choice and redistribution. Thus the significance of systems of administrative planning (the LEA) and institutional organization (the comprehensive school). Recognition of the complexity of professional purpose and practice shaped the mode of accountability. Public trust was afforded to the specialist knowledge of professionals and the necessary requirements of answerability could be fulfilled by delegating authority to heads, teachers, and advisors – only the trained eye could judge the quality of teaching and the pupil progress (cf. Kogan 1978). Their monitoring of progress was typically informal and ad hoc. Professional relationships, though located in administrative hierarchies, formally expressed partnership, collegiality, and trust between and within tiers of the service. The Education Committee formed the arena for dialogue on public accountability in which professional judgements were tested.

It was this professional accountability that the Ruskin speech was designed to challenge and reform when public trust in professional judgement evaporated. The quality of public services could not be a private matter for specialists to determine alone. The goods internal to a task could not be determined alone by teachers and their advisors but should be open to deliberation within the public sphere.

Neo-liberalism – marketisation (from early 1980s)

The distinctive interpretive schema that came to define how the public should hold public services to account was that of the Conservative regime of the 1980s. Their radical reconstruction of education was designed not merely to improve 'a service' but also to restructure a purported outmoded polity (King 1987; Levitas 1986). A new political order of 'neo-liberal' public accountability was constituted, based upon principles of rights designed to enhance individual choice. The public (as consumer) was empowered at the expense of the (professional) provider. Public goods, to achieve equity rather than equality, were conceived as aggregated private choices and interests that would better than public planning deliver the goals of opportunity and social change.

In education the new system of governance would provide parents with information to hold schools to account, choose schools, appeal and register complaints. A quasi market of increasingly differentiated and autonomous schools would, it was believed,[8] foster competition and improvement of performance, while services would become more accountable when they were made to respond directly to the choices of individual consumers. Information and choice in the marketplace provide an account for consumers that secures trust for public services. As in other forms of market exchange, the products which thrive can only do so because they have the support of consumers.

Neo-liberalism – contract management: strengthening legal regulation (from early 1990s)

Public services, moreover, would flourish more effectively if they modelled their management practice on the private sector. A 'new public management' (Hood 1992; Pollitt 1990; Stoker 1999) was promoted, asserting that there was one model of management and it was private. Services, Stewart and Stoker (1995) proposed, were encouraged to value the customer, plan strategically, target resources and, in particular, to adopt private sector models of contract management:

- *the separation of the purchaser role from the provider role:* in all parts of the public service there has been a separation of the role of determining what should be provided from the role of the provision of a service. The language varies: principal-agent; purchaser provider; client-contractor.

- *the growth of contractual or semi-contractual arrangements:* traditionally, public sector organisations have been structured for direct hierarchical control or reliance on professionalism; the purchaser provider developments reveal a new movement to control through contracts (Stewart and Stoker 1995, 3).
- *flexibility of pay and conditions:* national scales and conditions are challenged by market conditions and by performance related pay as the means of motivation.

Many authorities began their initiation into contracting in the early 1990s by introducing formal 'service level agreements' to ensure that services would be delivered between departments in a businesslike way, defining its range of customers, consulting and negotiating with them agreed levels of service to be incorporated in their development plans. As the contract culture spread (cf. Ainley 1999; Doogan 1999) some LEAs redesignated their whole organization as a client–contractor relationship so that services were rationalized and focused on customer demand; costs were defined and charging arrangements clarified; marketing of services was improved. LEAs created self-financing business units (including advisers, professional development and training, careers, and adult education) and began to plan for services to be 'externalized' or 'outsourced' to private sector providers.

Public management, it was argued, is improved by adopting the contract culture of the private sector to ensure the efficient delivery of services. Contracts enforce clear accountability for public servants, ensuring they are answerable for the service levels delivered, the resource targets set, and the outcomes achieved. The performance criteria for accountability embody clear, technical, means–end rationality. Trust is secured in the increased specification of purpose, task and condition of service delivery.

Neo-liberalism – product performativity: strengthening the audit state (from early 1990s)

This preoccupation with specification, which accountability generates, began to reach into the pedagogic core as well as the supporting services. A principal purpose of the 1988 Education Reform Act was 'above all to raise standards of attainment for all pupils by a better definition of what is to be taught and learnt...' believed necessary for enhancing quality and accountability and for securing the trust and confidence of the parent body in what schools were offering. The National Curriculum provided the vehicle for this greater specification of learning[9] enabling accounts of achievement to be presented in public league tables that would inform parents' market choices. In this way performance accountability and consumer accountability would become mutually reinforcing through improved school management.

It has been New Labour, however, that perceived increased definition of performance as the central vehicle for improving standards of attainment[10]: 'standards not structure' perceived as the key to standards. A new *Standards and Effectiveness Unit* at the DfEE in 1997 signalled the intention to draw together and codify the best knowledge from research and practice of school improvement and effectiveness and submit them to the regulatory power of the state. Improving the performance of schools required increasingly meticulous specification of the 'inputs', processes, and outputs that are expected of schools (cf. Gleeson and Husbands 2001; Fielding 2001): schemes of work are defined, learning outcomes targets set (especially in 'core skills' and at key stages); teachers' work is monitored and appraised; and schools prepare development/improvement plans defining a system of managing performance that head teachers are to lead and are accountable for. Husbands (2001, 11) deconstructs the model:

> School targets can be derived from national targets; and teacher and pupil targets from school targets. In the short term, it is almost certain that the sharper focus and defined targets brought by performance management systems will deliver higher levels of attainment in external tests and examinations...It is less clear that (these systems) will in the medium term produce a 'nation equipped for the challenges and opportunities of a new millennium.

This is because a sophisticated national system of regulations is put in place to measure and monitor a limited set of performances and outcomes – principally, test and examination results which inadequately represent the more comprehensive spiritual, cultural, moral, aesthetic, and intellectual values and purposes the nation has established for its schools (in Section 1 of the 1988 Education Act). What is constituted is performance accountability for marketability: what we are left unsure about in this account is the adequacy of learning and achievement in preparation for creating a community of educated citizens (cf. Pring 1996; Bottery 2000).

Neo-liberalism – partnership privatisation: strengthening corporate power (from late 1990s)

A distinctive form of neo-liberal accountability has developed over the past quarter of a century. Its principal dimensions – the market, contract, and inspection – have grown over time to become an intensive system of evaluating and accounting for educational practice. The most recent development – the strengthening of corporate differentiation and ownership of educational services and infrastructures – has inserted the regime of local regulation required to secure the organizing principles of neo-liberal accountability (cf. Glatter *et al.* 1997; Whitty *et al.* 1998; Whitty and Power 2000; Gewirtz 2001; Tomlinson 2001; Anderson 2001; Whitty 2002).

Private sector involvement in education has grown from 3% in 1979–80 to 7.5% in 1995–96 and to 10% in 1998–99 and is increasing (cf. IPPR 2001, UK Parliament 2002, Audit Scotland 2002). Beginning in the early 1990s, compulsory competitive tendering arrangements generated 'contracting out' or 'outsourcing' of services which LEAs would traditionally have delivered themselves. But private involvement continues to accelerate under New Labour (cf. Monbiot 2000; Whitfield 2001; Hatcher 2001; Hertz 2001[11]) including: outsourcing and franchising services; school inspections under Ofsted remain a contracted activity with many private sector teams carrying out inspections for profit; the control of Local Education Authorities and school; the creation of City Academies; and some teaching and the curriculum activities.

The activity generating the most significant acceleration in corporate privatisation of the education service is the rebuilding of the fabric of public institutions – for example, schools, hospitals, prisons, roads, bridges – following decades of neglect. Public–private partnerships, especially the PFI (Public Finance Initiative, building on the Conservative Government policy of 1992) seeks to encourage the private sector to invest in the regeneration of public service infrastructures. For school building and rebuilding, the PFI has largely become 'the only game in town'

(Parliamentary Select Committee 2002). The private sector designs, builds, finances and operates public sector capital works in return for future payments over time. The public sector retains control of the service provided within the building, which it begins to pay for with 'tax credits' once constructed. The buildings remain in private control until repayments are completed, typically 25–35 years (7–15 years for equipment).

These public–private partnerships present considerable benefits for government. The first is that, given the scale of need for rebuilding the infrastructure of public services and the limits on capital and public sector borrowing, the opportunity to draw upon private sector finance permits a vast programme of rebuilding to be undertaken in the short and medium term. The second purported benefit is to transfer the risks and costs of failure to private companies. A third is that PFI schemes allow the financing of building to be defined as revenue rather than capital because they are regarded as purchasing a service rather than a capital asset. Public infrastructure is thus renewed without increasing public sector borrowing. A fourth benefit, some argue, is to make the managerial skills and efficiencies of the private sector available to public services. It is not just the incentive to build on time and to budget, but that the discipline of PFI, ostensibly, is about 'outputs' rather than 'inputs': public sector managers are encouraged to think about the best use of buildings and the services they want to deliver from 'facilities'.

Yet the practice and prospect of PPPs remain subject to critical scrutiny (cf. Audit 2003). The principle of buying capital assets now and paying over time unreasonably mortgages the choices of future generations. The costs of building are judged excessive – higher than traditional means of public borrowing – justified, ostensibly, by the comparator used to calculate the (greater) risks undertaken by private sector companies (Kemp 1999; McFadyean and Rowland 2002). But when that risk is tested, the public sector inescapably has to step in to secure public need (Monbiot 2002). The purported efficiencies have often failed to materialize (Parliamentary Select Committee 2002). The long-term contracts, moreover, are inflexible, denying a defining characteristic of the public sphere of capacity to revise policies and practices in response to changes in need and understanding of good practice. The regime of legal regulation frustrates, rather than supports, public policy development. Most significantly public – private partnerships, by strengthening over time the private regulation and management of public institutions, subvert the practice of public democratic accountability of the public sphere (Whitfield 1999, 2000, 2001).[12]

A regime of neo-liberal accountability has been growing in extension over a couple of decades, each phase of policy development – market, contract, performativity, and now corporate influence – has intensified a regulatory regime of answerability. The discussion proceeds to ask whether there are limits and alternatives to this regime.

The limits and contradictions of the regulatory regime of answerability

The age of professionalism was built on a bedrock of public trust for professionals to deliver reliable public services of high quality. Yet, over the last 25 years, whether it has been the scandals of this or that school, care home or hospital, the contested practice of teachers, social workers and doctors has been called to account. Trust has dissolved in the face of public concern and inquiry. Public dependence on trusting the professional, authoritative judgement has been replaced by trust in mechanisms of explicit, transparent, systematic public accountability that seeks to secure regulatory compliance of professional practice.

This constituting of answerability over two decades has, however, set in train two interdependent and seemingly inexorable trends: from accountability being a 'general expectation' to being a process of increasing specification and regulation, and from being conceived as 'an event' to being embodied as a disposition. To require professionals to be accountable leads reasonably to definition: who is to be accountable to whom, for what, and how is this accountability to be effected over what periods of time? Yet specifications at any point of time, because they lack sufficient clarity, inevitably fail to realize their purposes and are superseded by ever more comprehensive and detailed specifications. A cycle of accelerating regulation begins. The purpose of accountability legitimates the creation of detailed regulations that ensure the compliance of professional practitioners. Fielding (2001) and the Gleeson and Husbands' (2001) collection illuminate the malaise caused by the detailed, prescriptive intervention into education at every level from state policy making to classroom pedagogic practice.

When 'formal answerability' is introduced to organizations, accountability is typically experienced as an instrumental event, as with the annual review or appraisal. Yet there is an inexorable tendency for the event to become a continuous process, an orientation to shape and reshape the course of practice. There is an orientation to action embodied in the purposes and relations of accountability. A critical evaluation of performance implies, and requires, a search to redeem and enhance performance in the future: practice can always be improved. The accounting for present performance and the improving of future performance are embodied in the expectations of accountability. Those who initiate schemes of accountability want it to become a routine disposition of public service professionals, shaping their modes of thinking, feeling, speaking, and acting.

The two trends – of increasingly specific regulation and internalized disposition – fuse together into an intensive system of performativity. Ball (1998, 2001a,b) captures how the rituals and routines of performance surveillance bite deeply into the attitudes, practices, and identities of state professionals. Performativity works from the outside in, through regulations, controls and pressures, but also from the inside out, colonizing lives and producing new subjectivities: what we see here is a particular set of 'practices through which we act upon ourselves and one another in order to make us particular kinds of being.'[13] Such performativity, experienced as a regime of externally imposed controls, generates identities disciplined by targets, indicators, measures, and records of performance. The preoccupation with these means of effectiveness often leads, moreover, as Ball points out, to the perverse fabrication of performance, constructions, and selections of the truth produced to create the most beneficial account'.

How is this intensifying regime of performativity to be explained? Organizational theorists have become interested in the tendency for institutions to develop momentum towards a 'design type', the tendency of organizations to evolve in one direction, realizing enhanced structural consistency and coherence: there is a 'gravitational pull' towards a design type (Ferlie *et al.* 1996; Greenwood and Hinings 1993; Hinings and Greenwood 1988). An organization which begins to operate with the rudiments of a design option will be pulled toward the option by the internal consistency, the 'logics of action', embodied in the dominant organizing principle. Institutions, therefore, find it difficult to move out of a dominant design mould. They become captured by the capacity of a system to institutionalize prevailing assumptions and 'myths' or culturally entrenched rules.

The historical narrative of the accumulating purposes and regulatory mechanisms of accountability suggests the temporal longevity of implementing public purpose expressed in the Ruskin speech 25 years ago. Moreover, it does indeed indicate an institutional system in the grip of a gravitational pull or momentum towards a design type revealed in the drive to intensify specification and control. But the codes of this design are to be discovered less in technical prescriptions of a service than in the organizing principles of the social and political order. The dominant relations of accountability are not value-neutral but reveal the practices, structures, and codes that shape the public sphere. The forms of accountability express: the public purposes that are valued; the knowledge claims that are regarded as authoritative; and whose authority acquires legitimacy. Answers to these questions in the public sphere define a conception of the public good underpinned by a structure of power and authority: accountability constitutes and evaluates the relationship of the public to the polity.

The principles informing the structuration of accountability over two decades have been a key aspect of the wider neo-liberal restructuring of governance: a political theory of performativity asserting that an effective public sphere will be one that makes public services answerable to the pressure of competition and the incentive of relative advantage in the marketplace. The historical coalescing and intensifying specification of practice – strengthening the consumer, contract law, state audit, and corporate power – are all designed to create the education service as a sphere of market exchange relationships, in which the actors are provided with an account of quantifiable performance that enables them to calculate their relative advantage in competition. This neo-liberal governance reveals its informing code of the public sphere: the neutral principles of negative liberty according rights to individuals and individual corporations to pursue their interests unfettered by any public authority which seeks to do more than regulate market exchanges in search of justice. Rights of possessive individualism override substantive conceptions of the common good. What this is eroding is any conception of the public good as collective good determined through democratic participation, contestation, and judgement in the public sphere. It seeks to replace politics (substantive rationality) with contract (technically rational solutions).

This regime of neo-liberal accountability, designed to restore trust to public services has, however, had the unintended consequence of further eroding public trust in the stewardship of public services because it has embodied flawed criteria of evaluation and relations of accountability. The dominant mode of answerability cannot deliver achievement because it defines a mistaken criteria of evaluating performance, emphasizing the external imposition of targets and quantifiable outcomes as the means of improvement. This is at the expense of a pedagogy that works 'inside-out', encouraging learners to recognize their capability and motivating them to enter into and remake the narratives that give meaning to their lives (cf. Geertz 1975; Bruner 1996; Bakhurst and Shanker 2001). The financier's accounts and tables cannot provide the conditions for achievement that grow out of acquiring the internal goods of reflective agency (MacIntyre 1999; Taylor 1995) within learning communities. The dominant system of relations of public accountability has, moreover, been transmuted into a system of corporate and state regulation in pursuit of external goods, that cannot deliver public trust because it cannot secure the agreements between diverse interests which form the condition for trust in the construction of public services.

This analysis suggests that an institution of public accountability that wishes to secure achievement and trust rests upon, at each level of the public sphere, processes of deliberation that enable understanding and agreement out of differing accounts of public purpose and service. At each level, whether the community of students or the wider community of citizens, the accounts to be deliberated are those of who we are and what we are to become.

This dialogue of accountability presupposes a public sphere informed by very different principles from the neo-liberal polity: a sphere of public goods to be determined through participation in collective deliberation in the purposes and conditions of citizenship.

In search of an alternative model of public accountability

The age of accountability rejected professional internal regulation and substituted a regime of neo-liberal corporate regulation. Neither are adequate models of public accountability: professional accountability omits the public, empowering the providers (though at least recognizing a distant representative democracy), while the regime of corporate accountability atomizes the public and empowers sectional interests. (The intriguing question is raised whether marketization has had the paradoxical effect of restoring the producer power, now as corporate power?)

Are alternative models of accountability available? Some (Elliott 2001; Macbeath and Mortimore 2001) strive to restore the paradigm of professional self-regulation, but the internal goods of learning – its meanings, purposes, and practices – cannot be determined alone by a specialist knowledge that superintends over the community of learning thus diminishing essential voices and accounts. The most influential proposal for 'restoration' has been O'Neill's (2002b) Reith Lectures, *A Question of Trust*. O'Neill (cf. 2002a) denies that there is a crisis of lost trust, while agreeing that the regime of target-setting answerability has been damaging, distorting professional purpose and erecting centralized bureaucratic control. The remedy is not the surveillance of market inspectorates, nor consumerist rights. Democracy and transparency are not the basis of, but rather depend upon, trust, which itself grows out the social capital of active, duties-oriented citizenship. The remedy is, she proposes, to restore good governance through self-governing institutions accountable to the knowledgeable independent specialist (for example, HMI). The claims of professionals should be scrutinized by an informed public that can depend on good libraries and an honest media for its opinions. This describes an archaic polity. The public is expected to restore control of public services to the professional specialist, whose accountability resides in the presentation of information. There is no recognition here that the internal goods of meaning and purpose are properly the subject of public deliberation requiring shared understanding and agreement if the conditions of learning are to be realized. More serious is the failure to recognize that it is precisely these democratic processes and conditions that constitute the social capital of active citizenship and trust. The conditions for trust may be established if citizens are included in the public space, and their voice heard in public deliberations that provide the basis for just public policy and distribution. It is the democratic institutions of the public sphere that constitute the conditions of trust and mutual accountability. Justice and voice are the foundation of dispositions of duty in civil society.

Others have sought to reform public accountability by fashioning a concept of partnership that integrates private and public into a ('third way') notion of hybrid accountability. Two models are of interest here: the Institute of Public Policy Research (IPPR 2001) *Commission on PPPs* and the New Local Government

Network's *Submission to House of Commons* (Stoker and Williams 2001). The IPPR argue that accountability is essential for the success of PPPs, which in turn can improve accountability if they display three principles: *transparency*, clarity of roles, and *responsibility* and *responsiveness* to adapt to citizens' needs. These principles necessarily inform different kinds of accountability. *Political* designates the appropriate level of democratic body which has responsibility for commissioning and monitoring particular public services. *Legal and financial* determine those provisions of public law, contract law, and auditing and accounting procedures with which the decisions of ministers and officials must comply. *Managerial* designates the setting of targets for performance, the provision of incentives, specification of contracts, measuring of results to ensure that the managers of particular services are responsible for the quality of services they deliver. *Citizen and user* designate the provision of information, forms of redress, and opportunities for consultation and participation both to the wider public and to particular groups of service users.

The IPPR Commission concludes that the traditional polarisation between public (democratic) and private (market) modes of accountability is now inadequate. Hybrid forms of public service organization require hybrid forms of accountability. Partnerships allow service users to exercise their democratic voice, while service providers will be encouraged by financial pressures to deliver high quality public services. Use of partnership boards also enables representatives to monitor performance whilst also acting as guardian of the public interest. In such ways 'the shift towards pluralism in procurement and/or provision ... can go hand in hand with more diverse and effective forms of accountability.'

Yet, though helpfully clarifying aspects of accountability, this report fails to capture the defining characteristics of accountability for the public sphere. The principles diminish the necessity for democratic *control* of partnerships in the public sphere. Democratic contestability, furthermore, needs to be strengthened to emphasize 'voice' but also collective deliberation, judgement and choice of partnership decision-making. Within boards, public representatives are more than monitors of performance, and will be unable to propose new forms of provision or act as guardians of public interest unless they have a controlling voice. The practice of 'boards' raises issues of power and representation in the public sphere. Can boards be democratic or are they illustrations of 'the new magistracies'? Are 'stakeholder' models appropriate to the public sphere selecting 'representative individuals' rather than democratically elected representatives? This illuminates the nature of boards as administrative rather than democratic public spaces such as forums or councils.

The New Local Government Network (NLGN) model of accountability improves on the IPPR Commission's democratic limitations. Public services of necessity require enhanced levels of public accountability to a broader range of stakeholders. Private or voluntary sector organizations have to work within these boundaries. Ultimate accountability for the delivery of a public service should always rest with the commissioner of the service – the public body. Thus public–private partnerships cannot mean 'outsourcing' the accountability for that service. To this extent, local politicians need to take the lead in explaining to the public why the council is engaging with a voluntary sector partner.

The NLGN recognize that the picture of accountability is a complex and developing one in local government. Recent changes to political structures and a clearer distinction between executive and scrutiny responsibilities of individual councillors have both helped (in clarifying responsibilities) and hindered accountability for the performance of PPPs (the scrutiny function focusing too much on the private sector neglecting the public partner). Local authorities should have the power to join up public service delivery agents at the local level when the effective achievement of service outcomes necessitates this. There is the need, it is argued persuasively, for the Government to impose a duty on other local public bodies to have regard to the community plan of the local authority as a practical tool for affirming local government's broader community leadership.

This perspective of the Local Government Network significantly strengthens the public dimensions of accountability. It emphasizes and secures public control. Yet the question arises whether partnerships can survive the implied hierarchy of control which privileges the public partners, and whether partnerships survive the flexibility of political choice that is a necessary characteristic of the public sphere. It is not just that risk cannot be transferred from the public to the sector, but that judgements of the collective good may change over time, and require to be expressed in the public choice. The NLGN's paper, therefore, although extending the scope of accountability, nevertheless lacks a conception of the public sphere and thus the defining characteristics of democratic public accountability. For this reason it remains unable to address the significant issues of the reconcilability of public and private goods, of contract and deliberation in the public sphere. Is an alternative available?

Towards democratic accountability in the public sphere

Corporate/contract accountability is inappropriate to the public sphere. The goods of effectiveness need to be subordinated to the internal goods of a service that can only be clarified through deliberation in the public sphere. The discussion about answerability turns on the need to clarify the democratic governance of public accountability. Rhodes (1997), Whitfield (2000), and Newman (2001) emphasize the need to reconstruct the governance of accountability as a democratic practice, yet its principal characteristics remain attenuated in their writing.

The public sphere is inescapably a political space because it is the space of collectivity, constituted to undertake the tasks that individuals cannot do alone but only together as a collectivity (Coole 2000; Peters 1996; Ranson and Stewart 1995). These are of three kinds: public goods and services (e.g. street lighting); establishing collective efficiency (e.g. regulating traffic congestion); and, most significantly, constituting collective rules and purposes. These are fundamental because the deep purpose of the public sphere is to constitute the social and political preconditions that make society possible, the agreements that enable social life to proceed: who is to be a member, what rights and duties are expected, and what will count as fair distribution of goods and opportunities. Such decisions will determine the basis of justice and well-being in society: they will remain essentially contested, only achieving legitimacy through democratic deliberation.

An alternative perspective of accountability begins by recognizing this agonistic plurality and contestation at the centre of the public sphere. Public services and institutions, serving and constituted by a plurality of actors, of publics, must reach shared understanding and agreement about what are their internal goods (meanings, purposes, and practices). Any linear, hierarchical and regulatory concept of answerability is misplaced in this context. The very language and discourse that construe the purposes and achievements of a public service will, and should, reflect a social and political process. That process will gain the consent of the constituent publics when it has enabled each to join a dialogue about the accounts, the interpretive schema, and normative grounds that should inform the practices of the public service. Accountability, in this understanding, even if initiated in requests for an account, will ensue in a narrative of the communicative action, the giving and taking of reasons, at the centre of the public sphere. Democratic governance of accountability, following these principles, would constitute the following practices.

Membership and the politics of presence: an inclusive democratic community would go further, however, striving to ensure that the multiplicity of differences within a community were present, rather than merely represented, within the governing body. Governance needs to be a space responsive to the politics of difference (Young 1990), recognition (Taylor 1992; Tully 1997) and the politics of presence (Phillips 1995) so that the voice of the marginalized is brought into the centre.

Participation, equality of voice and dissent: citizens acquire status and rights as members of the polity, but their principal obligations are to actively participate and contribute to life and deliberations of the public sphere. Voice is the most distinctive characteristic of the public space, capturing its essential feature of citizens speaking out to communicate their claims and protests (Hirschmann 1970). Others emphasize the need to recognize the source of this voice in the politics of different social and cultural identities, as well as the contested nature of public purpose (Gilligan 1982; Williams 1998). Each has a right to speak and have their say, including questioning, scrutinizing and opposing dominant groups and the status quo: 'the possibility of effective opposition is an essential require-ment of democratic justice' (Shapiro 1999, 39). Questioning enables information to be brought into the public eye and to be discussed, it allows evidence to be scrutinized and interrogated. Questions are the vehicle to ensure that the performance of a public institution is continually and reflexively monitored and evaluated (Giddens 1990, 1994). Scrutiny is the opportunity for learning in the space of governance.

Deliberation and the space of reason: opposition and challenge can only be resolved through a multi-sided conversation that allows the participants to deliberate their differences (cf. Benhabib 1996; Bohman 1996; Bohman and Rehg 1997; Dryzek 2000). The principle of democracy classically was that of 'proper discussions' – of free and unrestricted discourse, with all guaranteed a right to contribute in order to ground decisions in the force of the better argument, the open giving and taking of reasons as grounds for conclusions (cf. Dunn 1992).

> The deliberative process of democratic decision-making requires that each participant not only permit the others to express their views and offer their judgements but take others' views seriously into account in arriving at his or her own judgement. Clearly this does not require agreement with the views of others, but rather serious attention to, and respect for, their views. Such reciprocal respect also presupposes that disagreements be tolerated and not suppressed
>
> (Gould 1988, 88)

For Habermas (1984, 1990, 1996), the processes of argumentation which characterize discourse are oriented towards reaching shared understanding that grows out of a mutual commitment to enter the space of public reasons (cf. McDowell 1998; Scanlon 1998).[14]

Critics, anxious about the exclusionary possibilities embodied in any 'monolingual' concept of public reason, argue that participants should be allowed to speak in their own voices and customary ways so that by careful listening they can begin to grasp their common and interwoven histories (Tully 1995; Young 1990, 1997, 2000). There is no transcendental standard from which to judge the conversation: 'they can only listen to the voices of doubt and dissent within and reconsider their present arrangement'. Nor should participants be silenced or constrained to speak within the tradition of any particular institution. Gadamer (1975, cf. Warnke 2002) argues that this more inclusive process, through which individuals and communities enter a more and more widely defined community of shared understanding, learn through dialogue to take a wider, more differentiated view, and thus acquire sensitivity, subtlety and capacity for judgement.

Judgement and collective rule: The deliberative processes help them to lead to judgement about what is to grow out of the understanding – what is to be done. A faculty is required, Beiner (1983) argues, which avoids the illusion of determining objective decisions, while at the same time avoiding the immanent possibility of arbitrary subjectivism. Judgement offers this indispensable faculty which requires individuals through deliberation to reach detached reasons for decisions and action. The issues that we face in everyday public life are then made amenable to reflective reason, public discourse, dialogue, and common choice. Democratic governance embodies collective choice, and popular control over decisions (Beetham 1994, 1999; Weir and Beetham 1999). There is, however, no necessary one best decision rule for democratic civil society, Shapiro (1999, 36–7) argues: 'the goal is to take social relations as we find them and to discover ways to democratise them... [appropriate to]... the different domains of civil society'.

Accountability: Scrutiny and deliberation lead to collective choice and a return to public accountability. Accountability is a defining quality of the public sphere because it institutionalizes a discourse about purposes, practice, and performance. 'It is a social and political process' (Day and Klein 1987, 2). For Simey (1988) and Stewart (1999, 2000) the obligation to communicate with and explain to the public is the foundation of a democratic polity because the authority and consent for public services derives from the public, and without that the legitimacy of the public sphere withers. Public accountability articulates a theory of political authority grounded in the consent of society. That authority resides with the public and is delegated to representatives and officials on condition that they, in turn, account to the public. The structuring of the institution implies that consent has continually to be tested and reaffirmed. The traditional form of holding to account and of testing consent has been the periodic election. This by itself is inadequate and needs to be complemented by an active citizenship which alone can authorize and give consent to the polity.

Such structuration of power will embody the dominant values about the form of governance, of inclusion and exclusion, of citizenship and social justice. Because these classifications of who we are and what we are to become can be recognized as social constructions, we can also learn that they are amenable to revision. Systems of governance acquire authority if they are perceived as legitimate, that is, if they have wide support, and when legitimate they endure over time. This emphasizes the constructed nature of democratic governance.

Contradiction and change in community governance

The remedy for purported erosion of trust, of a regime of performativity and public accountability, has worked only to distort performance (by substituting a fabricated instrumental rationality) and has displaced the public it was meant to serve. This is because any framework of accountability reveals the polity it expresses. An instrumental, regulatory model of accountability has developed with increasing intensity over time because it has served to express and reinforce the neo-liberal polity of market exchange, and the incentives of relative advantage: competition, contract, corporate ownership have been constituted as the most effective means of formalizing accountability and evaluating performance.

This neo-liberal regime cannot realize its purposes of institutional achievement and public trust. Achievement grows out of the internal goods of motivation to improve (that follows recognition and the mutual deliberation of purpose) rather than the external imposition of quantifiable targets, while public trust follows deliberation of common purpose out of difference and discord, rather than forces of competition that only create a hierarchy of class advantage and exclusion.

Trust and achievement can only emerge in a framework of public accountability that enables different accounts of public purpose and practice to be deliberated in a democratic public sphere: constituted to include difference, enable participation, voice and dissent, through to collective judgement and decision, that is in turn accountable to the public.

Where is such a democratic accountability to emerge from when the public sphere is within the iron design type of neo-liberal corporate regulation? The spaces of contradiction in community governance may provide a glimpse of the possibility for securing transformation and renewal (cf. Engestrom 1999a,b; Daniels 2001). The institutional framework of community governance (including neighbourhood forums, institutional governing bodies, and local councils) are contradictory spaces, whose members – as Deem, Brehony and Heath (1995) powerfully argue in terms of school governing bodies – are configured both as conscripts of the state (implementing regimes of performance regulation) and as citizens (representing local communities in the public sphere).[15] Yet, whatever the present duality of tension embodied in these spaces of governance, they are, nevertheless, constituted enough as local arenas of citizenship to enable local communities to appropriate and develop them as democratic spheres. This can take place when communities learn to recognize that their identities and futures depend upon committing themselves to the internal goods of improvement embedded in institutional practices of democratic citizenship and governance (Hirst 2000; Nixon *et al.* 2001).

Notes

1   This paper has been developed as a background study of governance and accountability for the study of volunteer citizens in the governance of education, a project for the ESRC Democracy and Participation Programme (No. L215252043). I would like to thank a number of colleagues for their helpful critical commentary: Stephen Ball, David Beetham, Michael Fielding, Jon Nixon, Lindsay Paterson, Helen Sullivan, and John Stewart.

2   18 October 1976, Ruskin College, Oxford.

3   See also Ranson and Stewart, 1994.

4   For John Dunn (1988), trust as 'the capacity to commit oneself to fulfilling the legitimate expectations of others, is both the constitutive virtue of, and the key causal precondition for, the existence of any society', also Dunn (1996, 98) '...what politics consists in...is a huge array of free agents coping with each others' freedom over time. In politics so understood the rationality of trust will always be the most fundamental question'. See also Ranson and Stewart 1998.

5 cf. the work of Brian Friel (*Translations*) and James Kelman (*Translated Accounts*) who explore the contesting and negotiating of imperial 'official accounts' over indigenous accounts in the Celtic nations.

6 'Governance' will be defined, drawing on Stoker (2000), as the system of governing collective action in the public sphere and its pattern of legitimating authority. This is a neutral definition leaving open the particular forms governance might take (cf. Rhodes 1997, 2000, 2002; Pierre and Peters 2000; Richards and Smith 2002). Peters distinguishes between 'traditional governance' which focused on the capacity of the state to steer and control society, and 'the new governance' in which political institutions no longer necessarily exercise a monopoly of control, and collective action is networked through a plurality of differentiated centres of power across public, private, and voluntary sector boundaries.

7 Theorists of practice: Giddens, Bourdieu, MacIntyre, Foucault, Delueze.

8 Research studies have been sceptical of the beneficial effects of competition: cf. Gerwitz, S., Ball, S. and Bowe, R. (1995) *Markets, Choice and Equity in Education* (Buckingham: Open University Press); Gewirtz, S. (2002) 'School markets and locality: an exploration of difference in the English education market place', in C. Hudson and A. Lidstrom (eds), *Local Education Policies: comparing Sweden and Britain* (London: Palgrave); Fitz, J., Halpin, D. and Power, S. (1993) *Grant Maintained Schools: education in the market place* (London: Kogan Page); Whitty, G., Power, S. and Halpin, D. (1998) *Devolution and Choice in Education: the school the state and the market* (Buckingham: Open University Press).

9 The process had begun with a Consultative Document, *A Framework for the School Curriculum*, and continued with the White Paper *Better Schools*.

10 The key instruments of policy have been: White Paper, *Excellence in Schools, School Standards and Framework Act* (1998); Green Paper *Teachers Meeting the Challenge of Change*.

11 Regular commentaries on PPPs have been filed by Will Hutton in the *Observer*; Frances Beckett and George Monbiot in *the Guardian*; Nick Cohen in *The New Statesman* and the *Observer*.

12 Whitfield (1999, 2000, 2001) argues that it is unlikely that the private sector will sponsor buildings without regard for the performance of the institutions they support: 'In the longer term it is inconceivable that PFI projects will be confined to buildings and support services, or that only a relatively small part of the education infrastructure will be privately provided. PFI consortia have a vested interest in the quality of teaching and performance of schools they operate because this helps to maintain full capacity ad maximize income from third-party use of facilities'. The division between core and non-core public service is not inflexible. 'By their nature private companies are constantly searching for means of diversifying and expanding markets' (2000, 83). Whitfield envisages that the privatizing of the infrastructure will lead over time to the more general commercialization of education and the involvement of business in learning and teaching – for example, sales of ICT learning packages.

13 Ball, S. 2001a, 213 (quoting Rose, N. (1992)).

14 See Pinkard 1996 and 2002 for the roots of the space of reason in Hegel and in Sellars (1963).

15 Cf. Radnor, H., Ball, S. and Vincent, C. (1997) 'Whither democratic accountability in education?', *Research Papers in Education*, 12(2): 205–22; and Nixon, J., Allan, J. and Mannion, G. (2001) 'Educational renewal as democratic practice: 'new' community schooling in Scotland', *International Journal of Inclusive Education*, 5(4): 329–52.

Bibliography

Ainley, P. (1999) *Learning Policy: towards the certified state* (London: Macmillan).

Anderson, L. (2001) 'A "third-way" towards self-governing schools? New Labour and opting out', *British Journal of Educational Studies*, 49(1): 56–70.

Audit Commission (2003) *PFI in Schools: the quality and cost of buildings and services provided by early Private Finance Initiative schemes* (London: Audit Commission).

Audit Scotland (2002) *Taking the Initiative: using PFI contracts to renew schools* (Edinburgh: Edinburgh Accounts Commission).

Austin, J. L. (1956) *How to do Things with Words* (Oxford: Oxford University Press).

Bakhurst, D. and Shanker, S. (2001) *Jerome Bruner: language, culture, self* (London: Sage).

Ball, S. (1993) 'Educational markets, choice and social class: the market as a class strategy in the UK and USA', *British Journal of Sociology of Education*, 14(1): 1–20.

Ball, S. (1998) 'Performativity and fragmentation in "post-modern schooling" ', in J. Carter (ed.), *Post-Modernity and Fragmentation of Welfare: a contemporary social policy* (London: Routledge).

Ball, S. (2001a) 'Performativities and fabrications in the education economy: towards the performative society', in D. Gleeson and C. Husbands (eds), *The Performing School: managing, teaching and learning in a performing culture* (London: RoutledgeFalmer), pp. 210–26.

Ball, S. (2001b) 'Labour, learning and the economy: a "policy sociology" perspective', in M. Fielding (ed.), *Taking Education Really Seriously: four years hard labour* (London: RoutledgeFalmer).

Beetham, D. (ed.) (1994) *Defining and Measuring Democracy* (London: Sage).

Beetham, D. (1999) *Democracy and Human Rights* (Oxford: Polity Press).

Beiner, R. (1983) *Political Judgement* (London: Methuen).

Benhabib, S. (ed.) (1996) *Democracy and Difference: contesting the boundaries of the political* (Princeton, NJ: Princeton University Press).

Bohman, J. (1996) *Public Deliberation: pluralism, complexity and democracy* (Cambridge, MA: MIT Press).

Bohman, J. and Rehg, W. (eds) (1997) *Deliberative Democracy: essays on reason and politics* (Cambridge, MA: MIT Press).

Bottery, M. (2000) *Education, Policy and Ethics* (London: Continuum).

Bourdieu, P. (1999) *Practical Reason* (Oxford: Polity).

Bruner, J. (1996) *The Culture of Education* (Cambridge, MA: Harvard University Press).

Coole, D. (2000) *Negativity and Politics* (London: RoutledgeFalmer).

Daniels, H. (2001) *Vygotsky and Pedagogy* (London: RoutledgeFalmer).

Day, P. and Klein, R. (1987) *Accountabilities: five public services* (London: Tavistock).

Deem, R., Brehony, K. and Heath, S. (1995) *Active Citizenship and the Governing of Schools* (Buckingham: Open University Press).

DES (1980) *A Framework for the School Curriculum* (London: DES).

DES (1985) *Better Schools: White Paper* (London: DES).

DfEE (1997) *Excellence in Schools* (London: DfEE).

DfEE (1998) *School Standards and Framework Act* (London: DfEE).

DfEE (1998) *Teachers Meeting the Challenge of Change* (London: DfEE).

Doogan, K. (1999) 'The contracting out of local government services', in G. Stoker (ed.), *The New Management of British Local Government* (London: Macmillan).

Dryzek, J. (2000) *Deliberative Democracy and Beyond* (Oxford: Oxford University Press).

Dunn, J. (ed.) (1992) *Democracy: The Unfinished Journey: 508 BC to AD 1993* (Oxford: Oxford University Press).

Dunn, J. (1988) 'Trust and political agency', in D. Gambetta (ed.), *Trust: making and breaking co-operative relations* (Oxford: Basil Blackwell).

Dunn, J. (1996) *Interpreting Political Responsibility* (Oxford: Polity Press).

Dunsire, A. (1978) *Control in a Bureaucracy, The Executive Process*, vol. 2 (Oxford: Martin Robertson).

Elliott, J. (2001) 'Characteristics of performative cultures: their central paradoxes and limitations as resources for educational reform', in D. Gleeson and C. Husbands (eds), *The Performing School: managing, teaching and learning in a performance culture* (London: RoutledgeFalmer), pp. 192–209.

Engestrom, Y. (1999a) 'Activity theory and individual and social transformation', in Y. Engestrom, R. Miettinen and R.-L. Punamaki (eds), *Perspectives in Activity Theory* (Cambridge: Cambridge University Press).

Engestrom, Y. (1999b) *Expansive Learning at Work: toward an activity-theoretical reconceptualisation* (Helsinki: University of Finland).

Ferlie, E., Ashburner, L., Fitzgerald, L. and Pettigrew, A. (1996) *The New Public Management in Action* (Oxford: Oxford University Press).

Fielding, M. (2001) *Taking Education Really Seriously: four years hard labour* (London: Routledge Falmer).

Fielding, M. (2002) 'Ofsted, inspection and the betrayal of democracy', *Journal of Philosophy of Education*, 35(4): 695–709.

Fitz, J., Halpin, D. and Power, S. (1993) *Grant Maintained Schools: education in the market place* (London: Kogan Page).

Foucault, M. (1991) 'Questions of method', in G. Burchell, C. Gordon and P. Miller (eds), *The Foucault Effect* (Chicago, IL: University of Chicago Press).

Friel, B. (1981) *Translations* (London: Faber and Faber).

Gadamer, H.-G. (1975) *Truth and Method* (London: Sheed and Ward).

Geertz, C. (1975) *The Interpretation of Cultures* (London: Hutchinson).

Gewirtz, S. (12 July 2001) Where are we now and where are we going? Education policy after Blunkett. Paper given at King's College London.

Gewirtz, S., Ball, S. and Bowe, R. (1995) *Markets, Choice and Equity in Education* (Buckingham: Open University Press).

Giddens, A. (1984) *The Constitution of Society* (Oxford: Polity).

Giddens, A. (1990) *The Consequences of Modernity* (Oxford: Polity).

Giddens, A. (1994) 'Living in a post-traditional society', in U. Beck, A. Giddens and S. Lash (eds), *Reflexive Modernisation: politics, tradition and aesthetics in the modern social order* (Oxford: Polity).

Gilligan, C. (1982) *In a Different Voice: psychological theory and women's development* (Cambridge, MA: Harvard University Press).

Glatter, R., Woods, P. and Bagley, C. (1997) *Choice and Diversity in Schooling: perspectives and prospects* (London: Routledge).

Gleeson, D. and Husbands, C. (eds) (2001) *The Performing School: managing, teaching and learning in a performance culture* (London: RoutledgeFalmer).

Gould, C. (1988) *Rethinking Democracy: freedom and social co-operation in politics, economy and society* (Cambridge: Cambridge University Press).

Greenwood, R. and Hinings, C. (1993) 'Understanding strategic change: the contribution of archetypes', *Academy of Management Journal*, 35(6): 1052–81.

Habermas, J. (1984) *The Theory of Communicative Action* (London: Heinemann).

Habermas, J. (1990) *Moral Consciousness and Communicative Action* (Oxford: Polity).

Habermas, J. (1994) 'Three models of democracy', *Constellations: An International Journal of Critical and Democratic Theory*, 1(1): 1–10.

Habermas, J. (1996) *Between Facts and Norms: contributions to a discourse theory of law and democracy* (Oxford: Polity).

Hatcher, R. (2001) 'Privatisation and schooling', in C. Chitty and B. Simon (eds), *Promoting Comprehensive Education in the 21st Century* (Stoke on Trent: Trentham Books).

Hertz, N. (2001) *The Silent Takeover: global capital and the death of democracy* (London: Heinemann).

Hinings, C. and Greenwood, R. (1988) *The Dynamics of Strategic Change* (Oxford: Blackwell).

Hirschmann, A. O. (1970) *Exit, Voice and Loyalty* (Cambridge, MA: Harvard University Press).

Hirst, P. (2000) 'Democratic justice', in J. Pierre (ed.), *Debating Governance: authority, steering and democracy* (Oxford: Oxford University Press).

Hood, C. (1992) A public management for all seasons, *Public Administration*, 69(1): 1–180.

Husbands, C. (2001) 'Managing performance in the performing school', in D. Gleeson and C. Husbands (eds), *The Performing School: managing, teaching and learning in a performance culture* (London: RoutledgeFalmer).

Institute of Public Policy Research (2001) *Building Better Partnerships: the final report of the Commission on Public Private Partnerships* (London, IPPR).

Kelman, J. (2001) *Translated Accounts* (London: Secker).

Kemp, Sir P. (18 October 1999) Please stop fiddling the books, in Special Report: The Private Finance Initiative, *New Statesman*, pp. 28–9.

King, D. (1987) *The New Right: politics, markets and citizenship* (London: Macmillan).

Kogan, M. (1978) *The Politics of Educational Change* (London: Fontana).

Kogan, M. (1988) *Accountability* (London: Kogan Page).

Levacic, R. (1995) *Local Management of Schools: analysis and practice* (Buckingham: Open University Press).

Levitas, R. (ed.) (1986) *The Ideology of the New Right* (Oxford: Polity).

Lyotard, J.-F. (1997) *The Post-Modern Condition: a report on knowledge* (Manchester: Manchester University Press).

Macbeath, J. and Mortimore, P. (2001) *Improving School Effectiveness* (Buckinghamshire: The Open University Press).

McDowell, J. (1998) *Mind, Value and Reality* (Cambridge, MA: Harvard University Press).

McFadyean, M. and Rowland, D. (2002) *PFI vs Democracy: school governors and the Haringey Schools PFI Scheme* (London: The Menard Press).

MacIntyre, A. (1982) *After Virtue* (London: Duckworth).

MacIntyre, A. (1988) *Whose Justice? Which Rationality?* (London: Duckworth).

MacIntyre, A. (1999) *Dependent Rational Animals* (London: Duckworth).

Monbiot, G. (2000) *Captive State: the corporate takeover of Britain* (Basingstoke: Pan).

Monbiot, G. (18 June 2002) 'Public fraud initiative', *The Guardian*, p. 17.

Newman, J. (2001) *Modernising Governance: New Labour, policy and society* (London: Sage).

Nixon, J., Allan, J. and Mannion, G. (2001) 'Educational renewal as democratic practice: "new" community schooling in Scotland', *International Journal of Inclusive Education*, 5(4): 329–52.

O'Neill, O. (2002a) *Autonomy and Trust in Bioethics* (Cambridge: Cambridge University Press).

O'Neill, O. (2002b) *A Question of Trust* (The BBC Reith Lectures 2002) (Cambridge: Cambridge University Press).

Perkin, H. (1988) *The Rise of Professional Society: England since 1880* (London: Routledge).

Peters, B. G. (1996) *The Future of Governing: four emerging models* (Lawrence, KS: University of Kansas Press).

Phillips, A. (1995) *The Politics of Presence* (Oxford: Oxford University Press).

Pierre, J. (ed.) (2000) *Debating Governance: authority, steering and democracy* (Oxford: Oxford University Press).

Pierre, J. and Peters, B. G. (2000) *Governance, Politics and the State* (London: Macmillan).

Pinkard, T. (1996) *Hegel's Phenomenology: the sociality of reason* (Cambridge: Cambridge University Press).

Pinkard, T. (2002) *German Philosophy 1760–1860: The Legacy of Idealism* (Cambridge: Cambridge University Press).

Pollitt, C. (1990) *Managerialism and the Public Services* (Oxford: Blackwell).

Power, M. (1999) *The Audit Society*, 2nd edn (Oxford: Oxford University Press).

Pring, R. (1996) 'Values and education policy', in J. Halstead and M. Taylor (eds), *Values in Education and Education in Values* (London: Falmer), pp. 104–17.

Radnor, H., Ball, S. and Vincent, C. (1997) 'Whither democratic accountability?', *Research Papers in Education*, 12(2): 205–222.

Ranson, S. (July/August 1986) 'Towards a political theory of public accountability in education', *Local Government Studies*, pp. 77–97.

Ranson, S. and Stewart, J. (1995) *Management for the Public Domain: enabling the learning society* (London: Macmillan).

Ranson, S. and Stewart, J. (1998) 'Citizenship in the public domain for trust in civil society', in A. Coulson (ed.), *Trust and Contracts: relationships in local government, health and public service* (London: Policy Press), pp. 243–65.

Rhodes, R. (1997) *Understanding Governance: policy networks, governance, reflexivity and accountability* (Buckingham: Open University Press).

Rhodes, R. (2000) 'Public administration and governance', in J. Pierre (ed.), *Debating Governance: authority, steering and democracy* (Oxford: Oxford University Press).

Rhodes, R. (2002) 'The new public administration of the British state', in C. Hay (ed.), *British Politics Today* (Oxford: Polity).

Richards, D. and Smith, M. (2002) *Governance and Public Policy in the UK* (Oxford: Oxford University Press).

Rose, N. (1992) 'Governing the enterprising soul', in P. Heelas and P. Morris (eds), *The Values of the Enterprise Culture* (London: Routledge).

Scanlon, T. M. (1998) *All We Owe to Each Other* (Cambridge: Belknap Harvard).

Sellars, W. (1963) *Science, Perception and Reality* (London: Routledge).

Shapiro, I. (1999) *Democratic Justice* (New Haven, CT: Yale University Press).

Shotter, J. (1989) 'Social accountability and the social construction of "you"', in J. Shotter and K. Green (eds), *Texts of Identity* (London: Sage).

Simey, M. (1988) *Democracy Rediscovered: a study in police accountability* (London: Bedford Square Press).

Sockett, H. T. (ed.) (1980) *Accountability in the English School System* (London: Hodder and Stoughton).

Stewart, J. (1985) *A New Concern for Accountability* (Luton: Local Government Training Board).

Stewart, J. (1999) 'Towards democratic justice', in J. McCormick and A. Harvey (eds), *Local Routes to Social Justice* (London: Institute of Public Policy Research).

Stewart, J. (2000) *The Nature of British Local Government* (London: Palgrave).

Stewart, J. and Stoker, G. (1995) *Local Government in the 1990s* (London: Macmillan).

Stewart, J., Lewis, N. and Longley, D. (1992) *Accountability to the Public* (London: European Policy Forum for British and European Market Studies).

Stoker, G. (ed.) (1999) *The New Management of British Local Government* (London: Macmillan).

Stoker, G. (2000) 'Urban political science and the challenge of urban governance', in J. Pierre (ed.), *Debating Governance: authority, steering and democracy* (Oxford: Oxford University Press).

Stoker, G. and Williams, J. (2001) *Submission to the House of Commons Public Administration Select Committee Inquiry into Public Service Reform* (London: New Local Government Network).

Taylor, C. (1992) *Multiculturalism and 'the Politics of Recognition'* (Princeton, NJ: Princeton University Press).

Taylor, C. (1995) *Philosophical Arguments* (Cambridge, MA: Harvard University Press).

Thomas, H. and Martin, J. (1996) *The Management of Resources* (London: Routledge).

Tomlinson, S. (2001) *Education in a Post-Welfare Society* (Buckingham: Open University Press).

Tully, J. (1997) *Strange Multiplicity: constitutionalism in an age of diversity* (Cambridge: Cambridge University Press).

Tully, J. (2000) 'The challenge of reimagining citizenship and belonging in multicultural and multinational societies', in C. McKinnon and I. Hampsher-Monk (eds), *The Demands of Citizenship* (London: Continuum).

UK Parliament (2002) *Parliamentary Select Committee on Public Accounts* (London: HMSO).

Warnke, G. (2002) 'Hermeneutics, ethics and politics', in R. Dostal (ed.), *The Cambridge Companion to Gadamer* (Cambridge: Cambridge University Press).

Weir, S. and Beetham, D. (1999) *Political Power and Democratic Control in Britain* (London: Routledge).

Whitfield, D. (1999) 'Private finance initiative: the commodification and marketisation of education', *Education and Social Justice*, 1(2): 2–13.

Whitfield, D. (2000) The third way for education: privatisation and marketisation, *Forum*, 42(2): 82–5.

Whitfield, D. (2001) *Public Services or Corporate Welfare* (London: Pluto Press).

Whitty, G. (2002) *Making Sense of Education Policy* (London: Paul Chapman).

Whitty, G. and Power, S. (2000) 'Marketisation and privatisation in mass education systems', *International Journal of Education Development*, 20: 93–107.

Whitty, G., Power, S. and Halpin, D. (1998) *Devolution and Choice in Education* (Buckingham: Open University Press).

Williams, M. (1998) *Voice, Trust and Memory* (Princeton, NJ: Princeton University Press).

Wittgenstein, L. (1953) *Philosophical Investigations* (Oxford: Blackwell).

Young, I. M. (1990) *Justice and the Politics of Difference* (Princeton, NJ: Princeton University Press).

Young, I. M. (1997) *Intersecting Voices* (Princeton, NJ: Princeton University Press).

Young, I. M. (2000) *Inclusion and Democracy* (Oxford: Oxford University Press).

CHAPTER 13

REALISING POLICY
The *who* and *how* of policy production
Trevor Gale

Discourse: studies in the cultural politics of education, 2003, 24(1): 51–65

Introduction

I appreciate definitions of 'policy' as the 'authoritative allocation of values' (Easton 1953; Anderson 1979), not least because they draw attention to the *who* and the *how* of policy production. Prunty has argued similarly, that

> The authoritative allocation of values draws our attention to the centrality of power and control in the concept of policy, and requires us to consider not only whose values are represented in policy, but also how these values have become institutionalised.
>
> (1985, 36)

Such considerations are important because they expose the partiality (and, hence, fallacy) of rationality and consensus in policy production, or at least make room for such disclosure. In my view, traditional representations of the democratic process, in which policy is produced through mutual agreement while authority to produce it is invested in elected representatives (often supported by technical expertise) – consigning all else and others to the domains of implementation and consumption – are both theoretically naive and politically abhorrent. Drawing attention to the who of policy production enables the naming of values inherent in things that are seemingly technical (such as policy) and the foregrounding of a radical democracy (Lummis 1996) (which engages all people in public processes) as a legitimate basis for policy's authority. Whereas drawing attention to the how of policy production challenges not just the premise of rationality in policy making but also how particular individuals and groups are involved in various contexts as policy makers. In brief, the who and how of policy production are dialectically related. They are, as Bourdieu might describe them, much like field positions and stances: 'two translations of the same sentence' (Spinoza, in Bourdieu and Wacquant 1992, 105).

These are the issues I seek to explore in this paper: relations between the who and how of policy production and how these are connected to particular contexts of policy making. To borrow from Foucault (1972, 207), they represent the conditions of policies' realisation and are matters I have characterised elsewhere (Gale 2001) as the interests of critical policy historiography, specifically policy archaeology and policy genealogy. Regarding the first:

> critical policy archaeology asks: (1) why are some items on the policy agenda (and not others)?; (2) why are some policy actors involved in the production

of policy (and not others)? and (3) what are the conditions that regulate the patterns of interaction of those involved?

(Gale 2001, 387–8)

Whereas:

Policy genealogy...is not convinced by analyses of policy production explained by 'bounded rationality' (Simon 1960) or 'incrementalism' achieved through 'partisan mutual adjustment' (Lindblom 1959). Certainly, it asks (1) how policies change over time, but it also seeks to determine (2) how the rationality and consensus of policy production might be problematised and (3) how temporary alliances are formed and reformed around conflicting interests in the policy production process.

(Gale 2001, 389–90)

These interests, particularly (2) and (3) of both policy archaeology and genealogy, involve discerning the nature of 'social actors' engagement with policy' (Gale 2001) and are explored in this paper through analysing the production of Australian higher education entry policy during the period 1987 to 1996, with a particular focus on the production of Queensland higher education entry policy text in 1990 (Viviani 1990). In particular, data are drawn from 27 semi-structured, in-depth interviews with policy actors located at various levels of the Australian state: politicians and political advisers (PPA), bureaucrats and policy advisers (BPA), 'cowboys'[1] and independent authorities (CIA), and academics and university administrators (AUA).[2]

To put this research and its dataset in context, Australian institutions of higher education (universities and colleges), which were established through legislation by State[3] governments, initially managed their affairs under the auspices of their respective States. These arrangements began to change from the mid 1940s with increasing federal funding of higher education, following the federal government's takeover of income tax collection from Australian citizens, leaving the States with diminished primary sources of revenue. In the early 1970s, under an agreement between the federal and State governments, increasing federal involvement in higher education culminated in the States officially transferring their responsibility for financing and managing Australia's universities to the Whitlam federal Labor government. Federal responsibility for higher education was further strengthened in the late 1980s and early 1990s by the Hawke/Keating federal Labor government during the amalgamations of Australian universities and colleges into the Unified National System.

Despite these arrangements, the Australian States' residual legislative responsibility for higher education and the high 'unmet demand' for university places, peaking in the early 1990s, contributed to increasing political pressure from their constituents to address issues concerning the supply of Australian university places. In Queensland, for example, this 'under-supply' was perceived as a function of an unfair method of selecting students for university and, therefore, the responsibility of the State government. As a way of dealing with the politics of these arrangements – both the methods of selection and matters of university finance and governance – the Goss State Labor government, newly elected to power in Queensland, undertook a review of university entry policy in the State and produced what became known as the 'Viviani Review' (1990). It is in this complex mix of federal – State responsibilities for Australian higher education that the policy issues below are discussed.[4]

The paper begins by considering the political nature of 'policy speak', although this is primarily argued in relation to theoretical issues. It includes an account of the relations between policy makers and contexts of policy making or which policy actors tend to dominate particular stages of the policy process. The second section of the paper examines more empirically who has permission to speak policy and is interested in uncovering how the boundaries of 'who', 'where' and 'what goes on' are contested and, therefore, how particular production processes represent temporary settlements (Gale 1999) of policy vocalities. As noted above, this work is informed by a policy archaeology although I have refrained from engaging in a discussion of the specifics of this methodology, given that my account of such matters, drawing on similar empirical data, is recorded elsewhere (Gale 2001).

In exploring the how of policy production, the third section of the paper extends the analysis of 'what goes on' to consider the strategies policy actors utilise from particular positions within particular contexts to produce particular policies. That is, the interest is in the work of production: what policy actors do, more than what they produce, although these are not unrelated. Focused on one particular context of policy making, specifically the Viviani Review in Queensland, the contention is that what can be done by policy makers is related to where they are positioned within that context; that is, how they are related to other actors and contexts. Again, the policy genealogy that informs this account is not discussed in any great detail, given its previous elaborations (Gale 2001). Nevertheless, it is important to acknowledge that throughout the paper I am guided by what Troyna sees as the central questions in any critical analysis: specifically, to determine 'What is really going on?' and 'How come?' (1994, 72–3).

Policy speak: should politics be part of the vocabulary?

Traditionally, permission to speak policy has been vested in the state. In the academic literature, for example, definitions of policy often carry references to the state or to government[5] as a way of framing what is legitimate policy and what is, or what is not of particular significance. This literature also refers to distinctions such as 'public' policy and 'education' policy – references one could imagine as framed respectively by the 'context of outcomes' and the 'context of political strategy' (Ball 1994) – as ways of demarcating policy from other sociopolitical activities and actors. Many of these definitions are informed by 'executive' models of policy production, whereas others adopt a 'partnership' model (Yeatman 1998) and, hence, different conceptions of the nature of the state and how this defines the positioning of policy actors. Some extend this examination to questioning the legitimacy and adequacy of the state itself in producing policy in postmodern societies (see Dale 1992; Hoffman 1995). Others note that the rhetoric of withering nation states and policy relevance under the influence of market globalisation is not simply matched by empirical evidence (Keating and Davis 2000).

Such distinctions are informed by matters of 'policy speak': what is considered legitimate to say in policy contexts. Even though 'policy' and 'politics' are derived from the same root word (from the ancient Greek city-state of *polis*) and are indistinguishable in many European languages (*politik* in German; *politique* in French; and so on), some still view policy as 'concerned with outcomes, whereas politics is concerned with process – and in particular, with the participants' position in the game' (Colebatch 1998, 73). Drawing on Bourdieu and Wacquant (1992), I return below to such talk of positions and games but in a way that gives recognition to the politics of the policy process. That is, rather than viewing policy as static, the understanding here is that it invites its own distinctive type of politics that is 'internal to the policy process and is shaped by it' (Yeatman 1998, 22). In particular, it is a politics that speaks of a desired future: 'policy occurs when social actors think about what they are doing and why *in relation to different and alternative possible futures*' (Yeatman 1998, 19, emphasis added).

Such discussions are about the political and theoretical boundaries we draw around policy, including those who participate in its production (and those who do not) and under what conditions. The theoretical boundaries between those who produce and those who implement policy have undergone considerable debate in the policy literature (see, for example, Wilenski 1986) and are now well and truly dismissed as ill informed. Roger Dale, for example, has noted that

> Severing implementation from formulation of policy involves not only a distortion but a serious misunderstanding of the role of the state in education policy. It is a misunderstanding connected to the view that the State involvement in education implies ownership, control and operation of education systems, with a functional division of labour between formulation and implementation of policy.
>
> (1992, 393)

But the distinction lives on in the minds of many and in hegemonic ways that serve to privilege some policy actors and their activities in particular contexts at the expense of others. In short, advocating such separations on theoretical grounds amounts to political strategy. Yeatman, for example, notes that to define policy

> as *technical* in character...[is to privilege] the advice of experts not the participation of citizens. This is the function of the recent take-over of the policy agenda by libertarian neo-classical economics where the most important policy issues are represented as economic ones. This particular brand of economics is especially salient because it not only privileges the private power of business corporations who command enormous political influence but it seems to speak on behalf of the freedom of choice of the ordinary person.
>
> (1998, 25, emphasis in original)

What is clearly evident here is the political nature of the policy process or, more accurately, the political nature of attempts to deny the legitimacy of the policy process. In a political sense, 'for the conception of policy as a policy process to be possible, the work of state administration has to be conceived democratically' (Yeatman 1998, 17). Here Yeatman intentionally confuses politics and theory; a strategy she extends to conceptions of policy activism:

> I am offering a normative definition of *policy activist*...as anyone who champions in relatively consistent ways a value orientation and pragmatic commitment to what I have called the policy process, namely a conception of policy which opens it up to the appropriate participation of all those who are involved in policy all the way through points of conception, operational formulation, implementation, delivery on the ground, consumption and evaluation.
>
> (Yeatman 1998, 34, emphasis in original)

I appreciate the politics here but would want to theorise policy activism as also including the activities of those with commitments to less participatory interests, those who are committed to restricting the participation of others. However, I acknowledge the theoretical intent of aspects of Yeatman's account, particularly its broadening of Heclo's (1978) original conception of policy activism, as restricted to policy advisers, to include activists at all stages of the policy process.

We might imagine, then, a pairing, as illustrated in Table 13.1, where particular policy actors dominate particular policy contexts. What is envisaged are 'key media-tors of policy in any setting who are relied upon by others to relate policy to context or to gatekeep' (Ball 1994, 17). In other words, 'only certain voices are heard at any point in time' (Ball 1994, 16). What is not meant is a strict separation between contexts and their productive activities (see Gale 1999) nor a linear representation of the policy process despite this suggestion in Yeatman's (1998) listing of stages. As particular policy actors tend to dominate particular contexts, so they are dominated by particular activities but not exclusively so. Policy actors and their activities cannot be pinned down indefinitely but rather are temporarily settled in particular contexts. Similarly, contexts are not defined simply by their material properties but can be conceived as 'different descriptions of the same social reality' (Gale 1999, 404).

Another way of explaining these relations between policy contexts, actors and their activities is in terms of Bourdieu's notions of capital and field (see, for example, Bourdieu and Wacquant 1992, 98–9). In such terms, determining the limits of a policy field is one and the same thing as determining the capital valued within that field. In other words, at any one point in time certain cultural, social, economic and

Table 13.1 Policy making contexts and their policy makers

Produced where? *What kind of productive activity?*	*Produced by whom?*
Contexts of policy making (Bowe et al. 1992; Ball 1994) Stages of the policy process (Yeatman 1998)	*Interest groups (Lawton 1986) Policy activists (Yeatman 1998)*
• Context of influence (Bowe *et al.* 1992) • Setting the policy agenda and policy development (Yeatman 1998) • Context of policy text production (Bowe *et al.* 1992) • Policy formulation	• Politicians (Lawton 1986) • Government executives (e.g. cabinet), legislators, the judiciary (Yeatman 1998) • Bureaucrats (Lawton 1986) • Public officials – bureaucrats, public servants, public managers (Yeatman 1998)
• Context of practice (Bowe *et al.* 1992) • Policy implementation and policy delivery (Yeatman 1998)	• Professionals (Lawton 1986) • Direct service deliverers – e.g. those who staff a school, from principal to teachers to ancillary staff (Yeatman 1998)
• Context of outcomes (Ball 1994)	• The consumers, users, recipients of policy, and those subject to its regulation (Yeatman 1998)
• Context of political strategy (Ball 1994) • Policy evaluation and policy monitoring (Yeatman 1998)	• Policy analysts – analysis *of* and *for* policy (Gordon *et al.* 1977; Kenway 1990)

symbolic resources (capitals) tend to dominate any one policy context. Hence, as illustrated in Table 13.1, the capital seen to be required to formulate policy is privileged in contexts of policy text production. Further, it is not just the volume but also the structure of one's capital that determines a policy actor's positioning (his/her relative force in producing policy) and his/her strategic orientation within particular policy contexts. Hence, bureaucrats and public officials, for example, might be better positioned to write policy text and, therefore, dominate contexts of policy text production because they possess more of the relevant capitals that the context values. Bourdieu's analogy of a game to explain the interactions of and more fluid relations between (policy) actors within (policy) fields is instructive here. In negotiating the policy process or 'game', policy actors or

> players can play to increase or to conserve their capital [and, hence, their positioning in a particular policy context]...in conformity with the tacit rules of the game and the prerequisites of the reproduction of the game and its stakes; but they can also get in it to transform, partially or completely, the immanent rules of the game. They can, for instance, work to change...the exchange rate between various species of capital, through strategies aimed at discrediting the form of capital which the force of the opponents rests...and to valorize the species of capital they preferentially possess.
>
> (Bourdieu and Wacquant 1992, 99)

Permission to speak policy: the *who* of policy production

These are issues well illustrated in the production of Australian higher education policy during the period from 1987 to 1996. The players in this policy 'game' are those named above as politicians and political advisers, bureaucrats and policy advisers, cowboys and independent authorities, and academics and university administrators. And the rules of this policy game can be found in the withdrawing and redrawing of commitments, conditions of eligibility and manageability, and the sites of engagement with policy matters. These are matters discussed in turn.

Withdrawing and redrawing commitments

Changes in government are telling moments for policy actors. They can result in the repositioning of policy actors within policy contexts, a reduction in their status and/or legitimacy as policy producers and sometimes their exclusion from policy-making contexts altogether. The following interview extracts illustrate something of the effects the newly elected (1989) Goss Labor government in Queensland had on one set of policy actors identified with a particular independent authority (IA1) with considerable investments in issues of Australian higher education entry. As the incoming Minister of Education in Queensland described it,

> I had the boffins in [IA1] still telling me, 'look, the TE [Tertiary Entrance] score system's terrific. It really is the fairest thing.' I mean they were just totally convinced. They didn't want to change it, and they could sit down and draw up the graphs and the computer models all they liked, I told them, 'but', I said, 'out there, you've lost the battle. Whether it is the fairest system in the world or way up there with the best, it doesn't matter. You've lost. The war's over. People don't think it is.'
>
> (PPA1)

What is championed here by the Minister is the need to take account of politics within the policy process; an account that these policy actors were unwilling or unable to accept and which formed the rationale for withdrawing IA1's authority as the dominant policy maker and repositioning it as subservient to a second and new independent authority (IA2). The Minister's political adviser noted at the time that the intention was to create

> a more community orientation than [evident within IA1], and it has to [be community orientated] because it's a forum which has representatives from all different groups...That's not a criticism of [IA1]. It is a technical organisation... [That's] one of the reasons why [IA2's] there...to expose them and the other players to 'Well, hang on, what other views have the other groups?'
>
> (PPA3)

There is a certain politics in claiming technical expertise and

> it's quite easy for these authorities [such as IA1] to become branded as cowboys, and they are viewed typically as cowboys because they're not bound by the same level of accountability to the political process or the financial processes... Statutory authorities...are not obliged to account financially in the same way, and the political process is not as hard on them because they can always say, 'Well, we're an independent authority.'
>
> (BPA4)

But the effect of creating IA2 was to insert new interests into the policy-making context and to rework the regard for existing interests, diminishing previous levels of autonomy. It is as Bourdieu suggests: the policy field was (re)defined by the capital it valued. As illustrated in this example, such reconstruction

> put TAFE [Technical and Further Education] in there which changes the balance, they put the Department [of Education] in there as well, and the interest groups in the outer ring have changed that balance...the broader redistribution of power will follow from that. I think that it will be the case that [IA1's] powers have been diminished by this... [whereas] the universities have not been losers...they have retrieved their position.
>
> (Viviani)

And, as Colebatch (1998, 22) notes, 'in this context, the question is not simply, "Who needs to be included?", but also, "Who must not be left out?" – that is, whose exclusion would frustrate the policy or simply make it pointless?'

Conditions of eligibility

A further condition that determines policy actors' access to contexts of policy making is related to the particular structure of their capitals (the resources they draw on to produce policy) and how these are valued within the field. That is, the reconstruction of the policy context described above privileged different kinds of policy makers and capitals. In this particular context,

> Nancy Viviani was chosen because she's an expert at policy making, not because she knew anything about this particular [issue]... She's a very bright, able policy analyst. That's her background. And that's what they wanted.

They didn't want any educational person...That was the rationale behind choosing [Ken] Wiltshire [as Chair of the Reference Committee]...and Viviani [as the Reviewer]...that they're both policy people.

(AUA1)

Such positioning of 'education people' is not uncommon in contemporary contexts of education policy making, where their vocality within the field of education is seen as indicative of an inappropriate structuring of the capital that is required to produce education policy or, at least, to drive its production. In short, the strategy is to discredit the form of capital education people possess. Hence:

the people you negotiated with in [Australian] higher education were almost never the educators. They weren't from the Faculties of Education. The people who set the pace and had the views came from Engineering, or Medicine, or Physics.

(CIA6)

Emphasised here is the productive work within policy-making contexts and their associated capitals more than the content that might inform a policy text. This is the critique above of education policy that stresses education (expertise) rather than policy (expertise). Hence, in allocating permission to speak policy and to manage its production,

it's the capacity of people that's important more than their so called expertise in a particular area. That doesn't mean you pull people off the cane harvester and get them to do [a review of] tertiary education, but if they're broadly educated and well known in educational areas, it's much more important to pick a person with that strength of character and background which shows they can do things, rather than saying, 'well, let's find the person who is the expert in that area'.

(PPA1)

In this account, policy 'problems' are no longer dominated by the expert knowledge of specialist content areas but by policy expertise; that is, the politics of the policy process. This is what is valorised, as Bourdieu would say. Eligible policy actors, therefore, are those who possess a particular kind of political expertise, which necessarily has implications regarding the allocation of values.

Conditions of manageability

A second set of conditions regulating how policy actors are positioned within policy-making contexts more explicitly involve the structural relations established among policy actors. In producing Australian higher education entry policy, these structures were informed by certain time constraints that were mediated by a desire to incorporate a more participatory politics (noted above). Although, given the particular interests and historical dominance of some policy actors in this context, politicians and political advisers regarded participatory policy making as subservient to these time constraints. Hence, a particular kind of structuring of the policy context was required:

The idea of a single reviewer had been something which the British Civil Service had adopted some years ago – I think out of something called the

Rayner Review Process. Derek Rayner was Chief Executive of Marks and Spencer, I suppose one of the early quality managers... [He] came up with the idea of a single reviewer with a reference committee...in the belief that a single reviewer had a better chance of doing the job than a committee.

(AUA4)

Here, again, is the imperative of 'doing the job', getting it done, a focus on the political work of producing policy. And, according to the Minister who appointed this 'single reviewer', Viviani, and charged her with the responsibility of producing the policy text, this particular structuring of the policy context

was one of her ideas. It was a very good idea – a consultative committee... with the players in the field having a real chance to influence her...They'd be on this committee that worked one down from her, but it would be her report. Not their report. And they had a chance to help and not to dominate.

(PPA1)

A particular outcome was envisaged by these arrangements, one informed by 'the context of outcomes' (Ball 1994). That is, strongly influencing this particular context of policy text production was how current Australian higher education entry arrangements were perceived by the public and, more specifically, the immediate users of the Tertiary Entrance score that current policy settings delivered. The rationale, or fear, that informed this restructuring, then, was that

if you had a committee design it, you'd have different people doing different things all over the place. And you might not have ultimately a situation that everyone's happy with. But if you have a Reviewer, one person with the responsibility to produce a report to the government, who can use the views of experts and others in the field to bounce ideas off, but then, that person's held responsible for providing a report to the government, you've got a much better chance of an outcome, and it was an outcome that we really wanted.

(PPA3)

Illustrated here is that 'coherence is not so much one of the attributes of policy as one of the central problems: how to get all the different elements to focus on the same question in the same way' (Colebatch 1998, 3–4). Inevitably, this is a political issue.

Sites of engagement

A final area concerns the sites in which the politics of policy making are engaged. Certainly, formal meetings were featured in the research reported here but what should be noted is how the dominant policy maker in this context explicitly connected these formal meetings with other less formal sites of policy production and, therefore, drew them into the control features of the process. As she explains,

We would send the drafts out on a Monday by fax to everybody and then they [would] have a meeting the next Monday with their interest groups. They all had this very sophisticated networking processes of all these interest groups. And they would fax back the groups' comments. And then they would come to the [Reference Committee] meeting to reinforce it and then we'd go through the next stage. So we'd draft it. We'd draft it in committee, in those kinds of ways.

(Viviani)

Indeed, several policy actors used and even created informal sites of policy production with some effect. For example:

Queensland turned on some real power... it appears as if the Premier's Office itself insinuated itself strongly into the game, opened channels of communication directly through to the Prime Minister's Office, and so the two education bureaucracies – the [Queensland] State one of higher education [and] the Commonwealth [division of] higher education – were playing to a context created by Premier to Prime Minister Office contacts.

(BPA2)

Yet while politicians and political advisers were very aware of the need to engage with the policy process in less formal contexts, others were not. It was as if some of these policy actors (e.g. those associated with IA1) held to a theoretically naive executive model of policy production that could not or would not entertain the possibility of influencing policy text production within sites other than those officially designated. Hence, the need to engage with the media's criticism of current policy settings, for example, was not fully appreciated. However,

That's the reality we face. This is not the 1950s. This is an example of the [IA1's] failure to engage publicly. I mean given that reality, they should have got stuck into that, and they're the only ones who could demystify it, who could make it understandable, who could give out the comfort messages that we needed, and they tried once or twice and then gave up, and blamed the *Courier Mail*. And the *Courier Mail* was just outrageous – just outrageous but no worse than the *Sydney Morning Herald* when they first put league-tables in or anybody else. And it was – it's a failure to understand modern policy making which is a public phenomenon, and if you haven't got the skills or the drive to engage publicly, you lose. And the [IA1] could have done that better.

(CIA4)

Playing with the hand you've been dealt: the *how* of policy production

Focusing on the how of policy production provides another translation of this 'same sentence' (Spinoza, in Bourdieu and Wacquant 1992, 105): a reading of policy makers' 'strategic orientation toward the game' (Bourdieu and Wacquant 1992, 99) or what Lyotard describes as 'a "move" in a game' (1984, 10). More strongly, in producing Australian higher education policy, 'determining the "who" of policy production [their objective positioning] necessarily influenced aspects of their interaction' (Gale 2001, 388). The research disclosed six strategies in the negotiation of Australian higher education policy developed from the data: strategies of trading, bargaining, arguing, stalling, manoeuvring, and lobbying. While their separations imply a certain discreteness, they are more cogently understood as interrelated. For instance, a certain amount of stalling can be exercised in the process of bargaining, lobbying can involve a degree of trading and argument, while a strategic manoeuvre might involve several strategies of negotiation. Each of these strategies is illustrated in turn.

Trading: negotiating the exchange of interests

In the process of producing policy text for Australian higher education entry in Queensland,

> Viviani would come to the Reference Committee and she would listen to them and then she would say, 'No, I don't like that, I won't do that'...[but] she's a very good operator, because at the same time, when she is strong and makes her position, she'll tend to give a bit of ground somewhere else. So, she doesn't alienate people, or there's a minimum of that.
>
> (CIA7)

Interestingly, however, trading was not a strategy frequently engaged by policy makers in this policy context and was almost exclusively confined to politicians and their political advisers in other contexts of influence (Bowe *et al.* 1992) or in what Bourdieu refers to as broader fields of power.

Bargaining: negotiating the moderation of interests

In contexts of policy text production, policy makers were more frequently and discursively engaged in the to-ing and fro-ing (as in the Latin *discurrere*) of interests or what might more accurately be described as their moderation. Evidence of this can be seen in the bargaining over targets for new entrants into Australian higher education. For example, some Queensland policy actors

> went out publicly and got the school leaver targets back because the [Federal] Government was getting hit over the head with the huge retention increases to Year 12 – social pressure from parents and kids – and the universities themselves had argued with the Government that they needed to expand the sector in order to accommodate the Year 12 increases. So we thought at least on that we could hold them, so we included these school leaver targets. Then they came back to [us to] say by using them we were denying mature age access.
>
> (BPA1)

Arguing: negotiating the persuasion of interests

Similarly, there was struggle and conflict over more technical matters in which rational argument was used effectively by policy actors as a political strategy to persuade others of the legitimacy of their interests. The politics of these exchanges should not be under-estimated:

> We had a lot of big fights about important things...I tried very hard to talk them into one form of scaling – I tried really hard – and if you read [Graham] Maxwell's [academic appointed to the Reference Committee] argument (the first appendix) you can see why I couldn't and anyone who wants to get rid of one form of scaling, has to answer his argument. And that's why it's there as the first appendix [in the policy document].
>
> (Viviani)

Stalling: delaying the negotiation of interests

But policy actors did not always find it as easy to convince others purely on the basis of argument, particularly when the power relations were not balanced in their favour and when there was little appreciation of the politics involved. In the words of one of these policy actors,

> one of the sources of greatest frustration for me and for [IA1] through the early 80s was the fact that we could never ever get any dialogue with the Federal government. It was a stone wall...I went to Canberra on a number of occasions and interviewed numbers of different people...They'd always be interviewed off the record, particularly if they were senior public servants. Never on the record...We believed that Queensland was being given a raw deal in terms of allocation of places and funds and all the rest of it.
>
> (CIA7)

Manoeuvring: negotiating the circumvention of interests

When the shoe is on the other foot, differently positioned policy actors are able to manoeuvre their way around obstacles to the policy process. In the following example, the need to appease political interests and at the same time address compelling argument produced a political solution to the policy process that enabled the circumvention of such argument. As it unfolded,

> one group who'll be pushing it [a national system of university entry] is the Commonwealth, again because it'll get them off this policy hook about shifting load [to redress the imbalance of student places allocated to universities in different Australian States]. If they can say, 'Well, anyone can apply anywhere and go anywhere easily and there are no formal barriers to that', then that gets them a bit off that policy hook that they really need to put political pressure on Victoria to get rid of places. So they'll be supporting it. But the other bunch that are supporting it – this is what makes me really cross – is the bloody Directors of Admission Centres because they can become a national empire, you know.
>
> (BPA4)

What is worth reiterating here is the dominance of politics over rationality in the policy process.

Lobbying: negotiating the coalition of interests

Contrary to traditional rhetoric that positions bureaucrats as merely instruments of the political process, the research reported here revealed these policy actors as well versed in the politics of policy making. In particular, and more than most policy actors, they were adept at combining interests in ways that served particular policy agendas that held political currency while also advancing others. The use of particular economic discourses is a case in point. A number of these policy actors would

> imbibe all this macro stuff about the economic environment and we construct rationales that are influential in those terms. Now, a lot of it's unresearched and untested, but there's no doubt that we argue for certain things in terms of what we describe as perceived economic advantage. And then you also try to create a coalition of interests with what you know to be the Minister's personal interests... Some ministers are better than others at principles and policy broadly and some are much more framed by personal experiences and understandings.
>
> (BPA4)

Relations between policy actors and the (above) strategies they employ to produce policy are represented in Tables 13.2 and 13.3. Recognition needs to be given to the particular context in which these observations were made: the production of Australian higher education policy from 1987 to 1996, particularly the production of Queensland higher education entry policy text in 1990 (Viviani 1990). It should also be noted that these relations between policy actors and strategies are indicative rather than comprehensive. That said, Table 13.2 lists the most frequently used strategies by policy actors in contexts of policy text production while Table 13.3 lists the most likely policy actors associated with particular policy-making strategies. The point is to illustrate in tabular form that policy actors who are positioned in particular ways tend to employ some policy-making strategies more than others and, similarly, that particular policy-making strategies tend to be associated with certain policy actors more than others. The centrality of

Table 13.2 Most frequently used strategies by policy actors in producing Australian higher education policy, 1987–96

Policy actor	Strategy (most frequently utilised)
Politicians and political advisers	1. Bargaining 2. Arguing and lobbying
Bureaucrats and policy advisers	1. Manoeuvring and lobbying 2. Arguing
Cowboys and independent authorities	1. Stalling 2. Arguing
Academics and university administrators	1. Arguing 2. Bargaining and stalling

Table 13.3 Most likely policy actors associated with strategies for producing Australian higher education policy, 1987–96

Strategy	Policy actor (most frequent utiliser)
Trading	1. Politicians and political advisers, and bureaucrats and policy advisers 2. Academics and university administrators
Bargaining	1. Politicians and political advisers 2. Academics and university administrators 3. Bureaucrats and policy advisers
Arguing	1. Academics and university administrators 2. Politicians and political advisers 3. Bureaucrats and policy advisers, and cowboys and independent authorities
Stalling	1. Cowboys and independent authorities 2. Academics and university administrators 3. Politicians and political advisers
Manoeuvring	Bureaucrats and policy advisers
Lobbying	1. Bureaucrats and policy advisers 2. Politicians and political advisers

politics in the policy process should also be recognised and how, in this particular case, rationality was treated within the process.

Conclusion

In this paper I have argued a number of matters of policy, referring to aspects of the policy literature and drawing on research data from the production of Australian higher education policy. They are matters about the politics of the policy process. They are not about neat, rational debate and then consensus on entry issues in Australian higher education, nor are they concerned with an examination of the differences from one policy text to the next in order to determine the extent of the increment. I suspect that often it is a narrow focus on policy texts that produces accounts of policy production as informed by the 'characteristics of organized action...[that is,] *coherence, hierarchy* and *instrumentality*' (Colebatch 1998, 3, emphasis in original). Certainly, 'there is less written about what policy participants actually do than on almost any other aspect of policy' (Colebatch 1998, 100) and perhaps this provides some explanation. However, I suspect our inability to provide adequate theoretical explanations of the policy process is also an issue of politics.

Theoretically, then, critical policy sociology is well served by explanations of policy and the policy process that concern themselves with the *who* and *how* of policy production. As illustrated above, these are not separate endeavours but necessarily go hand in hand. Such explanations also require a less rigid account of policy contexts and their structural relations (Gale 1999). Moreover, these theoretical explanations of policy production also seem well served by policy methodologies of archaeology and genealogy. As I have discussed in more detail elsewhere (Gale 2001), policy archaeology involves an objectification of who is involved in producing policy, their structuring, whereas policy genealogy is interested in identifying the particularities of policy makers' activities and in various contexts.

It is in relating these matters of theory and politics, and the methodology implied in their analysis, that I conclude by drawing attention again to Yeatman's (1998) notion of policy activism and particularly to its normative elements. Policy is not only produced and reproduced in a theoretical sense by actors variously located within Western democracies. Such engagement by policy actors should also be acknowledged and encouraged as an expression of a radical democracy (Lummis 1996). In this account of policy making,

> the intent...would be to establish the conditions for new conversations (genuine expressions of interest, understanding and aspiration) and for new actions (proactive engagements with local and global constraints and opportunities); their newness deriving as much from *who* is involved and *how*, as from appreciation for new times.
>
> (Gale 2000, 132, emphasis added)

What is envisaged, then, are opportunities for policy actors: to focus on a wider sense of policy communities; for policy conversations across cultural and contextual boundaries, directed at collective commitments (rather than consensus); and for pursuing creative possibilities. This is a constant, ongoing task that is forever incomplete.

Notes

1   'Cowboys' is a term used by one of the interviewees (BPA4) to describe policy actors located in statutory authorities or quasi-government departments and who seem better positioned to resist the 'ministerialisation' or explicit politicisation of bureaucracies by government ministers.
2   When referencing the comments of interviewees, the acronyms 'PPA', 'BPA', 'CIA' and 'AUA' are used throughout to protect individuals' anonymity while also giving the reader a sense of the 'vocalities' of interviewees with respect to policy production in Australian higher education. Further, each interviewee is allocated a number to distinguish between those similarly positioned.
3   Throughout this paper, a distinction is made between: 'State' (first letter capitalised), which refers to one territory in a federation of territories that constitute a nation, as in 'the State of Queensland'; and 'state' (without capitalisation), which refers to a nation's collective political governance, as in 'the Australian state'.
4   A fuller account of these contextual issues can be found in Gale (1994a,b) and Gale and McNamee (1994, 1995).
5   I admit to some slippage here in referring to the state and government. In fact, they are different concepts supported by their own bodies of literature and present different implications for policy production. Hoffman (1995) provides a good account of such distinctions and the need for them. However, these discussions are beyond the scope and primary interest of this paper.

References

Anderson, J. E. (1979) *Public Policy Making*, 2nd edn (New York: Holt, Rinehart & Winston).
Ball, S. (1994) *Education Reform: a critical and post-structural approach* (Buckingham: Open University Press).
Bourdieu, P. and Wacquant, L. (1992) *An Invitation to Reflexive Sociology* (Cambridge: Polity Press).
Bowe, R., Ball, S. and Gold, A. (1992) *Reforming Education and Changing Schools: case studies in policy sociology* (London: Routledge).
Colebatch, H. (1998) *Policy* (Buckingham: Open University Press).
Dale, R. (1992) 'Whither the state and education policy? Recent work in Australia and New Zealand', *British Journal of Sociology of Education*, 13(3): 387–95.
Easton, D. (1953) *The Political System* (New York: Alfred A. Knopf).
Foucault, M. (1972) *The Archaeology of Knowledge* (London: Tavistock).
Gale, T. (1994a) 'University entrance in Queensland: post World War II challenges to the influence of the University of Queensland', *History of Education Review*, 23(1): 38–52.
Gale, T. (1994b) 'Story-telling and policy-making: the construction of university entrance problems in Australia', *Journal of Education Policy*, 9(3): 227–32.
Gale, T. (1999) 'Policy trajectories: treading the discursive path of policy analysis', *Discourse*, 20(3): 393–407.
Gale, T. (2000) 'Putting academics in their place', *Australian Educational Researcher*, 27(2): 121–36.
Gale, T. (2001) 'Critical policy sociology: historiography, archaeology and genealogy as methods of policy analysis', *Journal of Education Policy*, 16(5): 379–93.
Gale, T. and McNamee, P. (1994) 'Just out of reach: access to equity in Australian higher education', *Australian Universities' Review*, 37(2): 8–12.
Gale, T. and McNamee, P. (1995) 'Alternative pathways to traditional destinations: higher education for disadvantaged Australians', *British Journal of Sociology of Education*, 16(4): 437–50.
Gordon, I., Lewis, J. and Young, K. (1977) 'Perspectives on policy analysis', *Public Administration Bulletin*, 25: 26–35.
Heclo, H. (1978) 'Issue networks and the executive establishment', in A. King (ed.), *The New American Political System* (Washington, DC: American Enterprise Institute).
Hoffman, J. (1995) *Beyond the State: an introductory critique* (Cambridge: Polity Press).

Keating, M. and Davis, G. (eds) (2000) *The Future of Governance* (St Leonards, NSW: Allen & Unwin).

Kenway, J. (1990) *Gender and Education Policy: a call for new directions* (Geelong: Deakin University Press).

Lawton, D. (1986) 'The department of education and science: policy-making at the centre', in A. Hartnett and M. Naish (eds), *Education and Society Today* (Lewes: Falmer Press).

Lindblom, C. (1959) The science of muddling through, *Public Administration Review*, 19: 79–88.

Lummis, C. (1996) *Radical Democracy* (Ithaca, NY: Cornell University Press).

Lyotard, J. (1984) *The Postmodern Condition: a report on knowledge* (Manchester: Manchester University Press).

Prunty, J. (1985) 'Signposts for a critical educational policy analysis', *Australian Journal of Education*, 29(2): 133–40.

Simon, H. (1960) *The New Science of Management Decision* (Englewood Cliffs, NJ: Prentice Hall).

Troyna, B. (1994) 'Critical social research and education policy', *British Journal of Educational Studies*, 42(1): 70–84.

Viviani, N. (1990) *The Review of Tertiary Entrance in Queensland, 1990* (Brisbane: Department of Education, Queensland).

Wilenski, P. (1986) *Public Power and Public Administration* (Sydney: Hale & Iremonger).

Yeatman, A. (Ed.) (1998) *Activism and the Policy Process* (St Leonards, NSW: Allen & Unwin).

CHAPTER 14

POLITICS OF SOCIAL PARTNERSHIPS
A framework for theorizing

Terri Seddon, Stephen Billett and Allie Clemans

Journal of Education Policy, March 2004, 19(2): 123–42

Introduction

Recent issues of *Journal of Education Policy* have carried a series of articles mapping the features, dynamics, and conflicts of social partnerships. This body of work provides a helpful picture of these emergent structures for governance and learning within the broad field of education and training. However, when taken together, the sense is that this research is developing on a study-by-study basis rather than accumulating in ways that lead easily to higher order understandings of social partnerships and their implications.

In this paper we look across these various research reports and, in conversation with our own programme of empirical research, develop a framework for theorizing social partnerships and, in particular, their practical politics. To this end, we map critical moments within social partnerships where tensions and contradictions appear to coalesce in either overt conflicts or in situations of implicit conflict. Evidence of such implicit conflict includes expressions of unease or disquiet by participants within the social partnership or structural tensions that are evident within the organization and operations of partnerships.

This kind of analysis is, we believe, important for three main reasons. First, partnerships are a significant policy trend in many countries, not least the UK and Australia. They are also being promoted by global agencies, such as the OECD and World Bank. Partnerships are, therefore, an important feature in the current reconfiguration of education within the frames of neo-liberal governance. Second, given the place of partnerships in driving particular styles of working and resourcing educational practice in the current regime, it is necessary to interrogate this trend in order to clarify its practical consequences in education settings, the practical politics these developments embody, and the contradictions and conflicts that they call forth. Finally, this kind of critical policy scholarship can benefit education and educators because it provides a more systematic framework for analysing partnerships and their effects, and also provides a basis for identifying the kinds of political interventions that make sense in today's educational landscape.

The paper begins by clarifying the empirical basis on which our analysis is based. This is followed by a consideration of prior research on social partnerships that highlights a range of critical moments and tensions within social partnerships. Bringing these sources together permits the development of a framework for theorizing politics within social partnerships.

Politics within neo-liberalism

The paper builds on a programme of research[1] that, since the mid-1990s, has been documenting the impact of neo-liberal reform in Australian education and training with a special focus on teachers' and managers' work (Seddon *et al.* 1994; Seddon and Billett 2003). We have approached this work by focusing on the social relations of learning and the way they have been reconfigured through the design and implementation of neo-liberal policies and through the practical politics generated in these processes of institutional redesign. One feature of this contested process of education change has been the re-spatialization of education and training provision. Traditional sectoral boundaries have blurred (Anderson 1994) and choice policies have had variable effects across sectors, enterprises, and students (Anderson 2002, 2003), learning pathways have proliferated (Clemans 2000; Rushbrook 1997), and 'new learning spaces', such as social partnerships, work-based and community learning, have developed (Clemans and Bradshaw 1998; Billett 2001b; Bradshaw *et al.* 2001).

Drawing on recent theories of social space (Lefebvre 1991; McDowell 1999; Sojo 1996), we suggest that learning spaces (old and new) are produced by learning relations that shape material, cultural, and symbolic practices within each learning venue, and also learning outcomes. This conceptualization allows us to approach established institutions of education and training (e.g., schools, TAFE Institutes, universities) and social partnerships and other 'new learning spaces' (e.g. community settings, workplaces) from the same starting point in the analysis of the social relations of learning and the recognition that learning spaces (old or new) are never neutral sites. All learning spaces are shaped within relations of power – where the power of some is connected to the relative powerlessness of others. It means that these spaces carry with them certain assumptions about who should occupy them and the rightful activities that take place within them.

Our initial research, funded by the Australian Research Council, focused on neo-liberal reform in secondary schools (Angus and Brown 1997) and in Institutes of Technical and Further Education[2] (TAFE) (Brown *et al.* 1996). TAFE Institutes provide adult and work-related education, including vocational education and training, further education, second chance education, and access oriented general education for adults who have left school. The ages of students range from late teens to retirees, although there is a trend for growing numbers of young people to enter TAFE programmes through VET-in-schools programmes and as an alternative to the final years of secondary schooling. We were interested in the way neo-liberal governance was received in these different sites, and the way teachers' and managers' responses were differentially inflected as a consequence of the structural and cultural differences within these established learning spaces (Seddon and Angus 1999; Seddon 2000). It seemed that TAFE Institutes were subjected to more extreme neo-liberal pressures and that TAFE workers responded to these pressures by re-negotiating and re-norming their work (Angus and Seddon 1996) to a greater extent than in schools.

More recently, our focus has shifted from these established institutions of education and training to emergent, often hybrid, structures that blur the boundaries of formalized schooling and work, and public and private provision. These included private Registered Training Organizations (Seddon and Malley 1998; Seddon 2001a), workplaces (Billett 2001a); community settings (Clemans 2000), and social partnerships (Seddon *et al.* 2003). In each case, we are interested to see how educational practices related to work, learning, and governance are shaped through the agency of governments and education workers, and in learning spaces that are relatively new and, therefore, with relatively limited formal institutionalization and protection (unlike TAFE Institutes and, especially, schools). These studies are revealing the way participants within these different contexts assert particular traditions in educational practice; and how they re-negotiate them in the context of non-negotiable neo-liberal imperatives, including funding frameworks, interventions that shift the regulation of learning to outcomes and assessment, and changes in working conditions.

This research has been conducted primarily in Victoria, Australia, although some of our more recent work has been conducted in other Australian states. Victoria is distinctive amongst Australian States and Territories because, between 1992 and 1999, the conservative government engaged in a very energetic neo-liberal agenda of education reform. While similar agenda have developed elsewhere in Australia, they have not been prosecuted with such speed or energy. This means that Victorian education provides a distinctive research site for studying the implications of neo-liberal governance because its introduction was akin to an experimental procedure: a sudden intervention which destabilized established educational practices and identities and re-regulated them through neo-liberal political rationalities. This orientation persists under the now incumbent Labour Government, although there is a greater focus on social outcomes and co-operation than under the previous government.

This paper builds upon and extends these earlier conclusions, by drawing upon three specific projects that have examined the nature and operations of social partnerships. We define social partnerships broadly as sites of action in which:

> People and organizations from some combination of public, business, and civil constituencies come together in order to engage in voluntary, mutually beneficial, innovative relationships to address common societal aims through combining their resources and competencies.
>
> (Based on the Copenhagen Centre 1999)

The first partnership project was a Victorian Government-funded consultancy to evaluate the 16 first phase Local Learning and Employment Networks (LLEN) (Seddon *et al.* 2002). The LLEN were established by the Victorian Government, in two phases, in order to support community building that harnessed local opportunities and energies supporting young people in the transition from school-to-work and improve education, training, and employment outcomes, especially for 15–19 year olds. There are now 31 LLEN in operation across Victoria. The evaluation entailed a double data collection strategy. A snapshot of each Phase 1 LLEN was developed through an individual interview with the executive officer appointed by the LLEN and focus group interview(s) with other participants in the LLEN, generally the LLEN committee of management. A longer term assessment of LLEN development was facilitated through follow-up contact by phone and through various workshops and meetings. In addition, the evaluation team conducted interviews (individual and focus groups) with Department of Education and Training field officers, regional officers within the Office of Schools, and general managers. The analysis of data was consolidated in the final report which outlined the emerging character and challenges of LLEN and how their work might be facilitated (DE&T 2003).[3]

The second project was an investigation of social partnerships within the field of vocational education and training (VET), which was funded by the National

Research and Evaluation Committee (Seddon and Billett 2003). This project entailed a nation-wide desktop review of social partnerships relevant to VET. Forty social partnerships were followed up via a phone survey that obtained factual information about each partnership and more detailed stories that would provide richer information about the way the partnership worked, its governance processes, and the factors that contributed to success within the partnership. This broad review was complemented by four detailed case studies of social partnerships located in South Australia, Queensland, and Victoria. Each case study involved observations, conversations, and interviews with participants, and a review of relevant documents. These different sources of information were used to develop profiles of the partnerships.

The third project (Seddon *et al.* 2003) builds on the evaluation of LLEN, but with a specific focus on the reporting and accountability arrangements that are developing between government and the LLEN. This independent research project (funded by Monash University), currently underway, aims to develop a critical analysis of the power relations within and around social partnerships, and the way partnership work is being shaped through the practical politics between Centre and local partnership. The research process is based in ongoing dialogue with the executive officers employed by each LLEN, with a view to addressing the question of how the LLEN might intervene in existing reporting arrangements to better reflect the priorities, work, and achievements of the LLEN. This focus provides a valuable window on the dissonant definitions of success between Centre and LLEN, and the way these definitions of success create patterns of visible and invisible work in LLEN and problematize the priorities, identities, and achievements of LLEN.

In synthesis, this body of work indicates that neo-liberal governance facilitates the destabilization and reconfiguration of (old and new) learning spaces, reveals or establishes new traditions of learning, work, and governance, and is generative of emergent educational practices. The impact of neo-liberal reform appears to be contingent on a range of factors, including the consolidated traditions and existing protections within different learning spaces, and the extent to which agencies and individuals re-norm their work in ways that are attuned to the priorities of neo-liberal governance. The evidence, at least from the VET sector, suggests that once the shock of reform has past, individuals and agencies accommodate and routinize work, learning, and governance priorities that are complementary to the wider reform agenda (e.g., Harris *et al.* 2003). Our research indicates that this repositioning of educational work within the context of neo-liberal governance is framed and shaped by participants' prevailing educational commitments and identities, and the extent to which they have room to maneouvre within their local learning spaces (Seddon 2001b; Smyth 2001; Sachs 2003). However, such practical politics may not reach beyond specific learning sites into the wider field of education and training politics. Moreover, it is always subject to further review and reconfiguration as a consequence of subsequent government intervention. Our more specific findings on the politics of social partnership are outlined in the third part of this paper.

Politics within social partnerships

International research shows that there is a proliferation of social partnerships in public policy and service delivery (e.g. Osborne 2000). In many cases, these partnerships are promoted by governments as a means of achieving social goals, such as regional development, environmental health, sustainable communities, and improvements in health, welfare, and justice. These initiatives are now being taken up in education (Riddell and Tett 2001), although it seems that they are developing somewhat later than in some other areas of public provision.

Through the 1990s, much of the literature on neo-liberal reform in education tended to focus either on the general nature of neo-liberalism in education (e.g. Ball, 1990; Marginson 1997a,b) or on the impact of neo-liberal reform in school education (e.g. Bowe *et al.* 1992; Gewirtz 2000). More recently, this focus has broadened to take up the challenges posed by lifelong learning (Coffield 2000), reform in post-school contexts (Ainley and Bailey 1998; Slaughter and Leslie 1997), and emergent structures like social partnerships in education.

Education has had a long history of governance based in partnership (Centre for Contemporary Cultural Studies 1981; Alexiadou *et al.* 2000). There have been partnerships supporting disadvantaged learners (Connell *et al.* 1990) and community development (Sheil 2002) since the 1970s and, through the 1990s, there were moves to use partnerships as a form of professional mobilization (Sachs 2003, chapter 6). However, it seems that the 'new social partnerships' now emerging are different from those of the past. They often (but not always) build on arrangements or resources derived from earlier phases of public, private, and third sector (i.e. community) partnership activity, but are based in neo-liberal contractualism and often linked to public-private and/or volunteer resourcing arrangements.

The research on new social partnerships in education varies in the extent to which it acknowledges the neo-liberal framing of contemporary partnership. Some work, constrained by contractual and consultancy arrangements, accepts the framing of partnerships and focuses on what happens within partner relations between government and various stakeholder agencies (e.g. Seddon *et al.* 2002). Such research 'tells it like it is' rather than contextualizing the social partnership within wider social and historical frames in order to assess the meaning and implications of partnerships for education and society. In more independent research (e.g. Jones and Bird 2000), partnerships are contextualized, implicitly or explicitly, and the partners and patterns of institutionalization are interrogated in more depth to reveal contingent, and more persistent, and systematic, conflict and contradiction. The full range of work provides insights into the politics of partnerships. It reveals three broad forms of conflict and a series of critical moments when these forms of conflict are particularly evident.

Forms of conflict

The research on social partnerships can be roughly grouped into three main approaches, crudely: role conflict, interest conflict, and regime conflict. Each approaches the partnership and its parties in a pluralist fashion, yet makes different assumptions about the character, historical depth, and social significance of the actors involved.

Role conflict

There is a substantial body of research which documents the activities and tensions that exist between partners at a day-to-day level. For instance, Milbourne *et al.* (2003) provide a very detailed account of the process of developing a health-education partnership by documenting the experience of three women who took on the task of operationalizing the partnership. They draw attention to the difficulties of multi-agency social partnerships and their tendency to short time frames, managerialism with externally specified targets, pressure to include voluntary agencies, non-recognition of the time taken to build good relationships, and the continuing unpredictability of the wider policy context.

Such projects commonly report on the interactions between schools and young people, document the relationships among principals, community groups and individuals who broker employment opportunities, or highlight the tensions between the Centre and local partnerships (e.g. Kilpatrick *et al.* 2001; Stokes and Tyler 2002). These individuals or agencies are approached as different roles which are played out in the here-and-now. Conflict commonly relates to role conflict or ambiguities about the purposes and inter-relationships between roles. It tends not to be tracked back into longstanding relationships, interests, or identities, although these are often implicit within the accounts. For example, Kilpatrick *et al.* (2001) provide detailed accounts of particular partnership, explaining the roles, contribution, and inter-relationships of the school's principal, parent organization, management committee, apprenticeship co-ordinator, and local employers.

This work highlights the empirical complexities of partnership. It reveals that the rhetoric of 'partnership' sometimes masks complexities and tensions within localized decision-making processes (e.g., Ridell and Tett 2001). Yet, while such tensions and role conflicts seem complex, they shape the potential of social partnerships in ways that are situational, yet systemic. As Tett *et al.* (2003) show, there are a variety of different rationales for partnership, and these are accompanied, relatively consistently, by different expectations and barriers, such as:

- fragmentation and non-coterminosity of boundaries;
- differences in funding mechanisms and bases;
- differences in aims, organizational cultures, and procedures;
- lack of appropriate accommodation and resources;
- differences in ideologies and values;
- conflicting views about user interests and roles;
- concern for threats to autonomy and control and having to share credit;
- communication difficulties;
- lack of organizational flexibilities;
- differences in perceived power; and
- inability to deal with conflict (Tett *et al.* 2003, 40).

Interest conflict

The documentation of partnerships commonly focuses on the interests and identities involved in social partnerships and their unequal contribution and voice in decision-making processes. Rees (1997), for example, looks beyond individuals to focus on more established interests within the partnership process. He endorses local inter-agency decision-making because it can reflect the specificity of the region's industrial structure and patterns of productive organization, but he cautions against basing local needs analysis just on major enterprises, because these enterprises are frequently preoccupied with internal goals which can inhibit them from taking a broader perspective.

Billett and Hayes (2000) investigated support for localized decision-making amongst industry (i.e. Industry Training Advisory Boards, curriculum managers), enterprises (i.e. those who employ and sponsor VET provisions), community (i.e. representatives of key community interests), and individuals (i.e. those who seek to realize their personal or vocational roles through participation VET programmes). They found that there was a preference for local decision-making to proceed under the co-ordination of some governmental body on the grounds that this arrangement would overcome the problems of short-term market-based responses and uneven knowledge amongst the partners. Local decision-making processes were seen to be successful when they took all interests into account, including those most able to contribute (e.g. providers anxious to secure market share, powerful economic voices) as well as those whose interests may have been marginalized in centralized processes.

Jones and Bird's (2000) study of Education Action Zones (EAZ) reveals a wide range of partners involved in decision-making: public agencies, private partners, and a range of new hybrid 'public–private' enterprises that had developed in the context of market provision. However, they found that there was no necessary identity in the interests of any of these partners, and only some were really influential in the participative processes. This situation commonly led to the formation of strategic alliances between partners who were able to negotiate common cause. In these decision-making processes, government agencies were sometimes in an ambivalent position, torn between supporting local decisions and veering back towards more traditional bureaucratic ways of working. As a director from one of the public–private enterprises stressed, ' "conflicts of interests" are endemic to partnership' and should be 'recognized rather than disavowed'.

The analysis of interests within social partnerships quickly reveals that each partner is not just an abstracted decision-making agency, but is encumbered by its own history and culture. As a consequence, they each have different priorities and different definitions of social or individual 'need' (Tett 2003). Clegg and McNulty (2002) argue that each partner has a distinct organizational habitus, a set of dispositions, embedded values, and practices, which dictates what counts as 'ordinary ways of working'. These ordinary ways of working are rooted in the prior networking and cultural capital which are important resources for particular partners (Tett *et al.* 2003), but they can also be a source of conflict between partners. Conscious or unconscious assertion of particular ways of working within partnerships can be experienced as a kind of professional or institutional imperialism which denies other partners' knowledge, routines, and voice, and creates patterns of marginalization and exclusion. Organizational habitus is not just anchored in particular institutional or professional cultures, but is embedded in broader social relations based in gender, ethnicity, and class. These current and historical networks, gender dynamics, and politics of difference amongst activists within the partnership are important resources that are determinants of sustainability for partners and partnerships. Such cultural capital can influence the broader context for partnerships, creating distinct historical traditions in partnership working (Kearns and Papadopolous 2000). For example, Alexiadou *et al.* (2000) shows that the history and culture of Scottish resistance to English rule has created very different processes within partnership's localized decision-making.

Such research reveals social partnerships as socially embedded spaces in which the social relations of work, learning, and governance are shaped by the local legacy of established histories and cultures. This perspective turns attention to the way different agencies can mobilize resources and rules, and can protect their core interests and identities from encroachment by others. It raises questions about the conditions that enable the renegotiation of agenda to affirm positive cultural change that recognizes and endorses cultural diversity in meaningful ways.

Regime conflict

Within some research, the culturally-rich and encumbered interests and identities within social partnerships are explicitly contextualized within the contemporary regime marked by the shift from social democratic to neo-liberal governance. Much of this research analyses the discourses of neo-liberalism and its practical consequences in social, national, and individual formation and ways of working. For instance, Griffiths (2000) critiques culturally-thin neo-liberal policy rhetoric about partnerships highlighting the way it is framed within an abstracted and unreal liberal humanist discourse. She argues that this discourse presumes that individuals with sovereign rights meet as equals in collaborative decision-making processes. The outcome of their open, honest, and rational debate is seen to be the basis for consensus outcomes that provide everyone with an agreed and rational basis for action. The implication, she argues, is that the lived and messy practice of partnership is quite different to the image of partnership as some kind of *agora* or forum for debate and decision. Successful partnership working does not depend upon big binding decisions reached in the public decision-space. Rather, it rests upon the active negotiation of expertise and authority, careful networking and opportunism in pursuit of local action through a variety of inter-linked and hybrid public – private spaces where debate and action is collectively determined by relevant members. The consensus decision-making that occurred within LLEN meetings and work involved in negotiations prior to those meetings provides one example of these.

This political rationality reaches beyond partnership *per se* and is becoming the norm in a world marked by neo-liberal globalism and erosion of boundaries (Lawn 2001). In this context, governments reorient their work away from a societal level and, instead, operate increasingly through individual actors and the choices they make, for instance, pressing individuals to make choices about private and public education and health provisions. As Rose (1996, 327) notes, this work 'seeks to govern without governing *society*, to govern through regulated choices made by discrete and autonomous actors'. It constructs self-managing individuals who take-on risk and responsibility as personal concerns. It privileges performativity and accountability in terms of outcomes which drives a competitive culture based on the constant fabrication of instrumental representations (Ball 2000). It remainders the agora because the consolidation of interests in large decision-making agencies (e.g. corporatism) is incompatible with decentralization and marketization which is fundamental to neo-liberal governance (Power and Whitty 1999; Rose 1999).

Other research reaches beyond the discourse of neo-liberalism to consider the impact of regime shift within the material relations and practical politics of different social groups. In this work, the impact of neo-liberal hegemony is read in confrontation with established institutional forms, identities, and patterns of collective action. As Castells (1997) suggests, the destabilization of social orders is met with a range of, responses, including the assertion of fundamentalism, liberal institutionalism based in rule making, and socially transformative projects. It suggests that there is scope for building on older social democratic themes round nation-building, professionalism, and partnership as a basis for standing against the hollowing out of education and training (Lingard 2000; Ozga 2000). According to Ozga (2000, 94), the challenge is to work for localized responses in education that build on established institutional resources and professional identities but framed within an 'after-modernism', rather than 'post-modern', sensibility.

This might mean, for instance, engaging in partnership work that builds on established cultural and symbolic resources and relationships (e.g. commitments to community, profession, nation) in ways that recognize difference and inequality, and the responsibilities of government, as an anchor point for collective action at the local level.

Robertson and Dale (2002) take the political analysis a step further, arguing that neo-liberal hegemony confronts not just established histories and cultures but the ongoing and contradictory dynamics of capital accumulation. The state's continuing agenda – the contribution to enabling accumulation and profitability, reproducing an appropriately formed workforce, and addressing questions of legitimacy (Dale 1989) – persists within the context of neo-liberal hegemony, but is reoriented to address particular neo-liberal contradictions. They highlight the impact of neo-liberal governance in asserting decentralized provision of public goods and services on the grounds of increased responsiveness, and also driving marketization on the grounds of optimal distribution. However, these developments go hand-in-hand with intensified competition and market failure that creates winners and losers and institutionalizes inequality. Robertson and Dale suggest that these imperatives, that palpably increase inequality and decrease quality of life (e.g. Pusey 2003), and intensify problems of legitimacy, but the small state rhetoric means that conventional state responses, based in deploying public resources, are not available. Instead, the state has to represent generalized neo-liberal market failure as localized issues (e.g. failing schools, deficit communities) which are addressed through localized responses to crisis. Such 'local states of emergency' include interventions that allow failing students to choose an alternative to school, the proliferation of individualized case management to realize education and employment outcomes, provision of localized supports to patch up the safety net of existing (or failing) institutions and targeted initiatives to address supposedly deficit communities or regions. From this perspective, social partnerships can be seen to be an intervention which show that governments are doing something locally in response to the general problem of market failure and legitimacy within neo-liberalism.

This research on regime change does not always address social partnerships directly, but suggests ways in which tensions within social partnerships may be generated. For example, conflicts are likely to revolve around social partnerships if they are seen as, or permitted to become, a neo-liberal intervention aimed at fixing up individuals, communities, and established institutions (like schools). They are also likely to be subject to unpredictable shifts in government policy as governments reorient them to deal with new emergencies and issues of legitimacy. Social partnerships are being formed by established agencies and their longstanding interests and ethical norms may be in conflict with the priorities of government. Social partnerships may also be seen as a space within which new institutional alliances can be formed to endorse, resist, or turn the impact of neo-liberal political rationality in community relations. In this respect, social partnerships can be understood as a 'thirdspace' (Sojo 1996) where new (and old) identities can be (re)mobilized in nascent political action.

Critical moments in social partnerships

These three broad categories of conflict are all apparent in our studies of social partnership, but there are moments within the life cycle of social partnerships when some conflicts appear to be more significant than others. These patterns of partnership conflict are also moderated to some extent by the nature of the partnership. Drawing on our national review of partnerships, we suggest that there are three distinct types of social partnerships. These are:

- *Community partnerships* that constitute localized networks based in some combination of local community groups, education and training providers, industry, and local government to work on various local community and community-building activities. These community partnerships are driven from the bottom-up and are often regionally-focused or centre on particular issues or needs (e.g. women's small business networks).
- *Enacted social partnerships* that are constructed by sponsors that are external to the community for the purposes of realizing particular goals through direct or indirect funding. These enacted partnerships are often aligned to supporting local decision-making, community-building, and enhanced opportunities in vocational education and training (e.g. VET in schools programmes sponsored by the Employment and Careers Education Foundation (ECEF)).
- *Directed social partnerships* that are established and sponsored by government to achieve specific policy goals by bringing community, industry, and education and training providers together and shaping their activity in a relatively direct way. These can be seen as a sub-set of enacted social partnerships in which central control and direction is strong because it is coupled to direct policy, funding, and accountability arrangements (e.g. LLEN).

These different types of partnerships were revealed in the course of our NREC study (Seddon and Billett 2003) in which we became aware that tracking social partnerships was sometimes difficult. Directed social partnerships were easily identifiable and were often actively promoted by government as an innovation aimed at addressing particular social issues. The LLEN, for instance, have an individual, and a network, web-site which are a part of, and accessible from, the Victorian Department of Education and Training website (DE&T 2003). It is hot-linked to statistical resources which aggregate education, training, and employment data from the Department's statistical collections.

Enacted social partnerships were generally easily identifiable because they were also well established with web-sites and other resources. There were many partnerships associated with the Employment and Careers Education Foundation (ECEF 2004). This agency facilitates and supports social partnerships in education and training. It is well-resourced because the Commonwealth government sponsors the ECEF as a means of distributing funds to school-industry partnerships in the States and Territories that are in line with Commonwealth education, training, and employment policies. This funding arrangement exists because the constitutional division of powers makes education and training a responsibility of State Governments and restricts Commonwealth policy implementation in this field.

Community partnerships were sometimes harder to track. They were often small, sometimes just a few people, and often tended to meld into the life of the community. They were identified by word of mouth because they didn't have websites and, in many cases, appeared to have 'died' before we could make contact with them. For instance, in a study of how small business operators learned about the new Goods and Services Tax (GST), Billett *et al.* (2003) found that social partnerships were forged through shared concerns about the new taxation arrangements. These partnerships were based in networks amongst the wives of small business operators (who were also often the book keepers) who discussed the

GST while dropping off and picking up their children at school, and a group of small business operators who discussed their common concerns at the tennis club on Saturdays. In another case, a social partnership was enacted by local viticulturists who were concerned about workforce development and encouraging young people to take up training opportunities within their industry. Another group of vineyards collaborated in collectively promoting their region's wineries, and the accommodation and restaurant facilities they provided. This collaboration occurred, even though the vineyards were in competition with each other.

These examples provide some evidence for the idea of a partnership lifecycle. They suggest that partnerships are actively born through the initiative of external agencies or through the coalescing of friendship or collegial community networks in response to particular need. They also 'die' by dissipating or going out of existence. For instance, once the procedures to implement the GST had been met, the local discussions were likely to cease. In the case of enacted and directed social partnerships, these moments of birth and death are linked to sponsorship arrangements. On the basis of our data, we identified the following critical moments in the life cycle of social partnerships:

Establishment and closure

The determination of the 'birth' or 'death' of partnerships. Each partnership had its own birth story, which accounted for the decision processes leading to its establishment. These stories tended to provide a sanitized, sometimes heroic, account of the negotiations involved, although they inevitably entailed some negotiation of interests and agenda, both at a local and broader level. 'Death' stories were not accessed because our research focused on existing partnerships. Yet, clearly, the moments of partnership formalization and disintegration are crucial in realizing and shaping the partnership in ways that link to larger social, economic, and political dynamics. This was particularly clear in relation to the LLEN which were born as a consequence of policy and funding processes, tied to specified policy agenda and reporting requirements. These administrative technologies, coupled with the discursive affirmation of LLEN as leading the way in cultural change in schooling, framed the work and identity of the LLEN.

Sponsorship

The negotiation which leads to agreements about the sponsorship or funding of a social partnership, and the determination of the conditions and reporting requirements associated with that funding and support. In the case of LLEN, these discussions occurred within government when policy initiatives were signed off and resourced. In the ECEF enacted social partnerships, community networks approached the ECEF for funding and traded off community discretion for compliance with reporting arrangements. In community partnerships, resourcing was supported by the local partners (e.g. attending the tennis club where discussions of GST went on, establishing productive vines growing activities at local schools).

Auspicing

The locating or hosting of social partnerships in a particular social or institutional context, or place. In most, if not all, situations, social partnerships were located in ways that built upon existing affiliations or community interests and resources. For instance, In the small business community networks that formed around the GST, the partnerships were located in social places (e.g. the local tennis club) characterized by close affiliations, intimacy, and trust. These places were learning spaces whose culture and practices were very different to those of educational institutions. One of the early tasks of the LLEN was to determine where the LLEN office and employees should be located. This became contentious when different interests were suspicious of one another. Ultimately, some LLEN were auspiced by local government, others by educational institutions. In the former, the prevailing practices of representational and consensual decision-making provided competence in governance, yet also embedded the partnership in local politics. In the latter, existing educational networks provided a foundation for engaging community interests, although there was also suspicion that the LLEN might be 'captured' by education interests. Where LLEN were auspiced outside of local government and educational networks, an immediate task was to build networks and capacities for governance within the partnership.

Negotiating activities

The ongoing process of determining what kinds of activity the partnership should engage in and how different activities should be directed and prioritized. This process of negotiation was shaped by the interests that came together within the social partnership, although there is evidence to suggest that its character shifted as participants became more familiar with one another and learned to work together. As in group work, there was some evidence of a storming, norming, and conforming dynamic. In community partnerships, these negotiations occurred as an embedded process intimately associated with the development of sociability that addressed the needs of those within the network. By contrast, in enacted and directed social partnerships, these processes were more abstracted from the developing sociability within the network. LLEN, for instance, were required to conduct an environmental scan and engage in strategic planning as key steps in their establishment phase. Yet, these formalized planning processes commonly sat alongside the day-to-day LLEN activities which, as people got to know each other better, hinged more on the nature of sociable sharing of ideas and the opportunistic grasping of initiatives as they present themselves. This intimate level of LLEN work centred on the executive officer, employed by the LLEN, and the core participants (chair, members of working parties) who were active within the LLEN framework. The formalistic planning processes were more important for individuals and agencies who were linked to a LLEN, but less intimately involved in its everyday work. In particular, the formalist process was critical for government that sponsored the LLEN and needed to demonstrate that public funding was being spent in ways that were recognizable to politicians, bureaucrats, and the wider public.

Enabling achievements

Activities within the social partnerships that are less focused on the direct achievement of outcomes and more concerned with institutional redesign to facilitate the work of the partnership. Such work is oriented towards the creation of contexts that support partnership achievements. It entails a particular kind of strategic sensitivity to cultural diversity and organizational arrangements which allows the partnership to identify barriers to its successful operations, patterns of inclusion and exclusion, or marginalization that undercuts the voice and contribution of different groups to the partnership. For instance, in a South Australian education partnership between Indigenous communities on the 'lands', an urban residential support unit that coordinates education and training and support for Indigenous students and the South Australian Government, each party has moderated their ways of working to accommodate the distinctive features of this process of working together. The Department of Education adopted practices that demonstrated respect for the 'lands' community, including modifying bureaucratic staff selection processes to allow the 'lands' community to participate in the selection of new staff. The teachers' union modified their employment requirements to allow community members to be employed as education workers. Mandatory literacy tests in South Australia were adjusted to include English-as-a-second-language scales to better accommodate the language structures of the Indigenous students. A metropolitan LLEN has maneouvred so that it is represented in discussions about the opening of a new science high school in association with a local university. The executive officer argues that if government is supporting high-flyer science education, it should also be pressed to support students with more modest education and training ambitions.

Of course, such work was only possible when the partnership becomes aware of dissonance in work practices or patterns of marginalization, and surfaced these issues so that they could be brought into the planning process. In some cases, the organizational habitus (Clegg and McNulty 2002) of the partnership created marginalization or exclusion, despite their intentions. Trade unionists, for example, talked about the difficulty they found of developing a relationship with LLEN. Some employers were clearly reluctant to participate too. LLEN executive officers described this as employers being 'do-ers', rather than people who sit in committees.

Reporting outcomes

Reporting requirements, generally associated with sponsorship, through which the social partnership are required to show how funding has been used to realize its outcomes. In some cases, reporting requirements were relatively broadly defined, allowing the partnership considerable discretion in the way they do their work. In other cases, especially where there was direct government sponsorship, the reporting requirements were relatively tightly defined. For instance, the initial LLEN reporting schedule specified a series of administrative milestones as well as more general education, training, and employment outcomes for young people. The effect was to define 'success' in a particular way which did not always complement the actual work of the LLEN. Different LLEN contested the way the Department of Education and Training had defined success, arguing that the specified performance indicators overlooked their achievements in relationship building within the local community and did not acknowledge the complexity and time-consuming nature of this community-building work.

The common association between reporting and sponsorship downplays other accountabilities, such as the partnership's accountability to its local community and the local interests that are represented through its work. This localized accountability was not often acknowledged, yet it would seem to be critical in ensuring the legitimacy of the partnership as an agency working on behalf of, or for, local partners. An exception was the Indigenous education partnership where an education committee was established as a sub-committee of the Indigenous land holding body. It was legally constituted with formal office bearers and any community member can attend. They have 50–60 people participating in their meetings. The linkages between the education committee and each Indigenous community (based in community representation) mean that each community has a direct role in determining local priorities, directing school principals while also being accountable to their own communities through their local governing councils which have to be inclusive of all family groups.

A framework for theorizing partnership politics

Aligning these critical moments within social partnerships with the forms of conflict previously noted provides a rough matrix which offers a basis for more systematically theorizing the politics of partnership. This matrix is shown in Table 14.1. Each of the cells in this matrix flags a site of practical politics. The first three are interface sites where partnerships come up against external agencies or wider political dynamics. The last three are focused on practical politics within social partnerships.

Our data suggest that the politics playing out at each of these sites can be read in terms of the different manifestations of conflict – conflicts of roles, interests, and regimes. In much of the published research, politics internal to partnership tend to be interpreted in terms of role and interest conflict, while the negotiation of the partnership in relation to other agencies is more often interpreted in terms of wider social interests or regime conflict.

These are not necessary patterns however. It is important to interrogate the external and interface activities of social partnerships in terms of localized role and interest conflicts because these social partnerships are distinctively local in character. Such detailed analysis provides a deeper understanding of social partnerships as genuinely *localized* interventions rather than as a local format of some more generalized initiative.

Equally, it is important to bring the 'big picture' questions about social interests and regime change into the analysis of day-to-day partnership work, because this begins to reveal the workings of neo-liberalism and counter-rationalities at the level of individuals and their identities. Such analysis prompts questions about the nature of social partnership work and workers, their relationship with various political rationalities and political projects, and the way these activities map across wider social structures in terms of gender, ethnicity, class, and in relation to the state. Is social partnership working best explained as an expression of embodied neo-liberal sensibility mobilized through the 'competition state' (Cerny 1990) or a more contradictory form of middle class politics?

Table 14.1 Politics of partnership matrix

	Role conflict	Interest conflict	Regime conflict
Establishment & closure			
Sponsorship			
Auspicing			
Negotiating activities			
Enabling achievements			
Reporting requirements			

Conclusion

Social partnerships are an emergent structure within education and training, offering distinctive approaches to work, learning, and governance. They warrant research because they are an instrument and expression of neo-liberal governance and also a site of practical politics that encompasses both the prosecution of, and resistance to, neo-liberal political rationality. In these respects, they are similar to other established sites of education and training. Where they differ is in their polyvocal design, their formative character and in the challenges they present to established practices in education. Only time will tell what the significance and implications of these developments are.

This paper has suggested a framework for analysing these politics of partnership and their manifestations in complex and innovative patterns of partnership working. It is a resource that may assist the research effort by mapping domains of contention that are significant in shaping partnerships and muddying the conceptual frames which allow interpretation of their effects. If it counters the tendencies to celebratory narrative and premature closure about the implications, meaning, and significance of social partnerships, it will have done its job.

Notes

1   We acknowledge the funding received from the Australian Research Council (1994–7), Monash University (1999, 2003), the National Research and Evaluation Committee (2002–3), and the Victorian Department of Education and Training (1996, 2002).
2   TAFE Institutes are similar to Colleges of Further Education in England and Community Colleges in North America.
3   The Crown in right of the State of Victoria 2002. This publication is based on the Evaluation of the Local Learning and Employment Networks, first published in 2002 by the Department of Education and Training, Victoria. Reproduced with permission. Not an official publication. The State of Victoria accepts no responsibility for the accuracy of any part of this material and bears no responsibility for any modifications made. Except to the extent that a license is not required under the Copyright Act 1968, reproduction, modification, or adaptation without the permission of the State of Victoria is strictly forbidden.

Bibliography

Ainley, P. and Bailey, B. (1998) *The business of learning: staff and student experiences of further education in the 1990s* (London: Cassell).
Alexiadou, N., Lawn, M. and Ozga, J. (2000) *Educational governance and social inclusion/exclusion* (Uppsala: University of Uppsala).
Anderson, D. (1994) *Blurring the boundaries: TAFE and commercial colleges in the open training market* (Adelaide: National Centre for Vocational Education Research).
Anderson, D. (2002) 'The training market: a national overview of impacts on RTOs (Registered Training Organisations)' in CEET VET: *connections, costs and contradictions* (Monash University-ACER: Centre for the Economics of Education and Training (CEET)).
Anderson, D. (2003) 'Individual learners, choice and lifelong learning' in CEET *Strategic directions for VET* (Monash University-ACER: Centre for the Economics of Education and Training (CEET)), accessed 5 December 2003, available online at: http://www.education.monash.edu.au/centres/ceet/ceetcon2003/papda.pdf
Angus, L. and Seddon, T. (1996) Designing institutions and embodying designs, paper presented at the *Reshaping Australian Institutions Conference*, Australian National University, Canberra.
Angus, L. B. and Brown, L. (1997) *Making a school of the future* (Melbourne: AApress, Monash University Faculty of Education).
Ball, S. (1990) *Politics and policy making in education* (London: Routledge).

Ball, S. (2000) Performativities and fabrications in the education economy: towards the performative society, *Australian Educational Researcher*, 27(2): 1–24.

Billett, S. (2001a) *Learning in the workplace: strategies for effective practice* (Sydney: Allen and Unwin).

Billett, S. (2001b) 'Workplace pedagogic practices: participatory factors in localised arrangements', in F. Bevan, C. Kanes and D. Roebuck (eds) *Knowledge demands for the new economy* (Brisbane: Centre for Learning and Work Research, Griffith University).

Billett, S. and Hayes, S. (2000) *Meeting the demand: the needs of vocational education and training clients* (NCVER).

Billett, S., Hernon-Tinning, B. and Ehrich, L. (2003) Small business pedagogic practices, *Journal of Vocational Education and Training*, 55(2): 149–69.

Bowe, R., Ball, S. and Gold, A. (1992) *Reforming education and changing schools: case studies in policy sociology* (London: Routledge).

Bradshaw, D., Clemans, A., Donovan, C. and Macrae, H. (2001) *Room to move: why school/ACE partnerships expand opportunities for potential early school leavers* (Melbourne: Department of Education, Employment and Training).

Brown, L., Seddon, T., Angus, A. and Rushbrook, P. (1996) 'Professional practice in education in an era of contractualism: possibilities, problems and paradoxes', *Australian Journal of Education*, 40(3): 311–27.

Castells, M. (1997) *The power of identity* (Oxford: Blackwell).

Centre for Contemporary Cultural Studies (1981) *Unpopular education: schooling and social democracy in England since 1944* (London: Hutchinson).

Cerny, P. (1990) *The changing architecture of politics: structure, agency and the future of the state* (London: Sage).

Clegg, S. and McNulty, K. (2002) 'Partnership working in delivering social inclusion: organisational and gender dynamics', *Journal of Education Policy*, 17(5): 587–601.

Clemans, A. (2000) 'Metaphors of motion: pathways and adult community education', *Fine Print*, 23(3): 7–11.

Clemans, A. (2004) Educational work and community – so close to home PhD thesis, in preparation.

Clemans, A. (2005) Community Education Work. So Close to Home. PhD thesis, The University of Melbourne.

Clemans, A. and Bradshaw, D. (1998) *But who'll answer the phone – women in small business and the ACE sector* (Melbourne: Office of Training and Further Education).

Coffield, F. (2000) *The necessity of informal learning* (Bristol: Policy).

Connell, R. W., White, V. and Johnston, K. (1990) *Running twice as hard* (Geelong: Deakin).

Dale, R. (1989) *Education and the state* (Buckingham: Open University Press).

Department of Education and Training (DE&T) (2003) *Evaluation of the local learning and employment networks* (Melbourne, DE&T). Available online at http://www.det.vic. gov.au/det/post-comp/initiatives/llens.htm

Enterprise and Career Education Foundation (ECEF) (2004). Available online at http://www.ecef.com.au

Gewirtz, S. (2000) *The managerial school* (London, Routledge).

Griffiths, M. (2000) 'Collaboration and partnership in question: knowledge, politics and practice', *Journal of Education Policy*, 15(4): 383–95.

Harris, R., Simons, M. and Clayton, B. (2003) *Shifting mindsets: impact of changes to work in the VET sector on roles of VET practitioners in Australia* (Adelaide: National Centre for Vocational Education Research).

Jones, K. and Bird, K. (2000) ' "Partnership" as strategy', *British Educational Research Journal*, 26(4): 491–506.

Kearns, P. and Papadopoulos, G. (2000) *Building a learning and training culture: the experience of five OECD countries* (Adelaide, Australia: National Centre for Vocational Education Research).

Kilpatrick, S., Johns, S., Mulford, B., Falk, I. and Prescott, P. (2001) *More than an education: leadership for rural school – community partnerships* (Canberra: Rural Industries Research and Development Corporation).

Lawn, M. (2001) 'Borderless education: imagining a European education space in a time of brands and networks', *Discourse*, 22(2): 173–84.

Lefebvre, H. (1991) *The production of space* (Oxford: Blackwell).

Lingard, B. (2000) 'Federalism in schooling since the Karmel report (1973), schools in Australia: from modernist hope to postmodernist preformativity', *Australian Education Researcher*, 27(2): 25–63.

McDowell, L. (1999) *Gender, identity and place* (Cambridge: Polity).

Marginson, S. (1997a) *Educating Australia: government, economy and citizen since 1960* (Sydney: Allen and Unwin).

Marginson, S. (1997b) *Markets in education* (Cambridge: Cambridge University Press).

Milbourne, L., Macrae, S. and Maguire, M. (2003) 'Collaborative solutions or new policy problems: exploring multi-agency partnerships in education and health work', *Journal of Education Policy*, 18(1): 19–35.

Osborne, S. (2000) *Public private partnerships: theory and practice in international perspective* (London: Routledge).

Ozga, J. (2000) 'Education policy in the United Kingdom: the dialectic of globalisation and identity', *Australian Education Researcher*, 27(2): 87–97.

Power, S. and Whitty, G. (1999) 'New Labour's education policy', *Journal of Education Policy*, 14: 535–46.

Pusey, M. (2003) *The experience of middle Australia: the dark side of economic reform* (Cambridge: Cambridge University Press).

Rees, G. (1997) 'Vocational education and training and regional development', *Journal of Education and Work*, 14: 141–49.

Riddell, S. and Tett, L. (eds) (2001) *Education, social justice and inter-agency working: joined up or fractured policy?* (Research in Education Series) (London: Routledge).

Robertson, S. and Dale, R. (2002) 'Local states of emergency: the contradictions of neo-liberal governance in education in New Zealand', *British Journal of Sociology of Education*, 23(3): 464–82.

Rose, N. (1996) 'The death of the social? Refiguring the territory of government', *Economy and Society*, 25(3): 327–56.

Rose, N. (1999) *Powers of freedom: reframing political thought* (Cambridge: Cambridge University Press).

Rushbrook, P. (1997) 'Tradition, pathways and the renegotiation of TAFE identity in Victoria', *Discourse*, 18(1): 103–12.

Sachs, J. (2003) *The activist teaching profession* (Buckingham: Open University Press).

Seddon, T. (2000) 'Capacity-building: beyond state and market', *Pedagogy, Culture and Society*, 7: 35–53.

Seddon, T. (2001a) 'Exploring capacity-building: from functionalist to political analysis', *Australia and New Zealand Journal of Vocational Education Research*, 9(2): 61–86.

Seddon, T. (2001b) 'Identity formation within neo-liberalism: continuity or change?', *Education et Societe: Revue Internationale de Sociologie de L'Education*, 6: 139–66.

Seddon, T. and Angus, L. (1999) 'Steering futures: practices and possibilities of institutional redesign in Australian education and training', *Journal of Education Policy*, 14(5): 491–506.

Seddon, T. and Billett, S. (2003) *Building community through social partnerships around vocational education and training* (Adelaide: National Centre for Vocational Education Research).

Seddon, T. and Malley, J. (1998) *A staff development strategy for supporting research priorities in the state training service* (Melbourne: Office of Training and Further Education).

Seddon, T., Angus, L. and Rushbrook, P. (1994) Framing a social analysis of education, *Re-forming postcompulsory education* (Centre for Learning and Work Research, Griffith University). Brisbane, Australia.

Seddon, T., Fischer, J., Clemans, A. and Billett, S. (2002) *Evaluation of local learning and employment networks* (Melbourne: Department of Education and Training).

Seddon, T., Clemans, A. and Billett, S. (2003) Social partnerships: practices, paradoxes and prospects of LLEN, *Australian Educational Researcher*, under review.

Seddon, T., Clemans, A. and Billett, S. (2004) *Outcomes and indicators for the LLEN movement*, research project in progress.

Seddon, T., Clemans, A. and Billett, S. (2005) 'Social Partnerships: practices, paradoxes and prospects of Local Learning Network', *Australian Educational Researcher*, 32(1), 25–48.

Sheil, H. (2002) *Collaborative education for transformation: strategies for rural sustainability.* Unpublished PhD, Faculty of Education, Monash University, (Melbourne).

Slaughter, S. and Leslie, L. (1997) *Academic capitalism* (Baltimore, MD: John Hopkins University).

Smyth, J. (2001) *Critical politics of teachers' work: an Australian perspective* (New York: Peter Lang).

Sojo, E. W. (1996) *Thirdspace: journeys to Los Angeles and other real-and-imagined places* (Malden, MA: Blackwell).

Stokes, H. and Tyler, D. (2002) *Negotiating pathways: the evaluation of phase two of the pathways project in Victoria* (Melbourne: Department of Education and Training).

Tett, L. (2003) Collaborating for social justice: limits and possibilities for youth workers and school teachers in Scotland, unpublished paper.

Tett, L., Crowther, J. and O'Hara, P. (2003) 'Collaborative partnerships in community education', *Journal of Education Policy*, 18(1): 37–51.

The Copenhagen Centre (1999) *New partnerships for social responsibility*, accessed 21 March 2002, available online at www.copenhagencentre.org/main

CHAPTER 15

BOURDIEU AS EDUCATION POLICY ANALYST AND EXPERT

A rich but ambiguous legacy

Agnès van Zanten

Journal of Eduction Policy, November 2005, 20(6): 671–86

Introduction

Analysing Bourdieu's contribution in the area of educational policy appears at first sight a strange undertaking. We know that though he was intensely interested in, indeed fascinated by, the role of schools in advanced capitalist societies, he actually wrote very little on what is usually thought of as policy. As Wacquant (1997) noted in the Preface to the English translation of Bourdieu's (1989) *La noblesse d'etat*, and this applies even more to his earlier major works on the educational system, *Les héritiers* (Bourdieu and Passeron 1964) and *La reproduction* (Bourdieu and Passeron 1970),[1] there is little reference in his work on educational institutions to official state structures, policies or personnel. And even if we move from the level of policy formulation to policy enactment, i.e. what actually occurs inside educational institutions and classrooms (the main focus of Bourdieu's analyses), there is once again little analysis of the micropolitics of schooling: agents' reinterpretations, negotiations and resistances (Ball 1987). Should we then conclude that it is irrelevant or uninteresting to examine this major French sociologist's work on education from a policy perspective? I will argue that it is neither, for two main reasons.

The first is that, when closely examined, Bourdieu's writings on education reveal not one, but two or three competitive or complementary policy theories. Their common principle is the invisibility of policy as, in Bourdieu's view, the influence of the state and dominant classes in education is embedded in the cognitive classifications and everyday activity of institutions, and policy is thus a never-ending encoding process (Ball 1994). These theories differ, however, in the room they leave for policy action, and they have led to diverging political and pedagogical interpretations. The second reason is that Bourdieu not only wrote, if indirectly, on educational policy, but engaged in policy action. Although strongly reluctant to commit himself politically, he was invited to participate as a kind of special expert in the process of policy formulation. And at the end of his career, although he had stopped doing research on educational institutions and moved on to analyse other social fields, education still occupied a central place in his critical writings, political stances and radical public action.

Bourdieu as educational policy analyst: the production and reception of an ambiguous concept, 'relative autonomy'

The school, which in Bourdieu's view had replaced the church as the major agency for socialization and legitimation in modern societies, appeared to him to play an essential role in the symbolic reproduction of the social order; the school's institutional frames acted as both imposition and acceptance frames (Wacquant 1997). However, in order for schools to exert this influence, they have to develop specific forms of classification, segregation and evaluation and thus enjoy 'relative autonomy' from other institutions, the state and dominant social groups. The status of this 'relative autonomy' remains ambiguous in Bourdieu's work, however. And this ambiguity has led in turn to strikingly different interpretations of the political impact of his work.

School autonomy as an illusion

From *Les héritiers* (1964) to *La noblesse d'etat* (1989), Bourdieu's writings on education have developed a coherent, evolving theory on school autonomy as a deceptive device that helps legitimize domination by dissimulating the relation between school processes and the aims of the state and dominant groups. In this sense, 'relative autonomy' must be taken to mean that instead of reflecting society's divisions in the mechanical way of Marxist 'correspondence' theories (Baudelot and Establet 1971; Bowles and Gintis 1977), schools take over those divisions in complex, creative and frequently imperceptible ways. From this point of view, Bourdieu's sociology of education is a sociology of power relations centred on the specific contribution of symbolic forms such as education to the functioning, conversion and naturalization of those relations. Schools are a material and symbolic support of the social order; they consecrate social divisions by inscribing them in objective material distributions and subjective cognitive classifications (Wacquant 1997).

That school autonomy masks the relationship of school forms to social forms of domination may be discerned, according to Bourdieu, in educational expectations concerning language, verbal ease and style. Academic language is a historical product, an amalgam of different traditions, and in that sense a specific school form, but – and this is the essential point – it is not equally distant from the languages of different social classes. Bourdieu insists on the dependence of school style on the style of dominant social groups. According to him, the style still dominant in higher and secondary French education institutions was inherited from the Jesuits, who transposed the aristocratic vision of society and its 'cult of glory' into religious and educational institutions. Today, the privileged classes still find legitimation of their own cultural privilege in a style that can be called 'charismatic' because of the value it attributes to 'grace' and 'talent'; it allows them to disguise their social heritage by transforming it into personal merit.

The schemes that structure perception, appreciation, thought and action in socially oriented ways are also imposed through structuration, organization and evaluation of learning. Following a perspective similar to the one proposed by Michael Young in *Knowledge and control* (Young 1971), where one of his first papers on education was republished in English, Bourdieu also insisted on the intertwining of the intellectual and social hierarchies of disciplines. The structuring stylistic opposition between 'brilliant' and 'serious' students corresponds in fact to the opposition between dilettante upper class students and hard-working lower class students. This same opposition is transposed to the disciplines. French, philosophy and mathematics are thus associated with a capacity for abstract thinking and talent, while other disciplines, such as geography or the natural sciences, are associated with a sense of the concrete, work and study. This opposition is also at the basis of most evaluations, especially in oral examinations, where professors use the institutional freedom they enjoy to apply personal evaluation criteria that are in fact social criteria.

Legitimate symbolic violence through school mechanisms reaches its highest degree, however, in the conferring of credentials. Credentials are clearly a mark of school autonomy and give to their possessors a legal monopoly protected by the state. They are privileges, but privileges that imply some kind of technical competence, which means that pupils must submit to the demands of schools, demands that increase and grow more extensive as pupils move to the upper, most selective parts of the system. However, although the basis for credential conferring makes it appear a fair process of technical selection, credentials in fact validate a long series of acts of social segregation and aggregation in school contexts, as well as multiple ways of matching school requirements with class distinctions. And while credentials make reproduction more costly and uncertain for the dominant groups, they give strong legal, political and pedagogical legitimation to processes of social reproduction.

School autonomy as a historical reality and a result of class struggles

Looked at through these lenses, school autonomy may be said to ensnare both students and teachers. Nevertheless, Bourdieu's writings allow for two other competing, less deterministic interpretations. Although he himself never provided a comprehensive presentation of the internal basis for school autonomy, if we assemble various passages from his major books on education we can see the importance he gave to Durkheim's (1938) principle that schools have 'a life of their own'. An important concept here is 'inertia' or 'conservatism', the tendency of schools, like all other social institutions, to remain the same by replicating themselves and retranslating external influences into traditional forms. Modern schools were a church creation first and gradually became a church substitute. According to Bourdieu, who here takes his inspiration directly from Durkheim's (1938) *L'évolution pédagogique en France*, they have maintained a number of features of the Jesuit colleges which invented the school 'form' (Vincent 1980). Professors imitate priests and, influenced by Jesuit values, give pre-eminence to style over content and overvalue ranking and competition (Bourdieu and Passeron 1964, 1970). The lasting influence of religious features in modern education is made even more salient in *La noblesse d'etat* (Bourdieu 1989), where frequent reference is made to Durkheim's *Les formes élémentaires de la vie religieuse* (Durkheim 1912). Bourdieu analysed the process of elite formation in the 'classes préparatoires aux Grandes Ecoles' (for a small minority of students, the 'classes préparatoires' are the first two or three years of higher education in France, in preparation for admission to the most prestigious higher education institutions) as a process of 'ordination'. First comes a period of seclusion during which students are cut off from their normal environment and integrated into an all-enveloping educational community where they learn the values of asceticism, self-possession, competition among peers and docile obedience to institutional rules. Then comes 'consecration' through credentials, which are boundaries that segregate those who will occupy important social positions from everyone else, while simultaneously creating collective faith in the legitimacy of a new form of class sovereignty.

Two other dimensions contribute to the internal autonomy of educational institutions. One has to do with their bureaucratic nature. The development of a school bureaucracy, especially a sophisticated examination system, is for Bourdieu strongly linked to demands for social and technical selection generated by the overall process of rationalizing social and state activities as analysed by Weber, whom Bourdieu cites as a source for his thinking here. Although in contrast to the Mandarin system examined by Weber, the examination system in contemporary schools has not been able to make society accept the hierarchy of school values as the official principle of every social and value hierarchy, it has succeeded in creating a new principle that competes with other principles of social ranking. The second is teachers' corporatism. According to this view, examinations were developed by professors who, as members of the petite bourgeoisie and intellectual fractions of the bourgeoisie, were initially opposed to birth privileges and the preeminence of favouritism and nepotism in accession to desirable social positions. At the same time, however, meritocracy and examinations have become autonomous school forms and substitutive principles of power for a 'government of scholars', whose will is to have educational institutions submit all acts of political and civil life to their control.

The autonomy of the school also has an external basis in the dynamic nature of the class system. In *Les héritiers* (Bourdieu and Passeron 1964) and *La reproduction* (Bourdieu and Passeron 1970), Bourdieu and Passeron speak mainly about the dominant classes as a whole and implicitly present the relationship of these classes to the state as static, allowing for smooth reproduction of the social order. In *La noblesse d'etat* (Bourdieu 1989), however, written after *La distinction. Critique sociale du jugement* (Bourdieu 1979) and *Homo academicus* (Bourdieu 1984) and other books and articles on class, culture and intellectuals, Bourdieu adopted a very different view. He analysed this part of the educational system as strongly conditioned by power relations between two main upper class fractions, the economic bourgeoisie, represented primarily by managers, and the cultural bourgeoisie, whose emblematic representatives are professors. A careful analysis of the internal organization of this part of the education system and professor–student relations within it shows a particular form at work, very different from the one characterizing universities as analysed in *Les héritiers* and *La reproduction*. Here, professors are no longer priests and prophets but mere trainers, whose role is to create the conditions favourable to massive, intensive preparation for competitive examinations. Lectures yield to exercises and tests, and pupils are expected not so much to acquire a general culture and pose as intellectuals as to use formulae and short cuts to get a pragmatic grip on a wide variety of specific knowledge and skills. In fact, the work of teachers and students of and around the 'Grandes Ecoles' seems totally dependent on their function. These institutions work as 'schools for managers'; students here are preparing to exercise power rather than to conduct scientific research or embark on literary and artistic careers. In Bourdieu's view, this kind of training corresponds in a general sense to the reproduction and legitimation needs of the elite.

Nevertheless, the dominant pole, managers, and the dominated pole, intellectuals, have not developed the same relationship to these elite institutions, and this has important consequences for both social reproduction and school autonomy.

Holders of economic capital long relied on a domestic mode of reproduction and on private schools as an extension of the family. The transition from domestic to bureaucratic firms led them to turn to a school-based mode of reproduction and rely on credentials acquired in elite state institutions as a way of controlling access to firms and building internal cohesion among managers and high level employees. However, locating themselves on the side of efficiency and pragmatism in contrast to intellectuals, company heads and managers remain distrustful of credentials. This leads them to send their children to elite institutions such as the Haute Ecole Commerciale (HEC) or the Ecole Nationale d'Administration (ENA), where a concentration of students from similar economically oriented backgrounds, together with the curriculum and teachers' profile, reinforces inherited habituses rather than further inculcating a distinct school culture. On the contrary, members of the culturally oriented pole of the bourgeoisie have developed a much more intrinsic relationship to the kind of knowledge and world view promoted by schools and a higher respect for teachers as agents for the transmission of a valuable cultural heritage. They are also much more dependent on credentials for joining the elite than members of the economically oriented fraction of the bourgeoisie. That is why they tend to choose more meritocratic 'Grandes Ecoles', such as the Ecole Normale Supérieure (ENS) and Polytechnique.

This split has important consequences for the autonomy of schools and school agents. In the case of managers, school autonomy is limited because the school submits to worldly demands and agrees to validate earlier, extra-school acquisitions. Nevertheless, the need to attend elite institutions creates new problems and tensions in families as the reproduction of each individual family member's position is not guaranteed and requires major educational effort from both students and parents. Moreover, in the case of intellectuals, elite schools enjoy much greater autonomy. This is related to the nature of the knowledge required by the cultural fractions of the bourgeoisie, which cannot be acquired without specific teaching and learning. It is also related to the importance of credentials, which give schools the power to create a 'state nobility', i.e. an elite who can serve its own interests in the very act of serving the superior interests of the state. And although Bourdieu shows the relative decline of culturally oriented elite institutions that promote quasi-autonomous intellectual values, he concludes that the fact that elite schools have become one of the main fields for the struggles between different fractions of the bourgeoisie has two implications not just for school autonomy, but also social change. The first is that diversifying the fields where the main struggles between different fractions take place (the family, schools, work, politics, etc.) actually protects against tyranny, if tyranny is understood as the encroachment of one power on another or the intrusion of a power associated with one field into another. Another consequence is that struggles in the educational arena around the creation of new credentials or new institutions are much more likely to entail the universalizing of particular interests than are struggles in the family arena. This means that their results have implications for other social groups, including, to some extent, disadvantaged groups.

Relative autonomy and the reception of Bourdieu's work

Bourdieu and Passeron's first works on education have exerted a very powerful influence on the French vision of action and policy in the field of education and beyond. This influence is very difficult to assess, however, since it has had quite diverse and contradictory effects. On the one hand, the works widely diffused the idea that inequalities existed both in access to schooling and school success and failure as related to institutional and pedagogical processes. This definitively shattered the social beliefs prevalent at the time that the school functioned or should function as a neutral tool for modernization or a liberating force for working class students (Masson 2001). At the same time it enriched the French 'passion for equality' inherited from the 1789 Revolution with a more sociological perspective. It is certainly to a large extent thanks to these two major sociological works that the existence of education-related social inequalities has remained firmly at the fore of political and intellectual debates in France, much more so than in countries without such landmark sociological analyses. This has been so regardless of the political orientation of the French government and public leaders. A second, no less important, effect, however, has been to instil the belief that the influence of schooling is so powerful that it is impossible to do anything about it. Bourdieu and Passeron's works were perceived from the outset by many intellectuals, especially those directly concerned with educational reform or radical transformation of the educational and social system, as profoundly deterministic and pessimistic, and they were associated with the nihilist discourses of such authors as Ivan Illich (Prost 1970; Snyders 1976).

The influence of Bourdieu's works went beyond intellectual circles. Although many other historical and social processes must be taken into account to explain the strong distrust of policy and policy-makers in the French field of education, Bourdieu and Passeron's critical theory of education has played a key role in the formation of this point of view in the recent period. And this theory is also partly responsible for the scarcity of French research on education policy (van Zanten 2004). The first, more common interpretation of their analysis of school autonomy as an illusion whose main function is to legitimize domination has in fact helped discredit all discourse on the 'common good'. Indeed, in this perspective any discourse or action can be suspected of concealing particular interests and power relations, leaving no room for any decision-maker to justify changes in one direction or another on moral or political grounds. At the same time, policy changes seem extremely unimportant, and thus of little social and scientific interest, when weighed against structural processes. Bourdieu and Passeron's interpretation has also had an impact on teachers' and educational reformers' beliefs that pedagogical action is strictly limited in its ability to bring about change. This, in turn, is currently used by advantaged social groups such as middle class parents to justify and legitimate strategic individual action, such as school choice in socially and ethnically mixed urban contexts (van Zanten 2003). And, at the other end of the social spectrum, it has fostered discourses among youngsters from lower tatus and immigrant backgrounds in which they are much more likely to present themselves as 'victims of the system' than to try to contest it (Martucelli 2002).

Bourdieu and Passeron's books, however, were also perceived as radical and subversive, and ignored or rejected as such. The perception and reaction of teachers unions and some leftist political groups, especially the Communist party, still very influential in educational circles and in French society in general in the 1960s and 1970s, were particularly ambiguous. As Bourdieu himself pointed out, this was related to the trajectories, vision and political strategy of these political and educational militants. Many Communist leaders inside either the party or teacher unions were themselves school 'miracles', i.e. individuals from working class backgrounds who had succeeded in and thanks to school. They thus tended to ignore or minimize the importance of social determinants on school careers and to support the myth of the 'liberating' school. Moreover, the vision of the school that became dominant in the Communist party from the 1930s on was an essential element in the organization of the proletariat, its class education and ability to mobilize. This position was reinforced in 1947, when Communist intellectuals participated in developing the Langevin–Wallon education plan, which in turn became the basis for developing a comprehensive educational system, conceived as a remedy for educational and social inequality. Bourdieu and Passeron's work was perceived as undermining these central beliefs and, therefore, as a threat to the coherence of the Party line, especially since criticism from teachers could ruin the Party's political strategy of allying itself with teachers at both the local level, particularly in the municipalities of the Parisian 'red belt' periphery, and the national level (van Zanten 2001; Matonti 2004).

Bourdieu and Passeron's research was nevertheless used by student unions and leftist political groups to justify their own analysis of the educational system and played an important role in the debates and protest action of the May 1968 student movement. This in turn encouraged right-wing intellectuals and politicians to read their works, especially *Les héritiers*, as political pamphlets that had contributed to the development of a new form of generation-based social consciousness and fuelled political radicalism. This was one of the main factors in the break between Bourdieu and his former master Raymond Aron, a centre-right, classic liberal sociologist who had integrated Bourdieu into his research group, the Centre for European Sociology, which was largely funded at the time by the Ford Foundation. And it led Bourdieu to create his own first research group, the Centre for the Sociology of Education and Culture. Members of this group participated in the student movement in two distinct ways. In May 1968 they launched an appeal to organize an Estates-General of Teaching and Research whose general aim was to allow the entire population, especially the working classes, to debate on and contest educational matters and reform. They also prepared several written recommendations, based on Bourdieu's work, for changes in the organization and content of teaching and learning in schools and universities.

Bourdieu as policy expert: reforming educational institutions or radically transforming them?

To assess Bourdieu's contribution to policy studies we need to go beyond his academic work and take into account his voluntary or involuntary involvement as an actor in debates and decisions concerning educational institutions. The two dimensions interact in ways that are not always familiar to academic readers, especially non-French ones, and examining this interaction sheds new light on what he conceived as educational policy, the possible manoeuvring room for educational policy action and how intellectuals should intervene in educational policy-making.

A reformist parenthesis

Bourdieu's political attitude during the university crisis and student movement of 1968 is presented as ambiguous by some of his closest colleagues and friends, such as Robert Castel and Jean-Claude Passeron. In recent texts written in homage to Bourdieu after his death, both comment on his suspicion of any kind of political engagement during the 1960s and 1970s. Although he was sympathetic to the student movement, he was in fact extremely distrustful of the most activist groups, whom he reproached for having a petit bourgeois ethic and being politically irresponsible (Castel 2003). His own engagement in the student movement was extremely discreet and he only signed collective appeals and petitions. More generally, he distrusted all intellectuals who presented themselves as 'May leaders' and all sociologists who manifested their political engagement in intellectual circles or universities and in the press, radio or television. As he saw it, they were only expressing their own resentment and social fantasies and defending their social and academic interests, not participating in radical contestation of the social order. He was also extremely critical of the reforms that took place as a result of the May 1968 movement. They appeared to him as geared to eliminate the more visible authoritarian dimensions of the school and university system but not the authoritarian structure of the pedagogical relation and its power to legitimate educational inequalities (Poupeau and Discepolo 2002; Passeron 2004).

Bourdieu was, however, tempted by some reformist endeavours in the 1980s. Their content can be directly linked to his and Passeron's defence of a 'rational pedagogy' at the end of *Les héritiers*. Both authors believed at the time that one of the main vectors of inequality reproduction in French universities and secondary schools was the absence of explicit mediations between knowledge and learners, the existence of what Basil Bernstein (1975) called an 'invisible pedagogy', accessible only to students and pupils from privileged social backgrounds. Both saw the continuous and systematic clarification of educational expectations, content and methods by teachers recruited and assessed on the basis of their technical competence rather than their social attributes as a way of reducing the communication gap between teachers and working class students and limiting the advantages of middle class ones. Although it was totally unclear how a system devoted to the perpetuation of a cultural elite would introduce these changes, there was a definite attempt to link sociological descriptions and interpretations to pedagogical recommendations. However, despite these proposals for reform, Bourdieu seemed for more than 20 years little concerned with whether or how his analysis might be applied in educational policy.

Two factors seem to account for his transition from retreat to moderate engagement in reformist action in the 1980s. The first is related to the important changes in educational politics and policy that followed on the election of Socialist president Francois Mitterrand in 1981. The new government launched a series of social and educational initiatives, including a policy of 'Zones d'éducation prioritaires'. This policy was inspired by the English 'Educational priority areas' and the American compensatory education programs set up in the 1960s, but its focus on positive discrimination and specific pedagogical support for disadvantaged children was also directly linked to Bourdieu and Passeron's work. Moreover, the Socialist political elite, composed to a significant extent of university professors, also tried to create new relationships between policy-makers and researchers. Long reluctant to engage in reform and very rarely appealed to by government to do so, researchers were suddenly asked to participate in different educational commissions and working groups, prepare individual reports and, more generally, provide new ideas and new analysis for educational policy-making (van Zanten 2000). The second factor seems to be Bourdieu's 1982 recruitment into the Collège de France, an immensely prestigious institution, reserved to a very small elite of university professors and researchers who occupy personal lifelong chairs. It was from this institution that President Mitterrand himself commissioned two successive reports on education, and Bourdieu declared in interviews that he interpreted this appeal to the most prestigious representatives of science as 'a first order political act'. In fact, he thought he could use the collective intellectual reputation capital of this institution and the collective intellectual autonomy of its scholar members to promote change.

The first report, entitled *Propositions pour l'enseignement de l'avenir* (Collège de France 1985), and published as a collective contribution of professors from the Collège, details nine principles oriented toward developing rationality and justice in the educational system. Two of these principles, 'the diversification of forms of excellence' and the 'multiplication of educational opportunities', were directly inspired by Bourdieu and Passeron's analysis of educational inequalities, and in interviews Bourdieu insisted on their connection to two important negative education effects: hierarchization and definitive evaluations. Others, such as 'the unification of knowledge', implying a common core curriculum that all pupils should systematically acquire at each level, or the reinforcement of teachers' competence and engagement in educational activities are clearly influenced by the authors' vision of a rational pedagogy. Yet other principles, such as the need to reconcile the universal vision promoted by the natural sciences and the relativistic understanding of the human sciences, relate more to intellectual conceptions of knowledge.

More surprisingly, the report puts forward a principle much more in line with classic liberal thinking: the need for competition between autonomous, diversified educational institutions, which would be given a label of quality to guide users in their choice, while preserving disadvantaged individuals and institutions from segregation as a result of unfair competition. This point pertained first and foremost to higher education institutions, but could be extended experimentally, the report specified, to secondary schools. The underlying idea seemed to be that overt institutional autonomy linked to overt school choice could limit existing covert forms of competition and selection operating through cost, distance and limited access to information and that replacing competition among individuals by competition among groups and local powers could have beneficial effects (Léger 1986). As Bourdieu himself declared in interviews, the idea was in fact to propose a balance between state control and a classic liberal approach (Poupeau and Diecepolo 2002). The sources of this position are probably two-fold. One has to do with the political climate of the period, in which policies of decentralization, diversification and school autonomy could be justified as progressive in reaction to the authoritarian centralization and standardization of previous policy orientations. The other is more related to Bourdieu's belief that to guarantee a rational and just social order, the intellectual and scientific field – and therefore higher education institutions – had to enjoy broad autonomy.

The second report, entitled *Principes pour une réflexion sur les contenus d'enseignement* (Bourdieu and Gros 1989), published in 1989 by an ad hoc commission working under the direction of Pierre Bourdieu and François Gros, focused more on the intellectual organization of curricula and, to a lesser extent, the intellectual and material organization of teaching and learning. It restates some of the principles of the previous report, such as the need to reconcile universalism and relativism and to instate periodical revision of curricula so as to include new knowledge produced and required by scientific progress and social change. It also introduced new ideas, such as the importance of interdisciplinarity and both horizontal coordination between disciplines and vertical progression within them from one year to the next. The links between these proposals and Bourdieu's analysis of educational inequalities and suggestions for a 'rational pedagogy' are much more tenuous than in the previous report. As Bourdieu himself acknowledged in some interviews, there is no reference to reproduction or democratization. He justified this position as a pragmatic one: the impossibility of changing the educational system in depth meant that the best course was to make only modestly ambitious proposals to prevent that system from aggravating inequalities. In fact, closer examination of the content of the report and subsequent discussions bring to light Bourdieu's growing interest in the role of knowledge as an intellectual construction, in turn related to his thinking about science as a guiding principle for policy and action. This had somewhat superseded his concern about the social conditions of learning.

Academic radicalism

At first sight, these moderate reformist attempts seem to contrast starkly with Bourdieu's strong engagement in the public and political spheres in the 1990s and his public support of the major French strikes of December 1995. But while there are important discontinuities between these two positions, there are also significant continuities. Bourdieu's engagement had always been related to his vision of the crucial role of ideas in social struggles. This became particularly visible in his public engagement in the 1990s against neo-liberalism. He saw neo-liberalism as a symbolic force that intensified the material economic realities it started from and sought to develop; through their neo-liberal theorizing, researchers and policy-makers were the agents of this symbolic force. The increasing importance given to theory led Bourdieu to rethink his earlier understanding that there was no real connection between struggles internal to the intellectual field and external political struggles (Swartz 2003).

He became, in fact, convinced that while it was essential to protect the autonomy of the scientific field from political influence, it was also essential, in societies where science is to a large extent used by dominants to reinforce their domination, to allow the dominated to appropriate scientific results and instruments. Bourdieu's public engagement is also related to his professional trajectory. Passeron (2003) suggested that for many years he did not feel his intellectual power was solidly established enough to be able to use it in the political field. However, toward the end of his extraordinarily productive and influential career, which included international consecration of his work, he felt it possible to use his scientist status to develop and support new forms of expression aimed at producing powerful symbolic effects in the public arena.

Bourdieu's academic radicalism can be traced back to the publication of *La misère du monde* (Bourdieu 1993), which represents an important departure from his previous work in terms of the scientific representation of the social world, methodology and political alliances. As concerns theory and the representation of social hierarchies and power relations, a new key concept is introduced, that of 'poverty of position', a relative kind of poverty, distinct from but no less powerful than 'poverty of condition', i.e. massive poverty associated with social class and labour conditions. According to Bourdieu and the co-authors of the book, neo-liberalism, the dismantling of public services and ineffective policy attempts to reduce inequalities and exclusion have produced a whole new group of individuals who are 'relative failures' of the system and whose suffering is largely ignored. Schools have strongly contributed to this by creating an illusion of democratization coupled with continuous processes of segregation and exclusion that start inside classrooms and schools and accompany individuals throughout their lives. Analysis of these processes led Bourdieu and his collaborators to explore in more depth two main themes already present in Bourdieu's previous research on education: the symbolic violence of schools and the contradictory nature of educational heritage by social situation and individual trajectory. What is new, however, is that teachers and school personnel are no longer presented as deliberate or unconscious agents of social reproduction, but rather as victims themselves of the educational system. This is especially, but not exclusively, the case for those working in the most difficult peripheral urban areas. They share 'poverty of position' with many other state agents directly faced with problems of unemployment, violence and various forms of exclusion.

This new perspective was reinforced by a radical change in Bourdieu's methodological position. Drawing away from the Durkheimian principle of radical separation between subjects' and researchers' points of view that he had developed in *Le métier de sociologue* (Bourdieu *et al.* 1968) and put into practice in his previous work, Bourdieu stated in *La misère du monde* that analysis of 'difficult' places and 'poverty of position' supposes a comprehensive perspective. The researcher must abandon his god-like point of view in order to grasp and assist in the expression of the subjects' own self-analyses, thus allowing the expression of plural, frequently competitive points of view. As Lapeyronnie (2004) suggested, this radical change seems strongly related to a new form of political alliance between academic radicals such as Bourdieu and his collaborators and what they present as the middle class intellectual public service victims of liberalism, i.e. teachers, journalists, young researchers. Developing an alliance with these groups, for whom *La Misère du monde* can be seen to furnish a new social philosophy, appears crucial for at least two reasons: as representatives of public service these groups are the last bastion against liberalism and as intellectuals they are particularly likely to support the idea of rational political governance.

Consistent with this new radical perspective, Bourdieu developed new modes of communication in the 1990s aimed at making his theories more understandable and accessible, but also at substantiating the idea of a 'collective intellectual' capable of bringing together science and politics (Swartz 2003; Mauger 2004). After the success of *La Misère du monde*, which has even been adapted for the stage, Bourdieu created his own European journal, *Liber*, published until 1998. In a new European collection, *Raisons d'agir*, which he created just after the 1995 strikes, he published essays and articles mainly on neo-liberal public policies. Written by him and other social science researchers, these studies were attractive to larger audiences because of the style, length and journal price. He multiplied public appearances with protest leaders and artists and gave more and more speeches and conferences to highly diverse audiences. He also gave interviews and wrote short articles for opinion columns. These texts, frequently signed by a group entitled the 'Association de Réflexion sur les Enseignements Supérieurs et la Recherche' (ARESER), created in 1992 with Bourdieu as its president, often concerned education and research. They express a strongly critical view of all reforms proposed by government leaders on both the right and left, repeatedly pointing out the lack of real consultation with students and teachers, lack of resources, segmentation of users, excessive adaptation to the need of firms, limitation of curriculum content and the like. As Lapeyronnie (2004) judiciously pointed out, under the general accusation of liberalism, all types of reformism are denounced, including some that Bourdieu himself had promoted in the 1980s.

Conclusion

As underlined by Robert Castel (2004), Pierre Bourdieu's work and action, both generally and in relation to education, were characterized by constant tension between a sense of the power of social constraint and political voluntarism. In France his brilliant analysis of the educational process was perceived by many professional or lay readers as deterministic and was therefore understood to leave no room for political or pedagogical action. There are strong arguments in favour of this reading, and Bourdieu himself reinforced it in his oral presentations and interviews. He was profoundly conscious of social constraint and the crucial problem of the dominated's consent to domination. This led him to emphasize the force of reproductive mechanisms, visible and invisible, as well as the powerlessness of dominated groups and the more or less conscious exercise of privilege by dominant groups. In the coherent, all-encompassing theory he finally built on the foundations of an initially quite diverse set of research pieces the force of these mechanisms appears almost unlimited, as each social field makes its own specific contribution to domination and the legitimation of domination. However, a more detailed examination of Bourdieu's work in education shows that while the unveiling of processes of domination remained a priority for him, he could present those processes in a nuanced and sophisticated manner that leaves some room for autonomy and thus for policy action.

Bourdieu's political engagement was as rich and ambiguous as his theory is. For a long period he seems to have expected that his labour of gradually unmasking even the subtlest mechanisms of domination would almost magically create a broader and deeper social consciousness. He was also hopeful for some time that it could lead to concrete reforms, especially in higher education. Increasingly disappointed on these two points, and increasingly convinced that his theory had become a universal scientific and moral cause, he decided to step forcefully into the public sphere. Conscious that politics is not an individual but a collective process, he sought to build new alliances, both with other scholars – he had become much more assertive than he was early in his career about the scientific community's independence and capacity for sound political judgement, and he now worked to build a 'collective intellectual' – and at least potentially with all victims of liberalism, either working class or from the public sector intellectual middle class. Still, his position remained paradoxical until the end, as he tried to develop an emancipatory political line on the principle that only an elite of scholars can have access to universal truths and a radical political movement against economic forces that was based essentially on the symbolic power of words.

Although Bourdieu's intellectual career is atypical in terms of productiveness and influence, it exemplifies some classical crucial dilemmas of sociologists as intellectual workers and citizens. Most sociologists are both attracted to dissecting social mechanisms and processes of inequality and injustice in minute detail and trained to do so. This intellectual orientation leads them to emphasize social determinism or the unexpected, frequently negative consequences of social and political action (Hirschman 1991). They are thus more likely to contribute to a kind of social cynicism than to provide solutions and guidelines to action (Martucelli 2002). Many sociologists and intellectuals are also likely to hypertrophy the power of words and culture and to minimize, misinterpret or demonize economic processes; this in turn leads them to adopt insufficiently informed and strategic political stances. At the same time, although they tend to be morally and politically on the side of the 'victims' of society, as intellectuals, they are by profession and status on the side of power and the state. This means that they can always be suspected of confiscating the power of expression of the otherwise powerless groups they mean to represent.

Note

1 Reference throughout the article is to Bourdieu's initial publications in French but the English translations are indicated in References when relevant.

References

Ball, S. J. (1987) *The micro-politics of the school* (London: Methuen).
Ball, S. J. (1994) *Education reform. A critical and post-structural approach* (Buckingham, UK: Open University Press).
Baudelot, C. and Establet, R. (1971) *L'ecole capitaliste en France* (Paris: Maspéro).
Bernstein, B. (1975) *Class, codes and control*, vol. 3 (London: Routledge).
Bourdieu, P. (1979) *La distinction. Critique sociale du jugement* (Paris: Éditions de Minuit). Translated into English 1986 as *Distinction: a social critique of the judgement of taste* (London: Routledge).
Bourdieu, P. (1984) *Homo academicus* (Paris, Éditions de Minuit). Translated into English 1988 as *Homo academicus* (Cambridge, UK: Polity Press).
Bourdieu, P. (1989) *La noblesse d'etat. Grandes écoles et esprit de corps* (Paris: Éditions de Minuit). Translated into English 1997 as *State nobility: elite schools in the field of power* (Cambridge, UK: Polity Press).
Bourdieu, P. (ed.) (1993) *La misère du monde* (Paris: Éditions du Seuil). Translated into English 1999 as *Weight of the world: social suffering in contemporary society* (Cambridge, UK: Polity Press).
Bourdieu, P. and Gros, F. (1989) *Principes pour une réflexion sur les contenus d'enseignement* (Paris: Collège de France).
Bourdieu, P. and Passeron, J. C. (1964) *Les héritiers. Les étudiants et la culture* (Paris: Éditions de Minuit). Translated into English 1979 as *The inheritors: French students and their relation to culture* (Chicago, IL: Chicago University Press).
Bourdieu, P. and Passeron, J. C. (1970) *La reproduction. Eléments pour une théorie du système d'enseignement* (Paris: Éditions de Minuit). Translated into English 1990 as *Reproduction* (London: Sage).
Bourdieu, P., Chamboredon, J. C. and Passeron, J. C. (1968) *Le métier de sociologue* (Paris: Éditions de Minuit).
Bowles, S. and Gintis, H. (1977) *Schooling in capitalist America* (New York: Basic Books).
Castel, R. (2003) 'Pierre Bourdieu et la dureté du monde', in P. Encrevé and R.-M. Lagrave (eds), *Travailler avec Bourdieu* (Paris: Flammarion).
Castel, R. (2004) 'Entre la contrainte sociale et le volontarisme politique', in J. Bouveresse and D. Roche (eds), *La liberté par la connaissance. Pierre Bourdieu (1930–2002)* (Paris: Odile Jacob).
Collège de France (1985) *Propositions pour l'enseignement de l'avenir* (Paris: Collège de France).
Durkheim, E. (1912) *Les Formes élémentaires de la vie religieuse* (Paris: Presses Universitaires de France).
Durkheim, E. (1938) *L'évolution pédagogique en France* (Paris: Alcan).
Hirschman, A. (1991) *The rhetoric of reaction: perversity, futility, jeopardy* (Cambridge, MA: Harvard University Press).
Lapeyronnie, D. (2004) 'L'académisme radical ou le monologue sociologique. Avec qui parlent les sociologues?', *Revue Française de Sociologie*, 45(4): 621–51.
Léger, A. (1986) 'Débat autour d'un rapport', *Revue Française de Pédagogie*, 74: 87–98.
Martucelli, D. (2002) 'Sociologie et posture critique', in B. Lahire (ed.), *A quoi sert la sociologie?* (Paris: Éditions La Découverte).
Masson, P. (2001) 'La fabrication des *Héritiers*', *Revue Française de Sociologie*, 42(3): 477–507.
Matonti, F. (2004) 'Intellectuels "responsables" et intellectuels "libres"', in L. Pinto, G. Sapiro and P. Champagne (eds), *Pierre Bourdieu, sociologue* (Paris: Fayard).
Mauger, G. (2004) 'Résistances à la sociologie de Pierre Bourdieu', in L. Pinto, G. Sapiro and P. Champagne (eds), *Pierre Bourdieu, sociologue* (Paris: Fayard).
Passeron, J. C. (2003) 'Mort d'un ami, disparition d'un penseur', in P. Encrevé and R.-M. Lagrave (eds), *Travailler avec Bourdieu* (Paris: Flammarion).

Passeron, J. C. (2004) 'Le sociologue en politique et *vice versa*: enquêtes sociologiques et réformes pédagogiques dans les années 1960', in J. Bouveresse and D. Roche (eds), *La liberté par la connaissance. Pierre Bourdieu (1930–2002)* (Paris: Odile Jacob).

Poupeau, F. and Discepolo, T. (eds) (2002) *Pierre Bourdieu. Interventions, 1961–2001. Science sociale et action politique* (Paris: Agone).

Prost, A. (December 1970) 'Une sociologie stérile: la reproduction', *Esprit*, 851–61.

Snyders, G. (1976) *Ecole, classe et lutte des classes* (Paris: Presses Universitaires de France).

Swartz, D. L. (2003) 'From critical sociology to public intellectual: Pierre Bourdieu and politics', *Theory and Society*, 32: 791–823.

van Zanten, A. (2000) 'Les sciences sociales et l'école', in A. van Zanten (ed.), *L'école, l'état des savoirs* (Paris: Éditions La Découverte).

van Zanten, A. (2001) *L'école de la périphérie. Scolarité et ségrégation en banlieue* (Paris: Presses Universitaires de France).

van Zanten, A. (2003) 'La mobilisation stratégique et politique des savoirs sur le social: le cas des parents d'élèves des classes moyennes', *Education et Sociétés*, 9: 39–52.

van Zanten, A. (2004) *Les politiques d'éducation* (Paris: Presses Universitaires de France).

Vincent, G. (1980) *L'ecole primaire française* (Lyon, France: Presses Universitaires de Lyon).

Wacquant, L. (1997) 'Preface', in P. Bourdieu *State Nobility* (Cambridge, UK: Polity Press).

Young, M. F. D. (ed.) (1971) *Knowledge and control. New directions for the sociology of education* (London: Collier MacMillan).

NAME INDEX

SUBJECT INDEX